AMERICA'S
ANCIENT
TREASURES

AMERICA'S ANCIENT TREASURES

Guide to Archeological Sites and Museums

by Franklin Folsom

RAND McNALLY & COMPANY   New York   Chicago   San Francisco

Photo Credits

Illustrations for chapter openings, on pages listed, have been supplied by the following sources: Marmes Rockshelter Project, Laboratory of Anthropology, Washington State University, xiv; National Park Service photo by M. Woodbridge Williams, 8; Tom Myers, 42; Washington State Department of Commerce and Economic Development, 56; Manitoba Government, 74; National Park Service, 100; Wisconsin Conservation Department, 124; Rochester Museum and Science Center, 162.

Illustrations by RACHEL FOLSOM

Cover illustration by MARSHALL SMITH

Book designed by JEAN KRAUSE

Contents

Features

Foreword

The science of archeology has progressed far beyond what it was 122 years ago when Squier and Davis published their famous work, *Ancient Monuments of the Mississippi Valley,* as Volume I in the notable series, *Contributions To Knowledge of the Smithsonian Institution.* Today it is an activity engaging the energy of many governmental agencies as well as state and local organizations and private individuals. Digging up the prehistoric Indian past, visiting the sites where these remains are displayed, and interpreting the story of these remains are occupations that have become in some instances a profession, in others a pastime.

Those of us in the business of recovering the past, in one manner or another, are frequently asked, "Where can I go to see some Indian remains?" (A far cry from our European ancestors' statement: "the only good Indian is a dead Indian.") Mr. Folsom's book answers this question of "where to go" in an admirable fashion.

Squier and Davis's compendium of 1848 was largely concerned with prehistoric remains of the Mississippi Valley. Even with their complete maps and detailed descriptions, a tourist today would have difficulty in finding 85 percent of the Indian villages, mounds, burial grounds, and sites which Squier and Davis recorded. Most had vanished by A.D. 1900 through encroaching European civilization. Since A.D. 1900 the rate of destruction of prehistoric remains across the country has increased at an ever-accelerating pace.

New 20th-century technologies have given birth to new and expanding land uses: highways, superhighways, airfields, suburbia, industrialization, urban sprawl, massive large-scale reservoirs or other flood and water control projects, jumbo jet airfields. All of these are rapidly taking their toll of our heritage, all across the land.

In the middle and late 19th century a number of local societies became alarmed about the increasing loss of our historic heritage. An excellent example is the Mount Vernon Ladies Association which, in 1854, saved Mount Vernon, Washington's home, from oblivion. Not until 1906, however, did the federal government seriously get into the business of looking after its own historic resources. *The Act for the Preservation of American Antiquities* made it a federal offense to injure, damage, or destroy antiquities on federal lands. It also provided for the establishment of national monuments by presidential proclamation.

In the same year the famous ruins at Mesa Verde were set aside and protected from further vandalism as a national park open to all visitors. Today over 500,000 people a year enjoy and marvel at cliff dwellings and mesa-top pueblos of almost a thousand years ago.

Since then state and local communities have followed suit, so that today prime examples of historic and prehistoric remains are being kept inviolate from the depredations of our increasing technologies. The rate at which remains are saved, however, is not commensurate with the rate of destruction.

Although the task was past the capabilities of state and local organizations, it was not until the 1930s that the federal government entered the picture. Under the auspices of the Work Projects Administration a good deal of salvage archeology was done, especially in the Tennessee Valley where the TVA was building a series of dams. World War II interrupted this effort.

Following the war, the U.S. National Park Service sponsored a program of salvage archeology in other areas of the United States which were threatened by inundation from massive large-scale federal water control and impoundment projects. Since it was obviously impossible to save everything, or remove it to high ground before flooding, archeologists decided that with an adequate 10 percent sample they could recover 85 percent of the inherent scientific information within those remains. These sites are, of course, now gone, but the artifacts and information about them are now on display in various museums throughout the country.

When Squier and Davis compiled their compendium, they were mainly interested in survey and excavation of prehistoric remains as they understood those things in their day. Now, with new techniques, we can add ecological and environmental factors to the interpretation of our prehistoric remains, and this helps to put those remains in context with modern man and his struggle for an environmentally balanced way of life.

The Indian, too, had to compete, live with, and adapt to his environment. While not possessing the sophisticated techniques we do, he managed to make his adjustments and retain his culture patterns at least until the arrival of the Europeans. In view of our growing socio-technological problems, an understanding of how other people solved their problems in this same land is basic. One way to achieve this understanding is to visit the sites, park areas, museums, and institutions where these remains are displayed and interpreted.

Hopefully, visitors to the various sites and museums of this country will gain a greater appreciation of the long (maybe 20,000 years) past history of this country and a feeling for some of the unusual engineering and artistic feats achieved by the Indians. In turn then it is possible that the same visitor will do his best to help preserve these vanishing remains so other generations may enjoy them also.

Today, even more than before, it is necessary that we preserve the outstanding remnants of our past. The few we have left are fast disappearing. Some are set aside by federal law, others by state or local regulations, and a few by concerted efforts of private citizens and organizations. Mr. Folsom's guide provides a survey on how to visit these places.

John M. Corbett
Chief Archeologist
United States National Park Service

Preface

Prehistoric men in America did not know how to make symbols for the sounds of speech. They could not record the richness—or the bleakness—of their experience because they lacked the art of writing. This has meant that they could not talk to us, or even whisper to us, across the centuries.

Archeology has undertaken the task of trying to end this silence. And, here and there, archeologists have given some voice to a few of the millions of people who once were a part of the life on this land. Using a variety of techniques borrowed from a dozen other sciences, they have recalled fragments out of the past.

They have literally re-created dwellings and places of worship and indeed whole villages, and in the United States they have done so under a variety of auspices. On the federal level the National Park Service, the Bureau of Land Management, and the Forest Service have all joined in the work of protecting and presenting what Indians once built and archeologists have now studied and rebuilt. Certain state, county, and city agencies also have joined in the work of preservation, as have some privately financed institutions. All are saving some of the fast-disappearing past for the benefit of present and future generations. Thanks to these efforts we can move toward the world created by our predecessors and enjoy moments of close proximity to the people of yesterday while we listen to what they have to tell us. In archeological parks and monuments we can stand where Indians once built their dwellings or cooked their meals or said their prayers or made love. We can visit their ancient villages, revived for our delight. We can see the implements of their daily life, their works of art, their games, their religious paraphernalia.

Some of these things are displayed close to the homes where the people once lived. Other large collections of artifacts have been gathered in museums far from the sites where they were found. But there has been no convenient guidebook that would help the average present-day American to discover the American of an earlier era.

Now, in the pages that follow, you can find your way to all the archeological sites that have been prepared for public view in the area north of Mexico. Here, too, are the museums which tell with some clarity about America's aboriginal yesterdays. However, you will not find any road directions to the thousands of archeological sites in which exploration is still to be done, or to many of those which are being investigated at the moment. It would be impossible to list all of them. Nor could most tourists visit them. The roads are often rough; the lanes leading to sites are frequently unmarked. Moreover, if enthusiastic but inexperienced people try their hand at digging, the damage they may do is very great. So this book confines itself to sites that have been specially prepared for the enjoyment of visitors, including a number of excavations specially conducted so that visitors can watch what goes on.

In national parks, monuments, state parks, etc. where camping facilities are available this has been indicated. If facilities are within one hour's drive from the site this is indicated as "camping nearby."

There are, of course, many more museums than you will find listed here. A considerable number have good Indian exhibits. However, some of these have been omitted because they lack displays which illuminate *prehistoric* Indian life. By prehistoric is meant that period before the art of writing came to the New World and made possible the keeping of written records.

There are also many archeological sites which reflect human experience after European and Indian met in North America. These places, often called historic sites, are too numerous to be included here, as are museums devoted solely to materials recovered by workers in historic archeology. Another guidebook will have to be prepared to cover them.

A further word about the prehistoric sites which have *not* been opened to the public. Archeologists feel protective about such places. They know that thousands of glimpses into the past have been lost because well-meaning people have excavated and carried away evidence of ancient life. Almost all this evidence has gone into oblivion. It is fun to dig up arrowheads and potsherds and skeletons. But such digging is pure destruction unless it is done with real understanding and knowledge. Proper, minutely detailed reports must be carefully kept, and findings must be published. Otherwise the collection of artifacts does nothing but obliterate information—forever.

So don't, don't, don't dig unless you have the guidance of experts. But do look. Do photograph. Do draw. Do read. And do report any discovery you make. Pass your information along to museum authorities, archeological societies, or anthropology departments in universities. In these ways you can help to increase knowledge about that special kind of creature we happen to be—the kind that needs to understand himself and his past if he is to guide himself toward a livable future.

Franklin Folsom

Acknowledgements

A book like AMERICA'S ANCIENT TREASURES can appear to be the work of one author when it is in fact a collective enterprise to which many people have contributed their talents. However, since I alone among the contributors have been in a position to determine to what use the contributions were put, I alone must assume responsibility for any errors that appear in either judgment or fact.

At the outset I must emphasize that it has been possible to write AMERICA'S ANCIENT TREASURES only because a great many investigators have worked diligently. The result may seem to be that their findings are exploited as if they were a natural resource like air—the common property of all.

I am acutely aware that it is the massive and painstaking work done by others which I am reporting. My defense is twofold: first, I think scientific discoveries should be widely known; second, I have tried to avoid giving the impression that I had anything to do with making any of the discoveries reflected here. Moreover, all knowledge *is* a common resource, or should be. But, if I have misused knowledge in any way— if I have wasted this resource or thrown pollution into the intellectual atmosphere—then I should be taken to task.

However, the problem of acknowledging indebtedness cannot be solved by uttering words of general—anonymous—thanks. Perhaps the best way I can discharge part of my obligation is to refer readers to the bibliography on page 191–4. Each publication listed there has been helpful in some specific way, but a complete bibliography of material referred to would be far too bulky for this introductory guide. What I offer is frankly a compromise. I also acknowledge with thanks the many sources of the photographs I have used. But with these tabulations of indebtedness my words of appreciation have only begun.

Instead of making a last-but-not-least bow in the direction of Mary Elting Folsom, my wife, I want to start by acknowledging her contribution as co-researcher, file clerk, editor, critic, and collaborator.

To our daughter, Rachel, goes my very warm appreciation of the care she has devoted to the drawings that accompany the text, and the great amount of time she had to take away from painting to do them.

In many different ways, archeologists, both professional and amateur, have extended courtesies that directly or indirectly helped this book to take shape. To all the following I offer my sincere thanks and my apologies for not spelling out what each has done: George A. Agogino, David A. Armour, Alfred M. Bailey, James G. Bain, Charles J. Bareis, Robert E. Bell, Rainer Berger, George H. Bishop, Joseph A. Blatt, Elaine A. Bluhm, Calvin S. Brown, Bettye J. Broyles, William A. Buckley, Jr., Joseph R. Caldwell, Carl B. Compton, Charles R. De Busk, David De Jarnette, Violet L. Deming, G. T. Donceel, Jr., Don W. Dragoo, A. E. Ehly, Albert B. Elsasser, George Ewing, the late Carroll Lane Fenton, Joan E. Freeman, George Frison, Campbell Grant, H. Bruce Greene, Alfred K. Guthe, Wendell S. Hadlock, William W. Harvey, Orval L. Henderson, Jr., E. P. Henly, Henry E. Hertner, Donald H. Hiser, Ann Monseth Irwin, Cynthia Irwin-Williams, Herbert Jenkins, Virginia Jennings, Mary Gregory Jewett, Joye E. Jordan, James H. Kellar, A. R. Kelly, Barry C. Kent, R. S. Kidd, Marvin F. Kivett, George J. Knudsen, Thomas E. Lee,

Cara L. Lewis, Miles Libhart, Robert H. Lister, Roger Luebbers, Rita Lund, Howard A. MacCord, Sr., Patricia Marchiando, Gary M. Matlock, Iris McGillivray, Charles R. McGimsey III, Grevis W. Melville, Dan F. Morse, Jack W. Musgrove, W. E. Organ, Stewart Peckham, Martha A. Potter, Brian W. Preston, Alden Redfield, Roger C. Reif, Jon W. Roethele, Rudolph H. Rudeen, Howard R. Sargent, Julius J. Satre, Robert E. Schenk, Jack M. Schock, James A. Scholtz, James V. Sciscenti, Lawrence T. Shelton, J. A. Shotwell, Ruth D. Simpson, Jon E. Soderblom, Archie MacS. Stalker, Glenn G. Stille, G. Stuber, Earl H. Swanson, W. S. Tarlton, Ronald A. Thomas, James A. Tuck, Mary Vaughn, Elisabeth Walton, Merle W. Wells, Joe Ben Wheat, Elwood S. Wilkins, Jr., Edwin N. Wilmsen, John Witthoft, J. P. Wohler, Richard B. Woodbury, Wesley R. Woodgerd, James B. Work, H. M. Wormington, and Barton A. Wright.

In the field and in Washington, the members of the National Park Service have been exceedingly helpful. Aside from the generosity shown by John M. Corbett, Chief Archeologist, in writing the foreword to this book, specific and valuable courtesies have been extended to me by Roy E. Appleman, John P. Barnett, Michael J. Becker, Fred Bell, Guy B. Braden, Zorro A. Bradley, Robert G. Bruce, George E. Buckingham, Jr., George S. Cattanach, Jr., George J. Chambers, John L. Cotter, William W. Dunmire, John R. Earnst, Douglas B. Evans, Mildred L. Fleming, Neal G. Guse, George A. Hall, Sam Henderson, D. L. Higgins, Warren H. Hill, Warren D. Hotchkiss, Ronald J. Ice, Earl Ingmanson, Merritt S. Johnston, Ralph H. Lewis, David D. May, David C. Ochsner, Charles R. Parkinson, William J. Raymond, Roy W. Reaves III, Essy Schattilly, Horace J. Sheely, Bert L. Speed, Don S. Squire, William M. Taylor, Robert H. Utley, John R. Vosburgh, William F. Wallace, Gilbert R. Wenger, and Richard Wheeler.

For data about archeological sites administered by the Forest Service I am indebted to Richard O. Benjamin, Donald S. Girton, W. W. Huber, Gary P. Wetzteon, and James F. Wiley.

For data about archeological sites administered by the Bureau of Land Management I am indebted to Robert E. Anderson, E. I. Rowland, Garth H. Rudd, and Delmar D. Vail.

To the directors, curators, superintendents, or public relations officers of all the sites and museums listed in this book I am indebted for the information which they supplied and which I have used.

To Sylvia McNair and Rita Stevens of Rand McNally and Company I owe much for the care they have taken with the manuscript.

Finally, my thanks go in a very personal way to three winter neighbors in Roosevelt, New Jersey, and a summer neighbor in Ward, Colorado. Heidi Kaye helped to bring order into files and mailings, both in the initial stage and as the book neared completion. Judith Steigler worked at all hours to help launch the preliminary mailing of 1,600 letters, labored faithfully on the index, and typed much of the final manuscript.

Judith Warren of Ward kept the rapidly growing files in order and, along with many other chores, typed much of the first rough version of the book, and some of the final draft, too. Sarah Kevil, a patient and intelligent secretary, helped out in ways too numerous to mention.

AMERICA'S ANCIENT TREASURES

INTRODUCTION

Who was the first American?

No one has yet found a complete skeleton or even a complete skull which belonged beyond question to any of the very earliest inhabitants of America north of Mexico. As a result, we cannot be sure what the firstcomers looked like. We know Early Man in the New World mainly by his tools and by how and where he used them and left them. But if we know what work people do, we can understand a great deal about them. Therefore, the first American is not a complete stranger to us. We have learned something about how he hunted, what he ate, where he lived. We can be fairly sure that he wore clothes in cold weather, could make fire, and had religious beliefs or practices. We even have plausible notions about the size and structure of the social units in which he lived.

All this information has been put together by archeologists, with the help of other scientists who know about chemistry and physics, about rocks, soil, animals, plants, climate, and all their complex interrelationships.

When did the earliest immigrants come to America? The experts don't all agree on the answer. Some say about 20,000 years ago; others believe men reached here much longer ago than that. Whenever it was, much of the northern part of the continent must have been covered with glaciers, just as northern Europe was.

Bordering the ice sheets was a treeless zone of tundra, and in this zone lived enormous herds of mammals. Caribou grazed there. So did the huge elephants called mammoths. A male mammoth could achieve a weight of six or seven tons, living on a diet of arctic herbs and grasses. Far to the south, extensive prairies also furnished nourishment for mammoths, for giant bison, and for bands of horses and camels. Ground sloths and mastodons grew to great size near the edges of forests where they lived on a diet of leaves and twigs. Smaller game, too, was abundant—deer, elk, antelope, rabbit, and most of the other animals we know today. Apparently men hunted all these creatures but found it most efficient to kill the largest ones whenever they could. One spear thrust into the heart or lungs of a mammoth produced thousands of times as much meat as one spear that brought down a bounding rabbit.

To reap the harvest of Ice-Age meat, men needed good spears, tipped with ivory or bone or stone, that could pierce the thick skins of large mammals and reach the vital organs. For butchering, hunters found various ways to put sharp edges on

Archeologists, like these at work at the Marmes Site in Washington, bring to light and preserve the artifacts and remains of prehistoric man.

certain kinds of stone, thus shaping knives. These stone knives would cut easily through hides that were far too tough for fingers to tear or for teeth to pierce.

Besides food, men needed fire and shelter against the cold, as well as clothing which would produce a miniature warm climate close to their bodies. To make animal-skin clothing, they needed special tools: scrapers of stone or bone to remove from the inside of a skin the tissue that would make it unmanageable when it dried and hardened, awls for punching holes, and needles for sewing.

By burning animal fat and the long bones of mammals, which were rich storehouses of marrow, men could keep warm, even where there was no wood for fires. They could make shelters from the skins of most of the large animals they hunted, although mammoth skins, as thick as automobile tires, were quite unusable. However, in treeless country, mammoth ribs and the leg bones as big around as tree trunks could take the place of wooden frameworks, over which skins could be spread to make houses. With these inventions and a few others, human beings learned the trick of living under arctic conditions. And having learned it, they wandered far, following the herds of big game that were their food supply.

This wandering took some of them from Siberia into Alaska at a time when a vast stretch of prairie joined Asia to North America. In those days the ocean was lower than it is today because there was actually less water in it. Billions of tons of water had evaporated from the earth's seas, had then fallen in the form of snow, and remained unmelted. Each year more snow piled up on the land. There it was compressed into ice, which formed enormous ice sheets. Deprived of water, the oceans shrank, and land which had been close to the surface was now exposed.

One such area, known as the Bering Land Bridge, between Siberia and Alaska, was sometimes more than 1,000 miles wide, covered with arctic vegetation which fed game animals. Getting to Alaska was no special problem for hunters, and it was possible to live there because much of the land was never covered by ice, although most of Canada was.

No one yet knows how many people moved into Alaska during the Ice Age, or how long they remained there. But at least once, perhaps more than once, the ice sheet which covered Canada melted until a long strip of land, just east of the Rocky Mountains, became ice-free all the way from Alaska and northern Canada to the Great Plains. Vegetation invaded the strip. Then animals followed the plants, and at least once, perhaps many times, a band of hunters passed through this corridor, following game southward. After reaching the Great Plains they remained. The hunting was good, and it didn't matter that the glaciers grew again and met, closing the corridor behind them.

Because the food supply was ample, each band grew in size until it had to subdivide. On the Plains the number of bands steadily increased, and from this central starting point people spread out over all of North and South America.

In the heartland of North America the Big-Game Hunters, who are called Paleo-Indians, continued to use tools of the kind they had brought with them. But in time they made innovations and improvements. One very distinctive tool became popular—a type of spearpoint which the hunters fashioned from certain kinds of stone, such as flint, chalcedony, jasper, and chert. With great skill a point-maker thinned a fragment of hard rock and chipped its edges precisely. Then, striking two perfectly aimed blows, he knocked off flakes to form a groove or channel down its front and back. The groove, called a flute, set the point apart from others, and for this archeologists are grateful. Such an easily identifiable tool is almost a fingerprint of Early Man.

One kind of fluted point has been named the Clovis point because archeologists first excavated it near Clovis, New Mexico. The excavation offered clear proof that men had used points of this kind to kill mammoths about 9220 B.C. In excavations elsewhere evidence has appeared that men worked in groups when they hunted the huge elephants.

Wherever mammoth hunters went, they left points of the Clovis type. Literally thousands have been found in Kentucky, Tennessee, and Alabama, an area in which Paleo-Indians were relatively numerous. Between the years 11,500 B.P.

(meaning Before Present) and 11,000 B.P., a thin film of humanity spread over most of the United States and part of Canada. In the next thousand years (11,000–10,000 B.P.) a different kind of fluted point, called the Folsom point, replaced the Clovis point in popularity. Then fluting went out of fashion and for 2,500 or 3,000 years Big-Game Hunters brought down their quarry with points that were not fluted. All these hunters were Paleo-Indians, and all seem to have lived in much the same way. Their activities did not vary a great deal whether they lived in southern Arizona or the southeastern states or Massachusetts or Alberta or Nova Scotia.

Only one Paleo-Indian site has been prepared for public view—Sandia Man Cave in the Sandia Mountains east of Albuquerque, New Mexico. Several other Paleo sites have been designated National Historic Sites by the National Park Service, and some of these may be visited with a little difficulty, but there is usually nothing to see but a plaque. The excavation has been filled in, and the landscape has more or less the appearance it had before digging began.

Perhaps the most famous Paleo site is one near Folsom, New Mexico. Here a spearpoint was found between the ribs of a bison of a type that had long been extinct. It was this find, made in 1927, which established beyond a doubt the great antiquity of man in America. Up to that time most scientists did not dare to think that people arrived here more than 3,000 years ago. The Folsom spearpoints pushed the date back to 10,000 years ago, and subsequently the Clovis point discoveries pushed it back even further. The state of New Mexico made the Folsom Site into a State Monument, but the monument has now been closed to the public. Too many visitors dug there in the portion of the site that had not been scientifically excavated. Pending further professional work, it has been placed off limits to the public.

At this moment you will have to visit museums if you want to see what archeologists encounter when they dig in Paleo sites. Fortunately the museum exhibits are numerous and illuminating—perhaps more rewarding even than a visit to a site itself would be. Paleo-Indians left few tools or weapons in any one place, and really fine examples of such artifacts (archeologists call them "goodies") don't turn up every day in a dig.

On the archeologist's calendar, the Paleo-Indian Period came to an end about 6,000 years ago. By that time the great glaciers of the Ice Age had melted away. So had most of the great animals. The mammoths of North America were all gone. A little later the mastodons disappeared. The ground sloth and the giant bison that roamed the prairies vanished, as did the horses and camels.

Scientists disagree among themselves about the causes of this extinction. Some believe that the animals could not adjust to the changes in vegetation that came when the ice melted and the land grew warmer. Other investigators think that the reproductive cycle of larger animals was geared to Ice-Age seasons, and when the length of the seasons changed with warmer weather, offspring may have been born at times of year when they could not survive. Still others believe that the Paleo-Indians developed hunting techniques that were so efficient that they killed off the largest of their quarry.

At any rate, people had to turn from food that came in big units to smaller game. Men and women both began a more intensive search for things to eat. They developed new lifeways and fashioned new tools to provide a livelihood. To supplement their meat diet more than in the past, they gathered berries and plant food of various kinds, particularly seeds. By now the population had increased from a few bands to many thousands of individuals. All over America it had become necessary to exploit even the smallest kinds of food resource. This new stage with its new developments has become known as the Archaic.

Then, as now, the East differed greatly from the West. In the East heavy rains flowed off in numerous streams filled with fish and shellfish. Forests grew thick, and they sheltered smaller animals which were relatively fewer in number than the grazing herds on the grass-rich prairies. Nevertheless, ingenious fish weirs, extensive use of shellfish, or one-man hunting methods geared to the tree-congested forest all produced an ample food supply in certain places. There the people of the

Archaic could live in larger groups than had been possible in Paleo times.

One Eastern Archaic site open to the public is Russell Cave National Monument in Alabama where people first began to live 8,500 or 9,000 years ago. Another Eastern Archaic site is Graham Cave State Park in Missouri. But most Archaic artifacts, like those of Paleo times, are best displayed in museums.

The Archaic lifeway in the West has been called Western Archaic by some archeologists. Others prefer the name Desert culture, and well they might. The West had grown more arid as the Ice Age ended. Large areas had very little rainfall in the course of a year, and this lack of water shaped the kinds of plant that grew there. The plants determined the kinds of animal that lived on them, and these creatures differed markedly from those which lived on and amid lusher vegetation to the east. In turn, the people who lived on both animals and plants in the West worked out patterns of behavior which differed from those in the East. Men who had once hunted mammoths came more and more to depend on small animals, even the smallest, such as crickets and grasshoppers. But meat of any kind was scarce, and plant food became very important, particularly small seeds. People invented baskets for holding seeds and tools for grinding them. In the whole world no basketry has been dated as early as that found in the Great Basin.

About A.D. 850 Indians at Mesa Verde lived on the mesa top in dwellings built in a row. From a diorama in the museum at Mesa Verde National Park, Colorado.

Out of the Western Archaic or Desert culture developed a number of different and highly specialized ways of living. None of them, of course, followed the modern political state lines, and some in northern Mexico extended into the United States. As time went on, many ideas and institutions, inventions and customs flowed from Mexico farther northward into the present southwestern states of Arizona and New Mexico. It was primarily the ways in which people lived which shifted northward, rather than the people themselves. Recent excavations in the Southwest have shown that one particular group of Western Archaic people developed gradually, in one place, through stage after stage, until they became the modern Indians of Zia Pueblo.

In southern New Mexico and Arizona people became especially skilled in the exploitation of plant food. Their lifeway, which has been named the Cochise (ko-CHEEZ) culture, developed before 5000 B.C. This Cochise variety of the Western Archaic received many stimulating ideas from Mexico. Most important was the concept that by planting seeds in garden patches men could create food, not just find it. The result was that several hundred years before the beginning of the Christian era, there began a series of exceedingly important changes in the Southwest. These changes led to the creation of various distinctive house types and villages which can easily be visited today. Many prehistoric southwestern sites are open to the public, and finds from these sites may also be enjoyed in museums all over the country.

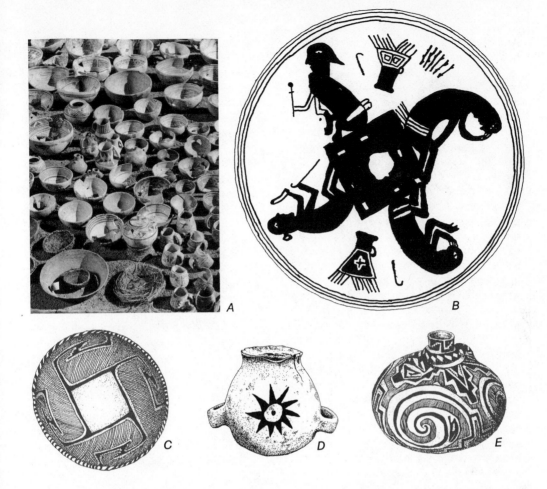

A B

C D E

Pot Hound or Pot Hunter

The rock hound is a collector of rocks and minerals; the pot hound is a collector of pots and other prehistoric Indian artifacts. A pot hound is a vandal when he digs in sites only to recover beautiful specimens to sell or to keep in his private collection. The collector who does not dig up artifacts himself encourages vandalism if he buys from those who have excavated solely for financial gain.

Amateur archeologists rightly object to pot hunters, but amateurs are no better than vandals if they dig without keeping careful, complete records of everything they do and find. Once an object is out of the ground it should be cataloged so that it can be located easily in a collection and so that all of the relevant information about it will be at hand.

If a collector arranges his artifacts in no order at all, or makes them into outlines of hearts or wheels, he shows a good deal about his own taste but reveals nothing at all about the people who made the artifacts. For storage purposes the great virtue is orderliness, but artifacts can also be arranged to show stages in their manufacture, to show how they lay in relation to each other in the ground, to show how they related historically to other artifacts, or to show how they related to the environment in which they were made and used. In other words, artifacts can be arranged so that they reveal something about people, and this after all is what archeology is all about.

Key to Archeological Sites

SOUTHWEST

ARIZONA
1. Besh-Ba-Gowah
2. Canyon de Chelly
3. Casa Grande Ruins
4. Grand Canyon
5. Kinishba Pueblo
6. Kinlichee Tribal Park
7. Montezuma Castle
8. Navaho
9. Oraibi
10. Petrified Forest
11. Pueblo Grande Museum
12. Tonto
13. Tuzigoot
14. Walnut Canyon
15. Walpi
16. Wupatki

COLORADO
17. Great Sand Dunes
18. Lowry Pueblo Ruins

19. Mesa Verde

NEW MEXICO
20. Abo
21. Acoma
22. Albuquerque Petroglyphs
23. Aztec Ruins
24. Bandelier
25. Carlsbad Caverns
26. Chaco Canyon
22. Coronado
28. Gila Cliff Dwellings
20. Gran Quivera
22. Jemez
31. Kwilleylekia Ruins
32. Laguna Pueblo
33. Pecos
24. Picuris Pueblo
24. Puyé Cliff Ruins
20. Quarai
24. San Juan Pueblo
22. Sandia Man Cave
22. Santa Clara Pueblo
24. Taos Pueblo
41. Three Rivers Petroglyphs
22. Zia Pueblo
43. Zuni Pueblo

UTAH
44. Alkali Ridge
45. Anasazi Indian Village
44. Arch Canyon Indian Ruin
46. Calf Creek Site
47. Canyonlands
48. Capitol Reef
49. Danger Cave
44. Grand Gulch
50. Hog Springs Site
44. Hovenweep
44. Indian Pictographs
44. Natural Bridges
44. Newspaper Rock
55. Parowan Gap Drawings
56. Zion

GREAT BASIN & CALIFORNIA

CALIFORNIA
57. Petroglyph Canyons
58. Calico Mountains Project
59. Clear Lake
60. Coyote Hills Park
61. Indian Grinding Rock
62. Joshua Tree

63. Petroglyphs
64. Sequoia & Kings Canyon

NEVADA
65. Lake Mead
66. Rocky Gap Site

NORTHWEST COAST

ALASKA
67. Katmai
68. Sitka

IDAHO
69. Alpha Rockshelter
70. Lolo Trail
71. Weis Rockshelter

OREGON
72. Collier Pithouse
73. Fort Rock Cave

WASHINGTON
74. Indian Painted Rocks
75. Indian Painted Rocks
76. Lake Lenore Caves
77. Neah Bay
78. Old Man House

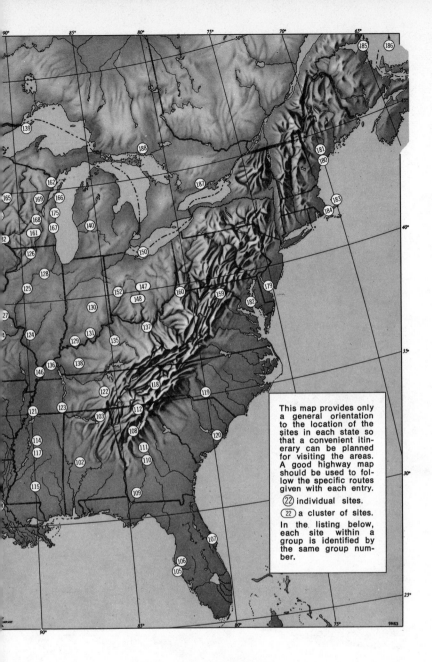

This map provides only a general orientation to the location of the sites in each state so that a convenient itinerary can be planned for visiting the areas. A good highway map should be used to follow the specific routes given with each entry.

㉒ individual sites.

㉒ a cluster of sites.

In the listing below, each site within a group is identified by the same group number.

9N63

SOUTHWEST

North of Mexico no places offer more abundant archeological remains than do Arizona, New Mexico, southwestern Colorado, and southern Utah. Millions, possibly billions, of pottery fragments lie in and on the soil. Surveys have revealed literally thousands of habitation sites. All these are reminders that creative men have long lived here, and all have a common history. The once-lived-in villages, of which the potsherds are the evidence, came into existence largely as a result of one special development that took place in Mexico six or seven thousand years ago. At that time people in the Tehuacan Valley, south of present-day Mexico City, began to domesticate a certain wild grass. The discovery that they could plant its seeds in garden plots changed their lives and the whole of Indian life in large sections of the American continents.

After men began to cultivate this wild grass, it changed greatly and evolved into the grain we call corn, or maize. As it changed it developed husks that wrapped more and more tightly around the seed-bearing cob. At last maize could no longer sow its own seeds. It could not live from year to year unless men removed the husks and planted the corn kernels. At the same time, people became so accustomed to eating corn, prepared in many ways, that their lives revolved around planting, cultivating, and harvesting the helpless but nourishing cereal. Corn and men became mutually dependent.

The idea of gardening spread northward. So did a knowledge of how to make long-lasting pots for cooking and storing the new food. With the ability to keep food in reserve, man's diet changed. Dwellings, too, changed under influences which swept into northern Mexico, then into New Mexico and Arizona. Along with corn there came a whole constellation of customs and ceremonies, such as corn dances and other planting and harvest-time rituals. Some of these are still observed today.

Perhaps as early as 2000 B.C. the Western Archaic people known as the Cochise had begun to add corn to their diet. They also added squash and beans. The beans were most important because they furnished protein which was lacking when farmers depended entirely on corn. Men could not live by maize alone. Life changed greatly with the arrival of this extraordinary plant. But the changes were not identical throughout the Southwest. They varied from place to place as men learned the new ways of creating food while continuing to be a part of the special kind of ecological system in which they had already found a place for

More than 600 years ago 12 or 15 families lived in this 19-room, five-story apartment house at Montezuma Castle National Monument.

themselves. In one sense, of course, all farmers were alike. They could give up the wandering existence of the hunter or gatherer and build more or less permanent dwellings. The differences in the details of how they built and created and elaborated on life are among the things that make Southwestern archeology fascinating to both the scientist and the layman.

Broadly speaking, four different lifeways developed under the stimulating influences that came with agriculture from Mexico: the Mogollon (MOH-goh-YOHN), the Hohokam (ho-ho-KAHM), the Patayan (PAH-tah-YAHN), and the Anasazi (AHN-ah-SAH-zee). Eventually there developed several variations or combinations of these four basic cultures.

The Mogollon Culture

By about 100 B.C. the new agricultural way of life had taken on a distinct identity in the highlands of the Mogollon Mountains, which lie across the present border between Arizona and New Mexico. In certain places the slopes of these mountains were ideal for raising corn. They duplicated to a considerable extent the conditions in the part of Mexico where corn was domesticated. Here in the mountains the Cochise had long based their pattern of existence on plant food. They were accustomed to grinding wild seeds in order to make them easy to chew and digest, and it was no problem for women to begin grinding corn as well. We know that the Cochise began to raise corn at a very early date; archeologists have excavated the tiny cobs and husks and even a few seeds of extremely ancient corn in Bat Cave and Tularosa Cave in New Mexico. (Neither of these sites is visitable, but some of the material from Bat Cave is on exhibit at the Peabody Museum, Harvard University, in Cambridge, Massachusetts.)

After the Cochise settled down and developed the characteristics now called Mogollon, they began to live in dwellings known as pithouses. To make such a house, they dug a circular pit two or three feet deep and set a strong, upright post in the center. Then over the pit they made a cone-shaped roof of saplings which leaned against the center pole from around the upper edge of the pit. Over the saplings they laid or wove small branches, and on top of the branches they spread a thick layer of mud. On one side of the pithouse a ramp led from ground level down to the floor inside.

A pithouse, part below ground and part above, and covered with a thick insulating layer of earth, was relatively cool in summer and warm in winter. As time went on, its shape changed from circular to oval to rectangular, and it came to be roofed in various ways, but it remained the standard home until very late in Mogollon history.

The pottery that Mogollon people made was at first red or brown without decoration. Later they invented or borrowed many different designs, and those who lived along the Mimbres River developed a unique style. They painted sophisticated, often humorous representations of animals, insects, fish, birds, and human beings on the surfaces of their dishes. A good collection of Mimbres pottery may be seen at the Palace of the Governors Museum in Santa Fe, at the Philbrook Art Center in Oklahoma City, and at the Peabody Museum in Cambridge, Massachusetts.

The Hohokam Culture

Just as some of the Cochise people adjusted to life in the mountains and later became the Mogollon, so other Cochise adjusted to life in the desert of southern Arizona. There they became the Hohokam (a Pima Indian word for "ancient ones"), after the knowledge of growing corn and other plants came to them from Mexico.

Along the Salt, the Gila, and the San Pedro rivers the Hohokam developed a special way of life. They dug canals and diverted water from the rivers to irrigate their fields far out on the semiarid desert land. Rich crops resulted from irrigation, and the River Hohokam not only had enough to eat, they had time to spare. Some of them became fine craftsmen, making lovely jewelry and figurines. The early Hohokam pottery was buff-colored with red geometric decorations. Later potters made decorations in the forms of birds or animals or people.

Hohokam houses resembled Mogollon houses in some ways, except that the builders did less excavation. Their homes were not true pithouses. In some places, late in Hohokam history, people built very large structures several stories high. These apparently were not dwellings but served for defense or ceremonial purposes or for storage. Near some of their villages the Hohokam made large, rather shallow excavations which some archeologists believe were courts on which men played a kind of ceremonial ball game similar to the game played with a solid rubber ball in Mexico and other places to the south. This idea has been challenged by those who think that the courts were used for some other kind of ceremony.

In the days of the Hohokam there was apparently somewhat more rainfall than there is today in southern Arizona. With more moisture people had more to eat with less work. So life was a little easier than it is for the present-day Pima and Papago Indians, who may be the descendants of the ancient Hohokam.

The Patayan Culture

In the valley of the Colorado River, which includes the western part of Arizona, lived a people to whom agriculture came later than it did to the Mogollon and the Hohokam. Here farming began only about A.D. 600. In the lowlands on the banks of the great river and in the high plateau country through which the Colorado had cut its deep channel, distinct lifeways developed.

Not a great deal is known about these prehistoric people, who are called Patayan by some archeologists and Hakataya by others. The reason is simple: much evidence of life along the riverbanks has been buried under layers of silt brought down by the Colorado River. Other sites have been washed away and lie now, lost forever, in the Gulf of California.

At the time when corn reached them from Mexico, the Patayan lived in flimsy shelters made of poles covered with brush. Later they began to make more permanent structures covered with mud. Finally some of them borrowed an archi-

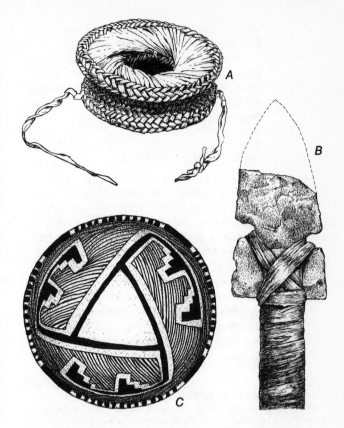

A. Basketry pad, found at Echo House, Mesa Verde, made for use in carrying heavy water jars on the head. B. Broken arrowhead, found with its hafting intact, showing how a point was attached to a shaft. Original in Colorado State Museum, Denver. C. Mesa Verde bowl, with a design made in black on a white background. D. Archeologists excavating four burials in a pithouse. National Park Service photo.

tectural idea from neighbors to the north and began to build stone dwellings.

People who live along the Colorado River today—the Havasupai, the Maricopa, and the Yuma among others—are probably descendants of the ancient Patayan people.

The Anasazi Culture

Still farther north of Mexico lies rugged country where high plateaus are cut by deep canyons and rimmed with steep cliffs. Here, along the southern part of Colorado and Utah and the northern part of New Mexico and Arizona, still another group of Western Archaic people made their home. Like other prefarming groups they hunted and harvested wild crops as they moved about. After the knowledge of corn reached them they did less hunting and adopted lifeways which archeologists call Anasazi. (This is a word

from the Navajo language meaning "ancient ones.")

As the Anasazi culture developed, changes were so very marked that archeologists have given special names to each of the stages. The first stage is usually called Basketmaker II. There is no Basketmaker I; the archeologists who named it have been disappointed. They expected some day to find evidence of a stage they could call Basketmaker I. They never did. At any rate these first Anasazi corn farmers tended to live in caves or recesses in the cliff walls where their nomadic ancestors had often camped. Sometimes they may have put up brush shelters in the caves, and they certainly stored food in slab-lined pits in cave floors. Later they learned to build pithouses for their own use. These resembled in many ways the pithouses of the Mogollon, but in Anasazi country the half-subterranean dwellings had an interesting later history which is best told at the museum in Mesa Verde National Park.

The Basketmakers did indeed make marvelous baskets. Thanks to the dry climate and their taste for living in caves, a great deal of their fine handiwork was protected from the weather and has survived for nearly 2,000 years. For the same

A. Ancient masonry methods: First, with a sharp-edged blade of chert, a deep groove was scratched on the surface of a slab of sandstone. B. Next the slab was placed over a pebble. C. Then, the groove was tapped with a hammerstone directly above the pebble to break the slab cleanly in two. D. Section of a wall built by this method, in Aztec National Monument. National Park Service photo by George A. Grant. E. Betatakin Ruin in Navajo National Monument. National Park Service photo by Fred E. Mang, Jr.

A

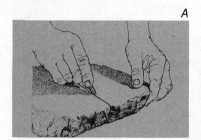

B

C

D

reason we also know what these people looked like. They buried their dead in empty storage pits, and in the dry air bodies became dessicated. Men wore their hair long, sometimes in braids; women cut theirs short and used it to make bags or rope.

By A.D. 700 the Anasazi had learned more about farming and had drawn together in larger groups than before. They were building houses of stone, one against another in communal dwellings. The Spanish word for these apartment-house villages was pueblo, and so archeologists have given the name Pueblo to the next stages in Anasazi culture.

In the next 600 years the Anasazi grew more and more skilled at building and pottery-making, and other crafts such as the creation of jewelry and fine cloth. Within the big general region where they lived, there began to appear three major centers of development. Each had a style of pottery and masonry and architecture that distinguished it from the others.

One center was near present-day Kayenta, in Arizona. There the finest achievements of the Kayenta Anasazi are preserved in Navajo National Monument. A second center was at Mesa Verde in Colorado. The third was in Chaco Canyon in New Mexico. From all these developments among the Anasazi one important fact emerges. Using corn, beans, and squash as sources of energy in an area which was far from ideal for agriculture, people managed to shape lifeways which became more and more sophisticated with the passage of time. They gathered together in villages and seemed to be approaching urban life, just as the agriculturalists did in the Tigris-Euphrates Valley at the beginning of the era of Middle Eastern civilization. Then a great convulsion affected the Anasazi world. In one village after another, men put aside their tools and women abandoned their cooking pots. With only what they could carry on a long journey, they set out to make new homes elsewhere.

Archeologists do not agree on what caused the change which left most Anasazi pueblos deserted forever and turned an expansive people to looking inward. Certainly there was such a change. The Anasazi withdrew from the wide area they occupied and went to live in a narrower one. From that time on they seemed to live with less energy. They grew protective of what they had and knew. Surviving, and surviving very skillfully, they became the ancestors of the Pueblo Indians of today.

E

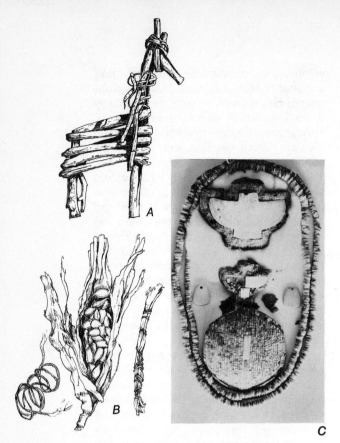

A. Figurine of a deer, made from split twigs about 3,000 years ago in the Grand Canyon area. Original in the Arizona State Museum, Tucson. B. Squash seeds were found in Canyon de Chelly, wrapped tightly in corn husk as shown on the right. Drawn from a National Park Service photo by Watson. C. Hohokam craftsmen at Casa Grande glued tiny bits of shaped turquoise onto seashells with mesquite gum. These are in the museum at the site. National Park Service photo by George A. Grant. D. Perpendicular sandstone walls tower above small clusters of masonry buildings in niches or on the canyon floor, in Canyon de Chelly. National Park Service photo.

Arizona

AMERIND FOUNDATION, INC.

From Tucson (too-SAHN) drive 64 miles east on Interstate 10, then 1¼ miles on local road toward Dragoon. Open free, by appointment only, Friday, Saturday, Sunday all year. Mail address: Dragoon, Arizona 85609.

This private museum contains a superb collection of prehistoric material from the area once called Pimeria Alta, which included southern Arizona and the northern part of the Mexican state of Sonora.

ARIZONA STATE MUSEUM

University of Arizona, N. Park Ave. at Third St., Tucson. Open free, 10 a.m. to 5 p.m., Monday through Saturday; 2 p.m. to 5 p.m., Sunday; closed Jan. 1, July 4, Labor Day, Thanksgiving, Dec. 25.

This remarkable museum has illuminating exhibits of all major cultures in Southwest prehistory. Displays include artifacts from: Ventana Cave, which was occupied by men for almost 10,000 years; Snaketown, occupied for a long time by the Hohokam people; the Naco and Lehner sites.

The latter site was discovered when a rancher in the San Pedro Valley saw some large bones exposed in an arroyo. He reported the find to Emil Haury of the Arizona State Museum. Haury excavated and found evidence that hunters, more than 11,000 years ago, killed nine mammoths and roasted some of the meat nearby.

An exhibit in the museum shows mammoth bones and the tools of mammoth hunters exactly as archeologists found them in the earth. Another display explains how prehistoric men made their stone tools. Dioramas show a mammoth kill, life around Ventana Cave 9,000 years ago, people of the Desert culture engaged in food collecting, and later people at work farming.

The museum also has rich collections of materials from all the Indian tribes that have lived in Arizona in historic times.

BESH-BA-GOWAH (besh-ba-GO-wah)

From the center of Globe drive south to the end of S. Broad St., turn right across the bridge, continue on Ice House Canyon Rd. to a directional sign on the right. Total distance 1½ miles. Open free, at all times. Camping nearby.

Anasazi people who moved down from the north settled in this area, where they became known as the Salado. At first they lived in small groups. Later they gathered together into sizable villages, of which Besh-ba-Gowah is one. It was inhabited from A.D. 1225 to 1400. The city of Globe sponsored the excavation and partial restoration of the site, which is now surrounded by a protective fence. Artifacts excavated from the ruin are on display at City Hall in Globe.

CANYON DE CHELLY NATIONAL MONUMENT (CAN-yuhn duh SHAY)

From Gallup, New Mexico, drive north 8 miles on U.S. 666, then 52 miles west on New Mexico-Arizona 264 through Ganado, then 33 miles north on Navajo 8 to monument headquarters and the Visitor Center at Chinle (chin-LEE). Open free, 8 a.m. to 5 p.m., Oct. through May; 8 a.m. to 6 p.m., June through Sept. Camping.

Protected by spectacular red sandstone walls, prehistoric Indians built hundreds of small villages and cliff dwellings in this canyon over a period of nearly a thousand years. Visitors can walk to a cliff dwelling called White House Ruin, following a trail that winds down from the canyon rim for about a mile. Other ruins can be seen only when visitors are accompanied by a Park Ranger or other official guide.

The Story. Beginning about A.D. 350, the canyon was occupied by people now known as the Anasazi, ancestors of the present-day Pueblo Indians. Then about A.D. 1300 the Anasazi moved out, leaving the canyon to occasional visits from their descendants or from the Navajo Indians who began to take possession of the area. During their thousand-year stay, the Anasazi gardened in small plots on the canyon bottom where there was flowing water at certain times each year. At other seasons the stream bed must have seemed completely dry, although there was usually enough moisture beneath the surface for crops of corn and squash.

Anasazi men also hunted—at first with spears, then with bows and arrows. Over the years house structures changed as much as hunting methods. Early inhabitants of the canyon lived in houses built partially underground. Their later dwellings, made of stone and entirely above ground, were joined one to another so that the whole village was one big apartment house. Still later they built some of their apartment houses in large dry caves in the cliffs.

About A.D. 1300 the Anasazi abandoned Canyon de Chelly, just as they moved out of other villages in the Four Corners area—the area where Arizona, Utah, Colorado, and New Mexico meet. Why they left is still something of a mystery. Archeologists have discovered that there was a severe drought at about this time, and for many years before they moved away the Anasazi had great difficulty raising crops. Quite possibly this was not their only reason for deserting the canyon. Many of the farmers may have ed from invaders—from the Utes, according to some archeologists, or the Navajos, according to others.

At any rate, Navajos did settle in the canyon nearly 300 years ago, and some of the paintings they made on its rock walls can still be seen. It was here that Kit Carson found the Navajos in 1864, rounded them up, and herded them into what amounted to a prisoner-of-war camp at Fort Sumner, New Mexico, 300 miles away.

The Museum. Contains exhibits of Southwestern archeological finds in the Four Corners area and also artifacts from later Navajo culture.

The Name. De Chelly (duh SHAY) is a mispronunciation in English of a mispronunciation in Spanish of the Navajo word *tsegi* which means "a rocky canyon."

CASA GRANDE RUINS NATIONAL MONUMENT
(KAH-suh GRAHN-day)

Halfway between Phoenix and Tucson, 1 mile north of Coolidge on Arizona 87. (Note: the National Monument is *not* in the town of Casa Grande.) Open 7 a.m. to 7 p.m. Admission: $1 per car or 50¢ for each adult who arrives by bus; children under 16 free when accompanied by an adult. Camping nearby.

This site offers an excellent introduction to the lifeway of the ancient irrigation farmers now known as the Hohokam. There are guided tours through one part of the ruins, 9:15 a.m. to 4:15 p.m., and a self-guided tour through another part.

The Story. The impressive four-story structure which gives the site its name (Casa Grande means Big House) was probably built about A.D. 1350 and was used until 1450. It may have been a ceremonial center or fortress or both. Its massive walls, made from a special kind of clay, are not typical of the Hohokam. The building is much more like those seen farther south in Mexico. The usual Hohokam dwellings were separate single-room houses made of brush and mud.

Throughout the semiarid Gila River Valley, the Hohokam managed to raise crops by irrigation. They built more than 250 miles of canals which were between two and four feet wide and about two feet deep. Some can still be seen today.

The Museum. Here may be seen artifacts of the Hohokam people and panels which explain their life.

The Name. The ruins were visited in 1694 by Father Kino, a Spanish explorer-priest, who named the place Casa Grande. The great size of the main building made it a landmark for later visitors, and the name has remained in use.

EASTERN ARIZONA MUSEUM AND HISTORICAL SOCIETY

Main and Center streets, Pima. Open free, 9 a.m. to 6 p.m., Monday through Friday.

Salado and Hohokam artifacts from the vicinity of Pima are on display here, together with some material from northern Arizona which is not identified.

GRAND CANYON NATIONAL PARK

The Park is divided by the canyon into two parts reached by very different routes. For the South Rim drive 59 miles north from Williams on Arizona 64 to Park headquarters. For the North Rim drive 30 miles south from Jacob Lake on Arizona 67 to the Park entrance, then 12 miles farther to the Ranger Station. Open (South Rim) all year; (North Rim) mid-May to mid-Oct. Admission: $1 per car. Camping.

Prehistoric men lived in and around this incredible canyon for a very long time. Some climbed into caves in the cliffs and left artifacts there. In recent years Dr. Robert Euler has explored the canyon walls and bottom lands by helicopter and found a great many archeological sites which no one knew about before.

A ruined village called Tusayan (too-sah-YAHN) on the South Rim may be visited all year. There are guided tours in summer.

On the North Rim a site called Cape Royal Ruin (G. C. 212) has been excavated and is open to the public.

A third site, G.C. 624, on the canyon bottom near the Colorado River, may be visited all year. The eight-mile Bright Angel Trail leads to the site from the South Rim. Experienced hikers can make the trip on foot in a day. Others are advised to go by muleback.

The Story. People of the Western Archaic or Desert culture moved into the Grand Canyon area three or four thousand years ago. They lived by

Fluted Points

When a projectile point has a channel or depression running lengthwise on one or both of its faces it is said to be fluted. Clovis points used by mammoth hunters about 11,000 years ago, and Folsom points, used by hunters of very large bison about 10,000 years ago, were fluted.

If fluting had any practical value, it was apparently that the thinned base could be easily inserted into the split end of a spear shaft. However, the labor involved in preparing these points was greater than the labor required to shape an unfluted point. In addition there was a great deal of breakage during manufacture. On the other hand, unfluted points seem to have been equally effective weapons, and they were more durable. This has led some archeologists to suggest that fluting may have had a ceremonial purpose.

How or when or where the practice of fluting began is not known. H. Müller-Beck, a Swiss archeologist, believes it may have started in Europe, possibly in southern Russia, at least 26,000 years ago. Other students of Early Man in America think fluting may have developed on the Bering Land Bridge where men once hunted mammoths. The Land Bridge is now submerged so all evidence of what went on there is lost. Still other archeologists believe that fluted points were first made in Alaska or on the southern Great Plains in the United States.

No matter where the custom began, it did not last long as archeologists measure time. By about 9,000 years ago point-makers had shifted from the fragile Folsom points to sturdier points which were easier to manufacture and less likely to break.

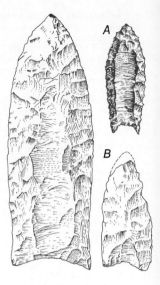

A. A Folsom point. B. Two Clovis points. Clovis points vary in measurement. These (which are pictured here about half actual length) were found along with mammoth bones at the Lehner Site in Arizona. After Haury et al.

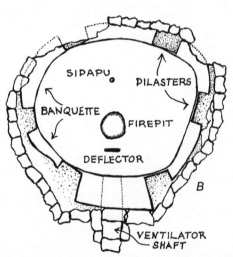

Anasazi Religion

Archeologists can't dig up a religious belief. All that comes out of the earth is an object. If the object resembles a prayer-stick used by Pueblo Indians today, it seems reasonable to suppose that the object may have been a prayer-stick in prehistoric times.

There are many similarities between present-day Pueblo religious objects and prehistoric objects which excavators have found.

The basic beliefs of modern Pueblo Indians have been studied. All things considered, it seems likely that the ancestors of the Pueblos had very similar views on life. If this was the case, the Anasazi religion said: "Man must live in harmony with nature."

A. A jar used in kiva ceremonies. The design was painted with a brush of yucca fiber and paint made of boiled plant juices. Original is in the museum at Mesa Verde. B. The ground plan of a kiva. After a drawing in the trail guide to Spruce Tree House, Mesa Verde.

gathering wild plant food and hunting, and they did what other hunters have sometimes done— they made figurines of deer or mountain sheep and left them in caves apparently in the hope that this practice would bring them luck. The figurines were fashioned of split twigs bent in ingenious ways. Sometimes these split-twig figurines were pierced by a twig spear for good measure. Archeologists have found many of the figurines in caves now almost completely inaccessible in the limestone walls.

Eventually people of the Grand Canyon area changed their patterns of living and became more like the Anasazi farmers who lived to the east and north. Some found their way down the canyon's high walls, built small villages, and raised their crops close to the thundering Colorado River. Others made their homes along the canyon rim. Tusayan, built between A.D. 1185 and 1200, housed about 30 people, but they did not stay long. By 1250 they had moved away, probably to the Kayenta region. One by one the other villages down near the river were also abandoned, and by the time the first Spanish explorers arrived the only Indians living in the canyon were the Havasupai, who have remained there to this day.

The Museums. At Tusayan Ruin the museum has exhibits with special emphasis on the culture of the people who lived there. Displays show how artifacts and pottery vessels were made. There are also exhibits of artifacts made and used by Patayan people called the Cohonina, who lived on the South Rim about A.D. 750 to 1100. The museum is open 8 a.m. to 5 p.m. in summer.

At the Visitor Center the museum is open all year, 8 a.m. to sunset. Displays here show artifacts of most people and periods in the area. Of special interest are the split-twig figurines.

Special Feature. In summer at Tusayan Ruin visitors can take a self-guided tour along a trail where plants are identified, with explanations of how each one played a part in the lives of prehistoric people who lived there.

HEARD MUSEUM OF ANTHROPOLOGY AND PRIMITIVE ART

22 E. Monte Vista Rd., Phoenix. Open 10 a.m. to 5 p.m., Tuesday through Saturday; 1 p.m. to 5 p.m., Sunday; closed Jan. 1, Dec. 25. Admission: adults, 25¢; children, 10¢.

Collections in this museum are built around artifacts of Indians of the Americas, including the Hohokam of southern Arizona.

KINISHBA PUEBLO

National Historic Landmark.
Drive 15 miles west of Whiteriver on Arizona 73. Open free, all year.

This partly restored Mogollon-Anasazi pueblo housed a thousand or more people between A.D. 1100 and 1350. It is one of the largest ruins in the Southwest. Despite its importance, the pueblo can only be viewed through a barbed wire fence which the White Mountain Apache Tribe has put up for the safety of visitors and for the protection of the site. When funds become available the tribe hopes to stabilize and restore the entire town, which includes two enclosed courtyards, and to reestablish the museum it once operated here.

Special Feature. An early excavator at Kinishba•

found the skeleton of a child around which was wrapped a necklace almost six feet long, made of 2,534 carefully polished turquoise beads. This astonishing piece of work is now in the Arizona State Museum at Tucson. Also in the necklace were 11 larger beads made of catlinite (pipestone), which may have been brought by traders from faraway Minnesota. Many other necklaces at Kinishba included coral, which came from either the Gulf of Mexico or Baja California, and shells from the Pacific Coast. Trade was obviously extensive in prehistoric America.

KINLICHEE TRIBAL PARK

On the Navajo Indian Reservation, drive west from Window Rock 22 miles on Navajo 3 (Arizona 264) to Cross Canyon Trading Post, then 2½ miles north on dirt road to Kinlichee and Cross Canyon Ruins. Open free, at all times. Camping nearby.

Anasazi people lived in this area for more than 500 years. Today, in a Tribal Park, the Navajo Indians are preserving the ruins of Anasazi dwellings, the oldest of which is a pithouse dated at about A.D. 800. Other ruins belong to the various Pueblo periods up to about 1300 when the large apartment house villages were abandoned. Wayside exhibits and a trail take the visitor on a self-guided tour which gives an opportunity to see how Anasazi architecture evolved. To help visitors visualize the life of the past one of the ruins has been completely reconstructed.

MONTEZUMA CASTLE NATIONAL MONUMENT

From Flagstaff drive 43 miles south on Interstate 17 to the main Visitor Center, east of the highway. Open 8 a.m. to 6 p.m., Memorial Day through Labor Day; 8 a.m. to 5 p.m., between Labor Day and Memorial Day. Admission: $1 per car or 50¢ for each adult who arrives by bus; children under 16, free.

The monument is in two sections—Montezuma Castle and Montezuma Well, seven miles apart. Footpaths lead to the beautifully preserved castle, a dwelling built in the cliff a hundred feet above the valley floor. Along the walk is a diorama with audio tape that explains what life was like in the dwelling more than 600 years ago. The ledge that supports the buildings has weathered so greatly that visits to the castle itself are no longer permitted. Ruins of other dwellings at the foot of the cliff, farther along the trail, may be visited.

At Montezuma Well two ruins overlook a sunken lake about 400 feet across and 55 feet deep. The well is fed by a huge spring from which flow 1½ million gallons of water every day.

The Story. Several groups of farmers with different customs contributed to the development of a distinct way of life in the valley of the Verde River. About A.D. 600 a group of Hohokam people moved into the valley from the desert country near modern Phoenix, where they lived in one-family, one-room houses made of poles covered with brush and mud. The Hohokam were farmers who dug irrigation canals to water their crops of corn, squash, beans, and cotton.

A second group of farmers lived north of Verde Valley. These people, who raised crops without irrigation, have been named the Sinagua (sin-AH-wah), Spanish for "without water."

In A.D. 1065 both these groups heard news that at a place now called Sunset Crater a volcano had erupted and covered a large area with a layer of

A

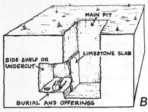

B

A. Reproduction of a painting of the Squash Blossom Girl from the Awatovi kiva, Museum of Northern Arizona photo. B. Diagram of an undercut grave at Montezuma Castle National Monument. After Shroeder and Hastings. C. Indian rock art in Petrified Forest National Park. National Park Service photo by George A. Grant. D. A view in the Keet Seel ruin, Navajo National Monument. National Park Service photo by Fred E. Mang, Jr.

C

D

cinders. These cinders helped the dry soil to retain moisture and made it good for farming. The result was a land rush which brought in from the east a third group of people called the Anasazi. Unlike the other farmers, these people built multiple dwellings of stone, sometimes two or more stories high.

Some of the Hohokam from Verde Valley joined in the land rush, and they mingled with the Anasazi and the Sinagua. But before long the cinder-covered land became crowded. Also there may have been a drought. At any rate, the area no longer seemed attractive to some of its inhabitants, and about A.D. 1100 a group of Sinagua moved south into Verde Valley. There they began to build the Anasazi type of stone house they had learned about during the land rush. Because they found water in the valley, they irrigated their fields, Hohokam-fashion, grew cotton along with food crops, and became excellent weavers. They also mined salt, which is always in demand wherever people's diet consists mainly of grain and other plant foods.

As a result of trade in salt and cotton and other products, new ideas came into the valley. So did many settlers who were attracted by the wealth there. One new idea served as a protection against rivals—the notion of building dwellings in cavities in cliffs. About 1250 the Sinagua began construction of a stone apartment house, with one room above another, in a cave overlooking Beaver Creek, which flows into the Verde River. This is the five-story habitation called Montezuma Castle.

For 200 years descendants of the original builders lived here in the valley. Then competition for the farmland along the creek and nearby river became too rough for the farmers, who seem to have been peaceful folk.

As aggressive newcomers—possibly the ancestors of the present-day Yavapai—moved into the valley, the Sinagua moved out. Very likely they went north and joined the ancestors of the present-day Hopi.

During their stay in Montezuma Castle, the Sinagua developed a unique way of disposing of their dead. They dug a grave straight down, then, near the bottom, hollowed out a side chamber for the burial and sealed it with a limestone slab. In spite of this special attention to the dead, the Sinagua in Montezuma Castle and around Montezuma Well apparently had no ceremonial rooms such as the Hopi were using at that time and are still using today.

The Museums. Each of the Visitor Centers at the Monument has a museum. Exhibits show and explain all the basic tools and utensils of the Hohokam and Sinagua in the area. Beautiful examples of weaving are displayed.

The Name. Early white settlers in Verde Valley mistakenly thought that Aztec Indians had built the dwellings at this site. So the five-story apartment house and the Well, several miles away, were both named in honor of Montezuma, last Aztec emperor. The name, although misleading, has stuck.

Special Feature. The prehistoric farmers here built irrigation canals from Montezuma Well to their garden plots. Because the water contained lime, the ditches became lined with a hard cement-like crust which has survived to this day.

MUSEUM OF NORTHERN ARIZONA

Fort Valley Rd., Flagstaff. Open free, 9 a.m. to 5 p.m., Monday through Saturday; 1:30 p.m. to 5 p.m.,

Sunday, June through Aug.; 9 a.m. to 12 noon and 1 p.m. to 5 p.m., Monday through Saturday; 1:30 p.m. to 5 p.m., Sunday, Mar. through May and Sept. through Dec. 24; closed Dec. 25 to Mar. 1.

Excellent displays give a very good idea of the lifeways of the Indians who have inhabited the Southwest. Exhibits cover all periods from the ancient Basketmaker through present-day Pueblo. Dioramas show ancient Anasazi village scenes and a ceremonial dance.

Special Feature. A full-scale reproduction of a Hopi underground ceremonial chamber, or kiva (KEY-vuh), is decorated with original murals taken from the ruins of the kiva at Awatovi, an ancient village on the Hopi Indian Reservation.

NAVAJO NATIONAL MONUMENT

From Tuba City drive 50 miles north on US 164, then 9 miles west on a paved road to the monument. Open free, 8 a.m. to 5 p.m. Camping.

Here visitors will find three superb cliff dwellings. Tours are conducted in spring, summer, and fall to the most accessible ruin, Betatakin (be-TAH-tah-kin) which means "ledge house" in the language of the Navajos who inhabit the region today. This is a village of 135 rooms, built in an immense cave which reaches 500 feet in height.

Dirt roads and a trail lead to a smaller ruin, now called Inscription House in memory of a Spanish explorer who scratched the date 1661 and some initials on a wall there. Visitors should inquire at the Visitor Center about road conditions before starting a trip to this part of the monument.

The third ruin, one of the largest in Arizona, is Keet Seel, which means "broken pottery" in the Navajo language. An eight-mile trail leads down into a canyon and along a stream to this splendid cliff village which has a remarkably new appearance although its 160 rooms have not been lived in for more than 600 years. A visit to Keet Seel takes a full day. The only way to reach it is on foot or on horses, which can be rented from Navajos by arrangement at Monument Headquarters.

The Story. About 1,500 years ago a special way of life began to develop in northern Arizona and New Mexico and in southern Colorado. People there had learned to farm, and so they could settle in small permanent villages which were scattered over a very large area. Little by little these communities joined to form bigger ones, and finally the population became oriented around three distinct cultural regions. One centered at Mesa Verde in Colorado, another at Chaco Canyon in New Mexico, and the third near Kayenta in Arizona. All of these people shared certain characteristics, and they have been given the general name Anasazi.

The Kayenta branch of the Anasazi built the three great cliff dwellings now called Betatakin, Inscription House, and Keet Seel. Like many other late Anasazi villages, these were abandoned in the 1300s for reasons that are still little understood.

Modern Navajo Indians, for whom the monument is named, avoided the ruins because they feared all things dead. Then in the 19th century John Wetherill, a trader with the Indians, and Byron Cummings, an archeologist, visited Betatakin and Inscription House. John Wetherill's brother Richard later discovered Keet Seel.

Special Feature. In the museum at the Visitor Center a slide program shows how the Anasazi lived and what they made. In summer there are campfire programs which introduce visitors to the history and archeology of the monument.

NAVAJO TRIBAL MUSEUM

From Window Rock drive 1 mile south to the Tribal Fairgrounds on Arizona 264 and proceed to buildings beyond sports arena. Open free, 8 a.m. to 5 p.m., daily; closed Jan. 1, Easter, Thanksgiving, Dec. 25.

Displays and dioramas show prehistoric Anasazi and other Southwestern artifacts, with special emphasis on Navajo history.

ORAIBI (Oh-RYE-bee)

National Historic Landmark.
From Tuba City at junction of US 164 and Arizona 264, drive southeast 50 miles on Arizona 264. Open to visitors who obtain permission from the village officials. Camping nearby.

Oraibi—or as it is sometimes called, Old Oraibi—has been inhabited continuously since about A.D. 1100. When scientists were working out a way to date ruins by studying tree rings, some of the most important information came from the wooden beams in ancient buildings in Oraibi. Visitors should respect the desire of the Hopi people for privacy in their homes and should honor their request that no photographs be taken or paintings or drawings made in the village.

PETRIFIED FOREST NATIONAL PARK

From Gallup drive 69 miles southwest on US 66 to northern park entrance and Visitor Center. Or from Holbrook drive 19 miles southeast on US 180 to Rainbow Forest entrance and Visitor Center. Open sunrise to sunset, June to Sept.; 8 a.m. to 5 p.m., Tuesday through Saturday, Sept. to May 5; 8 a.m. to 5 p.m., daily, May 6 to early June. Admission: $1 per car or 50¢ per person arriving by bus; children under 15, free.

This area, notable for its petrified trees, was once occupied by Anasazi farmers, ancestors of modern Pueblo Indians. Two of the 300 archeological sites in the Park have been prepared for visitors. One, Puerco Indian Ruin, 11 miles from the north Visitor Center, had about 150 rooms when it was occupied 600 years ago. It has been partially excavated. On a cliff about a mile south of this village, close to the road through the park, Indians at various times made pictures of animals and people by pecking with a hard rock on the softer sandstone.

Another ruin called Agate House, near the Rainbow Forest entrance, has been partially restored. Here the ancient builders used chunks of petrified wood in their construction. This site is reached by footpath from the parking lot.

Special Feature. In the museum at the southern (Rainbow Forest) entrance, exhibits show projectile points and other artifacts made of petrified wood.

PUEBLO GRANDE MUSEUM

4619 E. Washington St., Phoenix. Open free, 9 a.m. to 5 p.m., Monday through Friday; 1 p.m. to 5 p.m., Sunday and minor holidays; closed Saturday and major holidays.

Here, inside the city of Phoenix, are a large archeological site and a museum which illuminate the life of the Hohokam from about A.D. 1200 to 1400. Trails with explanatory signs lead to a large platform structure—a mound built of earth—upon which small buildings once rested. They may have served for defense or for ceremonial functions or for storage of food. Around this structure a village spread over an 80-acre area.

From the mound it is possible to see remnants of irrigation canals. A whole system of canals, totaling possibly 250 miles in length, once made the Phoenix area a very productive farming region. Corn, jackbeans, lima beans, kidney beans, tepary beans, amaranth, two kinds of squash, cotton, and possibly tobacco grew well here. Besides raising crops, the Hohokam people of Pueblo Grande gathered wild plant food and hunted desert animals of many kinds. They produced beautiful pottery and other artifacts, and made ornaments of shell imported from the Gulf of California.

Irrigation farming began between A.D. 500 and 700 in and around Phoenix. No one knows whether the Hohokam invented this practice themselves or borrowed the idea, but as soon as water flowed onto the dry land, food increased greatly and so did population. This abundance, however, brought problems. Apparently it attracted raiders who wanted food without the trouble of growing it, or who didn't know how to grow it in the first place.

In addition to enemies, the Hohokam around Phoenix had other problems. Salt in the water damaged the walls of their buildings. Life became increasingly difficult, and by A.D. 1400 the residents of Pueblo Grande and the surrounding area had all migrated from the Salt River Valley to the valley of the Gila River. Probably the Pima and the Papago Indians of today are descendants of the ancient Hohokam.

The Museum. Exhibits consist of materials recovered from this large site. Much of the excavation was done with the help of crews who were on work relief during the Depression. The museum building itself reflects the financial difficulties of that time. Its walls are of homemade adobe bricks. The beams are old trolley poles. The ceiling is made of staves from the old redwood water line which used to bring water to Phoenix. Many of the windows and doors were salvaged from old trolley cars. Inside this novel structure the exhibits show how the Hohokam lived and made use of the materials available to them. The museum and the archeological site are maintained by the city of Phoenix.

Special Feature. Visible here is a court in which the inhabitants may have played a ball game that was popular in prehistoric times in much of Mexico and Central America.

TONTO NATIONAL MONUMENT

From Globe drive 4 miles west on US 60, then 28 miles northwest on Arizona 88 to the monument entrance, then 8 miles to the Visitor Center. Open 8 a.m. to 5 p.m., daily. Admission: $1 per car.

Visits to the Upper Ruin can only be made by guided tours which must be arranged four days in advance.

On a self-guided tour to the Lower Ruin, which closes at 5:20 p.m. in summer and at 4:20 p.m. in winter, visitors follow a trail to cliff dwellings in which people lived 600 years ago. These ruins are particularly interesting for the richness of the details they have revealed about the lives of those who inhabited them.

The Story. At about A.D. 1100, farming people from the north and east moved into Tonto Basin—the area around Tonto Creek which flows into the Salt River. Here they lived peacefully with the Hohokam, who already farmed on irrigated land

along the stream. The newcomers and the old-timers quickly learned from each other, and the result was vigorous development. Pottery-making flourished. Expert weavers made cloth in intricate patterns, with fancy designs or colored stripes, and they used some dyes not found anywhere else.

For some reason, perhaps for defense, some of the people moved from the lower land about the year 1350. They built dwellings in three caves in the cliff, using chunks of very hard rock which they embedded in mortar of adobe clay. The outside was then plastered with clay to give a smooth finish. The cliff villages were lived in for only about 50 years, and then inhabitants moved away—no one knows where or why.

The unique lifeway of these people, and especially their pottery style, extended over much of the valley of the Salt River, and so archeologists have called them the Salado (sah-LAH-doh), the Spanish word for salt. The ruin of Besh-ba-Gowah is also an example of Salado architecture.

The Museum. At the Visitor Center you can see many of the items that the Salado made and used —pottery, beautiful cloth, tools, and weapons.

Special Feature. Those who lived here apparently wore more clothes than some others in the warm southern part of Arizona. At several places in the clay plaster on walls there are clear imprints of woven fabric at shoulder height. This seems to mean that people wearing cloth on their shoulders leaned against the walls when the clay was still moist.

TUZIGOOT NATIONAL MONUMENT
(TOO-zee-goot)

From Flagstaff drive 49 miles southwest on US 89A to Cottonwood, then 3 miles northwest to Monument entrance. Open 7:30 a.m. to 6 p.m., June 1 to Sept. 1; 8 a.m. to 5 p.m., Sept. 1 to June 1. Admission: $1 per car or 50¢ per person arriving by bus; children under 16, free when accompanied by an adult. Camping nearby.

Visitors follow a trail on a self-guided tour of this prehistoric hilltop town which once consisted of 110 rooms.

The Story. The earliest settlers at Tuzigoot were related to the Hohokam farmers who lived more than a thousand years ago near Phoenix. Later, about A.D. 1125, they were joined by people called Sinagua, who also settled at Montezuma Castle. The newcomers and others who arrived later built a village of stone houses along a ridge with a square, two-story structure on the hilltop. The village flourished and grew until the 1400s, when for some unknown reason it was abandoned. Perhaps there was an epidemic. Or the land may have ceased to be productive. Archeologists think that some of the people migrated northward, because modern Hopi and Zuni legends say that some of their families came from the neighborhood of Tuzigoot.

The Museum. Here are displays of artifacts recovered during the excavation of the site. One exhibit shows burial practices. Adults were placed, along with pottery and jewelry, in holes scooped from the village trash heaps. Children were buried beneath the floors of rooms.

The Name. Tuzigoot comes from a modern Apache word meaning "crooked water," referring to the nearby Verde River which winds back and forth through the valley.

WALNUT CANYON NATIONAL MONUMENT

From Flagstaff drive 7½ miles east on US 66 to directional sign, then 3 miles southeast to Visitor Center. Open 7 a.m. to 7 p.m., Memorial Day through Labor Day; 8 a.m. to 5 p.m., between Labor Day and Memorial Day. Admission: $1 per car or 50¢ per person arriving by bus. Camping nearby.

Visitors can take a self-guided tour along the rim of Walnut Canyon, then down to 25 cliff-dwelling rooms. From the trail about 100 other dwellings can be seen.

The Story. Very few people seem to have lived in this beautiful spot before the eruption in A.D. 1065 of Sunset Crater, a volcano about 15 miles to the north, near present-day Wupatki National Monument. Fifty or sixty years later groups of farmers called Sinagua moved into Walnut Canyon and built their stone houses in recesses in the cliffs. Here they lived for almost 200 years. Then, like their neighbors in this part of Arizona, they abandoned their homes and moved elsewhere. Possibly some of their descendants are now members of Pueblo Indian groups.

Special Feature. In addition to the cliff house, visitors can see a pithouse which has recently been excavated. This structure shows a way of life that was common before people began to build multiple dwellings of stone in the canyon.

WALPI

From Tuba City at junction of US 164 and Arizona 264, drive southeast 68 miles on Arizona 264, then north at directional sign. Camping nearby.

Walpi is a Hopi Indian village built on top of a high mesa. Some of the dwellings go back at least to 1680, and remains of prehistoric houses lie on the slopes below the present village. They are not open to exploration by visitors. No photographing is allowed in Walpi, and visitors are requested not to enter private homes.

Special Feature. Visitors may see at Walpi the Snake Dance ceremony in the late summer of odd-numbered years. This ceremony had its origin in prehistoric times. Information about the exact date and the place where the dance is held in even-numbered years may be obtained at the Hopi Indian Agency, Keams Canyon, or at Tribal Headquarters, New Oraibi.

WUPATKI NATIONAL MONUMENT (Woo-POT-key)

From Flagstaff drive 32 miles north on US 89 to the Wupatki-Sunset Crater Loop Rd. entrance, then 14 miles east to the Visitor Center. Open free, 8 a.m. to 7 p.m., May to Sept.; 8 a.m. to 5 p.m., Sept. to May. Camping in a nearby Forest Service campground, May to Sept.

There are about 800 ruins in the monument, nearly 100 of them within an area of one square mile. Visitors can take self-guided tours to the largest site, Wupatki, which has been partially excavated, and to one called the Citadel, which has not been excavated. At Wupatki archeologists have uncovered an ancient ball court, one of two in northern Arizona.

The Story. In A.D. 1065 a great volcano exploded and formed what is now called Sunset Crater. Volcanic cinders spread over 800 square miles. Instead of devastating the land, the cinders formed a kind of mulch which conserved moisture and so

A

B

A. At Tuzigoot National Monument the ancient town covered a ridge which rose 120 feet above the floor of the Verde Valley. In places the building was two stories high. National Park Service photo by Paul V. Long, Jr. B. Artifacts made by the Salado people at Tonto National Monument. National Park Service photo. C. Exhibits in the museum at Tuzigoot National Monument include a burial, showing how these people disposed of the dead. National Park Service photo by Zorro A. Bradley.

C

Kachinas

When the Spanish invaders arrived in the Southwest in 1540, every Indian pueblo except one had what the inhabitants called kachinas. These were men, costumed, masked, and painted with elaborate symbolism, who participated in ceremonies in the village plazas or in the kivas. They represented supernatural spirits that were themselves called kachinas, and the dancers were believed to have supernatural powers. Some of the dancers were very earthy clowns. Others were impersonators of spirits both good and evil. Occasionally paintings of kachinas were made on the walls of prehistoric kivas.

To teach children all the symbolism of the costumes, and to help them learn the stories about supernatural beings, men often carved and painted wooden dolls in the form of kachinas. Today the Hopi and Zuni Indians still have kachina dancers, and they make kachina dolls for children—and for anyone interested in buying them. Archeologists sometimes find kachina dolls in excavations.

Nokachok kachina doll from the Keams Canyon area. These dolls are made by Hopi and Zuni Indians for their children. Field Museum of Natural History photo.

Dirt Roads in the Southwest

Don't venture on a dirt road without asking people who know the road whether it is passable. A road that is safe in dry weather may be impassable and dangerous after a rain. Very often you can't tell by looking at one end of a road whether or not rain has fallen somewhere a mile or two or ten ahead.

Never stop your car in the bottom of a draw or arroyo. The sky may be clear above you but a cloudburst may be falling somewhere higher up on the watershed. A sudden flood—a flash flood—can pour down an arroyo and this can mean disaster.

In country you don't know take the advice of people who do know it.

Shifting sands at Great Sand Dunes National Monument sometimes reveal artifacts and campsites buried as much as 10,000 years ago. National Park Service photo by Robert Haugen.

promoted the growth of plants. This encouraged Indian farmers to move into the area. From the east and north came the Anasazi. Hohokam people who had farmed by irrigating crops came from the south. From the southeast came the Mogollon. And from the west came others who belonged to a group we call the Patayan.

All of these groups moved in upon farmers now called the Sinagua who had been living in the neighborhood before the eruption. Archeologists can be sure of this because they have excavated Sinagua dwellings which had been buried under a layer of cinders. And they have been able to calculate the year of the eruption by tree-ring-dating of the wood used in Sinagua houses.

The area around the volcano became a melting pot of Indian peoples. Several very different groups lived together and learned from each other for about 150 years. Perhaps by then the land was exhausted. For whatever reason, the last inhabitants left about A.D. 1225.

The Museum. Exhibits here show methods that prehistoric Indians used in making artifacts.

The Name. Wupatki, a Hopi Indian word, means "Tall House." It refers to a multistory dwelling which, during the 1100s, had more than 100 rooms housing perhaps 150 people.

Special Feature. Eighteen miles from Wupatki National Monument Headquarters, by the Loop Road, is Sunset Crater National Monument. Here may be seen the dead mouth of the volcano which spewed out cinders to cover the surrounding area.

Colorado
For additional listings see page 82.

GREAT SAND DUNES NATIONAL MONUMENT

From Alamosa drive 14 miles north on Colorado 17, then 18 miles east on Colorado 150 to Visitor Center. Open at all times. Admission: $1 per car or 50¢ for each adult who arrives by bus. Camping.

People have been leaving tools and weapons around the Sand Dunes for 10,000 years. Two archeological sites in the area have revealed the campgrounds of men who hunted giant bison, which are now extinct. Bones of the animals have been excavated, together with fluted Folsom points.

Later, hunters belonging to various groups, including some Pueblo Indians, once followed great herds of bison, antelope, deer, and elk which roamed the San Luis Valley near the Sand Dunes. Archeologists have discovered indications that whole families traveled along definite routes on these hunting expeditions from the south into the valley. Exhibits in the Visitor Center show artifacts of several prehistoric cultures.

Special Feature. Winds blowing across the San Luis Valley for thousands of years deposited sand at the foot of the mountains along the valley's eastern side, forming some of the world's highest dunes. Hiking is allowed on the dunes, which shift constantly and from time to time uncover a spot where Indians once lived and left artifacts. Visitors may look at but not loot such sites.

HOVENWEEP
See page 41.

LOWRY PUEBLO RUINS
NATIONAL HISTORIC LANDMARK

From Cortez drive north 18 miles on US 160 to Pleasant View, then 9 miles west on graveled road. Open free, at all times.

The Story. About A.D. 850 people began to garden at this site, and eventually they made their homes in a large masonry community dwelling several stories high. The 40 rooms that have been excavated were constructed by the Anasazi about A.D. 1075. Unlike other villages in the area it was not continuously inhabited. From time to time people abandoned it, then rebuilt and reoccupied its rooms. Finally everyone moved away for good, even before a great drought began in the year 1276. Perhaps too many people were trying to live on the land, which was already very dry. In any case they seem to have left without pressure from any hostile invaders.

Special Feature. In this ruin is one of the largest underground ceremonial rooms (called Great Kivas) in the Anasazi area. Apparently the village was a ceremonial center for people who came to it from neighboring places. It is one of a small but growing number of sites administered by the Bureau of Land Management. An information folder is available at the entrance.

MESA VERDE NATIONAL PARK
(MAY-suh VER-day)

Midway between Cortez and Mancos on US 160 turn south at park entrance, then drive 21 miles on the park road to Headquarters and museum. Open all year. Admission: $1 per car or 50¢ for each person arriving by bus. Museum open free, 7:45 a.m. to 7:30 p.m., summer; 8 a.m. to 6:30 p.m., winter. Camping May 1 to Nov. 1 within the park, 5 miles from entrance.

Mesa Verde is really a huge outdoor archeological museum which contains many different sites. The park occupies a stretch of high tableland, or mesa, which is cut by deep canyons with steep cliff walls. In many of the canyons prehistoric people found caves and rockshelters, and there they built some of the most beautiful and interesting villages to be found in the Southwest. On the mesa top other ruins can be visited. Because there is such a large number of visitable sites, each with its own special interest, each will be discussed separately in the following pages. All, however, share the same general history.

The Story. At about the beginning of the fifth century A.D. men started to cultivate small gardens in the semiarid Mesa Verde area. For 800 years they lived here, improving their farming techniques, eventually building dams and storage ponds and irrigation systems. Through one stage after another they developed a special style of architecture, and their pottery took on a beauty and quality that distinguished it from other pottery made in the Southwest in prehistoric times. Now and then the women who did the work of shaping and decorating pots adopted new ideas or fads, and these changes in fashion were often very marked. As a result archeologists have been able to use pottery types as an aid in determining the dates of certain events in the region.

Mesa Verde was one of the three regions where Anasazi culture reached a very high point before A.D. 1276. (The others were Chaco Canyon and Kayenta.) The year 1276 was important. At about that date people began to abandon the mesa top and the canyons where they had been living. Ex-

A. A courtyard scene as it appears in a diorama in the museum at the Visitor Center, Chaco Canyon National Monument. National Park Service Photo.   B. Mug House, one of the ruins on Wetherill Mesa, Mesa Verde National Park. National Park Service photo by Fred E. Mang, Jr.   C. Basketmaker mothers carried babies on cradles made of fiber. The child's head rested on the round pillow, and a pad of soft shredded cedar bark served as a diaper. After a Mesa Verde photo by Faha.   D. An Anasazi double mug. The original is in the Mesa Verde National Park museum.   E. Mesa Verde women used the beveled edges of bone tools to scrape flesh from hides. Originals of these fleshers are in the Colorado State Museum, Denver.   F. A black-on-white pottery ladle.   G. A pot made in the shape of a duck by a woman at Mesa Verde, between A.D. 750 and A.D. 1100. The ladle and the pot are in the Mesa Verde National Park museum.

A

B

C D E F G

A. BEFORE . . . When archeologists began excavation in Long House on Wetherill Mesa, this is what it looked like.
B. AFTER . . . As Long House appears now, ready for visitors when facilities are completed. National Park Service photo.

A

B

perts disagree on the reasons for the wholesale migration away from this ancient homeland. Some say that a 23-year-long drought set in; others believe raiders began to attack the villages seeking the food stored there. Possibly the Mesa Verde people began to have quarrels among themselves and to develop rival factions. They may have moved to other regions because of a breakdown in the general social structure on the mesa.

For whatever reason, everyone did move away nearly 600 years ago, and what you see now is the evidence of achievement in a far from lush environment over a period of eight centuries. For glimpses of the life led by descendants of the Mesa Verde people, visitors can go to present-day pueblos along the Rio Grande River and to the Hopi villages on the Hopi Mesas. It was in these areas that the emigrants made their homes after they left Mesa Verde.

For a clear and detailed picture of Mesa Verde life at each of its stages, visitors should start at the museum in Park Headquarters.

The Museum. Here well-arranged displays give an orderly and illuminating introduction to prehistoric life in the Mesa Verde area. Exhibits lead the visitor on a journey through time, beginning with the days when Basketmaker women ground corn kernels into usable cornmeal by rubbing them between a small stone called a mano and a large stone called a metate. For cooking, these women used baskets in special ways. Corn or other dry food might be placed in a broad, flat basket along with heated rocks and stirred till it was parched. Some baskets were so finely woven that they could hold water. To cook food in such a vessel, a woman dropped hot rocks into the water to make it boil.

Later at Mesa Verde women continued to weave baskets, but they also learned to make pottery. Men hunted with bows and arrows instead of depending on spears and spear-throwers as their ancestors had done. They were adept at manipulating fibers—yucca fibers, dog hair, human hair—all of which they made into cord. Using the cord they wove sandals, bags, belts, and nets for catching game. Combining cord and strips of rabbit fur they wove blankets. (The magnificent dog-hair sashes in the museum were not found at Mesa Verde but in Obelisk Cave in nearby northeast Arizona.)

By A.D. 600 people had begun to live in the kind of dwelling called a pithouse. This was a pit two or three feet deep, roofed over with branches and mud and entered by a ladder through a hole in the roof.

From this half-underground house, Anasazi architecture evolved in two different and fascinating ways, as an exhibit in the museum shows. Step by step, people learned to build homes of stone entirely above ground, but still with entrances through the roof. At the same time they dug deeper rooms entirely underground, and these they used as ceremonial chambers, now called kivas.

For a long time the stone houses clustered together in villages on the mesa top. Then people began to build in caves in the cliffs. For 75 or 100 years they lived in the cliff dwellings and tossed their trash down over the side. Refuse piled up, and very often it was entirely sheltered by the overhanging rock. In the dry Southwestern air the refuse did not decay, and the result was that archeologists found the trash heaps a mine of relics from the past. Many of their finds can be seen in the museum.

Very often the heaps were used as burial places, for it was much easier to dig a grave in trash than in hard clay. Bodies soon dried and became mummylike. However, before Mesa Verde was made a National Park, collectors carried away so much material from the ruins that there was no good mummy left to display there. The dessicated body of a young woman in the museum came from a cave near Durango, Colo.

Some of the best Mesa Verde exhibits must now be seen far from the Park. One is in the Palace of the Governors in Santa Fe, another in the Colorado State Museum in Denver. A beautiful woven blanket can be seen in the University Museum in Philadelphia, and most remote of all is an important collection in Helsinki, Finland.

Spruce Tree House, open 8 a.m. to 6:30 p.m., summer; 8 a.m. to 5:45 p.m., winter. Self-guided trip.

From the museum a good trail (walking time 45 minutes to 1 hour) leads to the Spruce Tree House ruin in the canyon nearby.

This is an unusually good place to examine a kiva, a type of ceremonial room which was hollowed out of the rock or dug into the earth. Such underground chambers were common at Anasazi sites in the Southwest.

Entrance to a kiva was by ladder through a hole in the courtyard floor. This entrance hole also allowed smoke to escape from the fire which furnished heat and some light. Fresh air came down into the chamber through a ventilator shaft built at one side. In front of the opening to the shaft inside the kiva an upright slab of rock deflected the incoming air and kept it from scattering ashes and smoke across the room. At intervals around the wall of the kiva stood masonry columns called pilasters.

The roof of a kiva rested on these pilasters, and it was ingeniously built. First, a row of logs, with their ends supported by the pilasters, was laid around the room. Then another row of logs was laid on top of this. In this second row each end of each log was placed in the middle of a log below it. On top of this second row another was similarly placed. The result of this cribbing was a dome-shaped structure. After the logs were all in place, they were covered with earth which was leveled off to serve as part of the courtyard floor.

In the kiva male members of a clan or a society held their ceremonies. Here also they lounged and sometimes worked at their looms. Apparently it was the men and not the women who did the fine Mesa Verde weaving. For special ceremonies women and children were sometimes admitted to these small male sanctuaries. In many places in the Anasazi Southwest there were also Great Kivas, each large enough to serve a whole community.

The history of the kiva seems to be something like this: Early Mogollon people lived in semi-subterranean pithouses. They may have conducted certain clan or society ceremonies in these dwellings. Or they may have had special large pithouses for community-wide ceremonies.

Then among the Anasazi the type of house changed. People began to build their dwellings entirely above ground. At the same time, following a conservative impulse, they continued to hold their ceremonies in the old-fashioned type of pithouse. Later apparently, they got the notion that if holding ceremonies partly underground was a good idea, it would be an even better idea to hold them in rooms that were all the way underground. So, fully subterranean kivas were built.

Ruins Road (two loops totaling 12 miles in length). Open 8 a.m. to 8 p.m.

If you follow this road, which runs along the mesa top, you will see ruins in the order in which developments took place during the course of Mesa Verde history.

1. A Modified Basketmaker pithouse built in the A.D. 500s.
2. Modified Basketmaker pithouses built in the A.D. 600s and 700s.
3. Pueblos of the Developmental Period, A.D. 850, 900, 950, 1000, and 1075.
4. Sun Point Pueblo, built in the early part of the Classic Period (A.D. 1100 to 1300). People then moved down into the canyon, taking with them material from the roofs and walls of their old homes to use in building new ones.
5. Sun Temple, a large ceremonial center, from the late Classic Period.
6. A cornfield, beside the road to Cliff Palace. Here Park Service workers plant Indian corn to demonstrate that normal rainfall will enable a crop to mature. The plants are specially adapted to survive in the dry conditions of the region, and they are set far apart so that each one can get the maximum moisture. Mesa Verde people cultivated their corn with digging sticks, and often they grew squash and beans in the same field. They stored their crops in granaries, a number of which can be seen in cliff walls farther along the road.
7. Cliff Palace (Classic Period). Ranger-guided tours start at the Viewpoint on the road, on the hour and half-hour, 9 a.m. through 6 p.m. in summer. The total walking distance is one-quarter mile; the time required, 45 minutes to one hour.

Mesa Verde people built their homes in this cave in the cliff, apparently seeking protection from enemies. Here, and at other cliff dwellings during the 1200s, the arts of weaving and pottery-making reached their peak. When Mesa Verde was abandoned, people left most of their possessions behind, and no invaders seem to have disturbed the vacant dwellings. Then one snowy winter day in 1888 two cowboys, Richard Wetherill and Charles Mason, discovered the pueblo and named it Cliff Palace. Although many walls had tumbled and dust had filled some rooms, Wetherill and Mason found treasures of pottery and other artifacts in the ruins. Many of these things are now in the Colorado State Museum in Denver.

8. Viewpoints. Along Ruins Road are a number of turnouts from which it is possible to see structures of several kinds in the canyon walls. Some are small granaries or storerooms. Others are pueblos of various sizes. One is a ceremonial site. These sites are not now accessible. To enter and leave many of them, the Mesa Verde people had to use small handholds and footholds they had chopped in the rock with hammerstones or axes made of harder rock.
9. Balcony House (Classic Period). Ranger-guided trips start at the Viewpoint sign in the Balcony House parking area on the hour and half-hour from 9 a.m. to 6 p.m. in summer. The total walking distance is one-half mile. The trip takes one hour.

In this village there is a second-story walkway or balcony, left intact from prehistoric times, which suggested the name for the ruin. Visitors may walk today through the courtyards high above the canyon floor, protected by the original wall, which has been reinforced for safety. However, archeologists have found evidence in the ruins that cliff dwellings were not always safe for those who lived in them. Skeletons of people whose bones had been broken have turned up in burials, as have crutches and splints.

10. Cedar Tree Tower (Classic Period). After completing the trip to Balcony House, visitors

should stop at Cedar Tree Tower on the drive back toward the park entrance. A road one-half mile long on the mesa top leads to this curious structure which was used for ceremonial purposes. From the round tower an underground passage led to a circular kiva, which is also connected to a small niche under an overhanging rounded rock.

No one knows exactly what ceremonies went on here—or elsewhere in Mesa Verde. Archeologists do know that among the Anasazi there were men who practiced healing and magical arts. A kit used by one of these men has been excavated and is on display in the Visitor Center. Archeologists also know how such kits are used in modern times, for they have studied the ceremonies of present-day Pueblo Indians, some of whom are descended from Mesa Verde people. It seems likely that ancient ceremonies resembled in some ways the modern Pueblo ceremonies. If so, they expressed the desire to have all the elements of the world working together in harmony.

11. Far View Ruins (Developmental Pueblo). Off the road between the park entrance and the museum a short side road leads to this group of ruins on the mesa top. The pueblos here were inhabited before people moved down into cliff dwellings.

Near the ruins is Mummy Lake which can be reached by a short trail leading past the ruins of another small pueblo. The dry basin called Mummy Lake was once an artificial reservoir. In ancient times a series of barriers or dams higher up on the mesa collected rainwater and channeled it into ditches which ultimately led into the reservoir. The water in the ditches was muddy, and to keep some of the silt out of the reservoir, the stone-age engineers who designed this facility worked out an ingenious device. They made a sharp curve near the end of the last ditch. The curve slowed the flow of water, and some of the silt settled out *before* the water entered the reservoir. From Mummy Lake a by-pass ditch ran along the sloping mesa, carrying water several miles to the area where Park Headquarters is now located.

Recent excavations close to Far View Ruins have added another Developmental Pueblo village to the Mesa Verde sites which can be visited. One feature of this new site is a round tower which stood close to a kiva.

12. Pictograph Point. Hikers who register with the ranger on duty in the park office near the Visitor Center may follow a trail to a place where Mesa Verde people made paintings on rock surfaces.

13. Above-ground kiva. From Morfield Campground a trail, which Park Rangers can point out, leads about one-fourth mile to a unique kiva on a hilltop. This kiva, which has been excavated and stabilized, is unusual in that it was not in a community, nor was it built underground.

14. The last stop on any day in Mesa Verde should be at one of the campfire programs, either in the Morfield Campground or in the amphitheater near Headquarters. Nightly at 8:30, from early June through Labor Day, a ranger talks on some aspect of Mesa Verde life. After Labor Day and until the campground closes, usually in mid-October, talks begin at 8 p.m.

The Future. A large additional area in the park, known as Wetherill Mesa, will be open in 1972 for public view.

In addition, the Park Service has acquired a large site at Goodman's Point, about 10 miles northwest of Cortez, in Montezuma Valley below Mesa Verde. When funds become available this site will be developed and opened to the public.

New Mexico

ABO STATE MONUMENT

From Albuquerque drive 45 miles south on US 85, then 26 miles east on US 60 to directional sign and 1 mile north on a local road. Open free, at all times.

Here, in addition to a 17th-century Spanish mission, is a mound, largely unexcavated, which covers a prehistoric pueblo first inhabited about A.D. 1300 by people who seem to have spoken a dialect of the now extinct Piro language. Descendants of the earlier settlers made an architectural innovation which has intrigued archeologists. Within the Roman Catholic Church complex at Abo, the Indians built a kiva suitable for use in continuing the practice of their traditional religion.

This site is administered by the Museum of New Mexico.

ACOMA (AH-koh-mah)

Between Albuquerque and Gallup leave US 66 at Casa Blanca and drive south 14 miles on New Mexico 23. Open all year, 6 a.m. to 6 p.m. Visitor's permit, $1.

Acoma, often called Sky City, is on top of a high sandstone rock. About A.D. 900, people began to live on or near the site of the present village. Ever since A.D. 1075, the pueblo has been continuously occupied. This means that visitors at Acoma are seeing a lived-in prehistoric site, although most of the structures which are visible are obviously of recent origin.

Visitors should respect the privacy of the people of Acoma and should obtain permits from the Governor of the pueblo if they wish to take photographs or do painting or drawing. The graveyards, the kivas, and the waterhole are out of bounds to tourists.

ALBUQUERQUE PETROGLYPHS

From Interstate 40 west of the Rio Grande River in Albuquerque, drive north one-quarter mile on Coors Blvd., then left on Atrisco Dr. A sign prepared by the real estate developer of Volcano Cliffs directs visitors to one petroglyph in a canyon in the basalt escarpment which parallels the Rio Grande River. Many other petroglyphs may be seen on rock surfaces in this area, which has been set aside by the developer to be a city park. Camping nearby.

At the north end of this same basalt escarpment there is another group of petroglyphs. To reach these drive north from Interstate 40 on New Mexico 448 (Mesa Rd.) to Paradise Blvd., then left to the Paradise Hills Golf Course, which is on the right. Opposite the golf course a dirt road turns off to the left. It is rough but usually passable. Drivers are warned to stay on the road, thus avoiding deep sand on either side. Four small canyons can be easily reached. In each of these are petroglyphs that show kachinas, birds, animals, flute players, and handprints.

AZTEC RUINS NATIONAL MONUMENT

From Farmington drive 14 miles north on US 550 to directional marker in the town of Aztec, then one-half mile west on Ruins Road to Monument entrance. Open 7 a.m. to 7 p.m., summer; 8 a.m. to 5 p.m., winter. Admission: $1 per car or 50¢ per adult arriving by bus; children under 16, free. Camping nearby.

This huge ruin was once a town built in the form of an apartment house around an open plaza. The beautiful masonry walls of its 500 rooms rose two and three stories high in places. A number of kivas—small round ceremonial rooms—were constructed within the building itself, and in the plaza was a very large kiva surrounded by a number of small rooms. This Great Kiva has been completely restored to show what the impressive ceremonial room must have been like 800 years ago.

The Story.   Aztec lies between two major areas of the Anasazi culture—Mesa Verde and Chaco Canyon. By A.D. 600 people at Aztec had begun to farm, and by A.D. 1000 they were being strongly influenced by their neighbors.

One idea the residents of Aztec borrowed from Chaco Canyon was the design for their town, with its central plaza and high walls. Another was the Great Kiva, which served as a ceremonial center for a large number of people.

Not long after the dwellings and the Great Kiva were completed, the inhabitants of this large village or pueblo moved away, possibly because in the middle 1100s the area was too dry for efficient farming. Rainfall then increased, and by 1225 people had moved back, bringing with them pottery designs and customs that were similar to those at Mesa Verde. Fifty years later the Aztec pueblo was again abandoned. This time the inhabitants left never to return.

The Museum.   Here are exhibits of pottery, baskets, various utensils, and tools made and used in the pueblo. Displays explain architectural features and show how the people once lived.

The Name.   Early pioneers, who were much impressed by what they had heard about the Aztec Indians in Mexico, called this ruin Aztec. There is, however, no known connection between the inhabitants of this pueblo and the Aztecs who lived in the valley of Mexico.

Special Feature.   One of the great archeologists of the Southwest, Earl Morris, who was born near Aztec, excavated this site and reconstructed the Great Kiva. When he began his careful work, he found evidence that the once-important ceremonial chamber had been used as a garbage dump before the pueblo was abandoned. Finally the roof caught fire and collapsed. Nevertheless Morris was able to figure out details of construction and rebuild the chamber.

BANDELIER NATIONAL MONUMENT
(Ban-duh-LEER)

From Santa Fe drive 18 miles north on US 285 to Pojoaque (po-WAH-kay) then 28 miles west on New Mexico 4 to the Monument entrance. It is 3 miles farther to the Visitor Center. Open 8 a.m. to 7:30 p.m., June through Aug.; 8 a.m. to 5 p.m., Sept. through May. Admission: $1 per car. Camping.

This beautiful and unusual site at the bottom of a deep gorge stretches out along a little stream called Rito de los Frijoles (REE-toh day lohs free-HO-less), Spanish for "Bean Creek." Along a two-mile trail visitors can see ruins of dwellings built near the cliff walls and behind them man-made caves. In a separate section of the monument, 11

A

A. Inside the Great Kiva at Aztec Ruins National Monument, after restoration. The T-shaped doorway in the center was popular in many Anasazi pueblos. The pits to the left and right may have been covered with boards and used as dance platforms or foot drums. National Park Service photo by George A. Grant.
B. A skeleton from Aztec Ruins still in its original wrapping. National Park Service photo by George A. Grant.

B

The Southwest

Only from the point of view of *norte americanos* (English-speaking people north of Mexico) is the southwestern part of the United States "the Southwest." From the point of view of Mexicans the area lies to the north. Moreover, in prehistoric times the area received great attention from people in Mexico and was widely influenced by Mexican culture.

To prehistoric Mexicans and also to the later Spanish *Conquistadores* the region was part of a large area that was known as the Gran Chichimeca, which extended northward from the Tropic of Cancer to the present vicinity of San Francisco, California, on the northwest and to Wichita, Kansas, in the northeast. The word *chichimeca* was descriptive. It meant, among other things, nomad. Gran Chichimeca was the Great Land of Nomads—people who were barbarians from the point of view of the more sophisticated inhabitants of the valley of Mexico. Some United States archeologists want to revive the name Gran Chichimeca and apply it to both northern Mexico and southwestern United States. Other archeologists, having no less respect for ancient Mexican culture and for present-day Mexican sensibilities, believe that the term "Southwest" is so deeply imbedded in usage that it is practically impossible to substitute the older name. So, bowing to current custom in the United States, this book calls the Gran Chichimeca the Southwest.

miles north of Frijoles Canyon, is an unexcavated ruin called Tsankawi (zahn-KAH-wee). Here visitors may take a self-guided tour on a two-mile trail.

The Story. At the end of the 13th century there was a great drought in much of the Southwest. Many Anasazi people moved from their homes seeking water. Some of them found it here in the deep canyons that cut into the Pajarito (PAH-hah-REE-toh) Plateau. (Pajarito is Spanish for "little bird.") In the bottom of Frijoles Canyon farmers planted fields of corn, beans, and squash and built a large pueblo called Tyuonyi (chew-OHN-yee), which means "a meeting place." At the same time, some inhabitants dug storage rooms and also living quarters in the rock, which is actually compressed volcanic ash.

People continued to live in the canyon until about A.D. 1550. Then for some reason they left, as did others from various parts of the Pajarito Plateau. Today people who are probably their descendants live at the Cochiti, Santo Domingo, and San Ildefonso pueblos along the Rio Grande River.

The Museum: A slide program at the museum in the Visitor Center interprets life in the canyon in ancient times. Exhibits show the arts and crafts of the people who lived there.

The Name. The first archeologist who came west to make a study of sites in New Mexico was Adolph Bandelier. In the late 19th century he walked thousands of miles over roadless areas of the state, learning Indian languages, often sleeping on the ground without a blanket, sometimes eating only the parched corn that was a food of the Indians among whom he lived. One of Bandelier's

discoveries was the prehistoric settlement in Frijoles Canyon. To explain what he thought life must have been like in this spot he wrote a novel, *The Delight Makers,* which is still very readable and informative. Because of his important services to archeology and his particular connection with Frijoles Canyon, the national monument was named in his honor.

Special Feature: Ninety percent of Bandelier National Monument is a wilderness in which roads will never be built. There are trails, however, and some of them lead to fascinating archeological sites. At one place, 7½ miles from Monument Headquarters, there are carved stone mountain lions unlike anything found elsewhere in the Southwest. At another site, 10 miles from Headquarters, is a very large cave where prehistoric people made paintings in color on the rock.

BLACKWATER DRAW MUSEUM

Midway between Clovis and Portales on US 70. Open free, daily, 1 p.m. to 5 p.m.

This museum is devoted exclusively to the story of man from his entry into America until the end of the Archaic period 2,000 years ago. Dioramas show the life of the Paleo-Indians and the mammals and other animals they hunted. Other displays show how artifacts were made and used. The museum contains many originals and replicas of material recovered from the very important Blackwater Draw Site nearby.

This site was discovered by C. W. Anderson and George Roberts, amateur archeologists, at the time when professional archeologists were just realizing that men had been in America for many thousands of years. On the surface, amid old sand dunes, Anderson and Roberts found some distinctive projectile points together with mammoth bones. Then in August, 1932, Anderson met a professional archeologist, Edgar B. Howard, in Carlsbad, N. Mex. He showed him the points, and told him about the bones. Howard immediately went to the site. He was much interested in what he saw, and scientific excavation soon began at Blackwater Draw. It has continued to the present time. The distinctive points found there have been called Clovis points, for the nearby town.

It is not yet possible to visit the excavation but a trip to the museum gives an excellent idea of what has been going on there for many years.

CARLSBAD CAVERNS NATIONAL PARK

From Carlsbad drive 18 miles south on US 62, then 7 miles west on Park Road to Visitor Center. Open free, June through early Sept., 7:30 a.m. to 9 p.m.; Sept. through May, 7:30 a.m. to 5 p.m. Camping outside the park.

Prehistoric Indians apparently never ventured far into Carlsbad Caverns, although they did camp in the shelter of the cavern entrance. They made black and red paintings on the rock wall of the entrance, and they prepared some of their food in heated, rock-lined cooking pits. Many such pits have been found in the area, some used much later by Apache Indians.

Along the park road in Walnut Canyon visitors may take a self-guided tour to a site where people once lived in a small cave. The tour follows what is called an ethnobotanical trail, meaning that it identifies plants and the uses to which they were put by Indians of the area.

Near the Caverns are many other caves, some of which prehistoric people used extensively. The National Park Service hopes to be able to open one of these, New Cave, for visitors.

An exhibit in the Visitor Center displays prehistoric cultural remains from the area.

CHACO CANYON NATIONAL MONUMENT
(CHAH-koh)

From New Mexico 17 at Bloomfield drive south 28 miles on New Mexico 44, then at Blanco Trading Post take unpaved New Mexico 56, 30 miles to Visitor Center. Or from US 66 at Thoreau drive north 28 miles on paved New Mexico 56 to Crownpoint, then 40 miles on unpaved New Mexico 56 to the Monument. Before leaving Blanco Trading Post or Crownpoint check the condition of the unpaved road ahead. It is sometimes impassable after a rain. Open free, daily in summer; closed Tuesday and Wednesday in winter. Camping; water is available but no other supplies.

Here, far from any present-day town, are a dozen large pueblos and about 300 smaller sites, the spectacular ruins of one of the three Anasazi culture centers. Easy trails from the main road lead to a number of the most important sites, and self-guided tours have been prepared for visitors at two of the ruins. In summer Park Rangers conduct guided tours through Pueblo Bonito, the largest of the sites.

Any visit to Chaco Canyon should begin at the Visitor Center, where exhibits in the museum tell the story of human life here. Dioramas and displays help to make clear how people could have

A. Artist Paul Coze's conception of life in one of the man-made caves in Frijoles Canyon. Photo by Glen Haynes, used by permission of Paul Coze. B. A diorama in the Palace of the Governors, Santa Fe, showing what a large pueblo in Bandelier National Monument may have looked like when it was inhabited. Photo by James DeKorne. C. Visitors entering the dwellings at Bandelier National Monument. National Park Service photo by Robert W. Gage.

A. *This is how Pueblo Bonito (in Chaco Canyon) looks when viewed from the top of the cliff which towers above it. National Park Service photo by George Grant. B. Three examples of the beautiful and distinctive pottery made by the Anasazi people who once inhabited Chaco Canyon. National Park Service photo. C. One of the many examples of rock art which appear on cliff faces in Chaco Canyon. Figures of this kind are found at many other places in the Southwest. Often their meaning is not known. National Park Service photo.*

prospered in a land which now seems dry and desolate. In summer there are special evening programs at the Visitor Center.

The Story. Twelve hundred people once lived in the 800 rooms of Pueblo Bonito, a village built in the form of a tremendous apartment house around inner courtyards. In this pueblo, and in others nearby, the art of stonemasonry reached its highest development in the Southwest. Great stretches of wall made from precisely cut and shaped stone remain standing today.

Chaco Canyon pottery was also distinctive and beautiful. Here, as elsewhere in the Southwest, a long history of development lay behind the greatest achievements. It began in the canyon with the Basketmaker people, who by A.D. 650 were building dwellings of the kind called pithouses. They were farmers and craftsmen, quick to adopt new ideas from neighbors or strangers.

Apparently the villages in the canyon were hospitable to outsiders. Immigrants from other parts of the Southwest came in steadily. In those days a pine forest probably covered the nearby mesas. The canyon bottom was well watered, and crops flourished. So did village life. Between the 11th and 12th centuries A.D. as many as 5,000 people were making their homes in and around the canyon. Craftsmen worked in turquoise and shell, fashioning mosaics, beads, and ornaments of various sorts. Each pueblo had its own small kivas where men met to conduct ceremonies or social activities. In addition there were Great Kivas where numbers of people from the larger community assembled for ceremonies.

In the early part of the 12th century the greatness of Chaco Canyon came to an end. Men had destroyed the forest on the mesas to get wood for fuel and for the ceilings and roof beams of their many homes and kivas. Without trees to hold back the moisture in the soil, rains brought devastating erosion in their wake. Water rushed down the canyon bottom, digging a deep arroyo in the flat land. Now the groundwater, which had once been close to the surface of the canyon floor, sank down to the level of the water in the arroyo bed. The roots of corn and bean and squash plants could no longer get moisture. Crops failed, and the people had to move. After they left, their great buildings filled up gradually with windblown sand and dust, and many of them were only mounds when the first United States soldiers passed through the canyon on an exploring expedition in 1849.

Pueblo Bonito, the largest of the ruins, has been thoroughly excavated and stabilized. Several other structures have been excavated and partially rebuilt. But many remain for future archeologists to study. An ambitious new excavation program is scheduled for Chaco Canyon. It will include exploration with the help of a satellite.

Special Feature. A trip through Pueblo Bonito (Spanish for "beautiful town") reveals fascinating details of ancient village life. Logs used for house beams show how stone axes cut into wood. Deeply worn sandstone slabs are still in place where women knelt to grind the corn that was the staple food.

The treasures of pottery and jewelry that archeologists found here have been removed to museums elsewhere. Some of the pottery is in the American Museum of Natural History in New York City.

Behind Pueblo Bonito an ancient trail leads up through a cleft in the cliff wall. Visitors may follow it to Pueblo Alto on the mesa top.

Across the arroyo from Pueblo Bonito a Great Kiva has been excavated and sufficiently restored to give an idea of the beauty and majesty of this ceremonial room. A pamphlet available at the ruin presents an excellent interpretation of the site.

Near the Great Kiva visitors may examine an interesting excavation of a pithouse.

CORONADO STATE MONUMENT

From Albuquerque drive north 15 miles on US 85, then west 5 miles on New Mexico 44 to the Monument entrance. Open free, 9 a.m. to 5 p.m., summer; 9 a.m. to 5 p.m., Tuesday through Saturday, winter; 2 p.m. to 5 p.m., holidays. Camping nearby.

Here on the west bank of the Rio Grande River a group of Anasazi people began to make their home about A.D. 1300. By the time the Spanish invaders arrived in 1540 the pueblo, known as Kuaua (KWAH-wah), had grown tremendously. There were about 1,200 ground-level rooms, and above them many other rooms, in places several stories high. The walls of the houses were made of adobe clay which was moistened and built up in layers, each layer being allowed to dry before the next was added.

In the courtyards of the pueblo were a number of underground ceremonial chambers, or kivas. When archeologists excavated one of them they found murals painted on its plastered walls. Further investigation revealed 17 other layers of plaster underneath, and on each layer were more mural paintings of ceremonial activities. The archeologists worked out an ingenious method of removing the murals a layer at a time. An exhibit in the Visitor Center at the Monument tells how they did it. Accurate reproductions of some of the paintings have been put on the wall of a reconstructed kiva at the site.

Because the Spanish explorers lived here and learned the language of the people, a great deal is known about them. They were farmers who grew corn, squash, tobacco, and cotton. They were good weavers and good potters, and they also made fine baskets. Many of their artifacts and religious objects can be seen in the museum at the Visitor Center.

The Name. The monument is named for the leader of the Spanish *conquistadores* who stayed at Kuaua for a while in the winter of 1540–41.

EASTERN NEW MEXICO UNIVERSITY ANTHROPOLOGY MUSEUM

On the campus of the University, Portales. Open free, 1 p.m. to 5 p.m., Monday through Friday; closed national holidays.

One large room in this museum emphasizes Early Man on the High Plains, with explanations of his way of life. The director of the museum, Dr. George A. Agogino, who is also director of the Miles Museum and the Blackwater Draw Museum, has arranged an unusual exhibit of photographs of Paleo-Indian sites throughout the western hemisphere, together with material about the archeologists who discovered and excavated the sites.

EL MORRO NATIONAL MONUMENT

From El Morro drive 2 miles west on New Mexico 53. Open free, 7 a.m. to 7 p.m., summer; 8 a.m. to 5 p.m., winter. Camping.

Although devoted primarily to preserving inscriptions made in historic times on a 200-foot high sandstone promontory, this monument includes hundreds of petroglyphs—symbols and designs which Zuni Indians pecked in the rock long before the first Spaniards arrived. On the mesa behind the cliff stand the ruins of two Pueblo villages, one of which has been partially excavated and stabilized. Visitors may take a self-guided tour of the site which includes a huge pool that is fed by rains and melted snow where inhabitants of the pueblos came for water. Handholds and footholds pecked in the rock show the route they followed up and down the cliff. Exhibits in the Visitor Center interpret the history of the monument, both ancient and modern.

FORT BURGWIN RESEARCH CENTER

From Taos (TOWSS) drive south 10 miles on New Mexico 3. The Research Center is east of Ranchos de Taos, on New Mexico 3. Open free, 8 a.m. to noon, 1 p.m. to 5 p.m., Monday through Friday, June, July, and Aug.

On display here are materials obtained from Pot Creek Pueblo, a 700-room site which was occupied between A.D. 1000 and 1350. Archeologists believe that the ancestors of both the Taos and Picuris (pee-koo-REES) Indians probably came from this Pot Creek Pueblo. Of special interest are the black-and-white pottery, corrugated utility ware, and manos and metates used in prehistoric times, together with tools and projectile points that were popular.

Several unusual exhibits are designed to show the techniques and methods that archeologists use for getting information about prehistoric cultures. Many of the materials which illustrate these archeological techniques come from local sites.

Other displays show cultural sequences and changes that developed in the pottery and stone tools and buildings from the Pueblo II period onward.

GILA CLIFF DWELLINGS NATIONAL MONUMENT (HEE-lah)

Drive 47 miles north of Silver City on New Mexico 25 and 527. Open free, 8 a.m. to 7 p.m., June 15 through Labor Day; 8 a.m. to 5 p.m., Labor Day through June 14; closed Jan. 1 and Dec. 25. Camping.

From the Visitor Center a half-mile trail leads along a tree-shaded stream to ruins built in large caves high above the canyon floor. In summer there are guided tours and evening campfire talks explaining the archeology of the region. Visitors may also take self-guided tours. Displays in the Visitor Center interpret prehistoric life in the area.

The Story. Perhaps as early as A.D. 100 Mogollon people began to live within the borders of the present Monument. They grew corn and beans, and for about 900 years they built dwellings that archeologists call pithouses because the floor was below ground level. About A.D. 1000, new ideas began to filter in from the Pueblo Indians to the north. Square stone houses above ground took the place of pithouses. New kinds of white pottery decorated with black designs were also borrowed from the north, replacing the older plain brown ware.

The Mogollon built some of the new square-roomed dwellings in caves in the cliffs, and some of these are the structures that have been stabilized and prepared for visitors to the monument. About A.D. 1400 the houses were all abandoned. No one knows why the inhabitants left or where they went. After they moved away, Apache Indians settled in the area, but they did not become cliff dwellers.

GRAN QUIVIRA NATIONAL MONUMENT
(grahn kee-VEE-rah)

From Mountainair on US 60 drive south 26 miles on New Mexico 10; or from US 380 at Carrizozo, drive north 56 miles on US 54 and New Mexico 10, a graded road. Or in good weather turn off US 380 at Bingham and drive north on New Mexico 41, a dirt road. Open free, at all times.

From the ruins of the 17th-century Spanish mission a trail leads through both excavated and unexcavated Pueblo Indian ruins in the monument.

The Story. Mogollon people built pithouses in the Gran Quivira area about A.D. 800. About A.D. 1100 they began to get many ideas from the Anasazi to the west. Soon black on white pottery became popular at Gran Quivira. So did underground ceremonial rooms called kivas, and much the same lifeways were observed here as in the pueblos in the Rio Grande Valley.

The Museum. In the Visitor Center, display cases show artifacts in their relation to the development of the culture of the people who lived at Gran Quivira.

JEMEZ STATE MONUMENT (HEM-ess)

From Los Alamos drive 23 miles west and south on New Mexico 4 to monument entrance on the northern edge of the town of Jemez Springs. Open free, 9 a.m. to 5 p.m., Wednesday through Sunday; 2 p.m. to 5 p.m., holidays. Camping nearby.

Here are the ruins of the pueblo of Giusewa (gee-EES-eh-wah), which dates from about A.D. 1300. It is known to have been very large, but how large is uncertain because only part of it has been excavated. In places the buildings are three stories high. The prehistoric people who lived here used the nearby hot springs as baths. Their descendants now live several miles down the canyon in Jemez Pueblo. The monument, a unit of the Museum of New Mexico, also preserves the 17th-century Franciscan mission of San Jose de los Jemez.

KIT CARSON HOME AND MUSEUM

E. Kit Carson Ave., Taos (TOWSS). Open 7:30 a.m. to 8 p.m., summer; 8 a.m. to 5 p.m., winter; 8 a.m. to 6 p.m., autumn and spring; closed Jan. 1, Thanksgiving, Dec. 25. Admission: adults, 50¢; children 12 to 15, 25¢; 6 to 11, 15¢; family rate, $1.50. Residents of Taos County and children under six with their parents, free.

One room in this museum is devoted to Indian culture and includes exhibits of prehistoric material from the Taos area dating back as far as 3000 B.C. Most of the archeological material is Anasazi after the year A.D. 1. The museum recently added a curator of archeology to its staff and is expanding its archeological exhibits.

KWILLEYLEKIA RUINS MONUMENT
(quill-lay-LAKE-ee-ah)

From Silver City drive northwest 30 miles on US 180 to Cliff, and from there follow directional signs 3 miles to the site and museum. Open 8 a.m. to 6 p.m., April 1 to Dec. 1. Admission: adults, 75¢; children over 12, 50¢.

This large and important site is privately owned by Mr. and Mrs. Richard B. Ellison, who bought it to save it from destruction. For a number of years they have engaged in careful excavation, and some of the materials they recovered are displayed in their museum at the site.

The Story. Following a drought which affected southwestern New Mexico from A.D. 1413 to 1425, a large number of Salado people moved from their villages on mesa tops and took up residence in the bottom of the Gila River Valley. At this site they built three blocks of houses with a total of about 300 rooms. Here they lived for about 150 years, farming, making beautiful pottery (good examples of which are exhibited in the museum), and cremating their dead.

Toward the end of that time, some Zuni Indians from far to the north moved into the pueblo, where they continued to make and use their own style of pottery, which was quite different from that of the Salado people. The name of the pueblo comes from these Zuni residents. Kwilleylekia is a Zuni word that means "the seventh village." Some people have said that this was the seventh of the seven legendary cities of Cibola.

In A.D. 1575, exceedingly heavy rains undermined the massive adobe walls of the pueblo, which began to crumble. The people tried to shore up the walls, and at the same time they began the construction of a new village. Soon a violent flood stopped all building at the new site. The inhabitants of Kwilleylekia gave up and moved away.

Unlike other Salado people who migrated to the south and finally settled in Mexico, those from Kwilleylekia moved northward with their Zuni friends, and took up residence in the Zuni pueblo of Hawikuh. This ancient village has been excavated, and from it have come a great number of Salado pots, exactly like those which had been made at Kwilleylekia. Also, the Kwilleylekia people at Hawikuh continued their practice of cremation. This was unlike the Zunis' own way of disposing of the dead.

It was at Hawikuh that the famous black explorer Estevan met his death in 1539. Estevan had traveled far, had visited many people who lived as hunters and gatherers, and was highly skilled at getting along with them. The best explanation of his sudden death at Hawikuh seems to be that he arrived there in the company of migratory Indians of the kind who had given the sedentary Zunis a great deal of trouble. More important, he looked different from any people the Zunis had ever seen, and he was dressed as if he might be a shaman or medicine man. The priests at Hawikuh were taking no chances with potential enemies, particularly potential rivals in the field of religion, and Estevan's large following gave the impression that he had special powers. So the Zunis killed the first great Negro explorer of America, who happened also to be the first explorer who entered New Mexico from Old Mexico.

Special Interest. Visitors may watch archeologists at work at Kwilleylekia. Competent archeologists conduct frequent tours and explain what is going on and what has been discovered.

LAGUNA PUEBLO (lah-GOO-nah)

From Albuquerque drive west about 45 miles on US 66. Open free, daylight hours. Visitors who

Size of Prehistoric Populations

There is no exact way of knowing how many people lived in a prehistoric community at any one time. However, archeologists have tried to find ways of making sensible estimates. One careful study has come up with a rough formula for use in some areas: One person for every ten square meters of floor space in a dwelling. To apply the formula, measure the number of square meters in the floors of all contemporary houses in a prehistoric Indian community, divide by ten, and you have a figure that represents the total number of people in the community at that particular time.

Classifying the Anasazi Cultures

The culture of the Anasazi people in the Southwest developed in rather clearly defined stages. You will find these stages referred to under two different sets of names, depending on which archeologist you are reading at the moment.

One set of names was agreed on at Pecos, New Mexico, in 1927, when a group of archeologists met there to exchange information and to work out terms they could all use. The arrangement of terms they adopted for the various stages in Anasazi culture is known as the Pecos Classification.

Later another archeologist, Frank H. H. Roberts, proposed a somewhat different classification, and his terminology is used by some writers.

Here are the two systems of classification, put down side by side for convenient reference (adapted from Jennings):

	Pecos	Roberts
A.D. 1700 to the present	Pueblo V	Historic
A.D. 1300 to 1700	Pueblo IV	Regressive (and Renaissance)
A.D. 1100 to 1300	Pueblo III	Great (Classic)
A.D. 800/850 to 1100	Pueblo II	Developmental
A.D. 750 to 900	Pueblo I	Developmental
A.D. 450 to 750	Basketmaker III	Modified Basketmaker
A.D. 1 to 500	Basketmaker II	Basketmaker
pre-A.D. 1	Basketmaker I	Basketmaker

A

B

A. Pecos ruins, which were first investigated by Adolph Bandelier, who drove out in a buggy from Santa Fe, 25 miles away. National Park Service photo.   B. Pecos Indians built this wall not for defense but to outline the area of the town which was closed to visitors at night.   National Park Service photo. C. The Palace of the Governors, Santa Fe, containing archeological exhibits, is the oldest governmental building on the soil of the United States. Spanish colonial authorities established it about A.D. 1609. In the arcade along the front of the building Indians from various pueblos sell their craftwork. Photo by Russell D. Butcher.

C

wish to draw or paint must pay a small fee and obtain a permit from the governor of the pueblo.

This pueblo is a lived-in archeological site. The ancestors of its inhabitants settled here about A.D. 1450.

MILES MUSEUM

On the campus of Eastern New Mexico University, Portales. Open free, 1 p.m. to 5 p.m.

Exhibits include general Southwestern archeological materials, natural mummies, and a large collection of prehistoric pottery.

MUSEUM OF INDIAN ARTS AND CRAFTS

103 W. 66th Ave., Gallup. Open free, 9 a.m. to 12 p.m. and 1 p.m. to 5 p.m., Monday through Friday; 9 a.m. to noon, Saturday; closed Sunday and national holidays.

Three of the 13 cases in this museum deal with prehistoric arts and crafts in the Southwest.

NEW MEXICO STATE UNIVERSITY MUSEUM

On the campus of New Mexico State University, at the southeast end of Las Cruces, off US 80. Open free, by appointment only.

This general museum contains Mogollon pottery and stone tools from the period A.D. 800 to 1350, together with a considerable quantity of Casas Grandes pottery from northern Mexico. Exhibits also include random local archeological finds and much ethnological material.

PALACE OF THE GOVERNORS

Palace Ave., on the Plaza, Santa Fe (administered by the Museum of New Mexico). Open free, 9 a.m. to 5 p.m., Monday through Saturday; 2 p.m. to 5 p.m., Sunday, May 15 through Sept. 15; closed Monday, Sept. 15 to May 15; Closed Jan. 1, Dec. 25.

This handsome building, which now houses one of the best museums in the Southwest, was formerly the residence of the Spanish governors. It was constructed on the site of a prehistoric pueblo, and sections of the original pueblo walls, more than four feet thick, now form part of the interior walls of the palace.

The archeological exhibits commence with the Paleo-Indian Period and go on to show the development of agriculture and sedentary communities, particularly the Hohokam, the Anasazi, and the Mogollon. In addition to displays of artifacts, there are dioramas and reconstructions of archeological sites. Excellent exhibits are also devoted to the Pueblo, Navajo, and Apache Indians of historic time.

PECOS NATIONAL MONUMENT (PAY-kohs)

From Santa Fe drive southeast 25 miles on Interstate 25 to Glorieta-Pecos interchange, then 8 miles on US 84A to the monument. Or from Las Vegas drive west on Interstate 25 to Rowe interchange, then 3 miles on US 84A to the monument. Open free, 9 a.m. to 5 p.m., summer; 9 a.m. to 4 p.m., winter. Camping nearby.

Here, near the Pecos River, are the ruins of a pueblo that may have been the largest center of population north of Mexico when Coronado entered the area in 1540. Visitors may follow a trail on a self-guided tour of the ruins.

The Story. About A.D. 1100 Anasazi people began to settle in small groups along the upper reaches of the river. In time these small settlements grew together into larger setlements, and by 1540 Pecos was a huge multistoried pueblo constructed around an open plaza. At least 660 rooms provided living quarters and storage space for about 2,000 people, and there were also at least 22 kivas.

The Pecos people were farmers, like all the Anasazi, but their geographic location led them into special activities. Their pueblo stood at a crossroads where Plains Indians met Pueblo Indians from the Rio Grande Valley, and where Indians from north and south along the Pecos River met. The pueblo was a great center for trade. So many strangers came to this spot that the Pecos people found it necessary to build a wall around the town in order to keep their living space for themselves. The wall was not for defense against enemies. It was merely a dividing line telling the foreign visitors that they must stay outside the wall at night.

Some time after 1540 the Franciscans built a huge church near Pecos and set about Christianizing the inhabitants. Apparently their success was incomplete. The pueblo continued to use numerous ceremonial kivas. But the friars did make converts who then built a new pueblo between the old one and the mission. Here there were no kivas.

In 1680 the Pecos people joined most of the other Pueblo Indians in a general revolt against the Spanish. They burned the church and drove the friars out. The church building which stands at Pecos today is much smaller than the original mission, signs of which were discovered only in 1967 during archeological excavations.

By 1838 the population of Pecos had dwindled from 2,000 to 17. Disease had killed many. Warfare, conducted largely by Comanche Indians, killed others. The few survivors moved to Jemez Pueblo where their descendants live today.

Between 1915 and 1925 Dr. A. V. Kidder made very important excavations at the Pecos site. A vast number of interesting artifacts came from the dig. Some of them can be seen in the Phillips Academy, Peabody Foundation, in Andover, Mass. Dr. Kidder's discoveries made it possible to bring order into the chronology of a large area in the Southwest. In 1927 all archeologists who had been working in the area came to Pecos to exchange information and to adopt a terminology that all of them could use and understand. Honoring that first Southwestern conference, archeologists still meet every year for a Pecos Conference at some place in the Southwest.

PICURIS PUEBLO (pee-koo-REES)

From Taos take US 64 west, then New Mexico 3 south for 16 miles, then turn west. Or from US 64, follow New Mexico 75 through Dixon. Or from US 64 at Riverside, follow New Mexico 76. Open all year, on payment of a fee, 8 a.m. to 5 p.m. Camping nearby.

Archeological excavations at Picuris have established that the pueblo was founded between A.D. 1250 and 1300. Those who built their homes at the present site moved from another pueblo that once stood near Talpa (on New Mexico 3). The excavated features at Picuris are open to the public and may be photographed.

PUYÉ CLIFF RUINS, SANTA CLARA INDIAN RESERVATION (poo-YAY)

From Espanola on US 84 drive southwest on New Mexico 30 to directional sign, then 9 miles west on New Mexico 5 to entrance gate. Open all year. Admission: a fee is collected by a representative of the Santa Clara Pueblo which supervises the ruin. Camping nearby.

Ancestors of the present-day Santa Clara Indians lived at Puyé Cliff. Some of their masonry dwellings were built along the base of the rock wall; other rooms were dug into the soft stone of the cliff itself, and on top of the cliff were about 2,000 additional rooms. Apparently the inhabitants moved away from Puyé Cliff seeking more fertile and better-watered lands, which they found near the site of the present Santa Clara Pueblo.

Parts of this very large ruin have been excavated and prepared for view by the public. The site is one of the few large prehistoric ruins administered by the descendants of the people who once lived there. Every year in midsummer the Santa Clara Indians hold an elaborate ceremonial at Puyé Cliff. The public is admitted.

QUARAI STATE MONUMENT (kah-RYE)

National Historic Landmark.
From Mountainair on US 60 drive north about 5 miles on New Mexico 10 to directional sign. Open free, at all times. Camping nearby.

In addition to walls of a 17th-century Spanish mission that can be seen here, there is a large rubble heap—the remains of an unexcavated pueblo ruin. The people who once lived at Quarai spoke the Tiwa language, and their culture was a combination of Mogollon and Anasazi. The village was apparently inhabited from about A.D. 900 until 1672.

SAN JUAN PUEBLO (san HWAN)

About 5 miles north of Espanola off US 285. Open free, daylight hours. A visitor's permit must be obtained from the governor of the pueblo. Camping nearby.

This pueblo was in existence when the first Spaniards arrived. The name San Juan is a shortened form of San Juan de los Caballeros, the name given the pueblo by the Spanish conquerors.

SANDIA MAN CAVE (san-DEE-ah)

National Historic Landmark.
From Albuquerque drive north 16 miles on Interstate 25, then east 12½ miles on New Mexico 44 to the parking area for the Cave. Or from Tijeras on US 66 drive north 6 miles on New Mexico 10, then northwest on New Mexico 44 about 12½ miles to the parking area. From the parking area a trail leads one-half mile to the cave itself. Camping nearby.

This cave is of interest because for many years archeologists believed that it had contained the oldest artifacts found in America. The remains of man's occupation were originally dated at about 20,000 years B.P. (Before Present). Recent restudy of the material has cast doubt on this early date, but the cave does remain of interest as one of the two places in which Sandia points have been found. These points seem to be at least as old as the Clovis points that have been associated with the hunting of mammoths.

Material from the excavation may be seen at the Museum of Anthropology, University of New Mexico, Albuquerque.

Sandia Man Cave is one of the very few archeological sites administered by the Forest Service of the U.S. Department of Agriculture.

SANTA CLARA PUEBLO

From Santa Fe drive north 24 miles on US 64 to Espanola, then 5 miles southwest on New Mexico 30. Open free, all year during daylight hours. Camping nearby.

This pueblo has apparently been on its present site since about 1500. Before the coming of the Spanish it was called Kapo. In earlier prehistoric times the Santa Clara people lived on the Pajarito Plateau in the region of Puyé.

SETON MUSEUM

From Cimarron at the junction of US 64 and New Mexico 58, drive 5 miles south on New Mexico 21 to Philmont Camping Headquarters. Open free, 8 a.m. to 5 p.m., Monday through Friday, June 11 through Aug. 31. Interested groups may request a tour of the museum at any time.

Each year the Ernest Thompson Seton Memorial Library and Museum, on the Philmont Scout Ranch, presents a different exhibit from its large collection of Southwestern Indian artifacts. These exhibits include some archeological material.

TAOS PUEBLO (TOWSS)

National Historic Landmark.
From Taos drive north 3 miles on New Mexico 3. Open all year, 8 a.m. to 6 p.m. Parking fee required. Camping nearby.

This pueblo has existed on its present site since prehistoric times, and the architecture of the buildings resembles closely the architecture of the pre-Spanish pueblo.

THREE RIVERS PETROGLYPHS

Drive 28 miles south from Carrizozo (care-ee-ZO-zo) on US 54, then 5 miles east at Three Rivers, following signs on a gravel road. Open free, all year. Camping nearby.

A 1,400-yard surfaced trail, with shaded rests along the way, leads through an area where people of the Jornada branch of the Mogollon culture made more than 500 rock carvings between the years A.D. 900 and 1400. Some archeologists have speculated that these petroglyphs were doodles made by prehistoric hunters to pass the time while they were waiting for game to appear. This interesting site is administered by the Bureau of Land Management.

UNIVERSITY OF NEW MEXICO, MUSEUM OF ANTHROPOLOGY

University and Roma NE, Albuquerque. Open free, 9 a.m. to 4 p.m., Monday through Saturday.

This excellent museum emphasizes archeology of the Southwest but has good exhibits on many other aspects of North American archeology as well. The oldest artifacts come from Sandia Cave. Authorities generally agree that the Sandia material is old, but not all of them accept the 18,000-year age placed on it by the museum. Other Paleo-Indian exhibits include Clovis points and Folsom material. The Anasazi exhibits contain a full range of the materials available from Basketmaker II through Pueblo IV. Other prehistoric cultures represented are: Plains, Northwest Coast, Eskimo, Hopewell, Adena, and Apache. A display of kachina dolls (kah-CHEE-nah) shows the various materials used in their manufacture and the stages in carving them. Another exhibit shows how Archaic craftsmen made stone tools by the flaking process. As part of a display of Southwestern Indian jewelry there are exhibits of prehistoric shell ornaments.

ZIA PUEBLO (TSEE-ah)

North from Bernalillo, 8 miles beyond Santa Ana on New Mexico 44. Open free, during daylight hours. Visitors are not allowed to photograph, draw, or paint in the pueblo. Camping nearby.

This pueblo has been on its present site since about A.D. 1300. Recent excavations by Dr. Cynthia Irwin-Williams suggest that the ancestors of the Zia people have lived in the same general area for nearly 8,000 years.

The symbol for the sun that the ancient Zia used has been adopted as the design at the center of the New Mexico state flag. These are the words of the official salute to the flag: "I salute the flag of the State of New Mexico, the Zia symbol of perfect friendship among united cultures."

ZUNI PUEBLO (ZOON-yee or ZOON-ee)

From Gallup drive south 30 miles on New Mexico 32, then 11 miles west on New Mexico 53. Open free at any time. Camping nearby.

Zuni Indians have lived on or near the site of the present town since prehistoric times. Several important digs have been conducted in abandoned Zuni villages, but the excavations are not open to the public.

Utah

ALKALI RIDGE

National Historic Landmark.
From Monticello drive 10 miles south on Utah 47 to directional marker, then 8 miles to site. Or from Blanding drive 5 miles north on Utah 47 to directional marker, then 10 miles to site. Open free, at all times. Camping nearby.

More than a thousand years ago a band of people settled in this land of cliffs and canyons. They hunted bighorn sheep, planted small fields of corn, and found it a good place in which to live. Their descendants continued to make their homes there for 500 years.

The firstcomers belonged to an early group of Anasazi people, called Basketmakers because they

Fremont Culture

In Utah about A.D. 900 many people began to live in somewhat the same way as the Anasazi farther south. Some archeologists call this Utah lifeway the Fremont culture and regard it as a subdivision of the Anasazi. Fremont people lived on the northern periphery of the Anasazi area and gathered wild foods, as their ancestors apparently had done for thousands of years, but they also raised corn. Unlike the Anasazi they wore moccasins rather than sandals. Much of their pottery was rather plain, and experts can easily distinguish it from Anasazi pottery which was often more decorated. Like the Anasazi, the Fremont people built dwellings of stone and adobe masonry, and they played games or gambled with carved bits of bone.

In the eastern part of Utah the lifeway of the Fremont people differed somewhat from that of their neighbors in the western part who are called Sevier (suh-VEER)-Fremont. Both the Fremont and the Sevier-Fremont left numerous examples of rock art on cliff walls throughout the area.

At the beginning of Pueblo III times the Fremont culture began to disappear. Perhaps some of the people moved south and took up life among the Anasazi. Others may have remained and resumed the older, simpler lifeway of the Western Archaic or Desert Culture. Possibly their descendants were the Utes and Paiutes who lived in the area when Europeans arrived.

Ball Courts

The Spanish who came to Mexico and Central America in the 16th century saw Indians playing a game with a solid rubber ball that weighed about five pounds. The players, divided into teams, tried to keep the ball in the air and scored points by bouncing it off the sloping side walls of a specially built court. The biggest score in the game seems to have been made when a player bounced the ball through the hole in one of the doughnut-shaped stone rings which were fixed high in the wall on either side of the court. Players were forbidden to hit the ball with their hands or feet. They could only direct it with blows from their hips or knees or elbows. Apparently the game had ceremonial significance, although it is not known exactly what this was.

In Arizona, archeologists have found in Hohokam settlements a number of large areas of hard-packed earth with sloping side walls which somewhat resemble the ball courts of Mexico and Central America. Presumably the Hohokam people borrowed the game from Mexico as they borrowed other elements of their culture. Excavation near one of the Arizona courts turned up a large ball similar to those used in Mexico. Nevertheless, one archeologist doubts that the Hohokam did play the ancient game. Edwin N. Ferdon, Jr. of the Arizona State Museum believes the large Hohokam courts were built for use in the Vikita ceremony, which is still conducted by some Arizona Indians—a ceremony to prevent the terrible effects of floods that can accompany violent rainstorms in the desert.

Prehistoric shields made of buffalo hide, which were found packed in juniper bark in a burial in the Capitol Reef National Monument area. National Park Service photo by George A. Grant.

were very skilled at weaving baskets of many kinds. As time passed they developed new skills, following the general pattern of all the Anasazi in the region. Students of archeology are especially interested in this settlement at Alkali Ridge because they can trace Anasazi life there, stage by stage, and also because the ceremonial kivas which mark Anasazi culture in the Southwest may have evolved in this particular area.

Alkali Ridge was excavated between 1931 and 1933 by J. O. Brew of the Peabody Museum at Harvard. Afterward, the site itself was covered over, and at present there is not a great deal for the casual visitor to see here. The Bureau of Land Management plans to reexcavate the site and provide interpretive facilities.

ANASAZI INDIAN VILLAGE STATE HISTORICAL SITE

East of Escalante on Utah 54. Open at all hours, April to October. Admission: Nominal fee. The Utah State Park system maintains a museum here at the site of an Anasazi village excavated by University of Utah archeologists.

ANTHROPOLOGY MUSEUM BRIGHAM YOUNG UNIVERSITY

On the campus, Provo. Open free, 8 a.m. to 8 p.m.

The museum contains archeological materials of the Fremont culture in Utah as well as materials of the Eastern Woodland and Southwestern cultures.

ANTHROPOLOGY MUSEUM UNIVERSITY OF UTAH

Building 411 on the university campus, Salt Lake City. Open free, 9 a.m. to 5 p.m., Monday through Friday; closed national holidays.

The archeological materials in this museum are primarily from archeological surveys and excava-

tions in the state of Utah. One famous site represented is Danger Cave.

ARCH CANYON INDIAN RUIN

About 15 miles southwest of Blanding off Utah 95. Open free, at all times. Camping nearby.

Visitors can hike along the bottom of Comb Wash about one-third mile to Arch Canyon where the remains of an Anasazi dwelling may be seen. The site is administered by the Bureau of Land Management.

CALF CREEK RECREATION SITE

On Utah 54 midway between Boulder and Escalante. Open free, at all times. Camping.

Anyone who plans to visit both Capitol Reef National Monument and Bryce Canyon National Park may wish to make the trip via Utah 54 (partly unpaved), which passes the ruins of two Anasazi villages. The sites are administered by the Bureau of Land Management.

CANYONLANDS NATIONAL PARK

To reach the Island in the Sky district of the park, turn west from US 160, 11 miles north of Moab. To reach the Needles district, drive west on the road that leaves US 160 about 12 miles north of Monticello. Both roads are graded dirt, slippery when wet, but passenger cars regularly use them. Open free, at all times. Camping.

Throughout the park there are numerous small ruins of dwellings, granaries, and kivas built by the Anasazi people between A.D. 900 and 1250. Visitors are invited to look at the ruins but are forbidden to enter them. The rock walls of the canyons offered innumerable flat surfaces for prehistoric artists, and a great deal of their work has been preserved. Visitors may see both pictographs, which are paintings on rock, and petroglyphs, which are pictures pecked or scraped on rock. Some of these, archeologists think, may have been made to mark game trails.

CAPITOL REEF NATIONAL MONUMENT

On Utah 24, 75 miles southeast of the junction of Utah 24 with US 89. Open free, all year. Camping.

The Fremont people once lived in this area and a portion of the Visitor Center museum is devoted to them. A pictograph is near the highway.

COLLEGE OF EASTERN UTAH PREHISTORIC MUSEUM

City Hall, Price. Open free, 9 a.m. to 8 p.m., daily.

This museum contains random local finds of Fremont culture materials and a diorama that shows prehistoric Indian dwellings.

DANGER CAVE STATE HISTORICAL SITE

One mile north of Wendover off US 40. Open free, at all times.

This famous site, although so far undeveloped, has been opened to the public by the Utah Park system. For its significance see page 44.

GRAND GULCH

From Blanding drive southwest 34 miles on Utah 95, then south 2 miles on Utah 261 to Cane Gulch. Then take hiking or horse trail down Cane Gulch to Grand Gulch. Open free, at all times. Camping nearby.

This is a deep canyon rich in archeological remains with many large, well-preserved Anasazi dwellings. There are three entrances, fenced for protection, and the area can only be traversed on foot or horseback. Guide service is available in Monticello. Inquire there at the Bureau of Land Management, which administers the site.

Pottery from Grand Gulch is now in the Museum of the American Indian, New York City. It was collected by Richard Wetherill, a member of a Quaker family who settled near Mancos, Colorado in the 1880s. From the home ranch he and his brothers, John and Clayton, went out on many exploring expeditions and made many archeological discoveries. In a cave in Grand Gulch Richard found, underneath layers of dust and debris containing things left by Pueblo people, artifacts made by Basketmaker people. This surely meant, said Wetherill, that the Basketmakers lived in the Southwest earlier than the Pueblos. Today the idea seems obvious, but at that time American archeologists had not made use of the principle of stratigraphy (the study of strata or layers in the earth), which had long been used in European archeology.

HOG SPRINGS PICNIC SITE

From Hanksville drive 37 miles south on Utah 95. Open at all times. Admission: $1 per car.

Near the picnic site is a rockshelter containing Indian pictographs, one of which is called the Moki Queen by local residents. Administered by the Bureau of Land Management.

HOVENWEEP NATIONAL MONUMENT

From Cortez, Colorado, drive north 18 miles on US 160 to Pleasant View; turn west at the Hovenweep directional sign and follow the graded road 27.2 miles to Square Tower Group, which is in Utah. Open free, all year, 8 a.m. to 5 p.m.

In this extremely isolated spot are imposing and well-preserved towers and other structures built by people who followed about the same lifeway as the ancient farmers of Mesa Verde. Exact dates and many details about the Hovenweep people are not yet known, because there has been no excavation at this site. Visitors take self-guided tours on a number of trails leading to the most interesting of the ruins.

Special Feature. Hovenweep is a kind of bank in which archeological riches are being kept for future generations of scientists to excavate and study. Archeologists approve this policy, because new techniques are constantly being developed which make it possible to learn more and more from the materials recovered at a site. When Hovenweep is excavated in the future it will yield information that might be lost if digging went on today. Once a site is excavated it is destroyed as a source of scientific information.

The Name. On September 13, 1874, a party exploring for the United States Government camped at this place. Ernest Ingersoll, a zoologist, and W. H. Jackson, a photographer, were members of the expedition. Ingersoll noted in his journal that the place was named by the explorers from two Indian words meaning "deserted canyon."

INDIAN PICTOGRAPHS AND PETROGLYPHS

South of Blanding, near Utah 95, just as the road starts down into Comb Wash. Open free, at all times. Camping nearby.

Indian rock art may be seen at this site, which is administered by the Bureau of Land Management.

NATURAL BRIDGES NATIONAL MONUMENT

From Blanding drive 45 miles west on Utah 95. Or from Mexican Hat drive north on Utah 261, then west on Utah 95. Open free, all year except when closed by rain or snow. The most pleasant season is from late April through October. Camping.

Within the monument are 200 sites once occupied by Anasazi people. Hikers who follow the trails will pass a cliff dwelling with several rooms, granaries, and kivas, which may be viewed but not entered.

NEWSPAPER ROCK, INDIAN CREEK STATE PARK

From US 160 at a point 12 miles north of Monticello, drive 12 miles west on the road to the Needles district of Canyonlands National Park. Open all year, daylight to dark. Admission: $1 per car. Camping.

Here a large cliff wall is covered with Indian rock art that may have accumulated over a period of 1,500 years. It seems likely that most of the petroglyphs were made by the Fremont people between A.D. 900 and 1200. Drawings depicting horses were clearly done in the historic period.

PAROWAN GAP INDIAN DRAWINGS
(pair-oh-WAN)

From Cedar City drive north 18 miles on US 91 to Parowan, then west on county road toward Utah 130. The site is next to the road. Open free, at all times. Camping nearby.

Drawings and designs seem to have been placed on the rock here by the Fremont people sometime between A.D. 900 and A.D. 1150. Administered by the Bureau of Land Management.

UTAH FIELD HOUSE OF NATURAL HISTORY

Natural History State Park, Main St., Vernal. Open free, 8 a.m. to 9 p.m., summer; 9 a.m. to 6 p.m., winter.

Within this natural history museum are archeological displays of prehistoric artifacts and mummies. The cultures represented are primarily the Fremont and Basketmaker. The materials range in date from the early Christian era to about A.D. 1200. A diorama shows the activities of Basketmakers at a campsite.

ZION NATIONAL PARK

From Kanab (kah-NAB) drive 17 miles north on US 89, then 24 miles west on Utah 15 to Park Headquarters. Or from Cedar City drive 32 miles south on US 91, then 27 miles east on Utah 15. Open all year. Camping.

The deep canyons and towering cliffs of this area were known to ancient Basketmaker and Pueblo people. A number of sites have been excavated, but none have been prepared for the public. An archeological diorama in the Visitor Center museum depicts prehistoric settlements in the park.

THE GREAT BASIN AND CALIFORNIA

 The peaks of the Rocky Mountains were a familiar sight to many a band of Big-Game Hunters 11,000 years ago. As men tracked mammoth and bison along the western edges of the Great Plains, they may have felt that the mountain range set a definite limit to their world. And indeed it usually did. At a few places, however, the Rockies presented no barrier to the hunters who wandered on foot. South Pass in Wyoming, for example, offered a route that rose like a broad gentle ramp, up and over the Continental Divide. Hunters could follow game across it without any sense that they were leaving the meat-rich Plains far behind, heading toward places where life would have to be lived in new ways.

Slowly little groups of people filtered across the Divide and down into a land which scientists call the Great Basin, an enormous stretch of country lying between the Rockies and the Sierra Nevada. Today this is a desert region, broken by short chains of rugged mountains. From much of the desert land there is no outlet to the ocean. Any water that flows down from the mountains must remain landlocked in swamps or in lakes, only one of which—the Great Salt Lake in Utah—is now very large.

In the days of the Big-Game Hunters the landscape looked quite different. Each of several basins within the Great Basin was filled with a huge body of water. But even in those days much less rain fell there than on the Great Plains, and men found desert shrubs growing instead of prairie grass. The reason for this seeming contradiction of little rain and vast expanses of water is simple: The basin lakes had been formed by the meltwater from Ice-Age glaciers and mountain snowfall. Following the Ice Age there was a rainy period for a while at least in the mountains, and the runoff fed the lakes. One of them, called by geologists Lake Bonneville, which had once reached a depth of about 900 feet, was still 90 feet deep by the time a small band of people began to visit its shore more than 10,000 years ago.

In this land of sparse vegetation game was less abundant than on the Plains. Mammoth hunting did not offer a way of life. Nor did bison roam in large herds. As a result human invaders had to look for other sources of food, and they had to try out new materials for some of their equipment.

Only two kinds of material existed in relative abundance—stone and fibrous plants—and people made the most of them. To the hunter's kit of stone tools, such as knives, scrapers, and projectile points, they added, in the course of time, flat stone

---

In these bedrock mortar holes prehistoric Indian women crushed seeds, particularly acorns, to prepare them for eating.

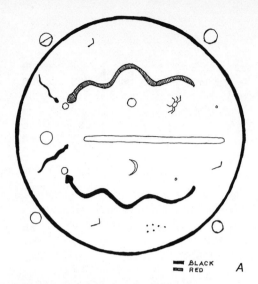

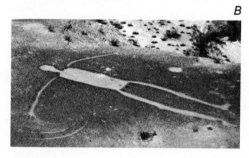

A. This design represents the world, the sun and moon, and snakes and animals with special powers. The Diegueño Indians used it in the puberty ceremony held for boys. After Waterman and Underhill. B. Prehistoric Indians shaped this gigantic figure, which is 105 feet long, and outlined it in gravel on the desert near Blythe, California. Photo by Michael J. Harner.

B

implements for grinding small seeds. From plant fiber they fashioned a variety of things that Big-Game Hunters had never found necessary. To hold the seeds that had become essential foods in the new environment they made deep carrying-baskets. Other baskets served for parching the seeds. Thin fibers could also be twisted into cord for nets, with which they caught small animals or birds. Other plant material went into sandals and aprons. Some men who lived near the lakes cleverly fashioned reeds into the shapes of ducks, which they floated on the water as decoys.

Those who came to the shores of Lake Bonneville sometimes took shelter in a cave now known as Danger Cave (so called because one of the archeologists who excavated it was almost buried beneath rock falling from its roof). There and in nearby caves people left signs of the extraordinary ways in which they managed to use whatever their harsh world offered. From layer after layer of debris archeologists reconstructed a picture of men constantly on the move, but not aimless wanderers. They had learned to take advantage of every edible thing in its own season, and they traveled from place to place according to a well-worked-out plan. Danger Cave, apparently, was a late-summer stopping place, where they harvested the tiny pickleweed seeds. Tons of dried stems from the plants accumulated over the years, after the seeds had been beaten out on the cave floor.

A Desert Culture

In other areas in the Great Basin groups of people adapted to the desert world in generally similar ways, although they may have come originally from different backgrounds. Some may have entered the far northern end of the Basin, then migrated southward, bringing with them a set of tools and a lifeway that has been called Old Cordilleran. Others, possibly descendants of the mammoth hunters, drifted across low passes in the Southwest. Wherever they came from, they developed a Western Archaic lifeway, known as the Desert culture, throughout the very large area that includes southwestern Wyoming, Utah, Nevada, and parts of California, Oregon, and Idaho.

After this desert way of life had taken shape, precarious though it was, it continued. The vast lakes, however, did not persist. As they dwindled, many groups of people moved on. Some of them migrated westward through passes into California, and in this new kind of country they found themselves forced to make adjustments in many different ways.

At this point there is disagreement among specialists on one important question. Did the migrants from the Great Basin find people already resident in California? And did these earlier people have a way of life so simple that it revolved around the use of large, clumsy tools made by chipping flakes from big pebbles or cobbles? The evidence is not all in and not all clear. Readers who wish to examine some of it firsthand may visit the Calico Mountains Project near Barstow, California.

When Europeans first reached California, they found many distinct groups of people speaking a great number of different languages or dialects. This probably meant that time after time a band of Indians, each with its own language, migrated from the east, found a niche for itself between the territories of other groups, and gradually took on some of the traits of its neighbors. (Some archeologists call this the "fish-trap" pattern of settlement, because the various bands seeking food entered California but never made their way out again.)

Migration for Food

All up and down the coast, and inland, too, people found life easier than it was in the Great Basin, but many of them continued the ancient pattern of local seasonal migration in search of food. Wherever they stayed they left evidence of their habits. At various places on the coast they gathered oysters and clams, and great heaps of discarded shells remained for the archeologist to use in reconstructing the past. Some groups came to depend almost entirely on the sea for their living. They fished with spears and hooks, and after they had become skilled boatmen they hunted seals and dolphins on the open ocean.

Elsewhere the early Californians gouged out pits in the rock to use as mortars for grinding seeds and nuts, and hundreds of these food-processing places are still visible. Like many other prehistoric Americans, these early Californians decorated rock surfaces and cave walls with paintings and peckings which are intriguing but not very well understood.

For all the variety in their languages and in the details of their lives, the California people remained gatherers of seeds and sea foods and hunters of small animals. In other words, their lifeway up until historic times remained at the stage we have called Western Archaic. Unlike the people of the Southwestern pueblos they never became farmers with solid permanent dwellings and all the habits that go with the raising of crops. Some Californians did live in good-sized villages where they had a year-round supply of food from the sea, but many continued their seasonal migrations, moving from one harvest to another. So too did the people who remained in the Great Basin. Like their ancestors thousands of years before, they journeyed from place to place, harvesting first one kind of food and then another as it ripened.

For a brief time some groups in one part of Utah and at the southernmost edge of Nevada did try farming. But by A.D. 1200 the Fremont people of Utah had given up, as had those who had built settlements along the Muddy River in Nevada. Apparently farming was not worth the struggle in this land of little rain. Those who had tried it reverted to gathering their food rather than growing it.

Baskets and Steatite Vessels

Because most of the Indians of California and the Great Basin were not farmers, the evidences of their lives are not easily seen today. They made lightweight, perishable baskets for gathering and storing their food, instead of manufacturing pottery, which was both cumbersome and fragile. And so the landscape is not littered with potsherds as it is in the Southwest. In a few places men did carve bowls and vessels from a soft rock called steatite, and a California people called the Canaliño, who lived near Santa Barbara, made elegant large steatite jars for storing water and for cooking. The latter were not placed over the fire. Instead they were filled with water which women kept at the boiling point by dropping in hot stones. It is interesting to note that on the East Coast of the United States some people also used steatite vessels before they made pottery.

Dwellings, like basketry, were made for the most part from perishable material, and people who stopped in caves did not build stone houses there as they did in the Southwest. The result has been that most archeological sites have not tempted park officials to restore them for visitors. Anyone who is looking for the artifacts and cultural remains of prehistoric Indians in California and the Great Basin will have to find them as a rule in museums. Fortunately there are excellent museums to be seen, so the search can be very rewarding.

California

ANTELOPE VALLEY INDIAN RESEARCH MUSEUM

15701 E. Ave. M. In Lancaster, on California 14, turn east onto Ave. J and drive to 150th St., then turn right and drive south to Ave. M, then left to museum. Total distance 18 miles from central Lancaster. Open 10 a.m. to 5 p.m.; closed Jan. 1, Thanksgiving, Dec. 25. Admission: adults, $1; children under 12, 50¢; children under 6, free in family groups.

In addition to displays showing Indian life in the historic period, this museum has exhibits on the Anasazi of the Southwest and prehistoric people of Alaska. An extensive exhibit of prehistoric California material includes some artifacts dated at 10,000 B.P.

BIG AND LITTLE PETROGLYPH CANYONS

National Historic Landmark.
At the Naval Weapons Center, Main Gate, in China Lake, obtain road directions. The access road is 45 miles long, about half of it hard-surfaced. Some parts of the area can be reached only by four-wheel-drive vehicles. Open free, 9 a.m. to nightfall, Saturday and Sunday, when range firing is not going on and when two vehicles, both sponsored by the Naval Weapons Center, make the trip together.

Possibly the largest concentration of petroglyphs in the world may be seen here. More than 20,000 have been counted. Apparently the carving was done over a long period of time and by people from at least two different cultures.

Visitors must leave everything in the area undisturbed.

BOWERS MUSEUM

2002 N. Main St., Santa Ana. Open free, 10 a.m. to 4:30 p.m., Tuesday through Saturday; 1 p.m. to 5 p.m., Sunday; 7 p.m. to 9 p.m., Wednesday and Thursday; closed Jan. 1, Thanksgiving, Dec. 25.

Exhibits in the Charles E. Bowers Memorial Museum show archeological finds from all the cultures of Orange County dating back 8,000 years. Several dioramas explain village life on the Great Plains and among the Eskimo.

Special Feature. One display contains 124 "cogged stones." The use of these gearlike objects is unknown, but they probably had some kind of religious significance. "Cogged stones" are unique to the southern California coast, and more than 90 percent of them have come from Orange County.

CALICO MOUNTAINS
ARCHAEOLOGICAL PROJECT

From Barstow on Interstate 15 drive east to the Minneola Overpass, then north on a local road past a cafe to the museum camp near the excavation. Open free, during daylight hours. Camping nearby.

Visitors are welcome to observe at this site even on working days. A tape recording has been installed to explain what is going on. Beginning in 1964, excavation was under the supervision of L. S. B. Leakey of Nairobi, Kenya, who gained worldwide fame for his discoveries about very early men in Africa. In immediate charge of the day-to-day work at the dig is Ruth De Ette Simpson of the San Bernardino County Museum in Bloomington, Calif.

Interest in the site began when an archeological survey party found on the surface of the ground numerous chipped rocks that appeared to be artifacts of great antiquity. Was it possible that men had knocked flakes from the sides of cobbles and shaped them to make knives and handaxes? Or had the rocks simply been broken by knocking against each other as floods washed them down from the mountains?

Excavation in undisturbed ground brought to light several hundred tools and flakes which the excavators consider to have technological significance. These, Dr. Leakey believed, were made by man between 50,000 and 80,000 years ago. If he is right, this may be the most important excavation going on in America. Some experts, however, feel that the objects Dr. Leakey called artifacts are merely accidental products of natural processes. In an effort to help settle the question, John Witthoft of the University Museum of the University of Pennsylvania studied the material in 1969 and came to the conclusion that it consisted of man-made artifacts.

CALIFORNIA STATE INDIAN MUSEUM

2701 L St., on the grounds of Sutter's Fort, Sacramento. Open 10 a.m. to 5 p.m.; closed Jan 1, Thanksgiving, Dec. 25. Admission: 25¢; children under 18, free.

This museum is devoted to the life of California Indians, past and recent, and includes many archeological exhibits.

Special Feature. A collection of photographs shows the California Indians as they were first seen by settlers from the United States.

CATALINA ISLAND MUSEUM

In the Casino Building at Avalon on Santa Catalina Island. Can be reached by boat from Los Angeles harbor or by plane from Long Beach airport. Open free, 2 p.m. to 4 p.m. and 8 p.m. to 10 p.m., daily, June 15 through Sept. 15; 2 p.m. to 4 p.m. and 8 p.m. to 10 p.m., Saturday and Sunday, Sept. 16 through June 14.

In prehistoric times men who were expert boatmen lived on Santa Catalina and others of the eight Channel Islands which lie off the coast of southern California. When Spaniards first arrived those who occupied the northern islands were Chumash Indians, and groups who spoke a Shoshonean language lived on the southern islands. However, archeologists often refer to the culture of all the islands at that time as Canaliño.

Included in the Catalina Island Museum are materials covering a period of about 4,000 years. Artifacts in the displays were excavated by archeologists from California universities and from the Museum of the American Indian in New York. The exhibits have been arranged to answer these questions: What did people use for dress and decoration? What did they use to make a living? What did they use in religious ceremonies?

CLEAR LAKE STATE PARK

From Lakeport on California 29 drive south on local road to Kelseyville, then northeast 4 miles on Soda Bay Rd. to park entrance. Open at all times.

Lovelock Cave

In northwestern Nevada, Lovelock Cave once opened out on Lake Lahonton, an immense body of water that existed during and after the rainy period at the end of the Ice Age. About 4,500 years ago, people began to visit this cave, and for a long time they used it as a place in which to store equipment. The implements they left there show how they exploited plant and animal life along the lakeshores. To attract ducks, for example, they used decoys fashioned from reeds that grew around the lake and sometimes made realistic with duck feathers woven along the sides. From reeds and a dozen other fibers, the cave's visitors made sandals, fishnets, mats, and baskets of various kinds. They used shredded fiber in clothing and wove blankets from animal fur and bird skins.

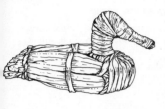

This duck decoy, made of reeds, was found in Lovelock Cave, Nevada. Some duck decoys were decorated with feathers. After Loud and Harrington.

The concern these people felt for weaving and basketry appeared in another way. In the cave they left sickles made of bone and mountain sheep horn that helped them harvest the grasses they used as fibers.

Few sites in the Great Basin area have yielded more information about the early people who lived there. Lovelock Cave itself has not been prepared for visitation by the public. Fortunately, however, some of the materials excavated there are on exhibit in the Nevada Historical Society Museum and in the Museum of the American Indian, New York.

Baskets, Bags, and Pots

Everywhere in the world people have usually found some way of making containers from such materials as were at hand. The art of weaving grasses and plant fibers into baskets seems to be older than the art of shaping and baking clay to form durable pots. Plant fibers were almost universally available, and when made into baskets the product was light and easily carried from place to place. On the other hand pottery was heavy, and it broke easily. So people tended to cling to basket-making as long as they were on the move looking for sustenance. When they had a food supply from farming, they could settle down—indeed, they had to settle down—and then they could economically use heavy pots.

In California and along the Northwest Coast, where food was relatively abundant without agriculture and where people lived together in large groups, they clung to basketry up to historic times. Apparently they felt satisfied with their old way of life and saw no great need for change. Pottery-making did come into southern California in relatively recent times when knowledge of the art spread from the Southwest and Mexico.

Baskets and baked clay pots were by no means the only kinds of container. In areas where steatite (soapstone) was available some people carved vessels from this soft material. In other places they carved bowls of wood or shaped wood into boxes or used tough-skinned gourds as canteens for holding water. In the northern woodlands they often shaped tree bark into containers. Hunters on the Plains made pouches and bags and boxes from the stomachs and intestines and hide of buffalo.

Prehistoric Indians mined steatite for cooking vessels. Smithsonian Inst. photo.

The advantages of containers for storing and carrying and cooking were endless—and so was man's inventiveness. He even used hollow buffalo horns for storing live coals and carrying them from one campground to another.

Admission: 75¢ per car, per day, or $3 per camp-site, May 1 through Sept. 30; $1.50 per campsite, Oct. 1 through April 30.

A group of prehistoric Indians who lived in much the same way as the Pomo Indians once had a settlement on this lake. Among the structures they used are two that have been restored and can be seen by visitors. The first of these is a sweat house.

Over much of North America the sweat house was important in prehistoric Indian life. In California it was usually a substantial earth-covered structure, a little smaller than the dwellings people lived in. Men came to the sweat house, often at night, much as men of other cultures go to clubs. They took the baths together and often slept all night in the house. Apparently sweat baths were more for pleasure than for reasons of health or because they had ceremonial significance. And men really sweated. They built a very hot fire, inside the house, and if the smoke got too thick they lay down on the floor where they could breathe fresh air. Often the houses were near streams or lakes or the ocean. After getting up a good sweat, the bathers plunged into the water. Then to dry themselves, some of them, in historic times at least, rolled in the sand.

The second structure that has been restored at Clear Lake is a ceremonial house. It, like the sweat house, is earth-covered. But it is much larger. People met here for dances and religious activities. California Indians never developed a priesthood. They had shamans or medicine men, and they had at least two simple religious cults that survived into historic times. One is called the Kuksu. Not much is known about it except that men impersonated mythological characters and initiations were very important. Another cult, called the Toloache, also placed great emphasis on initiation rites and on the use of Jimson weed, which has hallucinogenic properties.

No one knows which cult was connected with the ceremonial house at Clear Lake State Park, but we can be sure that the Indians in California, though they spoke many different languages, shared certain religious beliefs and practices.

A nature trail in the park, for which a folder has been prepared, identifies all the plants in the area and tells how they were used by the Indians who lived here. Along the trail is the site of an Indian village. It is marked by a mortar hole and a grinding slab. When a woman wanted to grind acorns, she took a special basket that had a hole in the bottom and placed it over the mortar hole. Then she filled this double receptacle with acorns, and used a stone pestle to crush them.

One of the plants identified along the nature trail is the California buckeye. This plant produces a fruit which is poisonous when eaten raw, but the Indians learned how to bake it and then soak it in a way that removed the poison. Roasted buckeyes were mashed or whipped much as we mash or whip potatoes.

COYOTE HILLS REGIONAL PARK

From Alvarado, near Fremont in Alameda County, drive south to the park on Patterson Ranch Road. Open free, 8 a.m. to 10 p.m., daily.

In this park are four shell mounds where people known as the Ohlone or Costanoans lived from about 1500 B.C. to perhaps A.D. 1400. Visitors may enter the site when accompanied by personnel of the East Bay Regional Park District or by a representative of the Treganza Museum of San Francisco

State College. One of the mounds has been made into an outdoor museum with signs to point out various features and a display which makes clear the time periods during which the site was occupied. Here visitors can have the unique experience of sitting in a small outdoor theater in the excavated area and hearing a lecture on the life of the hunting and gathering people who once inhabited the spot.

CUYAMACA RANCHO STATE PARK

From San Diego drive east on US 80, then north on California 79 to museum. Open free, daily. Camping.

An Indian exhibit in the former Dyar residence in the park deals with the story of the Diegueño Indians of the area.

DEATH VALLEY NATIONAL MONUMENT

From Las Vegas, Nev., drive northwest 85 miles on US 95 to Lathrop Wells, then south 23 miles on Nevada 29 to Death Valley Junction, then west 30 miles on California 190 to Visitor Center and museum at Furnace Creek. The museum is open free, 7:30 a.m. to 4:30 p.m., May through Oct.; 8 a.m. to 9 p.m., Nov. through April. Camping.

Exhibits in the museum tell briefly the story of human habitation of Death Valley from 6000 or 7000 B.C. to the present.

INDIAN GRINDING ROCK
STATE HISTORICAL MONUMENT

From Jackson drive east about 9 miles on California 88 to Pine Grove, then 1½ miles north on a county road. Open at all times. Admission: 75¢ per car. Camping.

The Story. Miwok Indians once lived at this site which they called Tco'se (sha-tzee). Here, on an outcrop of limestone 173 feet long and 82 feet wide, are 1,185 circular pits which have been worn in the rock. These pits are mortar cups—stationary basins in which women used pestles to grind up seeds, particularly acorns, as one step in preparing them to be eaten.

On this same outcrop are 363 petroglyphs which have been pecked in the limestone.

The Indians who lived at Tco se no doubt had many of the customs of other Miwoks. They probably used money made of shell or of small polished and baked cylinders of a rock called magnesite. They built cone-shaped dwellings, some wholly above ground, others partly below ground. Often they dug large pits and then erected structures over them to serve as assembly places or dance houses. Men had special houses in which they took sweat baths.

Certainly the grinding of acorns was not all that went on at Tco'se. For such large facilities there must also have been large storage arrangements. Wherever they lived the Miwoks seem to have erected granaries, which they built on posts, using a kind of basketry technique. Like other Indians of California, they had developed the art of basketmaking to a very high degree.

The baskets and other artifacts made by prehistoric Miwoks can be seen in various California museums. But nowhere is there a better example of the way these people turned bedrock into a tool essential to their livelihood.

JOSHUA TREE NATIONAL MONUMENT

74485 Palm Vista Dr., Twentynine Palms. The monument is open free, at all times. The Visitor Center is open 8 a.m. to 5 p.m., Thursday through Monday. Camping.

The Story. The Visitor Center has cases of archeological material devoted to the Pinto Basin culture, which once dominated the region and which takes its name from Pinto Basin in southeastern California. According to some specialists this culture may have begun as early as 6000 or even 7000 B.C. One archeologist, however, does not believe it began until about 3000 B.C. All agree that it lasted until at least 1000 B.C., and it is important because it marked for this region the beginning of the intensive use of crushed hard-shelled seeds for food. Evidence of this new adjustment to the arid environment—or evidence of adjustment to a newly arid environment, whichever the case may be—is that milling-stones and manos appeared here for the first time just when the distinctive Pinto Basin projectile points first appeared. Earlier people in the region, who belonged to the Lake Mohave culture, seem not to have made use of tools for pulverizing seeds.

The Pinto Basin people shared the tendency to engage in intensive exploitation of resources which marked the Archaic lifeway in every part of the continent. How, within this widespread Archaic pattern, they made their special adjustment can be seen here at the Joshua Tree National Monument. Exhibits at the Visitor Center also include one which shows how the distinctive Pinto Basin points were made. Another is devoted to more recent Indians who lived in the area from approximately A.D. 1000 to historic times: the Serrano, the Chemehuevi, and the Cahuilla people.

Within the monument visitors can see numerous examples of rock art in addition to archeological sites of other kinds. Rangers can give directions to some of the petroglyphs as well as other areas of archeological interest.

KERN COUNTY MUSEUM

3801 Chester Ave., Bakersfield. Open free, 8 a.m. to 5 p.m., Monday through Friday; 1 p.m. to 5 p.m., Saturday, Sunday, and holidays; 10 a.m. to 6 p.m., when Daylight Saving is in force; closed Jan. 1, Thanksgiving, Dec. 25.

Random local archeological finds are included here with more recent artifacts which are representative of Yokuts and other cultures in southern San Joaquin Valley. A diorama shows Yokuts basketweaving techniques.

LOMPOC MUSEUM

200 S. H St., Lompoc. Open free, 1 p.m. to 4 p.m., Saturday, Sunday; at other times by appointment.

Exhibited here is material from 50 Chumash sites in Santa Barbara County, mostly from the late prehistoric period. Among the exhibits is a cremation and an unusually large carved steatite vessel. From northern California there is an obsidian blade 26 inches long.

LOS ANGELES COUNTY
MUSEUM OF HISTORY AND SCIENCE

900 W. Exposition Blvd., Exposition Park, Los Angeles. Open free, 10 a.m. to 5 p.m., Tuesday through Sunday; closed Thanksgiving and Dec. 25.

Examples of Indian rock art can be seen in many canyon areas in California. These drawings were cut into a soft tufa cliff at Emigrant Wash in Death Valley National Monument. National Park Service photo.

Archeological exhibits include material from these southern California cultures: Oak Grove, Hunting, and Canaliño. Some materials date back as far as 8000 B.C.

Artifacts and displays are arranged to demonstrate how Indians made baskets, blankets, stone tools, and pottery. A diorama shows a Chumash village on the coast, and there are models that illustrate other phases of prehistoric life in California, including the preparation of acorn mush.

From the southwestern part of the United States there are displays of Hohokam and Anasazi materials.

LOWIE MUSEUM OF ANTHROPOLOGY, UNIVERSITY OF CALIFORNIA

2620 Bancroft Way, Berkeley. Open 10 a.m. to 5 p.m.; closed Christmas. Admission: free except when fees are charged for special exhibitions.

The Robert H. Lowie Museum has a vast collection of California and other American archeological material, parts of which are on display from time to time. There is no permanent display on North American prehistory.

MATURANGO MUSEUM

For road directions inquire at the Naval Weapons Center, Main Gate, in China Lake, north of Ridgecrest. Open free, 2 p.m. to 5 p.m., Saturday and Sunday and at other times by appointment.

In the Maturango Museum of Indian Wells Valley are exhibits of materials which span the period from Pinto Basin culture to recent Shoshonean culture in the Upper Mojave Desert. Displays include examples of Indian rock art from nearby Big and Little Petroglyph canyons.

MUSEUM OF EARLY MAN

Behind Stow House, Los Carneros Rd., Santa Barbara. Open free, all year, 2 p.m. to 4 p.m., Sunday only.

This museum, maintained by the Santa Barbara County Archaeological Society, specializes in prehistoric material from the coastal area in Santa Barbara County. It contains material used by the Milling-Stone, Hunting, and Canaliño people. One exhibit shows the evolution of the mortar and pestle.

OAKLAND MUSEUM, HISTORY DIVISION

Civic Center, between 10th and 12th streets, Oakland. Open free, 10 a.m. to 5 p.m., Tuesday through Thursday; 10 a.m. to 10 p.m., Friday; 10 a.m. to 5 p.m., Saturday, Sunday, and holidays.

Archeological materials from several Bay area sites are part of a large exhibit devoted to the ethnography and cultural ecology of California Indians. One exhibit is a reconstruction of an Alameda County shell midden.

PALM SPRINGS DESERT MUSEUM

135 E. Tahquitz Dr., Palm Springs. Open 10 a.m. to 5 p.m., Tuesday through Saturday and holidays; 1 p.m. to 4 p.m., Sunday; 7:30 p.m. to 9:30 p.m., Tuesday, Friday, and Saturday, Oct. 15 to June. Admission: adults, 50¢.

This museum displays some local archeological material.

PETROGLYPHS, NEAR BISHOP

From Bishop on US 395, a 50-mile circle trip passes five separate sites where prehistoric people made carvings in the rocks. A map showing the location of these petroglyph sites may be obtained from the Chamber of Commerce in Bishop. Open free, at all times. Camping.

Many of the pictures cut in the rock are recognizable deer and mountain sheep. Dr. R. F. Heizer of the University of California has suggested that the petroglyphs were designed to give magic powers to hunters. They are very often beside deer trails.

At one site called Fish Slough visitors can see not only petroglyphs but also signs of an ancient village. Circles of stone mark house locations. Deep pits in boulders once served as mortars where women ground seeds to make meal.

RANDALL MUSEUM

100 Museum Way, San Francisco. Open free, 10 a.m. to 5:30 p.m., Tuesday through Saturday; noon to 5 p.m., Sunday.

The Josephine D. Randall Junior Museum is designed primarily as a teaching aid for school groups and includes a variety of specially selected material on loan from the Robert H. Lowie Museum of Anthropology, University of California, Berkeley.

One exhibit identifies prehistoric artifacts found in a Costanoan shell mound and demonstrates the techniques used in excavating it. This model suggests how it is possible for archeologists to trace the development of Costanoan culture from the time when people began to live around San Francisco Bay in small, scattered clusters of dwellings made of poles covered with brush or mats. By studying the contents of the mounds, scientists have found that the Costanoans lived on or near these big heaps of oyster and clam shells only at certain seasons. This meant that people were elsewhere part of the time, gathering food that was different from the kind they could get along the shore.

Many aspects of Costanoan culture could not be preserved in the mounds. Baskets, for example, rotted and left little or no trace. So did canoes or rafts made of reeds. We know, however, from accounts written by early Spanish missionaries that the Costanoans made beautiful baskets and were clever at constructing watercraft from plants that grew in marshy places.

Beliefs, stories, myths, patterns of social organization are only dimly reflected in the artifacts that people discarded, but here again we can reconstruct some details from the accounts of Europeans. So the mounds, together with direct observation of historic people, give some depth to our picture of a lifeway that has entirely vanished. Costanoans have disappeared from the earth.

Special Interest. In cooperation with the San Francisco State College Department of Anthropology, the museum offers school children the experience of excavating an archeological site, finding artifacts, and recording data.

RIVERSIDE MUNICIPAL MUSEUM

3720 Orange St., Riverside. Open free, 9 a.m. to 5 p.m., Tuesday through Saturday; 1 p.m. to 5 p.m., Sunday; closed national holidays.

Dwarf Mammoths

On Santa Rosa Island off the California coast near Santa Barbara, excavators have found the remains of mammoths that apparently never attained a height of more than six feet. Elsewhere the crown of a mammoth's head was as much as 12 feet above the ground.

Some archeologists believe that men hunted the dwarf mammoths on Santa Rosa as far back as 29,000 years ago. Others think that the evidence for this is shaky and that fires attributed to men were really brush fires. Perhaps more excavation on the island will remove all doubt.

Santa Rosa is one of eight Channel Islands that lie off the California shore from San Diego northward. Two of them, Anacapa and Santa Barbara islands, have been designated a National Monument. At the present time only Anacapa can be visited, and no archeological site has been prepared for the public.

Acorns

The prehistoric population was more dense in California than in many other parts of America north of Mexico. Some specialists believe that about 150,000 people were living in the present area of California when the Spanish began to settle there. Obviously these Indians had a food supply ample for maintaining such a population, and the most important single element in their diet was acorns.

Most varieties of oak tree produce acorns that contain tannic acid and are bitter-tasting in their natural state. However, if acorns are soaked in water long enough the tannic acid disappears, and the nut that is left is sweet and nourishing. Archeologists don't know when Indians discovered this source of food; they do know that the technique of preparing it spread along the West Coast wherever oak trees grew.

The process of leaching whole acorns was slow. It took months to get out all the tannic acid. Finally someone made an invention to speed up the work. Using mortar and pestle of the kind that crushed hard-shelled seeds to make them edible, a woman ground the soft acorns into a flour. When this acorn flour was soaked in hot water, the tannic acid disappeared very quickly.

To do the leaching, a woman often made a small hollow in the sand beside a stream. In the hollow she placed a lining of leaves and poured in acorn flour. Then she filled a water-tight basket with water and dropped hot stones in it. When the water was hot she poured it over the acorn flour. Several dousings completely carried the acid away. What remained was a moist cake that could be eaten without delay or dried and saved for future use. The dried acorn flour, mixed with water, was served as a kind of thick soup or mush.

Acorn flour was not only tasty but nourishing. It contained about 21 percent fat, 5 percent protein, and 62 percent carbohydrate. Its fat content was much greater than that of either maize or wheat; its protein and carbohydrate content somewhat less.

Exhibits show a wide variety of artifacts made by the Luiseño, Cahuilla, and Diegueño people of the period from 1700 to 1750, just before they came into contact with the Spanish. Two exhibits explain how these people made baskets and pottery. Others contain some unique ceremonial objects.

SAN BERNARDINO COUNTY MUSEUM

18860 Orange St., Bloomington. Open free, 1 p.m. to 5 p.m.; closed July 4, Thanksgiving, and Dec. 25.

Although this museum has displays covering the Northwest Coast and Southwest, its main concern is with the prehistoric and historic Indians of San Bernardino County. The Serrano, Cahuilla, Chemehuevi, Panamint, and Mohave Indians are represented, as are ancient prehistoric cultures including Basketmakers, Amargosa, Paleo-Indian, and Calico. The Calico culture, represented by materials from an excavation in the Calico Mountains near Yermo, Calif., is creating widespread discussion in archeological circles. If the age of Calico material proves to be as great as some archeologists think it may be—50,000 years—then this museum will contain the oldest dated artifacts in the Americas.

SAN DIEGO MUSEUM OF MAN

Balboa Park, San Diego. Open 10 a.m. to 5 p.m., daily. Admission: adults, 75¢; children under 16, free; free for everyone on Friday.

This museum has rich resources of southern California and Southwestern material. The exhibits change frequently

As you go through California museums or read about Indians, you may be puzzled by two names which look somewhat alike—San Dieguito and Diegueño. San Dieguito refers to a very early culture. Diegueño refers to a very late culture which extended into historic times.

The San Dieguito culture began perhaps 11,000 years ago in the southern part of the Great Basin. At that time the people apparently did not specialize in any one method of getting food. They hunted, did some fishing, and dug up edible roots. As the centuries passed, they became gatherers and grinders of small seeds. Later, about 7,000 or 8,000 years ago, when some of them moved to the coastal regions in southern California, they became adjusted to a diet of food from the sea which supplemented their vegetable foods. Apparently because our first knowledge of this culture comes from sites close to San Diego, Calif., archeologists gave it the name San Dieguito. However, some important San Dieguito sites are a great distance from San Diego. One, for example, is at the lowest level of Ventana Cave in southern Arizona.

The Diegueño Indians, who also lived near San Diego, have attracted attention because they used a drink which they made from the pounded root of Jimson weed (Datura). Young men who took this drink hoped that the dreams it induced would bring them the help of powerful guardian spirits. The Diegueño also made paintings on the ground using fine powders for their colors. For white they used ground-up steatite (soapstone), iron oxide for red, powdered charcoal for black, and small seeds for other colors.

SANTA BARBARA
MUSEUM OF NATURAL HISTORY

2559 Puesta del Sol Rd., Santa Barbara. Open free,

9 a.m. to 5 p.m., Monday through Saturday; 1 p.m. to 5 p.m., Sunday and holidays; closed Dec. 25.

Archeological exhibits here are devoted largely to California Indians. Displays include grinding stones made by Oak Grove people 10,000 years ago; artifacts of the Hunting people 7,500 years ago, and of the Canaliño people from 4,000 years ago to 300 years ago. Dioramas show scenes of Canaliño, Oak Grove, California cave-dwelling and desert village life. One display demonstrates how steatite (soapstone) was traded from one of the islands off the California coast to other islands and to the mainland farther north. In another display is a most unusual burial in which the shoulder blade of a whale, inlaid with decorations, has been used as a bier.

Special Feature. Campbell Grant, an authority on American Indian rock art, has prepared two exhibits on techniques and materials used by Indian artists who painted on rock surfaces.

SEQUOIA AND KINGS CANYON
NATIONAL PARKS

Good roads lead to these two contiguous National Parks from either Fresno or Bakersfield. Open free, 8 a.m. to 5 p.m., summer. Camping.

Both the Lodgepole Visitor Center in Sequoia and the Grant Grove Visitor Center in Kings Canyon have displays of archeological material showing how Indians of the area made and used artifacts.

Special Feature. At Hospital Rock in Sequoia, Indian rock art can be seen, as well as a prehistoric village site.

SOUTHWEST MUSEUM

234 Museum Dr., Highland Park, Los Angeles. Open free, 1 p.m. to 4:45 p.m., Tuesday through Sunday; closed Jan. 1, July 4, Thanksgiving, Dec. 25, and for one month from mid-Aug. to mid-Sept.

Extensive exhibits are devoted to the Indians of all the Americas, with rich archeological materials from America north of Mexico.

There are particularly good exhibits of artifacts from California and the Southwest. Dioramas show prehistoric Indian life and structures. Artifacts on display include Sandia, Clovis, and Folsom projectile points dating back 10,000 to 12,000 years, and there is also a wide variety of Anasazi material.

TREGANZA ANTHROPOLOGY MUSEUM

San Francisco State College, 1600 Holloway Ave., San Francisco. Open free, 8 a.m. to 5 p.m., Monday through Saturday.

Materials on exhibit in the Adan E. Treganza Anthropology Museum represent most of the culture areas in northern and central California, beginning with Early Horizon times and coming up to the historic period.

TULARE COUNTY MUSEUM (too-LAIR-ee)

27000 Mooney Blvd., Visalia. Open free, 8 a.m. to 5 p.m., Monday through Friday; 9:30 a.m. to 6 p.m., Saturday and Sunday, April 1 through Oct. 15; 8 a.m. to 5 p.m., Monday through Friday, Oct. 16 to April 1; closed national holidays.

Exhibits illuminate the life of the Yokuts Indians, particularly as it was about 1800, before it was much influenced by European culture. A leaflet available at the museum gives a great deal of information about the activities, crafts, and skills of these inhabitants of the San Joaquin Valley.

Nevada

LAKE MEAD NATIONAL RECREATION AREA

Good highways lead into the area from Kingman, Ariz.; Needles, Calif.; Las Vegas and Glendale, Nev. Open free, all year. Camping.

Men have lived in Nevada for at least 11,000 years, and the tools and weapons that indicate their presence at an early date have been found in many places in the Lake Mead National Recreation Area. The waters of Lake Mohave and Lake Mead have not covered nearly all the campsites or petroglyphs left by men before the dawn of history.

The easiest place to see petroglyphs is in Grapevine Wash on the Christmas Tree Pass Road, near Davis Dam on Lake Mohave. Christmas Tree Pass can be reached from either Nevada 77, west of Bullhead City, Ariz., or from US 95 south of Searchlight, Nev. It is not known when or by whom the petroglyphs in this area were made, but they may be very ancient.

Not far from the recreation area, near Las Vegas, archeologists have excavated Gypsum Cave. In it they found a fairly complete collection of the implements that Western Archaic people had developed in the desert area for use in gleaning an

existence from so unpromising a terrain. Some of this material is in the Southwest Museum in Los Angeles.

The cave also yielded two quite unusual discoveries. One was a type of diamond-shaped projectile point that had not been seen before. The point seemed to be associated with the other novel feature—an unfamiliar kind of animal dung, apparently of great antiquity. Some very large animal had inhabited the cave and had left droppings on the floor; this happened after one group of men had been there and before another group took up residence. But what animal?

M. R. Harrington, who was excavating the cave, suspected the animal was a giant ground sloth, a creature that lived in the Americas at about the same time as mammoths. To make sure, he sent off samples of the dried dung to experts in natural history museums, and they agreed: a sloth had lived in the cave.

Since there were dates for sloths from other places, and since men's use of the cave seemed to be contemporaneous with the existence of the sloth, the time for men's use of Gypsum Cave appeared to have been more than 10,500 years ago. Long after the dung was discovered in Gypsum Cave, a radiocarbon date was obtained for it, and the date suggests that it may have been at least 10,500 years old.

Not all specialists are now convinced that the Gypsum Cave discovery proves that men hunted—or even lived—at the same time as sloths. But the discovery of sloth dung there does call attention to the importance of fossil fecal matter. Scientists are able to discover an amazing amount about the lifeways of prehistoric people by studying their droppings, which are called coprolites.

A

A. Vast numbers of petroglyphs (drawings pecked in rock) show the elusive bighorn sheep, greatly prized by ancient hunters but hard to get. The petroglyphs may have been connected with the belief that a hunter could win magical power over an animal by drawing its likeness. The pictures shown here were found in the Lake Mead National Recreation Area. National Park Service photo. B. This diorama indicates how prehistoric Chumash Indians in Southern California used caves as living areas and for storage. Santa Barbara Museum of Natural History photo.

B

LOST CITY MUSEUM OF ARCHEOLOGY

On Nevada 12 in Overton, near Lake Mead. Open free, 9 a.m. to 5 p.m.

This museum, operated by the state of Nevada, has extensive exhibits of materials which begin with the artifacts made by Gypsum Cave people. There are also materials here from ancient Basketmaker and Pueblo cultures. Of special interest are materials excavated in the Lost City area along the nearby Muddy River. Several hundred sites, which have been dated at about A.D. 500, were once inhabited by people who built pueblolike dwellings. These sites were covered by water after the building of Boulder Dam (now named Hoover Dam).

The museum also contains materials from the culture of the Paiute people, who apparently entered the area about A.D. 1100 and who still live in southern Nevada.

NEVADA HISTORICAL SOCIETY

1650 N. Virginia St., Reno, on the campus of the University of Nevada. Open free, 8 a.m. to 4 p.m., Monday through Friday.

In this museum are exhibits of artifacts from three important Nevada archeological sites.

Material from Lovelock Cave includes artifacts left there over a long period of time, beginning about 2500 B.C. Archeologists who have studied baskets, clothing, and weapons from the cave believe that its early visitors were probably ancestors of the Paiute Indians who were living in Nevada when Europeans first arrived.

The oldest artifacts from Fishbone Cave, also called Winnemucca Lake Cave, seem to have been used by men who entered this desert area about 11,000 years ago. Later people who used the cave as a storage place left fishing and hunting gear similar to that used near Lovelock Cave.

Pottery from Lost City, also called Pueblo Grande de Nevada, was made by farming people who built stone dwellings along the Muddy River in southern Nevada about A.D. 500. Their experiments with corn raising were apparently not successful on a long-term basis, and they abandoned the villages. Archeologists located several hundred sites in the area, all of which are now covered by water impounded by Hoover Dam.

Since neither the caves nor Lost City can be visited, the museum displays are of special interest.

NEVADA STATE MUSEUM

N. Carson St., Carson City. Open free, 8:30 a.m. to 4:30 p.m.; closed Jan. 1, May 30, Thanksgiving, Dec. 25.

Lives of Paiute Indians shown in this diorama differed little from the lives of their prehistoric ancestors. Nevada State Museum photo.

This museum has exhibits of archeological materials from Nevada, California, the Southwest, and the Great Plains. In addition to a life-sized display of a Paiute camp scene, there are dioramas of a Paiute fishing camp, of salt mining, of pine-nut harvesting, of a mud hen drive, and of an antelope hunt.

ROCKY GAP SITE

Red Rock Recreation Area. From Interstate 15 in Las Vegas turn west on Charleston Blvd. and drive 15 miles to Recreation Area, then follow directional markers to site. Open free, at all times. Camping.

The Bureau of Land Management, which administers the site (also known as Willow Springs), has made plans for an interpretive museum. Meantime, a sign gives information about the people who lived here about 900 years ago in pueblolike dwellings resembling those at Lost City, also in Nevada. Petroglyphs can be seen on rocks near the site.

UNIVERSITY MUSEUM OF NATURAL HISTORY

Desert Research Institute, University of Nevada, Las Vegas. Maryland Parkway, between Tropicana and Flamingo. Open free, 11 a.m. to 5 p.m., Monday through Friday; 10 a.m. to noon, Saturday; 2 p.m. to 5 p.m., Sunday.

Archeological displays are devoted to the problems of desert existence and the solutions which prehistoric men worked out. Several dioramas show details of Paiute life in the Great Basin; one is a model of techniques of archeological excavation.

VALLEY OF FIRE STATE PARK

From Las Vegas drive northeast 55 miles on US 91 to Crystal interchange, then southeast on Nevada 40; total distance 55 miles. Or from Overton drive south 16 miles on Nevada 12 and 140. The park is open free, at all times. The Visitor Center is open free, 9 a.m. to 5 p.m. Camping.

The Story. Because of the very limited water supply, there was apparently never a large or continuous occupation of the Valley of Fire. However, archeologists have found evidence that Anasazi people visited the area occasionally from about 300 B.C. to A.D. 1150. At various times, which cannot be exactly determined, the Indians left a large number of petroglyphs in the valley. Some of the designs are geometric. Others portray hands, feet, mountain sheep, birds, snakes, and lizards.

In the Visitor Center is a small display of material of archeological interest. A much larger archeological exhibit representing the area is in the Lost City Museum at Overton.

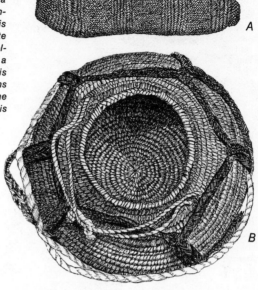

Two examples of basketry from the Mesa Verde area. A. The intricately woven pillow is in the Colorado State Museum in Denver, Colorado. B. Found in a Mesa Verde canyon, this basket contained charms used by the medicine man in performing his healing ceremonies.

Basketry

Almost everywhere Indians found that they could take grasses or shredded bark or other plant fibers and fashion them into implements that enriched life or—in very poor areas—made survival possible. Weaving and plaiting, they made baby-carriers, nets to catch game or fowl or fish, containers for food, and baskets so fine they could be used as canteens or as pots for cooking.

In the Great Basin, where people could not become great hunters because game was scarce, nor farmers because corn would not grow well, they found their own ways of exploiting the land. Basketry was the skill they used above all others. Strips of rabbit skin, woven basket fashion, formed their robes. Even their simple shelters were rather like big crude baskets.

On Visiting Excavations

Archeologists usually like to encourage people who want to learn about the science which they find so fascinating. But at an excavation everyone is usually too busy to explain what goes on. So, although they don't like to be rude, archeologists very often have to make an absolute rule that visitors may not come to their digs.

There are exceptions. If you want to watch the slow and painstaking work that goes into an excavation, you should ask the proper authorities if visitors are allowed. In National Parks, ask park rangers. It may be possible for you to see a dig from a good vantage point. There may even be a ranger assigned to explain what is happening.

Other digs, too, make special provision for visitors. At the Calico Mountains Project near Yermo, California, for example, visitors are invited to observe, and a tape recording has been installed which explains the whole operation. Visitors are also welcome at the Lyman Archaeological Research Center near Miami, Missouri, and at Kwilleylekia near Cliff, New Mexico.

NORTHWEST COAST

 At 4 o'clock in the afternoon, on March 28, 1778, the first white American to visit the Northwest Coast had his first glimpse of the Indian Americans who lived there. He was John Ledyard, aboard the *Resolution,* one of two ships with which Captain Cook was exploring the Pacific.

Ledyard had a special interest in Indians. He had lived for several months among the Iroquois in the Northeast, after dropping out of Dartmouth College, which was primarily a college for Indians. Now he was keen to observe the Nootkas whose village he had reached at the end of a sea voyage more than halfway around the world from New England. In the journal which he kept with his own unique spelling, he had this to say:

"It was a matter of doubt with many of us whether we should find any inhabitants here, but we had scarcely entered the inlet before we saw that hardy, that intriped, that glorious creature man approaching us from the shore. . . . In the evening we were visited by several canoes full of the natives. . . . The country around this sound is generally high and mountainous . . . intirely covered with woods. . . . We saw no plantations or any appearance that exhibited any knowledge of the cultivation of the earth, all seemed to remain in a state of nature. . . . We purchased while here about 1500 beaver, besides other skins, but took none but the best . . . Neither did we purchas a quarter part of the beaver and other furr skins we might have done. . . ."

Of the Nootka canoes he saw, Ledyard wrote: "They are about 20 feet in length, contracted at each end, and about 3 feet broad in the middle . . . made from large . . . trees. . . . I had no sooner beheld these Americans than I set them down for the same kind of people that inhabited the opposite side of the continent. They are rather above the middle stature, copper-coloured, and of an athletic make. They have long black hair, which they generally wear in a club on the top of the head, they fill it when dressed with oil, paint and the downe of birds. They also paint their faces with red, blue and white colours . . . Their clothing generally consists of skins, but they have two other sorts of garments, the one is made of the inner rind of some sort of bark twisted and united together like the woof of our coarse cloaths, the other . . . is . . . principally made with the hair of their dogs, which are mostly white, and of the domestic kind: Upon this garment is displayed very naturally

---

Animal symbols of ancient origin were often the figures which Northwest Coast Indians carved on totem poles.

---

the manner of their catching the whale—
we saw nothing so well done by a savage
in our travels. . . . We saw them make
use of no coverings to their feet or legs,
and it was seldom they covered their
heads: When they did it was with a kind
of basket covering made after the manner of the Chinese . . . hats."

Cannibalism

Ledyard then went on to describe an event
for which Europeans, for all their experience with killing in warfare, were not
prepared: "[the Nootkas] are hospitable
and the first boat that visited us . . .
brought us what no doubt they thought
the greatest possible regalia, and offered
it to us to eat: This was a human arm
roasted."

It is not clear what dark notion
prompted the Nootkas to make this cannibalistic offering to strangers whose civilization would soon devour theirs. There
is no doubt, however, that a form—or
forms—of religious cannibalism existed
on the Northwest Coast. Another coastal
tribe, the Kwakiutl, had established a
Cannibal Society. Members of this group
in moments of religious frenzy took bites
out of the arms of living people. They also
ate the flesh of the dead, often of slaves
killed for the purpose.

This cannibalism had nothing in common with the cannibalism practiced by
some farming people who sacrificed
things of great value—such as human
life—in an effort to obtain good crops.
Nor was the Kwakiutl custom like that of
people who ate brave enemies hoping
thus to gain courage. Something different
was involved. The Kwakiutls loathed the
flesh they ate. Very often they spat it out,
and the practice was regarded with re-
vulsion by the community which also regarded it with awe. After eating flesh a
man was isolated for a long time and
then had to go through elaborate rituals
before he could resume normal life.

It is difficult today to imagine what
religious frenzy accompanied the Kwakiutl cannibal rite, or what prized result it
was supposed to bring. But one thing is
clear: The Kwakiutls, and probably the
Nootkas, did not consider human flesh a
delicacy. And they certainly did not con-

sume it because they were hungry. No
people in America ate so well as the
Indians who lived on the Pacific coast
from northern California to southern
Alaska. These people had rich resourcs
in shellfish and fish—salmon, halibut, cod,
herring, candlefish. They could get quantities of meat from sea mammals—seals,
sea otters, porpoises, whales. They also
had a wide choice of land animals and
birds, and they could vary their diet with
berries of several different kinds.

The Northwest Coast Indians were indeed wealthy by prehistoric standards.
Besides ample food they had the beautiful skins of a number of animals to make
into clothing. They could weave garments
from the shredded bark of certain plentiful trees, and they fashioned rainproof
hats of fibers from cedar tree roots.

As Ledyard noted, they wove garments
from the long hair of dogs which they
kept especially to be shorn. Women in
certain coastal areas made expeditions
inland to collect the mountain-goat wool
that clung to bushes when it was shed.
This they combined with dog hair to make
fine blankets. Alone among North American Indians they wove with wool, and
alone on the Northwest Coast the women
around Puget Sound and in adjacent
British Columbia used true looms. Where
they got the idea no one knows. The
nearest looms in America were in the
distant Southwest, and there cloth was
made from cotton, not wool, until the
Spanish brought sheep to this continent.

Boards for Building

Another resource, one as important as
food and just as available on the Northwest Coast, was a special kind of wood
of exactly the right kind for making boats
and houses. In the forests that grew down
almost to the water's edge stood tall
cedar trees with unique properties: the
grain of the wood was straight, and men
using wedges could split it into flat, even
planks. These thick cedar boards made
possible the huge buildings that so impressed the artist who accompanied Captain Cook and Ledyard. Each dwelling—
it might be 40 by 30 feet with a high ga-
bled roof—was large enough to house
several families, and in some villages the

massive structures stood row on row along the beach. Those who lived farther north than the Nootka—the Haida and Tlingit people—built the grandest houses of all. A dozen families could live in one of them.

The social relations between these villagers were unlike those in most parts of prehistoric North America. The differences were largely due to the fact that their easy food supply allowed them time to accumulate a wealth of possessions. One custom based on their economy of abundance was known as the potlatch, or gift-giving, ceremony. This is how it went: Suppose a chief's son was growing up and approaching the time when he was to be given a new name. Far in advance the chief would make preparations to celebrate the occasion by giving away property. When he had accumulated piles of blankets, furs, boxes of whale oil, con-

tainers filled with berries, and vast quantities of food, he sent out messengers in canoes to deliver invitations to people in other villages up and down the coast. At the appointed time the guests assembled, and the big plank house was taxed to capacity. Between great meals the chief ceremoniously gave away everything he had—and much that he had borrowed from relatives. The biggest gifts went to the most important guests, and everyone present remembered who got what.

Behind this intemperate generosity was a rather simple notion. A man—any man, not just a chief—could assert his

Indians made innumerable pictures and designs on rock surfaces, particularly in western North America. Archeologists differ about the meaning of this rock art, but agree that it is not a form of writing. These designs were pecked into a rock in southeastern Oregon. Photo by Donald Martin, courtesy of Campbell Grant.

importance by gift-giving. The more lavish his gifts the higher his status, and nothing in Northwest-Coast life was more essential than status. Those who had received the gifts, of course, had to proclaim their own importance by holding potlatches to which the giver was invited. And so in the end a man was likely to get back what his potlatch had cost him. Among the Kwakiutl this way of asserting superiority had a special quirk. The potlatch was often used to embarrass and humiliate a rival by giving him more costly gifts than he could possibly give in return. A man could not refuse a gift, even though he might have to sell himself into slavery to make a reciprocal gift.

Totem Poles

In historic times the rich men among the Haida often held potlatches to commemorate the raising of totem poles. A totem was an animal which was associated in some way with a man's family. Or it might be a monster or a supernatural being. Figures of these creatures were carved on masks or worn as crests on helmets. An important family might be entitled to a number of different crests. In prehistoric times people may have made small carvings to represent their totems, and later—in the 18th century—when they got steel tools, they began to carve the figures, one above the other, on huge wooden poles.

A totem pole could be rather like a coat of arms—advertising the ancestry of the man who raised it beside his house. Other totem poles were memorials to people who had died. Still another type, the ridicule or shame pole, might be set up to shame an important person who had failed to carry out some obligation, with a portrait of him carved upside down.

The property-conscious Northwest Coast Indians were aggressive and competitive in many ways. They were also creative. They had many ingenious implements for fishing, for hunting, for storing food, for killing whales, for keeping off rain, and their art was highly developed and unique in style.

Establishing the date at which their elaborate culture began is a problem which archeologists are not sure they have solved. Certainly it took time to de-velop, and certainly it was based on earlier lifeways. All American prehistory, of course, began in Alaska during the latter part of the Ice Age, when Siberia was joined to North America by the Bering Land Bridge, a thousand miles wide. Some of those who wandered across the bridge continued eastward following game. Along the Arctic Ocean shore they found an easy travel route, and when they reached the mouth of the Mackenzie River, good hunting led them south. After traveling the whole length of the river valley, they crossed where there was no natural barrier, from the headwaters of the Mackenzie into Alberta. There the open Plains spread out endlessly to the south.

Archeologists have found sites where these hunters camped and dropped their tools. One, known as Kogruk, is on the slope of the Brooks Mountains near the Arctic coast in Alaska. Another, called Engigsciak, is at the mouth of the Firth River in the Yukon. At the latter site, excavation indicates that hunters who followed the British Mountain lifeway perhaps 18,000 years ago, when the local climate was warmer, killed bison of a kind that has long been extinct. Neither of these sites is open to the public. Indeed, visitors to Alaska and northwest Canada will find little evidence of prehistory on display. For one thing, travel is difficult in much of the area. For another, archeologists have only begun to examine this vast but little-inhabited portion of the continent.

Descendants of some of these earliest wanderers developed the big-game-hunting Paleo-Indian culture. At the same time other southward-moving groups sifted into the high plateau region between the Continental Divide on the east and the coastal ranges on the west. In this Interior Plateau region those who began to live along rivers found an abundance of fish. As early as 11,000 years ago fishermen left tools at Five Mile Rapids on the Columbia River. Not far away, at a place called The Dalles, men also camped and caught salmon that ran in the river for nine months of the year. Farther up one of the river's tributaries, at the Marmes Site, archeologists have found the bones of people who arrived between 10,000 and 13,000 years ago. In Idaho radiocarbon dates show that men left stone and bone tools at Wilson Butte Cave at least 14,500 years ago.

Very early, in other words, human beings found a way of living in the Interior Plateau by exploiting the food resources of the rivers that cut through it. They also gathered camas bulbs in spring and summer and ate them raw or cooked. Roots and tubers of other plants were another source of nourishment. Women ground some of them into a kind of flour which they made into cakes and stored. They also harvested berries, sunflower seeds, and wild carrots.

As far as archeologists can now tell, it was these Riverine Plateau people, who eventually moved down the rivers to the coast, and became the ancestors of the Northwest Coast Indians. Once they reached the food-rich ocean they developed new tools, new food-gathering techniques, and social customs that were unique in all America. Their unusual lifeway spread throughout the long narrow coastal region between northern California and southern Alaska.

Because steep mountains and thick woods came down to the edge of the water in the fjords which cut deeply into the land, travel had to be almost entirely by water. People paddled great distances in canoes, and in time they met others to the north who had their own ways of managing life along the shore. From these northern people, who were Aleuts and Eskimos, the Northwest Coast tribes learned many things. The Aleuts and Eskimos, for their part, had ideas which had come from people who lived on the coasts of Asia. Thus some of the ideas borrowed by the Northwest Coast Indians came indirectly from Asia. In addition, it is possible that some Asian traits reached them directly. Fishermen, possibly from Japan, may have been blown off course and drifted to America on the Japan current, which also brought the warmth and rain that distinguish the climate of the Northwest Coast from the cold and snowy inland climate in the same latitudes.

By combining the ways of living that they had developed along the rivers on the Interior Plateau with ideas that came from Asia, the Northwest Coast people produced a unique culture. Ideas even

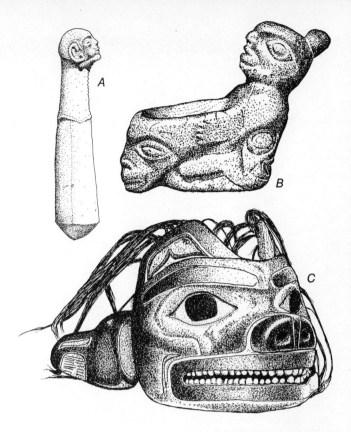

A. A Stone club from British Columbia that may have been used in battle or ceremonies. B. Ancient Northwest Coast Indians were expert carvers in bone, wood, and stone. This figure, made of steatite (soapstone) represents a guardian spirit. C. British Columbian Indians used this ceremonial mask which represents a bear. Originals of A, B, and C are in the Museum of the American Indian. D. An archeologist digs through 8,000 years of debris accumulated in the Alpha Rock Shelter near the Salmon River in Idaho. Idaho State University photo.

A

A. Prehistoric Indians on the Interior Plateau and the Northwest Coast often gave artificial shapes to the heads of their babies. This Chinook woman had her head flattened when she was very young, and now she is giving her own baby a fashionable head shape. Apparently this practice had no ill effects on the brain. Redrawn from Catlin. B. The lifeway of prehistoric people in a cave in the Grand Coulee area is re-created in a diorama at the Interpretive Center in Dry Falls, Washington. Washington State Parks photo.

B

came from coastal dwellers in California, but there is no hint of Mexican influence. This absence of Mexican traits is one thing that sets the Northwestern lifeway apart from much of the rest of prehistoric Indian life in North America.

The stimuli coming from Alaska reflected an adjustment to coastal living that may have begun when the Bering Land Bridge still joined Siberia and Alaska. The coast of the Land Bridge curved around the North Pacific, with one end at a mountain which now appears on the map as Umnak Island in the Aleutians. At the other end lay the Japanese island of Hokkaido. Along the intervening shore people moved from Asia toward America, exploiting bird and fish and sea-mammal resources along the way. Before the end of the Ice Age, some of these wanderers from Asia had reached the vicinity of the Umnak Island mountain. Then the ocean rose, swollen by water from melting glaciers, and forced people onto higher ground. Some of them took refuge on the mountain, which the sea eventually surrounded and cut off from adjacent land.

Among the descendants of these settlers on Umnak Island two separate traditions developed, beginning perhaps 4,500 years ago. Some of them, seeking new places to live, spread out along the other Aleutian islands where the ocean remained open all year. There they developed a dialect, then a distinct language, Aleut. Other groups moved north from Umnak. Their language, too, changed, becoming Eskimo. Most of the Eskimo people lived on the edge of water which was covered over with ice for much of each year. Intense cold required them to make adjustments quite unlike those of their relatives on the Aleutian Islands.

This drift of Umnak people in two different directions, and along two different types of shore, resulted in two separate cultures—the Aleut and the Eskimo. Both of them were distinct from any Indian cultures, and both the Aleuts and Eskimos were physically different from Indians. They were more Mongoloid in appearance than any Indians, and they differed in blood type. No Indian has blood type B, but this type is not uncommon among Eskimo-Aleuts, and it is present in modern Mongoloid people in Asia.

Physical anthropologists believe that the Mongoloid race appeared relatively recently and was still evolving when the earliest ancestors of the Indian entered North America. Mongoloids then continued to evolve in Asia and reached their characteristic present-day form less than 15,000 years ago. It was apparently from this modern Asian base that the ancestors of the Eskimos and Aleuts split off when they migrated to North America.

New Skills and Inventions

Later, when the Umnak people themselves split and some of them took up residence on the Aleutians, they developed certain special skills. They made elegant baskets from the fine grasses that grew on the windswept islands. Since sea mammals were less abundant than they had been on Umnak Island, the Aleuts made increased use of fish and birds. Although Aleuts were largely dependent on driftwood for any wood they had, they developed a unique custom of carving wooden hats, and they were skilled carvers of masks for their ceremonies, some of which were very much like those of the Northwest Coast Indians farther south. Apparently the Aleuts borrowed ideas from their southern neighbors, who in turn borrowed from them.

The Umnak people who moved to the mainland—the Eskimos' ancestors—learned to protect themselves from the cold in a variety of ingenious ways. They invented clothes capable of retaining body heat, thus creating a microclimate in which man could survive. They developed sleds, and some Eskimos trained dogs to pull them. They learned how to harpoon seals in every season—in spring as the animals basked on shore, in summer on the open ocean where hunters pursued them in light skin boats called kayaks. In winter they searched out the holes in the ice where seals came to breathe and drove their harpoons down from above. Many Eskimos also hunted caribou.

Wherever they were, at any time of year, Eskimos were able to build dwellings. In summer they used tents made of poles, possibly collected as driftwood, over which they stretched a cover made of skin. Some developed the dome-shaped winter igloos made of snow. Others made semisubterranean winter houses roofed with driftwood covered with earth or sod. For light and heat they had lamps—shallow stone dishes filled with seal oil in which a burning wick floated.

To judge from the discoveries archeologists have already made, a surprising amount of material left by Aleuts and Eskimos and their ancestors still lies in the earth waiting to be excavated. But there are great areas of Alaska and Canada that have not yet been studied, and for the most part visitors to this area of few roads will not be able to see archeological sites. There are, however, some excellent museum exhibits. The University of Alaska Museum displays artifacts from three particularly important sites—St. Lawrence Island, Ipiutak, and Cape Denbigh. At the Haffenreffer Museum in Rhode Island, there are fine displays of material from Ipiutak, Denbigh, and Krusenstern sites which give insight into Arctic prehistory.

Included in this prehistory are Indians as well as Aleuts and Eskimos and their predecessors. In southwest Yukon, beginning perhaps about 5500 B.C., men who hunted in the subarctic forest made distinctive tools from tiny blades of flint, which they struck from larger chunks. No one knows with certainty who they were, but some archeologists suspect they may have been the ancestors of the Athapascan Indians who still live in the area. The Athapascans seem to have been late arrivals from Asia, and they could have brought with them the habit of making small-blade implements which are known to have been used in Eurasia after the end of the Old Stone Age.

One other type of culture existed in part of the area included here with the Northwest Coast and Interior Plateau—that is, in southeastern Oregon and southern Idaho. This region is geologically part of the Great Basin, and the prehistoric Indians who lived there developed lifeways similar to those of Desert culture people to the south. Indians who lived along the rivers of the Interior Plateau seem to have borrowed some traits from their Great Basin neighbors, but since they are described elsewhere in this book, there is no need to dwell on them here.

Alaska

ALASKA STATE MUSEUM

Juneau. Open free, 4:30 p.m., Monday through Friday; 1 p.m. to 4:30 p.m., Saturday, Sunday; 7 p.m. to 10 p.m., evenings, June to mid-Sept.; 1 p.m. to 4:30 p.m., Monday through Saturday, mid-Sept. to June.

Archeological materials are used in this museum along with ethnological materials to interpret the cultures of native Alaskans whose home areas are shown on a large map: Tlingit and Haida in the southeast, Athapascan in the interior, Aleut on the Aleutian Islands, and Eskimo on the coast of the Bering Sea and the Arctic Ocean. Explanations accompany each exhibit, and museum assistants are on duty to answer questions.

One display focuses attention on a highly decorated object called a Rain Screen, which once stood in a Tlingit community house. Dwellings such as this were often very large, and several families, who belonged to the same clan, shared them. The screen separated the chief's part of the house from the quarters of other people who lived there.

Other exhibits show the life of prehistoric Athapascan Indians who shared a common ancestry with the Navajos and Apaches who later migrated to the southwestern United States. Athapascan economy was based on fishing and on hunting caribou. Exhibits of caribou skin clothes indicate the skill of Athapascan women at sewing and ornamenting garments with dyed porcupine quills. Some of the prehistoric crafts of these Indians have survived to the present time—basketmaking, for example, and the construction of birchbark canoes.

Aleuts, who are distinct from Indians but share a common ancestry with Eskimos, depended mainly on the sea for their living. Exhibits, including two types of skin boat, suggest their marine orientation in prehistoric times, and there is also material that shows the impact of Russian traders on their culture.

Several groups of Eskimos have had lifeways based entirely on the sea, as exhibits show. Seal, walrus, and fish provided their food and clothing and much of the material for their tools and weapons. Other Eskimos combined hunting sea mammals with hunting caribou. Art objects made by members of both groups are a prominent part of the exhibits.

ANCHORAGE HISTORICAL AND FINE ARTS MUSEUM

121 W. 7th Ave., Anchorage. Open free, 10 a.m. to 10 p.m., daily, June 1 to Sept. 1; closed Tuesday and Sunday morning, Sept. 1 to June 1.

This expanding museum displays prehistoric artifacts made during a long period of time by the Indian, Aleut, and Eskimo peoples of Alaska.

KATMAI NATIONAL MONUMENT (KAT-my)

From the King Salmon Airport on Bristol Bay, scheduled commercial flights go to Brooks River Lodge in the monument. Open free, from about June to Sept. 15. Camping.

National Park Service Rangers conduct trips from Brooks River along a nature trail to Kashim. This is a large ceremonial house that was in use about 1,000 years ago. The site has been excavated and roofed over. Some artifacts found in the excavation have been left in place and are open to view.

SITKA NATIONAL MONUMENT

Visitor Center, Metlakahtla and Lincoln streets, Sitka. Open free, at all times.

Though not strictly devoted to a prehistoric site, this monument preserves 14 Alaskan totem poles and several carved house-posts which were part of the Alaska exhibit at the St. Louis Exposition in 1904.

Tlingit Indians occupied the area around Sitka when white men—Russian fur traders—first arrived. Like other coastal people the Tlingits were great craftsmen. Woodcarvers even made into works of art the clubs that men used for killing the seals they harpooned. After they got steel tools from traders, they turned their skills to carving the huge totem poles that they had not made previously. A few small Tlingit artifacts are on exhibit in the Visitor Center.

UNIVERSITY MUSEUM

University of Alaska, on the campus, College (four miles from Fairbanks). Open free, 1 p.m. to 5 p.m., daily, mid-Sept. to mid-May; 9 a.m. to 5 p.m., daily, mid-May to mid-Sept.

With materials gathered in the course of an active archeological research program, this museum in-

terprets pre-Eskimo and Eskimo lifeways. Artifacts and environmental exhibits show the adjustment man has made to life on the tundra.

The artifacts on display come from many of the most important digs in Alaska, including St. Lawrence Island, a large treeless island in the Bering Sea southwest of Nome, only 40 miles from Siberia. Eskimos who live there are much like the Siberian Eskimos, and, until recently at least, intermarried with them.

In 1878 Russian traders obtained furs from the 1500 people on St. Lawrence, giving alcohol in exchange. Three years later the naturalist John Muir and an ethnographer visited the island and found the Eskimo dwellings filled with skeletons. Most of the people on St. Lawrence had died in the winter of 1878-79, either of starvation or of an epidemic which accompanied it. Alcohol, brought by the traders, had caused the disaster. The Eskimo men had been drunk during the hunting season when they normally obtained their winter food supply.

None of the traders who visited the island, nor Muir himself, realized that St. Lawrence harbored a rich record of human life stretching back for at least 2,000 years. More recently archeologists have excavated mounds on the island and studied a series of beaches that have been exposed on the Northeast Cape. People have lived on each of these beaches in turn and left the remains of their dwellings, the oldest being farthest from the present seashore. Driftwood used for beams in the dwellings apparently had floated down the Yukon River, and the wood made it possible to date some of the houses by the tree-ring method. Thus a picture of cultural change could be constructed in a spot which is remote from present-day life but close to the route from Asia followed by those who peopled America many thousands of years ago. The archeological sites at Gambell on the Northwest Cape of St. Lawrence have been made a National Historic Landmark.

Excavated sites on the tiny Punuk Islands near St. Lawrence have yielded artifacts, many carved from ivory, which are on exhibit at the University Museum.

Artifacts from Point Hope Peninsula may also be seen. They come from the Ipiutak Site where the earliest Eskimos lived, and many objects are similar to those found in Siberia. The site itself is large, covering 200 acres and including a cemetery and more than 600 houses, not all of which were lived in at the same time.

Another important area represented in the museum is Cape Denbigh on Norton Sound. Here archeologists found evidence of a lifeway that

flourished between 6000 B.C. and 4000 B.C. and included the use of very small, very delicate flint blades. The makers of these tools lived in the same area where the Eskimos appeared much later. The Iyatayet Site, where Denbigh artifacts were first found, is a National Historic Landmark.

British Columbia

BRITISH COLUMBIA PROVINCIAL MUSEUM

Belleville St., between the Parliament Buildings and the Empress Hotel, Victoria. Open free, 10 a.m. to 8:30 p.m., Monday through Saturday; 1 p.m. to 4:30 p.m., Sunday, summer; 10 a.m. to 4:30 p.m., Tuesday through Saturday; 1 p.m. to 4:30 p.m., Sunday, winter.

In its new building this museum has temporary displays reflecting the Indian life and art of the Northwest Coast. These are changed on a periodic basis, exhibiting additional artifacts and material drawn from the museum's extensive archeological collections.

Special Interest. The museum supervises Thunderbird Park in Victoria, where there are reproductions of totem poles from various parts of British Columbia and a full-scale Kwakiutl Indian house that is sometimes used for Indian ceremonies. Visitors to the park may watch several Kwakiutl woodcarvers at work on totem poles, masks, and other objects, some of which are for sale.

A. This engraving from the report of Captain Cook's third voyage, in 1778, shows a communal dwelling of the kind that Indians had long used on Nootka Sound in British Columbia. B. An unusual stone bowl with a human effigy carved into the bottom in which Eskimos burned oil for heat and light. C. Prehistoric Eskimos carved these goggles from antler horn. Redrawn from Giddings. D. Carvings of ivory from a burial at Ipiutak Site, Point Hope, Alaska. Redrawn from Larsen and Rainey. E. A hat shaped like an eagle's head, used by Tlingit Indians in ceremonies. F. This 64-foot ocean-going canoe, carved from a single log, is now at the American Museum of Natural History in New York.

CAMPBELL RIVER MUSEUM

Centennial Bldg., Tyee Plaza, Campbell River. The town of Campbell River is about 40 miles south of Kelsey Bay on British Columbia 19, on the east coast of Vancouver Island. Open, 1 p.m. to 5 p.m., 7 p.m. to 9 p.m., Tuesday through Friday; 10 a.m. to noon, 1 p.m. to 5 p.m., Saturday, May 15 to Sept. 30; closed statutory holidays. Admission: adults, 25¢; children 6 through 15, 10¢.

The Indian exhibits concentrate chiefly on the Kwakiutl, but there is also some Nootka and Haida material. Displays include old but not necessarily prehistoric masks, prehistoric projectile points, scrapers, stone clubs which are popularly called slavekillers, and a ceremonial club. One exhibit is devoted to local Indian mortuary practices.

CENTENNIAL MUSEUM OF VANCOUVER

1100 Chestnut St., Vancouver. Open noon to 5 p.m., Monday; noon to 10 p.m., Tuesday through Friday; 10 a.m. to 10 p.m., Saturday, Sunday, holidays. Admission: adults, 50¢; children, 25¢; free on Monday, except when Monday is a holiday.

In the archeology section of this museum are random local finds and excavated materials representative of the lifeways in Fraser Canyon from 11,000 B.C. to 400 B.C. and of lifeways in the Fraser Delta from 1000 B.C. to A.D. 1808. One display shows how adze blades were manufactured from nephrite, sometimes called jade. Many artifacts are grouped by their function—for example, woodworking tools in one display, bone-shaping tools in another. Some exhibits show how artifacts were made. Behind a number of exhibits are very large photographs of excavations in progress.

KAMLOOPS MUSEUM ASSOCIATION

207 Seymour St., Kamloops. Open free, 10 a.m. to 9 p.m., Monday through Saturday, summer; 3 p.m. to 5 p.m., 7 p.m. to 9 p.m., Monday through Saturday, winter.

Here are displayed baskets which Thompson River Indians made in ways that were common in prehistoric times. Other exhibits include artifacts recovered from burial mounds. These mounds were very much smaller than those found in the eastern part of the United States. Indeed they were simply low heaps of earth or rock, and were often so shallow that planks, used to line the graves, protruded a little above the mounds.

'KSAN INDIAN VILLAGE

Hazelton. Open free, 10 a.m. to 11:30 a.m., 1:30 p.m. to 5 p.m., 7 p.m. to 9:30 p.m., daily, May through Oct. Camping.

This is a reconstruction of a Gitskan Indian village staffed by Indians, some of whom can be seen engaged in the practice of ancient crafts, including woodcarving. One of the buildings called "Stone Age House" is a replica of a large prehistoric communal dwelling. In it visitors may see how Gitskans used feathers, bone, skins, and especially cedar bark in making clothes, tools, and utensils.

MUSEUM OF ANTHROPOLOGY

University of British Columbia, in the library, on the campus, Vancouver. Open free, 1 p.m. to 5 p.m. Monday through Saturday, during school session; closed May, June, Sept., and national holidays.

Collections representing cultures of the Northwest Coast Indians, the Plains Indians, and the Eskimo include archeological materials. The museum maintains sections of Totem Pole Park in Vancouver where totem poles and two Haida Indian houses are exhibited.

MUSEUM OF ARCHEOLOGY, SIMON FRASER UNIVERSITY

Burnaby, 2.

For information about this museum, write to Roy L. Carlson, Director, at the above address. It will be opened to the public on a limited-hour basis late in 1971.

MUSEUM OF NORTHERN BRITISH COLUMBIA

First Ave. and McBride St., Prince Rupert. Open free, 9 a.m. to 9 p.m., Monday through Saturday, 2 p.m. to 5 p.m., Sunday, May 1 to Sept. 30; 9 a.m. to 4 p.m., Tuesday through Saturday, Oct. 1 to April 30.

This museum preserves and exhibits three large totem poles carved from tree trunks and a number of small totem poles carved from a rock called argillite which resembles slate. Although large totem poles everywhere date from the historic period when steel woodworking tools became available, the traditions and beliefs which inspired the poles had their origins in prehistory.

Other materials in the museum reflect the customs and the arts and crafts practiced in the area before the arrival of Europeans. Some elaborate ceremonial robes and masks are on display, along with objects used in a ceremony called the potlatch.

OKANAGAN MUSEUM AND ARCHIVES ASSOCIATION (oh-kah-NAG-ahn)

470 Queensway Ave., Kelowna. Open free, 2 p.m. to 5 p.m., Tuesday through Sunday, Sept. to May; 10 a.m. to 5 p.m., 7 p.m. to 9 p.m., daily, June through Aug.

Archeological exhibits here emphasize people who were ancestral to the Interior Salish people of historic times. Two burials are exhibited together with grave goods. A diorama shows a semisubterranean winter Salish house. Also on display is cedar-root basketry of the kind made in early historic and in prehistoric times.

Archeological study of the Okanagan Valley has only recently begun, and the dates of the materials being found have not yet been fixed.

PENTICTON MUSEUM AND ARCHIVES (pen-TICK-ton)

785 Main St., Penticton, which is 265 miles east of Vancouver on the southern Trans-Canada Highway. Open free, 1 p.m. to 9 p.m., daily, summer; 2 p.m. to 5 p.m., Tuesday through Saturday, fall and winter; closed Jan. 1, Good Friday, Nov. 11, Thanksgiving, Dec. 25, and Boxing Day (Dec. 26).

In addition to random local finds, some materials from organized excavations are on display here. Most of the artifacts were made by Salish Indians or their predecessors. Some materials were excavated by Washington State University archeologists.

THUNDERBIRD PARK

See British Columbia Provincial Museum, page 65.

Idaho

ALPHA ROCKSHELTER

From Salmon drive 20 miles north on US 93 to North Fork, then follow the Forest Service Road down the north side of Salmon River past Shoup, then cross the Salmon on the Pine Creek Bridge and continue along the south side of the river about 4 miles to a marker which indicates the site. Open free, at all times.

From a platform erected for the convenience of visitors it is possible to look into this rockshelter which has been excavated. Paintings are visible on the roof of the overhang.

Occupation began here about 6000 B.C. and continued until 1000 B.C. After that it was visited intermittently until about A.D. 1300. Broken animal bones and freshwater mussel shells show that the site was used by hunters and fishermen. Milling-stones found among the debris indicate that women collected seeds and ground them to make them edible.

The people who lived in this and other rockshelters followed what is called the Bitterroot way of life. They may have been ancestors of the Northern Shoshoni who inhabited the valley when Lewis and Clark visited it in 1805.

IDAHO STATE UNIVERSITY MUSEUM

University Library Building, on the campus, Pocatello. Open free, 8 a.m. to 5 p.m., Monday through Friday; 7:30 p.m. to 9:30 p.m., Wednesday, when the university is in session; closed holidays.

In addition to semipermanent displays of local archeological materials, which are arranged chronologically, there are other exhibits that change from time to time, including some installed for college students who are doing introductory work in archeology. The museum also conducts special programs for school children.

LOLO TRAIL

National Historic Landmark.
From the Idaho-Montana line, this old trail parallels US 12 for 4 miles. Open free, at all times.

This ancient Indian trail generally follows the ridge of the mountains north of the Lochsa River and extends for 150 miles through wilderness. It is not passable for ordinary tourist vehicles. In prehistoric and early historic times, Nez Perce Indians traveled along it to reach buffalo country in Montana. Lewis and Clark followed it in 1805 on their expedition to the West Coast.

LOST TRAIL PASS VISITOR CENTER

On US 93 at Lost Trail Pass, between Idaho and Montana. Open free, 8 a.m. to 5 p.m., daily, June 15 to July 1; 9 a.m. to 7 p.m., daily, July and Aug.; closed about Sept. 10 to June 15.

Exhibits and dioramas in the Center interpret Alpha Rockshelter and other rockshelters near Shoup,

A

A. In September 1805 prehistory and history met on this meadow, now Nez Perce National Historical Park, in Idaho, when three Nez Perce boys and six men of the Lewis and Clark expedition came face to face. People in the village from which the boys came fed the white men and gave them a horse load of roots and salmon to take back to the main body of the expedition. National Park Service photo by William S. Keller. B. Weis Rockshelter in Idaho was excavated between 1961 and 1964 by archeologists from Idaho State University who discovered evidence of occupation going back 8,000 years. Idaho State University photo.

B

A

A. From the summit of Fork Rock, 300 feet above the prairie, visitors can see the butte in the distance where archeologists, digging in a cave, found sandals and basketry. These were radiocarbon dated at about 7000 B.C.—earlier than any other woven material then known anywhere in the world. Oregon State Highway photo.

B. This remnant of a sandal from Roaring Springs Cave in Oregon shows a type of weaving mastered by early people in the Great Basin. After Cressman.

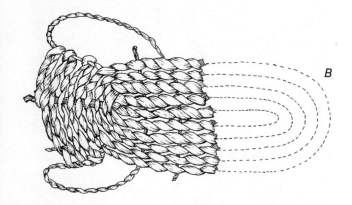

B

Idaho, where prehistoric Indians of the Bitterroot culture lived for about 8,000 years.

McCAMMON PETROGLYPHS

From Pocatello drive about 18 miles southeast on Interstate 15 to a roadside rest between Inkom and McCammon. Open free, at all times. Camping nearby.

Here, protected by a fence, are several large boulders on which prehistoric Indians pecked designs and pictures. A State Historical sign reads: "Over much of western North America, Indians made rough drawings like these, mainly in areas where they hunted and gathered food. Often called rock writing, these drawings are really not writing at all: their meaning—if any—could be interpreted only by the people who made them. Some probably are forms of magic, some ceremonial, some religious, and some may have been made simply for fun. Many of them, including these, range in age from a few centuries to much older, but dating them precisely is difficult at best."

Other examples of rock art in Idaho have been found along the Snake River and in the south central part of the state.

MIDVALE QUARRY

On US 95 near Midvale.

Here a historical sign labeled "An Early Industry" indicates a nearby quarry that is of archeological interest but is not open to the public. The sign reads: "At the top of this hill 3 to 5000 years ago, prehistoric men had a rock quarry where they made a variety of stone tools. Projectiles, knives, and scrapers were among the tools made by these early people who camped at the foot of the hill. These nomads hunted deer and other game, collected plant foods, and fished in the river here. They had spears and spear-throwers for hunting and fishing, and mortars and pestles for grinding roots and berries. Archaeologists have not yet determined when this industry shut down."

NEZ PERCE NATIONAL HISTORICAL PARK
(NEZ PURS)

Park Headquarters is in Spalding, on US 95, 9 miles east of Lewiston.

The park itself consists of 18 separate areas, one of which—the Weis Rockshelter—is an archeological site open to the public. Weippe Prairie, though not strictly an archeological site, has interest because it was here that Lewis and Clark first met Nez Perce Indians who had never before seen white men.

WEIS ROCKSHELTER

At Cottonwood, on US 95, a Nez Perce National Historical Park interpretive marker calls attention to the site. From this marker drive south 8 miles on the graveled Grave Creek Canyon Road. Camping nearby.

Weis Rockshelter is one of a series of niches in cliffs along the western slope of the Rocky Mountains in Idaho. People lived here for about 8,000 years, but their culture was somewhat different from that of the occupants of Alpha Rockshelter near Shoup.

During excavation archeologists found many

tools, including bone awls and needles for piercing and sewing skins, chipped stone projectile points for hunting, and antler wedges for splitting wood. The hunters who made these tools may have been ancestors of the Nez Perce Indians of historic times.

The Weis Rockshelter is one of many separate areas which make up the Nez Perce National Historical Park.

WILSON BUTTE CAVE

On Idaho 25 near Wilson Lake reservoir.

Here a historical sign labeled "Prehistoric Man" indicates a nearby cave which is of archeological interest, but which is not open to the public. The sign reads: "Archeological excavations show human occupation of the Snake River Plains for more than 10,000 years. Early man left weapons and other gear in a cve in nerby butte. Bones show that they hunted game which is now extinct—camels, ancient horses, and ground sloths. In succeeding thousands of years, the climate grew extremely dry, much drier than it is today. Still later, it became less arid again. Through all these changes, man succeeded in adapting and remained here."

A radiocarbon date indicates that the earliest visitors left their crude stone tools in the cave between 14,500 and 15,000 years ago.

Northwest Territories

Archeologists have excavated sites in the upper Arctic, and recently they have done some investigation farther south. Most of the sites in both areas are inaccessible by road, and none are yet open to the public. Some material from the region is in the collections of The National Museum of Man in Ottawa.

Oregon

COLLIER STATE PARK, PITHOUSE

From Klamath Falls drive 40 miles north on US 97. Site is on the east side of the highway. Open free, at all times. Camping.

Archeologists from the University of Oregon have excavated a semisubterranean house here, then restored part of it to show what a pithouse must have been like when people lived in it.

FORT ROCK CAVE HISTORICAL MARKER

National Historic Landmark.
On the east side of Oregon 31, about 18 miles north of Silver Lake.

This roadside marker indicates Fort Rock Cave at the foot of a butte which can be seen about four miles away, although it is not open to the public. (The cave is named for a nearby volcanic formation called Fort Rock.)

No one knows exactly when Indians first took shelter at this spot. By 9,000 years ago they had already left in the cave some of the baskets and sandals which they wove with great skill from sagebrush fibers. Apparently they did not have a permanent camp there. At least they were all away from home one day when volcanic eruptions at Newberry Craters north of Fort Rock filled the air with glowing cinders and ash. The hot layer of ash that settled in the cave charred, but did not destroy, some of the 75 sandals scattered about on the floor. Later, people returned to the cave, and their household debris accumulated on top of the older layers.

When archeologists excavated the cave they could establish a radiocarbon date not only for the charred sandals—and for the people who had made them—but also for the volcanic eruption. The sandals turned out to be the oldest woven artifacts so far discovered in North or South America—or anywhere in the world. Moreover the sandals and basketry found here and at other Oregon caves were not the work of people who had recently taken up the art of weaving. A long period of experimentation, innovation, and practice obviously lay behind the fashioning of any artifact so intricate.

In other Oregon caves, and at open campsites, there is evidence of even earlier visitors to the area. At one place archeologists found very primitive chopping tools. The signs of weathering on these tools indicated that they had been manufactured originally at some unknown date in the distant past. Then about 9,000 years ago they were picked up, sharpened, and reused.

The remains of daily life in caves known as Roaring Springs, Paisley, and Catlow indicate a scene quite unlike the present semidesert landscape. These caves, like Fort Rock, were all formed by the action of waves at the edges of lakes which filled the valleys at the end of the Ice Age. Eventually the lakes dried up. Until then the people who lived on their shores had food resources different from those available today—and much richer.

In Catlow Cave archeologists found several objects which helped them to remember with a certain poignance that real people lived here. First they came upon two small sandals, about right for a child of five or six. Nearby were two tiny baskets and a small dart of the kind used in a well-known Indian game. For some reason a little girl one day left her sandals and her toys on the cave floor and never returned. Nor did anyone else disturb them for thousands of years.

PORTLAND ART MUSEUM

Southwest Park and Madison, Portland. Open Tuesday through Sunday, noon to 5 p.m., Friday to 10 p.m. Admission: free, except for occasional major exhibitions.

Materials chosen primarily for esthetic value make up the collections devoted to Northwest Indian art and prehistoric art from elsewhere in America.

TILLAMOOK COUNTY PIONEER MUSEUM
(TILL-ah-mook)

2106 2nd St., Tillamook. Open free, 9 a.m. to 5 p.m., Monday through Saturday; 1 p.m. to 5 p.m., Sunday; closed Monday, Oct. 1 to May 1.

On display here are materials from Umnak Island in the Aleutian Islands, together with surface finds from dry lake beds in Oregon.

UNIVERSITY OF OREGON
MUSEUM OF NATURAL HISTORY

On the campus, Eugene. Open free, 8 a.m. to 5 p.m., Monday through Friday, during the academic year; 8 a.m. to 4:30 p.m., summer.

The museum staff has conducted significant excavations, and archeological exhibits of material from the Northwest Coast and Columbia Plateau areas are on display here. Dioramas show prehistoric cave dwellings. One extensive exhibit contains material from Fort Rock Cave. Another deals with a large site at The Dalles, now flooded by a dam.

WINQUATT MUSEUM

On US 197 one-half mile east of the Columbia River toll bridge at The Dalles. Open free, 9 a.m. to 5 p.m., Wednesday through Monday, May through Sept.; 9 a.m. to 4 p.m., Wednesday through Monday, Oct. through April.

Archeological materials from numerous sites along the Columbia River are displayed here. Many different cultures and fusions of cultures are represented, because many different peoples came to this place to fish and trade.

Among the displays are 26 petroglyphs which prehistoric Indians carved on hard basalt rock. These were removed from their locations behind The Dalles Dam in order to save them from being lost to view under water. Many of the designs in the carvings are abstract. Some show eyes enclosed in circles. Others seem much like the designs which also appear in basketry. Dates are uncertain for almost all the petroglyphs, but some may be as much as 9,000 years old.

The petroglyphs seem to have had various functions. Some were apparently used to show that a particular family or group used this spot for fishing; others seem to have been connected with magic. All required skill to make, because basalt is a very hard stone.

The Name. Winquatt is a word used by local Indians meaning "high hills."

Special Interest. Jeanne Hillis at the museum has worked out a technique for transferring petroglyph designs to paper, and she has preserved in this way many examples of rock art that are now under the water impounded by the dam. These reproductions, much like rubbings, are available for exhibits.

Washington

DRY FALLS INTERPRETIVE CENTER

From Coulee City on US 2 drive 2 miles west to junction with Washington 17, then follow directional markers. Open free, at all times.

This building with a spectacular view of the Grand Coulee area contains exhibits intended chiefly to explain geological phenomena. However one display is devoted to the nearby Lake Lenore Caves, which were inhabited in prehistoric times.

EAST MUSEUM

Civic Center, 5th and Balsam, Moses Lake. Open free, 9 a.m. to 5 p.m., Tuesday through Friday; 2 p.m. to 5 p.m., Saturday, Sunday, May through Aug.; 1 p.m. to 5 p.m., Tuesday through Friday, Sept., Oct., March, and April, and by appointment for groups; closed Easter, May 30, July 4.

This museum houses a large number of artifacts collected by Adam East along the Middle Columbia River. Detailed information about these finds is often lacking, but many of them were made by Salish Indians and their prehistoric predecessors.

Some very crude scrapers on exhibit are said to have come from *under* a moraine. Since a moraine is a mass of rock and gravel deposited by a glacier, these tools would be evidence of man's presence in the area before the last glacier of the Ice Age. Scientists are not sure with what care the scrapers were excavated and are cautious about accepting them as proof that man existed in America in preglacial times.

EASTERN WASHINGTON
STATE HISTORICAL SOCIETY

West 2316 First Ave., Spokane. Open free, 10 a.m. to 5 p.m., Tuesday through Saturday; 2 p.m. to 5 p.m., Sunday; closed Jan. 1, July 4, Labor Day, Thanksgiving, Dec. 25.

As part of regional historical exhibits, there are displays of Plateau Indian artifacts, some of which are prehistoric.

FORT SIMCOE MUSEUM (SIM-kweh)

Fort Simcoe State Park. From Toppenish drive 26 miles west on Washington 220. Open free, 6:30 a.m. to 10 p.m., Tuesday through Sunday; April 15 through Sept.

Some prehistoric but undated artifacts appear here among local ethnological materials.

GINKGO PETRIFIED FOREST STATE PARK
INTERPRETIVE CENTER

From Ellensburg drive 27 miles east on US 10 to Vantage, then follow directional signs to park. Open free, 9 a.m. to 8 p.m., daily, April 1 to Oct. 16; 10 a.m. to 5 p.m., Oct. 16 through March.

At an unknown date early inhabitants of the Columbia Plateau region pecked many designs and pictures into basalt cliffs along the Columbia River. The rising water of Lake Wanapum, behind Wanapum Dam, would have covered all of these had not some been removed and placed where they are now, south of the balcony in the Interpretive Center. An exhibit in the center shows how the petroglyphs were made.

INDIAN PAINTED ROCKS

Northwest of Spokane near the Rutter Parkway Bridge over Little Spokane River. Open free, at all times.

Pictographs on the rocks here are similar to those found at Indian Painted Rocks near Yakima.

INDIAN PAINTED ROCKS

From Yakima city limits drive 3 miles northwest on US 12. Open free, at all times. Camping nearby.

Present-day Indians in the area have no idea who may have made paintings on the cliffs at this spot. They resemble many others found in western North

America and are sometimes interpreted as depicting religious experiences. They may also have been records of hunts or of meetings between people of different tribes. This particular display of rock art stands beside a modern highway that follows an old Indian trail leading to the Wemas Mountains.

LAKE LENORE CAVES

From Coulee City on US 2 drive 2 miles west, then 10 miles south on Washington 17 to directional sign, then one-half mile east to parking area. Open free, at all times. Camping nearby.

A trail leads to seven caves in Lower Grand Coulee that were inhabited by prehistoric Indians who apparently used them as temporary shelters while on hunting expeditions. Many small stone scrapers have been found in the caves and these are taken as evidence that people who lived here prepared skins.

At Dry Falls Interpretive Center, an exhibit is devoted to Lake Lenore Caves.

NEAH BAY (NEE-ah)

Makah Indian Reservation, at the western end of Washington 112. Open free at all times, but visitors should be careful not to invade the privacy of the residents.

This village is not, strictly speaking, an archeological site, and although tourists are welcome, nothing has been done here to interpret the prehistory of the place. However, the 500 Makah residents of Neah Bay live on a huge shell mound which their ancestors built up over a long period of time.

The Makah are related to Nootka Indians of Vancouver Island, British Columbia, and their prehistoric culture was much like the culture of southeastern Alaska. The Makah were an aggressive people famed for their great skill in the manufacture of canoes. One type was a small dugout specially shaped for use in shallow streams. Another was huge and carried many men on the open ocean on whale-hunting expeditions.

OLD MAN HOUSE

East of Poulsbo on Bainbridge Island. Open free, at all times.

This is the site of a very large communal dwelling, built of hand-adzed cedar slabs, which existed at the time the first settlers arrived in the area. Chief Sealth, for whom the city of Seattle was named, once lived here. The house survived until 1870, when it was destroyed by order of the U.S. Army.

OLYMPIC NATIONAL PARK, PIONEER MEMORIAL MUSEUM

2800 Hurricane Ridge Rd., Port Angeles. Open free, 8 a.m. to 9 p.m., mid-June to Labor Day; 8 a.m. to 4:30 p.m., Labor Day to mid-June; closed Thanksgiving, Dec. 25. Camping in the park.

A large amount of ethnological and archeological material, mostly undated, from 25 Northwest Coast tribes is stored here and is available for scientific study. A small selection of this material is exhibited in the museum.

PACIFIC NORTHWEST INDIAN CENTER

On the Spokane River, near Gonzaga University, Spokane.

An ambitious building, recently opened to the public, houses a considerable amount of archeological material. The center is located on the site of an early camping area of the Spokane Indians.

ROOSEVELT PETROGLYPHS

On Washington 14 about a mile east of Roosevelt. Open free, at all times.

Here, in a special park, the citizens of Roosevelt have installed and protected a group of petroglyphs collected from nearby sites along the Columbia River. These sites have been flooded by the reservoir behind John Day Dam.

SAKAJAWEA STATE PARK MUSEUM
(SOCK-ah-jah-WEE-ah)

From Pasco drive 6 miles southeast on US 395 to directional sign. Open free, 8 a.m. to 5 p.m., daily.

Random local finds of stone artifacts are displayed here.

SEATTLE ART MUSEUM

14th Ave. E. and E. Prospect St., Volunteer Park, Seattle. Open free, 10 a.m. to 5 p.m., Tuesday through Saturday; 7 p.m. to 10 p.m., Thursday; noon to 5 p.m., Sunday and holidays; closed Jan. 1, Memorial Day, Labor Day, Thanksgiving, Dec. 25.

In a large general collection, which has been selected for artistic merit, are some archeological objects from the Northwest Coast and the Upper Mississippi Valley.

SNOQUALMIE VALLEY HISTORICAL MUSEUM
(sno-KWAL-mee)

45 Fourth Ave. E., North Bend. Open free, 7 p.m. to 9 p.m., Tuesday and by appointment.

Included here with historical exhibits are a display of undated Snoqualmie Indian artifacts and a collection of baskets.

STATE CAPITOL MUSEUM

211 W. 21st Ave., Olympia. Open free, 10 a.m. to 5 p.m., Tuesday through Friday; noon to 5 p.m., Saturday; 1 p.m. to 5 p.m., Sunday; closed major holidays.

Here are examples of Northwest Indian art and material culture, including undated prehistoric stone artifacts from the Columbia River region.

WANAPUM TOUR CENTER

From Ellensburg drive 27 miles east on US 10 to Vantage, then 5 miles south on Washington 243 to the Wanapum Dam. Open free, 9 a.m. to 6 p.m., about April 15 through June 10; 8 a.m. to 9 p.m., about June 11 through Sept. 15; 9 a.m. to 6 p.m., about Sept. 16 through Oct. 31.

Displayed here are projectile points, net sinkers, knives, scrapers, pipes, drills, needles, and other prehistroic artifacts found in the vicinity of the Wanapum and Priest Rapids reservoirs.

Points

Redrawn from Giddings

Archeologists use the word "point" for the tip on a spear or an arrow. They also call a stone implement a point even when it served as a knife and not as the tip on a projectile.

Examination by microscope often reveals whether or not a point has been used as a knife; certain wear-marks appear on it. Sometimes it is even possible to tell what kind of material was cut by the point.

If a stone tool was used as a scraper this too can be discovered by studying the edge with a microscope. The wear-marks left by scraping are very different from those left by cutting.

The three views above show a flint blade that has been turned into a point only 1⅝ inches long. This delicate workmanship was done by pre-Eskimo craftsmen at Cape Denbigh in Alaska.

Carbon-14 Dating

An archeologist can often learn the age of a site if it contains charred wood or bone. He sends samples of the charred material to a laboratory where radiocarbon or Carbon-14, or C-14, dating is done.

Carbon is part of the nourishment of every living thing. Plants get it by taking in carbon dioxide from the air; animals and men get it from their food, which may be either plants or plant-eating animals. Among the carbon atoms which living things take in, some are radioactive. These radioactive atoms, called Carbon-14, or C-14, are not stable. They decay, giving off tiny bursts of energy, which can be detected in a laboratory. After a C-14 atom decays, what remains is an atom of ordinary carbon.

When a plant or animal dies it ceases to take in food, and therefore it ceases to take in C-14 atoms. But it continues to lose them. The C-14 atoms in a dead object decay at a steady pace. Half of the radioactivity in a dead plant or animal is gone at the end of 5,730 years, give or take 40 years. Scientists say that C-14 has a half-life of 5,730 plus or minus 40 years.

By measuring the radioactivity that remains in a given quantity of dead plant or animal material, a scientist can calculate how long ago the plant or animal died. He cannot tell the exact year of death, and he always makes allowance for error. Therefore a C-14 date is usually written this way: 5,000 ± 250. This means that the date of death falls between 4,750 and 5,250 years ago.

The C-14 method is not perfect. It cannot date anything that died more than 70,000 years ago. Sometimes an object may accidentally acquire extra C-14 atoms, and thus it will appear to have died more recently than it actually did. But C-14 dating has been a useful tool for sorting out information from the past. It has helped archeologists to put all kinds of happenings in their proper order and thus to know more about the real meaning of events which took place before history was written.

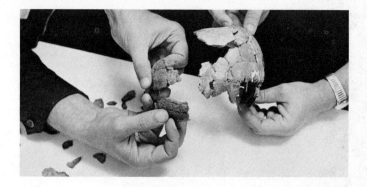

On the table and in the hands at the left are pieces of a child's skull that were found at the Marmes Site in the State of Washington. In the hands at right is the skull cap of a young adult, also found at Marmes. These fragments have been dated as more than 10,000 years old. Photo by Marmes Rockshelter Project, Laboratory of Anthropology, Washington State University.

WASHINGTON STATE HISTORICAL SOCIETY

215 North Stadium Way, Tacoma. Open free, 9 a.m. to 4 p.m., Tuesday through Saturday; 2 p.m. to 5 p.m., Sunday; closed national holidays.

This museum, which emphasizes Northwestern history, displays some prehistoric artifacts.

WASHINGTON STATE UNIVERSITY ANTHROPOLOGY MUSEUM

Johnson Tower, on the campus, Pullman. Open free, 1 p.m. to 5 p.m., Monday through Friday during the academic year.

In this general teaching museum, an exhibit devoted to basketmaking in the Northwest illuminates basketry techniques which derive from prehistoric times. A special diorama is devoted to Pomo basketry.

Archeological materials are also included in a display on Northwestern Indian culture, with artifacts from Ozette, a 6,000-year-old site on the Washington coast, and St. Lawrence Island in Alaska.

Special Feature. Staff members at the museum are now studying material taken from the Marmes Site, one of the most important Early Man sites in America, which cannot be visited because it now lies under 40 feet of water in a reservoir in the southeastern corner of Washington. When completed an exhibit of the items, prepared under the supervision of archeologists who excavated the material, will give valuable information about Paleo-Indian culture.

The Story. For several years Washington State University conducted excavations in the Marmes Rockshelter, named for its owner. Here, in the Palouse River Valley near the junction with the valley of the Snake River, archeologists found layer after layer of debris which indicated man had first lived there 10,000 years ago. About 250 whole or partial skeletons were uncovered. Nowhere else in America had excavation revealed such a quantity of burials spanning such a long period of time. With the skeletons was rich evidence of how people lived at each stage.

One day a member of the expedition—a geologist—decided to have a trench dug in a terrace below the shelter. He called in a bulldozer to clear away the soil quickly, and as he walked behind the machine, he saw a fragment of bone. It turned out to be human bone. The bulldozer was replaced by trowels, and careful digging revealed portions of three skulls. Since these skulls lay underneath material which was radiocarbon dated at 10,000 years old, the bones had to be older than that. Since

they lay on top of soil known to have been deposited no more than 13,000 years ago, the skulls were somewhere between 10,000 and 13,000 years old.

With parts of the human skulls were found a spearpoint made of animal bone and a very small, delicately made bone needle with an eye in it. This was taken to mean that the people who lived here, more than 10,000 years ago, may have sewed animal-skin clothing. Indeed, the needle was so small that experts think it may have been used to sew watertight seams, as Eskimos are known to have done in much later times.

The Marmes discovery was very important, but those who made it excavated only part of the site, because they felt sure that more illumination of the lifeways of very early Americans would come from studying what they already had before they dug further. However, a dam was under construction downriver, and when it was completed, water rose rapidly behind it and approached the level of the rockshelter. People who were interested in the scientific importance of the site persuaded President Johnson to order the Army Corps of Engineers to protect it. A coffer dam was built around it, but someone had overlooked the nature of the soil under the coffer dam. It was gravel through which the water from the reservoir seeped very readily. Now it will take millions of dollars to drain the Marmes Rockshelter area so that excavation can be resumed.

YAKIMA VALLEY MUSEUM (YAK-i-maw)

2105 Tieton Dr., Yakima. Open free, 10 a.m. to 4 p.m., Wednesday through Friday; 2 p.m. to 5 p.m., Sunday; closed holidays.

The principal Indian exhibits here are Yakima, Klickitat, and Sioux. A small amount of undated prehistoric material is included.

Yukon Territory

MacBRIDE CENTENNIAL MUSEUM

First Ave. and Steele St., Whitehorse. Open 10 a.m. to noon, 2 p.m. to 5 p.m., 7 p.m. to 9 p.m., daily, May 19 to mid-Sept. Admission: 50¢.

Although no archeological sites in Yukon Territory are open to the public, some finds of prehistoric materials are exhibited in this museum, which also displays more recent Indian materials along with relics of pioneer and Gold Rush times.

GREAT PLAINS

"I observed the remains of an old village which had been fortified," Captain William Clark wrote in his journal on Oct. 19, 1804. He and other members of the Lewis and Clark Expedition noted several of these abandoned sites along the Missouri River before they stopped at a vigorous and hospitable settlement of Mandan Indians near present-day Bismarck, North Dakota. There for the next five months the exploring party camped on the very edge of prehistory.

The daily lives of the Mandans, their ceremonies and rituals, may well have resembled those of Indians whose villages and garden plots had been sprinkled along rivers in the flat heart of America for the preceding thousand years. Even before that, transient hunters left evidence of their wanderings over the Great Plains, just as they had in other parts of the country. The Plains environment, however, was unique. Accordingly man's adjustments to it had special qualities.

This huge region extends from central Texas northward to southern Alberta, Saskatchewan, and Manitoba. On the west it begins at the foothills of the Rocky Mountains, and it stretches eastward through much of Oklahoma, all of Kansas and Nebraska, part of Iowa, and all of South and North Dakota. A feature common to most of the Plains is grass. In the east it grows tall, and the tall-grass country is often called prairie. The west, where the land is higher and rainfall less, is short-grass country.

When Europeans began to explore here they assumed, as have most people since then, that the prairies were very ancient. However, this may not have been the case. In the not too distant past, trees grew in some places where white men found only grass. Forests covered large sections of the Plains at certain periods. Just when or why they disappeared is not altogether clear. Possibly a slight decrease in rainfall, together with forest fires, destroyed much of the tree cover. The grasses could survive, but perhaps the slower-growing trees then succumbed to the Indian's habit of setting grass fires to make hunting easy.

This change in vegetation had its effect on animal life. It gave bison a virtually limitless supply of food. Herds multiplied and roamed freely. Perhaps 30 million of the big animals were grazing on Plains grasses by the time Europeans first saw them. With such a resource men, too, could make the grasslands their home. Bison fed the Plains dweller. Their hides gave him

An aerial view of part of the Ojibwa Boulder Mosaic area in Whiteshell Provincial Park in Manitoba.

robes for warmth and skins for clothing and containers. Sinews were useful for sewing. Horns could be made into spoons, certain bones into scrapers. Dried bison dung (buffalo chips) made excellent fuel.

Even before the buffalo hunters there were small groups on the Plains who followed the giant bison, as well as mammoths, camels, and other game that is now extinct. Mammoth kill sites have been found in Oklahoma, Colorado, and Wyoming, and associated with the bones were projectile points of the kind first discovered at Clovis, New Mexico. A whole series of other points were also used to kill large game animals on the Plains. These too are identified in museums by the names of the sites where they were first found—Scottsbluff, Eden, Milnesand, Hell Gap, and others. Although they vary in shape, all are of beautifully worked stone. Perhaps it was the efficient use of these points that helped to bring extinction to several species of animal. At any rate the big game of Paleo-Indian times disappeared, and by about 5000 B.C. the lifeway of hunters on the Great Plains began to undergo change.

Archaic Period

Hunting continued in the next period— the Archaic, but in the absence of the large meat animals people ate more of the smaller ones, even squirrels, rats, and mice, which already had a place in their diet. They also accepted plants as food. Grinding-stones to make seeds edible now appear in places where Archaic campsites come to light. Not many of these sites have been found. Perhaps no one has looked hard enough for them; or the climate may have been to blame. According to some weather experts a hot, dry period began about 5000 B.C., and vegetation declined in the western sections of the Plains. This could have meant that animal life was scarce, and men who depended on both plants and animals would have had little reason to stay in the area. Some dispute this idea, but archeologists have found few traces of man's presence during the next 2,500 years.

Eastern sections of the Plains were not arid, and there the life style resembled that of Archaic people who inhabited the heavily wooded areas from the Mississippi to the Atlantic coast. (Although archeological material from eastern Oklahoma is listed in this section of the book, it is culturally related to the Southeast.)

No mountain barrier separated the Plains from the woodlands. On the contrary, waterways linked the entire region from the Rocky Mountains to the Alleghenies, and Woodland people could and did move freely along them. Ideas traveled too, but not always very fast. Pottery-making, for example, had begun in the East by 1000 B.C. It took about a thousand more years for that very useful art to reach the eastern Plains and even longer for it to spread into short-grass country.

Partly because pieces of broken pottery are numerous and easy to see, man's record on the Great Plains becomes clearer. The advent of gardening and corn-raising makes the record clearer still, because farmers stay longer in one place and hence leave more debris in one place than hunters do.

How agriculture entered the Plains is a matter of discussion among the experts. Some believe it came from the south and west. Others think it may have been brought by people who moved westward out of the valleys of the Ohio and Illinois and Mississippi rivers. Apparently a migration did begin about A.D. 1 when a group settled on the Missouri River where Kansas City now stands. With them came customs typical of a lifeway known as Hopewellian that centered in Ohio and Illinois. After that, settlements appeared farther and farther up the Missouri.

As the people moved northward the women, who did the planting, had a basic problem—the farther they went, the shorter was the dependable season of warm weather for crop growing. This meant that not all of their corn seeds would produce mature plants before frost. Nevertheless, along the Missouri River and elsewhere, they managed to save some hardy, early-ripened seeds each year, and gradually, by a process of selection, they developed strains suited to the climate of each area they settled.

Wherever corn became a successful crop village life was possible for at least part of the year. Although these Plains settlements had much in common, they

A

B

D

B

C

Strange stone heads from the southern Plains may be among man's earliest works of art in the New World. A. The Frederick Head was carved from sandstone. B. and C. The Malakoff Heads (only the faces are shown here in reproduction). D. Paleo-Indian Big-Game Hunters of the Plains used these projectile points: Midland (left); Hell Gap (center); and Scottsbluff (right). Redrawn from Irwin and Wormington. E. A mammoth kill site was excavated at Domebo in Oklahoma by the Museum of the Great Plains. This is an artist's conception of how the kill took place, displayed in a diorama at the museum. A, B, C, and E photos from Museum of the Great Plains.

E

varied in many ways that intrigue the archeologist. Life in regions where farming developed early differed from life where it came late or not at all. And so, for convenience in reporting, archeologists who have been most concerned with the Great Plains area divide it into five subareas: Southern Plains, Central Plains, Middle Missouri, Northeastern Periphery, and Northwestern Plains.

There are several reasons why the Middle Missouri has yielded the most archeological "goodies." Along this stretch of the river, as it crosses South Dakota and North Dakota to its junction with the Yellowstone, the land was suited to the needs of village dwellers. It offered good soil for gardens. Men had access to hunting grounds. There was plenty of timber for building the distinctive Plains Village houses. These are known as earthlodges because their framework of poles and upright logs was banked with earth or sod. A frequent house shape was a half-dome, like those which Lewis and Clark saw among the Mandans, with roofs which sometimes covered a surprisingly big area. A hole in the center provided an escape for smoke and a source of light. In bad weather the smoke hole could be covered with an inverted bull boat—a circular craft made of bison skin stretched around a wooden frame.

In varying sizes and shapes—sometimes round, sometimes rectangular or square—the earthlodges housed Plains Village Indians along the Missouri from about A.D. 1000 to historic times. After they were abandoned they attracted little attention until, at the end of World War II, dam-building for flood control began along the Missouri. A program of salvage archeology in this rich area yielded much fascinating material that may be seen in the Museum of Natural History in Washington, D.C., and also in western museums and at a few sites noted in this section.

Archeologists have done less excavating in the eastern Dakotas and southern Manitoba (the Northeastern Periphery subarea). As a result they are not altogether sure what happened there during the Plains Village period. They do know that at some time men built a good many burial mounds. Just when they began is not certain, but they may have

continued into historic times. Perhaps the first mounds were the work of people who shared in the widespread Woodland lifeway. Almost certainly they were not farmers but hunters.

Woodland people did inhabit the longgrass part of the Central Plains subarea, which includes the westernmost part of Iowa, all of Kansas and Nebraska, eastern Colorado, and a little of southeastern Wyoming. Here were resources for men who hunted and for women who may have done a little gardening but who certainly had the knack of gathering seeds and roots. What happened to these groups after about A.D. 500 remains a mystery. All we know is that people with an entirely different life style moved in and stayed.

Changing Lifeways

These newcomers were village dwellers. Like their predecessors they hunted bison, but they were also gardeners, and they made new use of one particular part of the bison—they turned the shoulder blades into hoes for their cornfields. Along one river valley after another the Plains Village communities spread westward through the Central Plains. Proof that they were not transients appeared when archeologists dug into a site inhabited by people of the Mill Creek culture in Iowa. During the years they spent here—from perhaps A.D. 800 to 1400—they piled up a rich collection of trash 12 feet deep over a two-acre area.

Somewhat less wealthy were the earthlodge builders who settled in the upper valley of the Republican River in Nebraska. However, they must have had large surpluses of corn, beans, squash, and sunflower, for they dug innumerable food storage pits both inside and outside their dwellings. The Upper Republican women were good potters; the men efficient hunters of deer, antelope, and bison. Why they disappeared shortly before the arrival of Europeans, archeologists cannot say. Possibly nomadic raiders from the west stole their surplus food and forced them to move toward safer places in the east. Or perhaps it was drought that robbed them of food.

A little farther to the west, where the prairie gives way to the shortgrass coun-

Prehistoric Fire-Power

Stone weapons changed a great deal in the millenia of their use. Very early in the Old World men learned to extend their grasp by jabbing a pointed stick into small creatures they could not easily reach with their bare hands. They also learned how to break certain kinds of stone to get sharp edges that were good for cutting or gouging. Then came a big innovation. Men fastened a stick and a sharpened rock together—and made a spear.

At first this new tool was probably used only for poking, but it was effective. In America men could apparently kill even mammoths with thrusting spears. They increased the range of their weapons when they found they could hurl a spear as well as thrust it. The spear had become a javelin—a projectile. Next its range was extended with the aid of a spear thrower, also called a throwing stick or atlatl (AT-ul-AT-ul). Men who used atlatls often made the shafts of their spears lighter than the shafts of thrusting spears, and these small spears or javelins are often called darts. Dart points, too, were likely to be smaller than the points on heavy thrusting spears.

For thousands of years American Indians got much of their protein food with the aid of darts and atlatls. Then came a device with which a man could put still more power behind projectiles—the bow. The bow acted as a spring: It stored up muscle power and then released a lot of it all at once.

As men increased the power behind the projectile, they continued to decrease the size of its shaft and points. Arrows and arrow points were smaller than darts and dart points.

Since arrows were easily transported in quantity, they made possible a great increase in fire-power, and man's destructiveness multiplied. Not only could he kill more animals and thus obtain more food; he could also kill more men. So, paradoxically, as soon as human beings were better able to provide for themselves, they also became less sure of surviving.

Archeologists may never know how it happened that some genius in the Old World about 5,000 years ago invented the bow. They do know that it spread from the Old World to the New. Exactly how it got here is not clear, but it had reached as far into America as the Southwest by about A.D. 450. In general, bows appeared late in the Archaic stage in North America, and together with other Archaic inventions marked a stepped-up effort by man to survive in an environment that was not as lush as it had been.

The wood that went into making bows varied from place to place, depending on what was available. Some were made of several small pieces of wood ingeniously fitted together. Some were reinforced with sinews. Bows were long. Bows were short. Bows curved in different ways.

Some arrows may have been only sharpened wooden sticks. Some shafts were made of sturdy reeds. Very often a man identified his own arrows by painting on them some special mark or symbol.

Arrow points are abundant in areas where people depended heavily on hunting for food. In other areas, where most of the food came from agriculture, arrow points may be much less frequently found. In the largest ruins of the Southwest, for example, they are often far from numerous.

The spear thrower, also called a throwing stick or atlatl, extended the distance a spear could be hurled. Men who used atlatls often made the shafts of their spears lighter than the shafts of javelins or thrusting spears. The projectile launched by an atlatl is often called a dart. A dart point was smaller than the point of a thrusting spear but was larger than the point of an arrow used with a bow. After Indians discovered the greater accuracy and efficiency of the bow and arrow, they stopped using the atlatl and dart.

try of the High Plains, lived the Dismal River people, who did little gardening but lived primarily by hunting. Instead of building earthlodges they made shelters of poles with roofs of skin or bundled grass. Probably they were the ancestors of the Plains Apaches who followed the buffalo herds on horseback in historic times.

Farther south in the Oklahoma and Texas panhandles, which are part of the Southern Plains subarea, people of the Antelope Creek culture had an interesting mixture of traits. Some of their patterns of living seem to have come from Upper Republican contacts; another custom— their way of building square houses of masonry and adobe mud—certainly reached them from the Pueblo people across the mountains in New Mexico.

Close by these settlements lay the Llano Estacado—the Staked Plains— where, long before, Paleo-Indians hunted mammoths. Because the hard sod and the uncertain climate made farming almost impossible, this remained hunting country. Countless bison roamed there, and in late prehistoric times Comanche Indians made it their home.

Elsewhere in northern Texas and Oklahoma, village Indians resembled in many ways those of the Central Plains. The Washita River people, for example, built rectangular houses but daubed the outside with clay instead of banking the walls with earth. They gardened and hunted and also did some fishing. Similar villages dotted parts of north central Texas.

Although south Texas is not strictly a part of the Great Plains, it is included here for convenience. This was not a hospitable or comfortable land. Along the coast plenty of rain fell in the course of a year, but it often did not fall at the right time for corn-growing. Inland the climate was very dry. As a result, people who lived either on the coast or inland never took up agriculture, and so they did not gather in permanent farming villages. They simply subsisted on what was at hand—roots, nuts, seeds, and the fruit and stems of cactus. Along the coast they found fish and mollusks, and shell heaps accumulated as they did along the Pacific and Atlantic coasts. Man's way of life, in short, was a continuation of the Desert culture from which the farming cultures of the Southwest developed. Possibly these South Texans were immigrants

who came to North American very early and were pushed into so harsh a land by later people. One basis for this theory is their language. It resembles the Hokan tongue which survived into historic times in California and which scholars believe is the oldest of all California languages.

Almost as difficult as south Texas are some parts of the Northwest Plains which include Wyoming, Montana, the western Dakotas, and the southern end of Alberta and Saskatchewan. Corn did not prosper here, and people could not base their lives on farming. Instead they continued to live century after century much as their ancestors had in Archaic times. Some pottery did appear about A.D. 500, but it was never very useful to nomadic hunters because it was fragile and awkward to transport. More suitable containers could be made from hide and from the stomachs and intestines of bison.

Ways of hunting bison varied. The most spectacular was also the most productive—and wasteful. To secure a large quantity of meat with least trouble, men would drive a whole herd over a cliff. Indians used this technique, called the buffalo jump, both before and after they obtained horses.

Some of the buffalo hunters of historic times—the Blackfeet, Arapaho, and Assiniboine—were probably descendants of the prehistoric Northern Plains people. Others who hunted here after the arrival of horses had different origins. The Cheyenne and the Sioux were latecomers. Their ancestors had been Plains Village dwellers farther east—farmers who gave up farming and lived entirely by the chase, once horses were available, which made them mobile.

From the colorful riders of historic times to the early makers of simple stone tools the range of Plains life was wide and, like the Plains themselves, surprisingly varied. Our knowledge of it is far from complete but has accumulated very rapidly in recent years. As a result of decisions to build huge flood-control dams in the Missouri River Basin, the Smithsonian River Basin Survey and the National Park Service undertook a large and intensive salvage archeology program, especially in the Dakotas. The work done by the Survey—and work done everywhere else on the Plains—has been well summarized and interpreted by Waldo R. Wedel in a very illuminating book, *Prehistoric Man on the Great Plains*.

A. This diorama in the Pawnee Indian Village Museum in Kansas depicts a moment of contact between white traders and a Pawnee village group. Kansas State Historical Society photo. B. The Pawnee Indian Village Museum in Republic County, Kansas, is constructed over and around the remains of a large Indian dwelling. The village of which it was a part was in use during historic time, but it closely resembled those of prehistoric time. The museum building is designed to resemble a Pawnee earthlodge, and it houses artifacts recovered in the course of excavating the site. Kansas State Historical Society photo.

B

Alberta

EARLY MAN SITE

From Fort MacLeod drive 12 miles northwest on Alberta 2. Open free at all times.

A cairn erected by the Provincial government marks the site where Indian hunters built an enclosure, or pound, into which they drove bison. In this trap they could conveniently slaughter the animals which were difficult to kill when on the run.

GLENBOW MUSEUM

530 Seventh Ave. S.W., Calgary. Open 10 a.m. to 9 p.m., Tuesday through Friday; 10 a.m. to 5 p.m., Monday, Saturday, and holidays; 11:30 a.m. to 6 p.m., Sunday. Admission: adults, 50¢; children, 10¢; children under 16 accompanied by an adult, free.

Archeological exhibits devoted to the Northern Plains are featured along with historic and ethnographic material which places some emphasis on western Canada.

Very little systematic archeological work had been done in Alberta until 1955 when the Glenbow Foundation began to sponsor research. Since then it has conducted an active program of investigation at a number of important sites. One of them, the Old Women's Buffalo Jump, is unusual because hunters killed buffalo there almost continuously for about 1,500 years, whereas most other jumps were used only sporadically. Excavation through heaps of bones more than 20 feet deep revealed, among other things, the development of projectile points from the large, wide kind that tipped ancient spears to the small, triangular arrowheads of later times.

LUXTON MUSEUM

Birch Ave., Banff. Open 10 a.m. to noon, 1:30 p.m. to 5 p.m., Tuesday through Sunday; closed Monday, except holidays. Admission: adults, 50¢; children under 16 with parent, free.

Included with western Canadian ethnographic material in the museum are archeological specimens from this part of Alberta. A diorama portrays a buffalo jump.

THE RIBSTONES

From Viking drive 6 miles east on Alberta 14. Open free, at all times.

Here on a farm is a Provincial cairn which points out the ribstones—a kind of artifact found more in Alberta than in any other Plains province or state. A ribstone is a boulder on which prehistoric hunters pecked grooves which often resemble animal ribs. The Cree Indians in historic times thought that these petroglyphs represented buffalo ribs and that the boulders were dwelling places of the animals' guardian spirits. Sometimes a buffalo head was pecked near the grooves in a ribstone, along with circular depressions. These holes, according to the Crees, allowed arrows (and bullets in historic times) to pass through without harming the guardian spirit within the stone.

UNIVERSITY OF ALBERTA ANTHROPOLOGY EXHIBITS

Henry Marshall Tory Bldg., on the campus, Ed-monton. Open free, 8 a.m. to 6 p.m., Monday through Saturday, when the university is in session.

In the hallway on the main floor of the building are display cases of archeological material representing all stages of Alberta's prehistory from Paleo times up to the period of contact with Europeans. There are also recent Eskimo artifacts.

WRITING-ON-STONE

Off Alberta 4, on the Milk River 75 miles southeast of Lethbridge. Open free, at all times.

Here in the valley of the Milk River, near sandstone cliffs, the Provincial government has erected a cairn to indicate where Indians pecked various designs in the rock.

Some of the petroglyphs show men on horseback. Although horses roamed the Plains in Paleo-Indian times, they disappeared and were reintroduced by the Spanish in the 16th century. The pictures showing men on horseback must have been made sometime after A.D. 1730, which is thought to be the date when horses reached Alberta. Representations of men with bows and shields may have been made earlier.

Archeologists who have examined the site believe that much of this rock art is prehistoric. Possibly the figures of animals were made by young men as part of a religious rite called the guardian spirit quest. A youth in search of a guardian spirit went off alone to some remote spot where he fasted and tried to dream of an animal which would become his protector and helper in later life.

Colorado

For additional listings see page 23.

COLORADO STATE MUSEUM

E. Fourteenth Ave. and Sherman St., Denver. Open free, 9 a.m. to 5 p.m., Monday through Friday; 10 a.m. to 5 p.m., Saturday, Sunday, holidays.

This museum has a large amount of material obtained from the Wetherill brothers who were the first to explore the cliff dwellings at Mesa Verde. In addition there are Anasazi materials from other areas in southwestern Colorado. Dioramas deal with these prehistoric cultures: Mesa Verde, Upper Republican, and Dismal River. There are ethnological exhibits which throw light on prehistory, particularly that of the Utes.

DENVER MUSEUM OF NATURAL HISTORY

City Park, Denver. Open free, 10 a.m. to 4:30 p.m., Monday through Saturday; noon to 5 p.m., Sunday, Labor Day to June 1; 9 a.m. to 5 p.m., Monday through Saturday; noon to 5 p.m., Sunday, June 1 to Labor Day.

This museum first gained fame in the world of archeology for its excavation of the Folsom site in New Mexico, and it displays the original Folsom point, as it was found, between the ribs of an extinct bison. Murals show Folsom hunters, Cochise food gatherers, Hohokam canal builders, Basketmakers, Pueblo people, the Betatakin cliff dwellings, and California Indians.

Numerous and varied exhibits contain material from Chaco Canyon, from Kayenta, and from Mogollon, Basketmaker, and Hohokam sites in the

Very Old Sites in Alberta

In 1961, about three miles north of Taber, Alberta, a geological field party found fragments of the bones of a young child buried under 70 feet of earth and gravel. Unfortunately the fragments were too small to permit dating by the radiocarbon method, but scientists have ways of estimating how long ago the gravel was deposited at the site. A geologist, A. MacS. Stalker, who studied the deposits, came to the conclusion that the bones were at least 37,000 years old and perhaps as much as 60,000 years old. If Stalker is correct, these human remains may be the oldest so far found in the Americas.

At another site, near Medicine Hat in Alberta, Stalker's attention was called to a gravel bed in which chipped stones appeared. Some of these showed that they had been additionally flaked as if to sharpen a knife-edge. The sharpening, Stalker believes, must have been done by man, because he knows of no natural process that could have accomplished the flaking. In this same bed appeared wood and mollusk shells. Radiocarbon dates for this material indicate an age of between 30,000 and 36,000 years. Stalker also found the bones of mammoth and other extinct animals in this bed, but there was no proof that they were associated with the tools of men who might have hunted them.

The pebble tool was one of the earliest implements developed by man. Archeologists have not yet determined who made them in the New World or when, but thousands have been found in various parts of the United States. These two views are of a pebble tool from Alabama, where many such artifacts have been discovered. After Lively and Josselyn.

Pebble Tools

If a man knows the trick, he can pick up a certain kind of water-worn pebble or cobble, strike it a few times with a hammerstone, and make it into a useful tool for chopping. Pebble tools of this kind were among the earliest created by men, and they have been found by the ton on the surface of the ground in certain parts of Alabama.

Did recent Indian hunters knock out these artifacts for one-time or emergency use? Or were the choppers made a very long time ago by men whose tool kit was very, very simple? These questions occurred to archeologists, both amateur and professional, as they encountered thousands of rounded stones that had distinct chopping or cutting edges. Often the stones looked very old because they had weathered deeply. Always they resembled tools found in the Old World which were known to be very ancient. However, there seemed to be no way to discover the exact age of the Alabama artifacts. Even when the tools were found buried in the earth, luck has not been with the diggers. So far dating has been uncertain or impossible.

As a result, a fascinating mystery remains unsolved. Some archeologists suspect that the pebble tools are evidence that men who did not know how to make stone projectile points lived in America before the days of the big-game-hunting Paleo-Indians. Other archeologists think the pebble tools may have been made in a hurry by much later people who regarded them as expendable. Whatever the true explanation turns out to be, interest in the tools is considerable in Alabama and elsewhere, and the Alabama Archeological Society, University of Alabama, Box 6126, University, Alabama, can tell interested persons where examples of the artifacts may be seen.

Southwest. Also displayed are Upper Republican, Woodland, Hopewellian, and Mississippian artifacts. Ethnological exhibits include one which shows the effect of the horse on Indian culture.

Special Feature. One exhibit in the museum has an interesting history: A summer cloudburst in 1932 exposed some large bones near the Dent railroad station along the South Platte River, 39 miles from Denver. Railroad workers reported the bones to Reverend Conrad Bilgery, S.J., a teacher at Regis College near Denver. Father Bilgery excavated and found under the pelvis of a mammoth a large point that had short flutes on each face near the base. This Dent Site is not open to the public, but bones and Clovis points found there may be seen in the museum.

KOSHARE INDIAN MUSEUM, INC. (ko-SHAH-ray)

From US 50 in La Junta drive south 18 blocks on Colorado Ave., then west 1 block. Open free, 9 a.m. to 5 p.m., 7 p.m. to 9 p.m., summer; 1 p.m. to 5 p.m., winter.

This museum on the campus of Otero Junior College contains archeological materials and dioramas showing prehistoric Indian life. The collections have been assembled partly through the activities of an extraordinary troop of Boy Scouts who call themselves Koshares. The Koshares also perform Indian dances in authentic costumes before audiences throughout the United States.

PIONEERS MUSEUM

25 W. Kiowa St., Colorado Springs. Open free, 10 a.m. to 5 p.m., Tuesday through Saturday; 2 p.m. to 5 p.m., Sunday. Camping nearby.

Artifacts from Colorado and New Mexico make up the archeological displays in this museum. There is a special collection of 90 pieces of Mesa Verde pottery and another of more than 300 stone artifacts collected in the Southwest. Eight-hundred-year-old materials, excavated from a site in Chama Valley, New Mexico, are also on display.

ROCKY MOUNTAIN NATIONAL PARK, MORAINE PARK VISITOR CENTER

From Estes Park drive 2 miles west on Colorado 66 to park entrance, then follow directional signs within the park 4 miles to Moraine Park Visitor Center. Open free, 8 a.m. to 5 p.m., summer. Admission to the park: $1 per car; 50¢ for each person arriving by bus. Camping.

Included among the exhibits are displays that show how prehistoric Indians of the area made axes, hammerstones, arrow points, and scrapers; how they used the bison for food and materials; how they built stone forts and walls to control the movements of game being hunted. The Indians who made use of the Rocky Mountain National Park area in prehistoric times are thought to have been the ancestors of the Utes and Arapahoes.

TRINIDAD STATE JUNIOR COLLEGE MUSEUM

Library Bldg., on the campus, Trinidad. Open free, 8 a.m. to 5 p.m., Monday through Saturday when the college is in session.

Here on display along with ethnological materials are archeological exhibits from the Trinidad area and also from the Southern Plains and the Texas Panhandle. The early history, geology, paleontology, and anthropology of the local region are shown in detail. A diorama shows the Tinchera Rock Shelter with artifacts which date from the Archaic period.

UNIVERSITY OF COLORADO MUSEUM

On the campus, Henderson Building, Boulder. Open free 8 a.m. to 5 p.m., Monday through Saturday; 2 p.m. to 5 p.m., Sunday and holidays; closed Dec. 25.

The Hall of Man in this museum includes numerous displays that illuminate North American prehistory, particularly in the Plains area and the Southwest, beginning with the entry of man into this continent.

One exhibit dramatizes a mass bison kill at the Olsen-Chubbock Site in Colorado, which was excavated under the direction of Joe Ben Wheat, the museum's curator of anthropology. In this dig archeologists exposed about 200 bison skeletons and recovered 27 projectile points and a few stone tools. That, plus a study of the terrain, was all Dr. Wheat and his colleagues needed for putting together a complete scientific detective story.

The Story. In May or June about 6500 B.C. a band of perhaps 150 hunting people sighted a herd of buffalo. Because the wind was blowing toward the hunters, the animals were not alarmed. This gave time for men, women, and children to station themselves in two long lines leading up to a steep-banked arroyo. With the trap arranged, a few men stampeded the buffalo across the prairie, between the lines, straight into the gulch, where they were killed either by the fall or by hunters' spears.

Butchering and feasting started immediately. Tongues and tender favorite cuts were eaten first, while the tough parts were dried for future use. Probably the fresh meat lasted for three weeks before it spoiled. After that the band moved on, carrying loads of preserved meat and fat to eat until the next big kill.

A few of the clues to the story are these: Buffalo calves are born in May or June, and the calf skeletons at the site were those of animals only a few days old. Projectile points told the approximate century of the kill. They were similar to points found at other sites which had been dated by the radiocarbon method. The positions of skeletons in the arroyo led to reconstruction of the stampede procedure. All of the big bones were laid in more or less orderly piles after the meat was cut off, but tongue bones were scattered about, suggesting that people ate the fresh tongues as they worked. The size of the band was estimated by calculating the amount of meat cut from the carcasses, taking into account how much of it could be eaten fresh and how much was tough and had to be dried for future use.

The Olsen-Chubbock display is one of many in the museum. Others are devoted to the Hohokam, Mogollon, Fremont, and Anasazi cultures. One exhibit shows how archeologists have been able to determine the age of material found at Southwestern sites by the use of tree-ring dating. Another display presents various types of Hopi kachina dolls.

Special Interest. The Anasazi material on exhibit was collected by Earl Morris, famous for his archeological work in the Southwest and Yucatan. His papers are in the custody of the museum, and his biography has been written by Robert Lister of the Anthropology Department of the University of Colorado, in collaboration with Mrs. Lister.

A Plains Indian Garden

A living garden can scarcely be prehistoric, but it can be a reasonable facsimile of an ancient Indian's vegetable patch—provided the modern gardener can find authentic seeds. Most varieties of vegetables grown today are very different from the ancestral plants which Indians cultivated. The new, improved types of corn, beans, and squash have become so widely used that the older types have almost disappeared. To save them from extinction became the hobby of Charles E. Hanson, Jr., an engineer in the U. S. Department of Agriculture. With the help of his wife and children, he collected and planted seeds of the old-time varieties, some of them rare or even the last in existence. Now a flourishing garden which resembles those of the Plains Indians is sponsored by the Nebraska Historical Society. It can be seen at the Museum of the Fur Trade, three miles east of Chadron, Nebraska, on US 20.

Plants for Food

Indians north of Mexico used an astounding total of 1,112 different species of plant for food. Of these, 86 were cultivated, and among the cultivated plants, 58 were imports from Mexico or Central America. The others were native, 19 in the Southwest and 9 in the East.

In the East, the earliest plants to be cultivated were gourds, squashes, and perhaps pumpkins. These all came from Mexico. Maize, which also came from Mexico, arrived a little later.

Sunflower, pigweed, goosefoot, and marsh elder were also cultivated in the East at an early date, but evidence that they were cultivated *before* the arrival of the Mexican plants has not been found.

The date when people began cultivation varied from place to place, but generally speaking it was about 1000 B.C.

In the Midwest, people who practiced the Hopewell Cult were the first to grow maize. The addition to their diet of this new source of energy probably had a good deal to do with the tremendous vitality they developed.

As an indication of the continuing importance of plants derived from Indians, economists say that in the state of Georgia alone in 1960 crops from plants of European origin were worth $21,334,000; at the same time the value of plants domesticated by American Indians was more than ten times that amount—$241,736,000.

UTE INDIAN MUSEUM

From Montrose drive 4 miles south on US 550. Open free, 9 a.m. to 5 p.m., daily from about April 15 to about Oct. 25.

The collection here consists mainly of ethnographic material but includes stone tools and baskets made by the prehistoric inhabitants of Colorado and Utah. Some of the material has been dated as early as 2000 B.C.

UTE TRAIL

Rocky Mountain National Park. From Estes Park drive 2 miles west on Colorado 68 to park entrance, then follow directional signs to Trail Ridge Road. Open free, daily, in summer when Trail Ridge Road is open. Admission to the park: $1 per car; 50¢ for each person arriving by bus. Camping nearby.

This ancient Indian trail crosses Trail Ridge Road above timberline, opposite the place where a service road turns off to several nearby stone service buildings. It is possible to explore the trail for some distance on foot, following cairns which mark a portion of the route which prehistoric Utes took when they crossed the Continental Divide in this area.

A large wall map of the entire trail is displayed in the Visitor Center farther west on Trail Ridge Road.

Kansas

ELLSWORTH COUNTY MUSEUM (HODGDEN HOUSE)

Main St., Ellsworth. Open free, 10 a.m. to noon, 1 p.m. to 5 p.m., Tuesday through Saturday; 1 p.m. to 5 p.m., Sunday.

One room here is devoted to about 20 replicas of petroglyphs which prehistoric Indians pecked in sandstone outcroppings in central Kansas. Some prehistoric artifacts are also on display.

A number of the figures in the petroglyphs represent animals. Although their exact meaning is not known, archeologists have speculated that they may be of religious significance. Quite possibly the petroglyphs were symbols of the visions young men had or sought during their guardian spirit quests.

INDIAN BURIAL PIT

National Historic Landmark.
From either Niles exit or Camp Webster Corner exit on Interstate 70, near Salina, follow directional signs to the site. Or from Salina follow directional signs on old US 40, now Kansas 140, about 4 miles to the site. Camping nearby.

More than a thousand years ago, farming people built a little village here near the Smoky Hill River. They were not especially wealthy, but they did make a practice of burying gifts with the dead —shell ornaments, stone tools, and sometimes a piece of pottery. Graves in their cemetery came to light after modern farmers began to cultivate the land. More than 140 of these have been meticulously excavated and protected inside a building,

so that visitors may now see the burials just as they were found.

Excavation at the village site has only begun. However, enough is known about it and similar hamlets along the river to give a general picture of the Smoky Hill lifeway. Houses were sturdy structures of poles against which earth or sod was banked. The men did some hunting of deer and antelope and bison to supplement the crops that were raised in garden plots. For winter use, corn, beans, and sunflower seeds were stored in grass-lined underground caches.

Indian Burial Pit, which is operated as a private commercial enterprise, is known in archeological literature as the Whiteford Site or the Price Site, named for successive owners. No place in Kansas has been more carefully preserved to give a glimpse into the past.

INSCRIPTION ROCK

Lake Kanapolis State Park. From Ellsworth drive 15 miles east to junction with Kansas 141, then south to junction with Kansas 241, then west one-half mile to park entrance. Open at all times. Admission to park: $1 per car. Camping.

Prehistoric Indians pecked designs and figures on sandstone boulders in this area. A leaflet guide to the sites in the park is available at the park entrance. Replicas of some of the petroglyphs may be seen at the Ellsworth County Museum, Ellsworth.

KANSAS HISTORICAL SOCIETY

Memorial Bldg., 120 W. 10th St., Topeka. Open free, 8:15 a.m. to 5 p.m., Monday through Friday; 8:15 a.m. to 4 p.m., Saturday; 1 p.m. to 4:30 p.m., Sunday; closed national holidays.

In a gallery devoted to Kansas Indians are dioramas of Indian life and displays of archeological specimens from Paleo, Archaic, Middle Woodland, and Central Plains cultures.

PAWNEE INDIAN VILLAGE MUSEUM

From Belleville on US 36 drive 8 miles north on US 81, then 15 miles west on Kansas 266. Open free, 10 a.m. to 5 p.m., Tuesday through Saturday; 1 p.m. to 5 p.m., Sunday; closed Jan. 1, Thanksgiving, Dec. 25.

Here, on the carefully excavated site of a Pawnee village, is a museum which the Kansas Historical Society has constructed over and around the remains of a large dwelling. Although the village was inhabited after the arrival of Europeans, it closely resembled those of prehistoric times.

Like many other people of the Central Plains, the Pawnees and their predecessors lived a divided life. Twice a year the entire community picked up and left for buffalo country to the west. During the buffalo hunts they camped in tipis. Afterward they returned to their home base, a settlement of perhaps 20 huge circular houses built near the fields where they raised corn, beans, and squash. Each of these dwellings, called earthlodges because the framework of logs was covered with blocks of sod, sheltered as many as 40 people.

In the museum building, which somewhat resembles an earthlodge, display cases contain artifacts recovered in the course of excavating the site. Outside the museum a walk takes the visitor past underground storage pits and lodge floors which have been exposed.

ST. BENEDICT'S COLLEGE MUSEUM

Science Hall, on the campus, Atchison. Open free, 2 p.m. to 5 p.m., Monday, Tuesday, Thursday, Friday, and by appointment.

Exhibited here are Hopewellian artifacts from Easton, Kan., from Weston, Mo., and from the important Renner Site in Kansas City, Mo. Other materials come from a Kansas village site in Doniphan, Kan. The prehistoric Southwest is also represented by artifacts of the Mimbres Culture. One display is devoted to the manufacture and use of certain artifacts.

UNIVERSITY OF KANSAS, MUSEUM OF ANTHROPOLOGY

Dyche Hall, on the campus, Lawrence. Open free, 8 a.m. to 5 p.m., Monday through Saturday; 1:30 p.m. to 5 p.m., Sunday.

Official university expeditions on the Great Plains produced most of the archeological material on display here. Dioramas show reconstructions of activities of prehistoric people.

Manitoba

MANITOBA MUSEUM OF MAN AND NATURE

190 Rupert Ave., Winnipeg. Open free, at times to be announced.

In its new building this museum has archeological exhibits dealing with Manitoba and adjacent areas. Displays are centered around man's relation to his environment—in the arctic, sub-arctic, boreal forest, parkland, and grassland areas. Used in the exhibits are materials from a far-northern culture known as pre-Dorset, from burial mounds, and from Eskimo sites. Paleo-Indian and Copper culture artifacts are also featured, along with rock paintings and boulder effigies.

OJIBWA BOULDER MOSAICS (oh-JIB-way)

Whiteshell Provincial Park. From Trans-Canada Highway 7 at the Manitoba-Ontario border, which is also the border of the park, drive about 20 miles west on Manitoba 44, then follow Manitoba 307 about 20 miles north to the site. Open from about the third weekend in May to about the last weekend in Sept. Admission to the park, 50¢. Camping.

Exposed here are granite expanses which are interesting because the rock is perhaps the oldest in the world. It was scoured clear of soil by glaciers of the Ice Age. This bare granite serves as a background for large designs which prehistoric men laid out, using both small rocks and huge boulders which had been pushed along by glaciers and left when the ice melted. Some of the designs are geometric; others are effigies which include turtles and snakes. The snakes vary in length from a few feet to about 300 feet. One human figure is 90 feet long.

Who built the effigies and when is not known. Estimates, based on slight evidence, date them

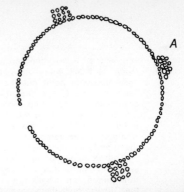

A. This circle, the significance of which is unknown, is outlined in boulders in Stutsman County, North Dakota. Redrawn from American Anthropologist. B. A closeup view shows one of the Ojibwa Boulder Mosaics in Whiteshell Provincial Park in Manitoba. Manitoba Government photo. C. The hunting technique of driving buffalo herds over a cliff and then harvesting the meat began among the Indians about 4,000 years ago. At Madison Buffalo Jump, a Montana State Archeological Site, there is much information about this ancient practice. Montana Fish and Game Department photo.

variously at a few hundred years ago, or at as much as 7,000 years ago. To support the older age, observers point out that the large boulders used in some of the designs have protected the granite under them from weathering. Beneath the boulders, the polishing effect of glacial movement is clearly visible, whereas around the same rocks, weathering has removed the polish and lowered the granite as much as three-quarters of an inch.

Ojibwa medicine men apparently used the "mosaics" in connection with ceremonies in the historic period, but it does not necessarily follow that the Ojibwas built them. In addition to these visitable effigies there are many others in Whiteshell Provincial Park which are not accessible to the public.

At two places, towers have been built to enable visitors to see the effigies from above.

The Museum. Near the mosaics a log building houses exhibits of tools, weapons, and ornaments made by prehistoric inhabitants of the area.

UNIVERSITY OF WINNIPEG ANTHROPOLOGY MUSEUM

515 Portage Ave., Winnipeg. Open free, at times to be announced in 1972.

Archeological exhibits in this museum will concentrate on prehistory in the Boreal Forest and Northern Plains areas.

Montana

GALLATIN COUNTY COURT HOUSE (GAL-ah-tun)

Bozeman. Open free, 8 a.m. to 5 p.m., Monday through Friday.

In the second floor lobby is a collection of artifacts from the Madison Buffalo Jump, together with a display of projectile points from other sources.

MAC'S MUSEUM OF NATURAL HISTORY

On US 212 in the center of town, Broadus. Open free, on request at any hour, any day.

This private collection includes more than 4,000 Indian items, some of which are prehistoric. A few are like artifacts which have been radiocarbon dated at about 2500 B.C. Others are more recent. Most of the Montana material has come from bison traps in Powder River country.

MADISON BUFFALO JUMP

From Interstate 90 at Logan drive 7 miles south on a local road to Visitor Center. Open free, at all times.

On the eastern approaches to the Rocky Mountains, between central Wyoming and southern Alberta, several hundred places have been found where Indians killed bison by driving them over cliffs or bluffs. More than half of these sites are in Montana. The Madison Buffalo Jump is the first one to be preserved and prepared for the public.

Whenever possible, Indians chose for the drive a gently rising stretch of prairie ending in a steep dropoff which the bison could not see until it was too late to turn back. To guide the animals' approach the hunters set up piles of rocks in two lines—far apart on the open prairie and funneling in toward the cliff. At some jumps the lines stretched out for as much as two miles. The rock piles were often large enough to conceal and protect the men who would spring up suddenly, wave blankets, and frighten the bison on toward the jump. Smaller rock piles could support a pole with something attached to flutter in the wind. Once started into the funnel, a herd ran faster and faster, then plunged over the brink. Any that were not killed by the fall could be dispatched with weapons.

In some places, where the jump was not very high, hunters might build a sort of corral or pound at the foot of the embankment. This would contain the bison until they could be killed with spears or shot with arrows.

At Madison Buffalo Jump, archeologists found evidence that Indians made their last drive about 200 years ago. They used it at intervals for about 4,000 years before that.

Near the jump stand five tipi rings—stones arranged in circles, supposedly to hold down the edges of skin tipis. Here the hunters camped while they butchered and dried the buffalo meat, cured the skins, and made implements of bone and horn. As they worked they feasted. Some of the meat they roasted over fires, and some they stewed in skin containers. To make a stew a woman filled a skin pouch with water, then heated it and kept it boiling by dropping hot rocks into it. Many of these rocks have been found at the site.

At the top of the cliff are other tipi rings. Perhaps these mark shelters for lookouts who watched for bison or for enemies. Other small stone enclosures are something of a mystery here as they are elsewhere on the Plains. Some archeologists think they may have been eagle traps. Covered with brush they could conceal a man who waited for an eagle to dive for bait—perhaps a rabbit—fastened outside. When the bird struck, the man could seize its legs.

The stone enclosures may equally well have been shelters for young men who were fasting and seeking religious visions. Indians in historic times said they were fireplaces used in smoke signaling.

MUSEUM OF THE PLAINS INDIANS

Immediately west of Browning at the junction of US 89 and US 2. Open free, 8 a.m. to 8 p.m., June 1 to Sept. 15; 8 a.m. to 5 p.m., Sept. 15 to Sept. 30.

As part of its effort to improve understanding of Plains Indian cultures, past and present, this museum displays some prehistoric artifacts, along with early historic material.

Special Interest. The museum sponsors tours of sites on the Blackfeet Reservation. On one circle drive visitors may see prehistoric tipi rings and the site of a buffalo drive.

MUSEUM OF THE ROCKIES

Montana State University, on the campus, Bozeman. Open free, 8 a.m. to 9 p.m., June 1 to Sept. 30; 1 p.m. to 5 p.m., Oct. 1 to May 31; closed Jan. 1, July 4, Thanksgiving, Dec. 25.

In addition to random local finds, this museum has Paleo-Indian material from the MacHaffie Site near Helena, where artifacts were discovered in three different layers during excavation. In the deepest and oldest level were fluted Folsom points, along with stone tools and the bones of extinct bison.

Tipi Rings

One form of evidence of man's presence on the Northern Plains is a large number of sites where Indians collected stones and laid them in circles. There are perhaps half a million of these circles in the Canadian province of Alberta alone. What were they for? Many archeologists think that the stones held down the edges of tents or tipis. Hence the name "tipi rings." Some rings, however, seem too small for tipis. Were they made to hold down children's play tents? Or were they small tipis in which medicine men did conjuring tricks? Other rings seem too big and elaborate for tipis. Did they have ritual significance? That was certainly true of other outlines made of rocks in the shape of animals, men, and women.

Aerial photography in the Central Plains has disclosed another type of ring made by digging a circular trench and heaping the earth into a mound inside the ring. Each such circle seems to have had a central position at a village site, and each one has signs of breaks in the circle at just the spots where the sun's rays would fall at sunrise at the time of the equinoxes. Were they calendar rings? Some archeologists think so.

The U. P. Site

In 1960 Ivan Hayes was operating a dragline on the Union Pacific Railroad's right-of-way near Rawlins, Wyoming. In the muck, around the spring he was clearing, the dragline caught on some huge bones. Hayes reported this to Dr. George A. Agogino, at that time Professor of Anthropology at the University of Wyoming. Agogino quickly got money from the National Geographic Society. Then he persuaded Henry and Cynthia Irwin, a brother-sister team of archeologists, to bring their student crew from a dig elsewhere in Wyoming. Battling against mud and water, the excavators unearthed proof that hunters had butchered a mammoth at this spot. Its crushed skull indicated that they had probably killed it by hurling down rocks from the top of a bank above the stream where it had come to drink. Materials from the U.P. Mammoth Kill Site are in the Peabody Museum at Harvard University.

PICTOGRAPH CAVE STATE MONUMENT

From Billings drive southwest toward Hardin across an overpass, then turn right and follow directional signs about 7 miles to monument entrance. Open free, at all times. Camping nearby.

When this large cave was discovered in 1937 its most obvious features were the pictographs on its walls—designs and figures of men and animals painted in red, white, and black. Interesting though these were, material that was even more valuable to archeologists lay in the cave floor. When they dug down through 23 feet of earth and debris that had accumulated there, they uncovered evidence of at least three different periods of occupation.

The first visitors were hunters who took shelter in the cave perhaps 5,000 years ago. Among the projectile points they left, two seemed to belong to a much older period. Very likely the Pictograph Cave people had picked them up somewhere and decided to reuse them. The limited number of deer and migratory bison they managed to kill provided a rather meager living, and they relied partly on smaller animals. Still they had some leisure for carving out little pieces of bone to use in gambling games of some sort.

In the layers of debris above these early remains, archeologists found evidence of a much richer existence. Although people who lived farther east on the Plains had by now begun to do gardening, those who sheltered in the cave remained hunters. Their increased wealth apparently came from better hunting techniques. Possibly they had learned to use buffalo jumps, one of which was uncovered within the nearby city of Billings. Or they may have driven herds into corrals in narrow canyons. At any rate they now had spare time for

making ornaments, baskets, and later the paintings on the cave walls.

The upper layers of trash indicated the presence of hunters in late prehistoric times.

After Pictograph Cave had been excavated, a museum and trail for visitors were prepared. Unfortunately vandals damaged the museum and destroyed the parts of the cave that archeologists had left for future investigation. However, the pictographs remain in fair condition and are worth a visit.

Nebraska

FORT ROBINSON MUSEUM

Fort Robinson, 4 miles west of Crawford on US 20. Open free, 8 a.m. to 5 p.m., Monday through Saturday; 1 p.m. to 5 p.m., Sunday, May to Oct. 1. Camping.

As part of its interpretation of the story of man's occupation of the Plains, this museum has displays on the life of prehistoric Indians, with special attention to bison hunting.

UNIVERSITY OF NEBRASKA STATE MUSEUM

Morrill Hall, 14th St., on the city campus, Lincoln. Open free, 8 a.m. to 5 p.m., Monday through Saturday; 1:30 to 5 p.m., Sunday and holidays; closed Dec. 25, Jan. 1.

A

B

Like their prehistoric ancestors, Mandan Indians lived in round earthlodges along the Missouri River in North Dakota. A. When the artist George Catlin visited them in 1832 they allowed him to watch and sketch their ceremonies. From Catlin's Eight Years, *Vol. 1. B. Farming people in many parts of the world have sought to increase crops by sacrificing precious things to some god or spirit who, they thought, controlled fertility. Anxious for good crops, members of the Wolf Clan of the Pawnee tribe sacrificed a captured maiden every spring to Mars when it was the Morning Star. This diorama showing the sacrificial ceremony is in the Nebraska State Historical Society at Lincoln. Nebraska State Historical Society photo.*

Six of this museum's ten displays on Indians are devoted to archeology north of Mexico. A great deal of the material comes from important sites which the museum has excavated. One of these, the Lipscomb Site in Texas, seemed puzzling at first. There the skeletons of a dozen bison lay in a very small area, most of them facing in the same direction and actually overlapping each other. In among the bones were projectile points, scrapers, stone knives, and charcoal from fires. Had hunters managed to lay out their game so neatly? If so, why—and why the charcoal?

Probably, the archeologists decided, the Indians had simply been lucky enough to find the animals caught in a deep snowdrift, huddled together and headed away from the wind. After the kill, the hunters apparently built fires, made camp on the spot, took some of the meat, but left most of the carcasses as they had fallen.

A section from the Lipscomb Site, removed with a Folsom point in place among the bones, is on exhibit in the museum. Other Paleo-Indian material on display came from the Scottsbluff Bison Quarry in Nebraska, where a different type of projectile point appeared with bison bones, and from the Red Smoke and Allen sites, also in Nebraska.

At a much later time, about 2500 B.C., hunters began to camp on top of a high, isolated hill called Signal Butte, which stands tall above the surrounding valley of the North Platte River. They and their descendants stayed for a good many years—long enough to leave a layer of debris a foot thick. In it the museum's archeologists found hearths, the bones of animals people cooked and ate, tools, and the storage pits where they kept food for winter. After these earliest visitors left, wind covered the site with 18 inches of dust and sand before others began to camp there off and on until historic times.

North Dakota

The first six sites are largely undeveloped, pending the time when the State Legislature appropriates funds.

CROWLEY FLINT QUARRY SITE

From Eagle Nest on Interstate 94 drive north on county road. The quarry is 17 miles north of Hebron. Open free, at all times.

Prehistoric Indians from North Dakota and neighboring areas obtained flint at this quarry which is on the north side of the Knife River Valley. The site is administered by the State Historical Society.

DOUBLE DITCH HISTORIC SITE

From Bismarck drive north on US 83 to marker. Open free, at all times.

One of the largest Mandan villages in North Dakota once stood here on the east bank of the Missouri River. Apparently the site had been abandoned by 1804 when Lewis and Clark visited the area. The outlines of earthlodges, refuse heaps, and two moats, now dry, are clearly visible. A shelter has been constructed by the State His-

torical Society to protect maps, drawings, and a description of the site.

FORT CLARK HISTORIC SITE

From Interstate 94, just west of Bismarck, drive north on North Dakota 25 to Fort Clark. The site is just north of the post office. Open free, at all times.

A Mandan village was standing here when Fort Clark was built in 1829. The location of the village is clearly visible, and a small shelter constructed by the State Historical Society contains maps and a description of the area. The Mandans here all died in a smallpox epidemic in 1837. Arikara Indians occupied the site after that date.

HUFF INDIAN VILLAGE HISTORIC SITE

From Interstate 94 at Mandan drive south on County Road 1804 to Huff on the west bank of the Missouri River. The site is one mile south of Huff. Open free, at all times.

A marker describes the large Mandan village which once stood here. The rectangular outlines of individual house-sites are clearly visible, as is a dry moat. At one time, in addition to the moat, there was a protective palisade, along which ten bastions were built.

MENOKEN INDIAN VILLAGE HISTORIC SITE

From Menoken on Interstate 94 drive 1¼ miles north on county road. Open free, at all times.

A marker describes this former Mandan village which occupied 14 acres. House sites and a dry moat are clearly visible.

MOLANDER INDIAN VILLAGE HISTORIC SITE

From Interstate 94 at Mandan drive north on county road on the west bank of the Missouri River to Price. The site is 3 miles north of Price. Open free, at all times.

Here, clearly visible, are the remains of an earthlodge village which was once surrounded by a moat.

SLANT INDIAN VILLAGE

Fort Lincoln State Park. From Mandan drive 4½ miles south on North Dakota 6. Open 9 a.m. to 5 p.m., daily, May, Sept., Oct.; 9 a.m. to 9 p.m., daily, June, July, Aug. Admission: adults, 25¢; children 6 to 12, 10¢; under 6, free. Camping nearby.

Mandan Indians, who were living at this site about A.D. 1750, chose an unusual location for their houses. Instead of building on level ground, they placed their dwellings on a slope. Hence the name Slant Village. Five of the dwellings have been restored and are much like the circular earthlodges of late prehistoric times.

The Indian collection in the museum interprets the history of North Dakota tribes, with special attention to Mandan agriculture, hunting, home activities, and social life.

The Story. At some unknown date, perhaps a thousand years ago, people began to cultivate gardens around little communities along the Missouri River in central North Dakota. They grew sunflower, beans, squash, and a remarkable variety of corn. Ordinary corn is a plant that needs warm temperatures and a long growing season. Certainly that was the kind the Indians first tried to raise in this cool northern climate. They must have been disappointed and hungry very often before they managed to develop a new variety which ripened in only a little more than two months.

Perhaps it was the ancestors of the Mandans who became corn experts. At any rate, they were prosperous farmers when white traders first met them here and at other large neighboring villages. By 1837, as the result of a devastating epidemic of smallpox that spread to the villages from a passenger on a river boat, only a few Mandans remained.

STATE HISTORICAL SOCIETY MUSEUM

Liberty Memorial Bldg., Bismarck. Open free, 9 a.m. to 5 p.m., Monday through Friday; 9 a.m. to 4 p.m., Saturday; 1 p.m. to 5 p.m., Sunday, June through Aug.; closed holidays.

This museum has conducted excavations for many years, and its exhibits reflect its work. Among its activities has been salvage archeology aimed at saving valuable information before it was lost under rising water behind dams on the Missouri.

WRITING ROCK HISTORIC SITE

From the junction of US 85 and North Dakota 5, at Fortuna, drive southwest on county road to the site. Or from Grenora on North Dakota 50 drive north on county road. Open free, at all times.

Here the State Historical Society preserves a large glacial boulder on which are many Indian petroglyphs.

Oklahoma

CREEK INDIAN MUSEUM

On the Town Square, Okmulgee. Open free, 9 a.m. to 5 p.m., Monday through Saturday; 1 p.m. to 5 p.m., Sunday.

In the archeology room are displays of prehistoric artifacts of the Caddoan culture and material which was excavated from the Eufaula and Spiro mounds.

EAST CENTRAL MUSEUM

East Central College Library, Ada. Open free, 8 a.m. to 5 p.m., Monday through Friday; by appointment, Saturday and Sunday; closed national holidays.

Exhibits in this museum are devoted to Anasazi culture of the Southwest, the archeology of Texas and Arkansas, and six sites in Oklahoma, all dated at about 1,000 years ago. One display presents prehistoric carvings and a reproduction of a painted wall in a cave about six miles from Ada. Another identifies different types of projectile point from various parts of the United States, and gives the time periods during which they were

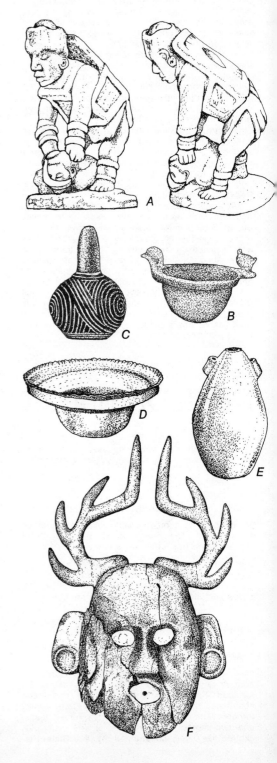

G

H

A. Front and side views of a tobacco pipe made of clay found at Spiro Mound in Oklahoma. The pipe represents a human sacrifice. After Hamilton. B, C, D, and E. Women in the Southeast made their pottery in many different shapes. C, D, and E are from Spiro Mound. Originals in the Stovall Museum, Norman, Oklahoma. F. Prehistoric people often used masks in ceremonies. In the Southeast many were carved from wood. This one from Spiro Mound is of red cedar, with shell inlays for eyes and mouth. Original in the Museum of the American Indian. G. Mississippian people made intricate carvings on pieces of conch shell. Found at Spiro Mound, this is in the Stovall Museum at the University of Oklahoma. H. A gorget, a neck ornament, has the weeping eye symbol which often appears in art of the Southeast. It was carved from conch shell and found at Spiro Mound. Original in the Museum of the American Indian.

Spiro Mound

On the bank of the Arkansas River near what is now Spiro, Oklahoma, a remarkable village stood in late prehistoric times. Its people followed the Mississippian lifeway and built temple mounds, eight in all. They were excellent craftsmen, particularly adept at carving intricate designs on conch shells, which came all the way from the Gulf of Mexico. Women fashioned beautiful pottery in a great variety of styles, and much of it was buried with the dead, together with other grave goods. The elaborately furnished Spiro burials were a rich storehouse of information about one way of living on this earth—until the day when a modern farmer's plough exposed the handiwork of an earlier farming people.

Soon a business operation began. Men formed a corporation and began literally to mine the mound using road scoops and dynamite. The miners sold great quantities of pottery, pearls, and other material, just as gold miners sold what they took out of the ground. Before long the mounds had been gutted, to the modest enrichment of the diggers and to the enormous impoverishment of science.

Slowly, painfully, Mr. and Mrs. Henry W. Hamilton, amateur archeologists, set about undoing what little of the damage could be undone. For 16 years they traced artifacts to their buyers and recovered them whenever possible. The result of this patient endeavor was a surprisingly large amount of material which revealed a culture akin to, but also distinct from, the cultures at Etowah in Georgia and Moundville in Alabama.

Thanks to the Hamiltons and to various scientific excavations that managed to glean data from part of the site not totally destroyed, it is now possible to get glimpses of Spiro culture in a number of museums, including these: Museum of Natural History of the Smithsonian Institution, Stovall Museum, University of Arkansas Museum, Oklahoma Historical Society Museum, Museum of the American Indian, Woolaroc Museum, Philbrook Art Center, Nebraska State Historical Society, and Creek Indian Museum.

used. There is also an exhibit showing how prehistoric Indians made artifacts of stone.

GILCREASE INSTITUTE

2500 W. Newton St., Tulsa. Open free, 10 a.m. to 5 p.m., Monday through Friday; 1 p.m. to 5 p.m., Saturday, Sunday, and holidays.

The Thomas Gilcrease Institute of American History and Art has in one gallery an extensive display of projectile points. These include Clovis, Folsom, Archaic (some Old Copper), Woodland, and Mississippian points. There are several examples of each type, labeled to give information about age and distribution. One display is devoted to harahay knives, a rather uncommon type with beveled edges. These have been found at some sites on the Great Plains, in western Arkansas, and northwest Louisiana.

An exhibit on bone pathology in prehistoric times shows how diseases among the Pecan Point people of Mississippi altered their bones and how head-flattening changed the shapes of their skulls.

Mississippian artifacts are displayed along with a burial removed in a block from the Banks Village Site near Clarksdale, Okla.—all material is dated about A.D. 1535.

From time to time the museum arranges special temporary exhibits which make simultaneous use of its extensive ethnological and archeological resources.

INDIAN CITY, U.S.A.

From Anadarko drive 2 miles south on Oklahoma 8. Open 9 a.m. to 6 p.m., summer; 9 a.m. to 5 p.m., winter. Admission: adults, $1.50; children, 75¢. Camping.

Here visitors may see reconstructions of various house types which were common in early historic and late prehistoric times. In a kind of large outdoor museum the living arrangements of the Navajo, Chiricahua Apache, Wichita, Kiowa, Caddo, Pawnee, and Pueblo Indians are brought to life. Many of the houses are furnished with typical tools, household equipment, toys, weapons, and musical instruments. A herd of buffalo graze in a pasture adjoining the Indian City grounds.

All buildings here were constructed under the supervision of the Department of Anthropology, University of Oklahoma. An Indian-owned corporation operates the enterprise, and Indians serve as guides.

MUSEUM OF THE GREAT PLAINS

In Elmer Thomas Park, off US 62 West, in Lawton. Open free, 10 a.m. to 5 p.m., Tuesday through Saturday; 2 p.m. to 5 p.m., Sunday; 7 p.m. to 10 p.m., Tuesday, Thursday; closed Jan. 1, Memorial Day, Thanksgiving, Dec. 25.

This museum offers exhibits of Paleo-Indian, Plains Archaic, and prehistoric Plains farmer materials. Some displays interpret the relationship between prehistoric peoples and the Plains environment. One diorama shows how women in a Wichita Indian village constructed a typical grass house. Another shows hunters who have trapped a mammoth. This is based on the museum's excavation of the Domebo (DUM-bo) Site in Oklahoma where a mammoth skeleton was recovered in association with artifacts.

A unique artifact on display is a naturally rounded ball of sandstone in which human features have been pecked. This crudely sculptured head was found near Frederick, Okla.; it may be very old. It was discovered more than 15 feet below the surface in a gravel bed, but unfortunately no datable material accompanied it, so archeologists can only speculate about its origin and age. Somewhat similar carvings, called the Malakoff Heads, are now in the Texas Memorial Museum, Austin, Texas.

NO MAN'S LAND HISTORICAL MUSEUM

Panhandle State College, on the campus, Goodwell. Open free, 1 p.m. to 5 p.m., Sunday through Friday, when college is in session.

Archeological exhibits include Oklahoma Basketmaker material and artifacts of the Plains area, from Folsom times up to the contact period.

OKLAHOMA HISTORICAL SOCIETY

Lincoln Blvd., Capitol Complex, Oklahoma City. Open free, 8 a.m. to 4:30 p.m., Monday through Friday; 8 a.m. to 6 p.m., Saturday; 1:30 p.m. to 4:30 p.m., Sunday.

In this historical museum are several archeological exhibits. One is devoted to materials excavated at the Spiro Mound in eastern Oklahoma. Others contain artifacts from the western Oklahoma Basketmaker culture, and from the Ozark Cave cultures in eastern Oklahoma.

PHILBROOK ART CENTER

2727 S. Rockford Rd., Tulsa. Open 10 a.m. to 5 p.m., Tuesday through Saturday; 1 p.m. to 5 p.m., Sunday; 7:30 p.m. to 9:30 p.m., Tuesday; closed legal holidays. Admission: adults, 25¢; children under 15, free.

Rich archeological and ethnological materials are intermingled in this museum, which has excellent collections of baskets and pottery. In addition to the exhibits of pots, which are mostly from the Southwest, there is one on pottery-making.

An entire gallery is devoted to ornaments, pipes, beads, and other material from the Spiro Mound on the eastern edge of Oklahoma. Although this mound was destroyed by commercialized mining for artifacts, careful scientific excavations produced significant information about the site. In its most flourishing period, the people who lived there were followers of the Southern, or Buzzard, Cult, which was widespread in the Southeast from about A.D. 1400 to A.D. 1700. In connection with this exhibit, a large map shows the distribution of mounds throughout the United States and Canada.

One exhibit is devoted to models of Southwestern prehistoric structures; another deals with craftsmanship in stone. Some of the artifacts displayed are easily recognizable as tobacco pipes or axes or spearpoints. Some resemble nothing utilitarian and are extraordinarily fanciful.

STOVALL MUSEUM

University of Oklahoma, on the campus, 1335 Asp Ave., Norman. Open free, 9 a.m. to 5 p.m., Monday through Friday; 1 p.m. to 5 p.m., Saturday, Sunday, holidays.

In this museum's extensive displays of prehistoric material, some sections are accompanied by photographs showing how excavation was done; others identify artifacts according to use.

A special exhibit gives clear explanations of the four basketmaking techniques—coiling, twining, wickerwork, and plaiting. With these is a display of finished baskets, showing their role in the household, in ceremonies, and for storage.

Other exhibits contain materials from various periods and cultures. Artifacts from sites along Fourche Maline Creek include atlatl weights, a reconstructed atlatl, bone hairpins, rings, and other ornaments. Two burials are shown as they appeared after excavation.

Some of the most interesting displays are devoted to Spiro Mound, notably the so-called Lucifer pipe made of polished red sandstone.

WOOLAROC MUSEUM (WOOL-ah-rock)

From Bartlesville drive 14 miles southwest on Oklahoma 123 to entrance to the Frank Phillips Ranch, then 2 miles on ranch road to the museum. Open free, 10 a.m. to 5 p.m., Tuesday through Sunday.

In addition to historic displays this museum tells the story of prehistoric man in America, particularly in Oklahoma. Included in the archeological exhibits are materials 3,000 years old representing the Oklahoma Basketmaker culture in the neighborhood of Kenton. Several cases contain artifacts from the Spiro Mound, from Washita culture sites in western Oklahoma, and from Hopewell culture sites in northeastern Oklahoma. Other exhibits contain materials from Alaska and from the vicinity of Phoenix, Ariz.

Special Interest. In rugged woodland adjoining the museum, herds of bison graze just as they did in prehistoric times.

Saskatchewan

BATTLEFORD NATIONAL HISTORIC PARK

E. 13th St., Battleford. Open free, 9 a.m. to 8 p.m., daily, June 16 to Labor Day; 10 a.m. to 5 p.m., Monday through Saturday; noon to 5 p.m., Sunday, for the balance of the season, May 1 to Oct. 31.

In addition to Cree and Sioux ethnological material, this museum displays some random local finds of prehistoric artifacts.

SASKATCHEWAN MUSEUM OF NATURAL HISTORY

Wascana Park, College Ave. and Albert St., Regina. Open free, 9 a.m. to 9 p.m., daily, May through Sept., 9 a.m. to 5 p.m., Monday through Friday; 2 p.m. to 6 p.m., Saturday, Sunday, holidays, Oct. through April.

Here in the Hall of Man are ten cases devoted to prehistory in Saskatchewan. In addition to random local finds, there is considerable material from excavations conducted by the museum staff. Exhibits include artifacts from various periods and cultures from Paleo-Indian to historic times. Special displays are devoted to a reconstruction of an Indian burial, to hunting, and to religion, ceremonies, and customs.

South Dakota

BADLANDS NATIONAL MONUMENT

From Rapid City drive 70 miles southeast on Interstate 90, then 9 miles south on US 16A to Visitor Center. Or from Kadoka drive 18 miles west on Interstate 90 to US 16A, then 9 miles south to Visitor Center. The Visitor Center is open free, 7:30 a.m. to 8 p.m., daily, early June through Labor Day; 8 a.m. to 5 p.m., daily, Labor Day to early June. Camping.

In the course of trying to stamp out a religious movement known as the Ghost Dance, which was spreading among Plains Indians, a unit of the U.S. Army arrested more than 250 Sioux three days after Christmas in 1890. All night these people, two-thirds of whom were women and children, camped at Wounded Knee Creek in South Dakota, surrounded by 500 soldiers. In the morning the soldiers disarmed the Sioux men and then proceeded to shoot indiscriminately, using rapid-fire guns. Almost all the unarmed captives were killed on the spot, but a few women escaped and ran for several miles before soldiers overtook and shot them. This was the massacre of Wounded Knee, and one of the two Indian exhibits in the Visitor Center here is devoted to it. The other exhibit traces Indian life in the Badlands from 10,000 years ago through the Woodland culture of about A.D. 500, the Village Indians of about A.D. 1500, and the Sioux of A.D. 1800.

CROW CREEK VILLAGE

From Chamberlain drive 15 miles north on South Dakota 47. Open free, at all times. Camping nearby.

A marker on the highway calls attention to this village site, one of the few large prehistoric sites in the region which has not been covered by water impounded behind new dams on the Missouri River. It is possible to walk over the village area and see evidence of a defensive ditch which once surrounded it.

Although open to the public, the site is not yet protected, and visitors are earnestly urged not to do any souvenir hunting.

OVER DAKOTA MUSEUM

University of South Dakota, Clark and Yale streets, Vermillion. Open free, 10 a.m. to 4:45 p.m., Monday through Friday; 10 a.m. to noon, 2 p.m. to 4:30 p.m., Saturday; 2 p.m. to 4:30 p.m., Sunday.

In the W. H. Over Dakota Museum exhibits devoted to material culture emphasize the development of implements and their uses from Paleo times to the historic period. Following the Big-Game Hunters and the Archaic Foragers, people in this part of South Dakota began to build large rectangular houses in groups of 25 or more along terraces above streams. They certainly did some hunting, for they left implements made of buffalo bone. And they must have done gardening, because one of their implements was the hoe made from the shoulder blade of the buffalo.

These people, whose lifeway is called the Over focus, resembled the Plains Indians in many ways. But their pottery and their tobacco pipes were more characteristic of groups who lived to the east in Wisconsin. Some archeologists think they may have been ancestors of Mandan Indians who stopped here on their way westward.

Other exhibits are devoted to a much later people who also combined elements of two cultures. Their lifeway, called Coalescent, was studied at the Scalp Creek Site. A diorama of the Scalp Creek village shows round earthlodges surrounded by a stockade and a ditch.

Other dioramas show a mound of the Woodland Period and Mandan and Arikara earthlodges. There are also several maps showing the locations of important archeological sites.

SHERMAN PARK INDIAN BURIAL MOUNDS

Sherman Park, West 22nd St. and Kiwanis Ave., Sioux Falls. Open free, at all times. Camping nearby.

In this municipal park are several mounds built by people who followed the Plains Woodland lifeway, 1,600 years ago. One mound has been excavated by the W. H. Over Dakota Museum of the University of South Dakota. Material recovered by the dig, including artifacts and the skulls and large bones of four people, is at the museum in Vermillion.

SOUTH DAKOTA STATE HISTORICAL MUSEUM

Soldiers Memorial Bldg., Pierre. Open free, 8 a.m., to 5 p.m., Monday through Friday; 10 a.m. to 5 p.m., Saturday; 1 p.m. to 5 p.m., Sunday.

After current renovation is completed, this museum will have exhibits showing two different Middle Missouri earthlodge village sites that have been excavated by archeologists in cooperation with the River Basin Salvage Archeological Program. Also there will be exhibits covering the entire range of South Dakota prehistory from Paleo through Forager (Archaic) and Woodland times up to the period of contact with Europeans.

WIND CAVE NATIONAL PARK

From Hot Springs drive 13 miles north on US 385. Or from Custer drive 19 miles south on US 385. Open free, 8 a.m. to 5 p.m., daily, May to Sept. Camping.

One exhibit case here includes Arikara and Mandan pottery and projectile points. There are also a few random finds of points and other artifacts from earlier periods.

Texas

ALIBATES FLINT QUARRIES AND TEXAS PANHANDLE PUEBLO CULTURE NATIONAL MONUMENT (AL-ah-bates)

Near Sanford Recreation Area, Sanford.

Although this site has not been formally opened to the public, visits may be arranged by making reservations for a guided tour along a one-mile trail (which includes one very steep hill). Tours begin at 9:30 a.m. every Saturday and Sunday and end at noon. Requests for reservations must be received at least five days before the tour date. Write to Superintendent, Sanford Recreation Area, Sanford,

Henry Hertner (at left), an amateur archeologist, led the campaign to have the Alibates Flint Quarry made into a National Monument. In this area prehistoric Indians made projectile points, knives, and scrapers from multicolored flint that they found there in large deposits. The quarry and a nearby prehistoric masonry pueblo may be seen by arrangement with the superintendent of the monument. Texas Highway Department photo.

Tex. 79078, giving date and number of persons in the party.

When the entire new national monument is open, it will make available to visitors a large area which was used by prehistoric man over a long period and in two very different ways.

The word "Alibates" is supposedly derived from the name of Allen Bates, son of an early ranch foreman in the area.

The Story. Here, above the Canadian River, Paleo-Indians found a large outcrop of excellent stone—a varicolored flint which has an easily recognized marbled appearance. At least 12,000 years ago men began to quarry it for use in making projectile points, knives, and the scrapers with which they removed hair and tissue from hides. Many Clovis points used for hunting mammoths in New Mexico were made of Alibates flint. It remained popular with Paleo-Indians who lived in the Texas Panhandle up to 7,000 years ago. It was also sought by people who followed the Archaic lifeway at a later time. Hunters of the Woodland Period obtained flint at the quarries, and they left evidence of their presence nearby.

About A.D. 900, farming people settled near the flint outcrop. They built a village, somewhat like the villages of the Pueblo Indians of New Mexico, but they made their houses of a material that was different. Instead of using sandstone, they built with limestone and adobe. Their dwellings were well suited to the area, insulated against cold in winter and against heat in summer. These farmers combined raising crops with mining flint, and the flint was exchanged, sometimes over great distances, for such things as pottery, baskets, obsidian, catlinite, olivella shell beads, and turquoise.

Estimates of the extent of the mining are astonishing. The Panhandle Pueblo people apparently dug out thousands of tons of flint. Their quarries extended for about a mile and were nearly 400 feet wide. More than 500 pits are visible.

Alibates flint continued to be sought by Indians of the Plains. Even in historic times they made it into weapons whenever they could not get metal.

EL PASO CENTENNIAL MUSEUM

The University of Texas at El Paso, on the campus, University Ave. and Wiggins Rd. Open free, 10 a.m. to 5 p.m., Monday through Friday; 1 p.m. to 5 p.m., Saturday, Sunday.

Exhibits emphasize prehistoric cultures of the El Paso area, including material from caves in the nearby Hueco Mountains. Other displays are devoted to the Mogollon culture and to pottery and ornaments from the Casas Grandes area of northwestern Mexico. A diorama shows prehistoric Pueblo life near El Paso.

FORT WORTH MUSEUM OF SCIENCE AND HISTORY

1501 Montgomery St., Fort Worth. Open free 9 a.m. to 5 p.m., Monday through Saturday; 2 p.m. to 5 p.m., Sunday; closed Jan. 1, July 4, Labor Day, Thanksgiving, afternoon Dec. 24, Dec. 25.

In addition to ethnographic exhibits on numerous Indian tribes in many parts of North America, the Hall of Man contains much archeological material. Special emphasis is given to prehistoric life in Texas, beginning with Paleo-Indian times. Dioramas show the manufacture and use of a number of

prehistoric implements and artifacts, such as the atlatl and pottery. Some show daily activities of cliff dwellers and other peoples.

Additional archeological material is exhibited in the historical sections of the Hall of Medical Science.

LUBBOCK RESERVOIR SITE

North of Clovis Rd., off Loop 289 in Yellow House Canyon and Comanche Park which is being developed near Lubbock. For information about the date of opening of the park inquire at Texas Tech University Museum in Lubbock.

The University Museum reports that it has found evidence at this site of very early human activity. Buried under deep layers of earth were spear-points and the fossil bones of extinct animals, indicating visits by Paleo hunters. Visits by later people continued at intervals thereafter.

PANHANDLE-PLAINS HISTORICAL MUSEUM

2401 Fourth Ave., Canyon. Open free, 9 a.m. to 5 p.m., Monday through Saturday; 2 p.m. to 6 p.m., Sunday; closed Dec. 25.

In addition to a large collection of Comanche and Kiowa ethnological material, this museum displays random local finds and artifacts excavated by the Works Progress Administration in the 1930s. In the archeological exhibits are Clovis, Folsom, and Plainview projectile points used by hunters in the Paleo Period, also Archaic materials and artifacts of the Panhandle culture from the South Canadian River, dated about A.D. 1300 to A.D. 1540.

One display explains how Indians made tools of flint. Another shows what archeologists can learn from pottery.

STRECKER MUSEUM

Baylor University, West Basement, Sid Richardson Science Building, on the campus, Waco. Open free, 9 a.m. to noon, 2 p.m. to 5 p.m., Monday through Friday; and by appointment.

In addition to random finds of prehistoric artifacts from central Texas, this museum displays materials from a Bell County rockshelter of about A.D. 1000 and a basket burial of about A.D. 700 from Reeves County.

SUL ROSS UNIVERSITY MUSEUM OF THE BIG BEND

On the campus, Alpine. Open, 1 p.m. to 5 p.m., Tuesday through Friday; 1 p.m. to 6 p.m., Saturday; 2 p.m. to 6 p.m., Sunday. Admission: adults, 25¢; children under 12, 15¢.

The prehistoric materials here are mainly from the Texas-Oklahoma Basketmaker culture. There are also Apache and Comanche materials, some of which may be prehistoric.

TEXAS MEMORIAL MUSEUM, UNIVERSITY OF TEXAS

Trinity and 24th streets, Austin. Open free, 9 a.m. to 5 p.m., Monday through Saturday; 2 p.m. to 5 p.m., Sunday; closed national holidays.

This large museum has many archeological exhibits of several different kinds. Dioramas show a central Texas flint quarry, Archaic life, and Bonfire Shelter, which was the site of a bison jump. Technological exhibits demonstrate flint chipping and the manufacture of pottery and baskets. Other exhibits introduce North American archeology as a whole or concentrate on specific subjects such as the Paleo, Archaic, and later periods. A cross-section of an Archaic midden appears in one exhibit; in another, Archaic points are identified. A display is devoted to influences that came into Texas from the Southwest. Another shows Caddoan cultural stages.

Special exhibits are based on these sites: Blackwater Draw in New Mexico; the Kincaid Shelter, a stratified site; the Malakoff Site, where carved stone heads were found.

Of particular interest is material from the Plainview Site in Texas. Here archeologists found the skeletons of about a hundred giant bison—a type now extinct. With them were 18 points, which resembled Clovis points except that they did not have a flute or groove down the center. Apparently the bison had become mired at a waterhole or stream crossing where hunters found and dispatched a good many of them with their stone-tipped weapons. Later this same type of projectile point was found elsewhere on the Plains, as far away as the Dakotas, and it took its place as an indication that Paleo-Indians had passed that way.

TEXAS TECH UNIVERSITY MUSEUM

Indiana Ave. and 4th St., Lubbock. Open free, 9 a.m. to 5 p.m., Monday through Saturday; 2 p.m. to 5 p.m., Sundays and holidays; closed Dec. 25.

Exhibits in the Hall of Earth and Man are devoted to two Archaic cultures—Trans-Pecos and Edwards Plateau. There are also exhibits and dioramas based on the Lubbock Reservoir Site, which is maintained by the museum.

Wyoming

BUFFALO BILL MUSEUM
AND PLAINS INDIAN MUSEUM

836 Sheridan Ave., Cody. Open 7 a.m. to 10 p.m., June through Aug.; 8 a.m. to 5 p.m., May, Sept. Admission: adults, $1; children, 50¢.

The lower floor of the new addition to this museum is devoted to Plains Indians. One wing of the addition contains prehistoric artifacts and the dessicated body of an adult male (Mummy Joe) found in a cave about 35 miles west of Cody.

GATCHELL MEMORIAL MUSEUM

10 Fort St., Buffalo. Open free, 9 a.m. to 9 p.m., June 1 to Labor Day; closed July 4.

In addition to random local finds the Jim Gatchell Museum displays prehistoric artifacts recovered in a dig conducted by the University of Wyoming at a buffalo jump nearby.

MAMMOTH VISITOR CENTER,
YELLOWSTONE NATIONAL PARK

From the north entrance to the park on US 89, drive south to Mammoth Hot Springs. Open free, 8 a.m. to 7 p.m., mid-June to Labor Day; 8 a.m. to 5 p.m., May 1 to mid-June and Labor Day to Oct. 31. Camping.

Five exhibits in the Visitor Center contain material about Indians in the park. One has a map and other information about the Bannock Indian Trail. Others contain material on the Blackfeet, Crow, and Sheepeater Indians who lived in the area in historic times. One exhibit concentrates on prehistoric art work and artifacts collected in the park.

OBSIDIAN CLIFF

In Yellowstone National Park. From Mammoth Hot Springs drive about 12 miles south toward Norris. Park gates open 7 a.m. to 11 p.m., May through Oct. Admission: day pass, $1 per car. Camping nearby.

East of the road may be seen a dark mass of stone known to pioneer explorers as Glass Mountain. It is quite literally that—a mountain of volcanic glass, or obsidian.

Prehistoric hunters made projectile points and knives of obsidian, which can be chipped to an edge as sharp as steel. However, sources of the material are rather rare, and early archeologists were puzzled when many obsidian artifacts turned up in the burial mounds of Ohio and Illinois. Was it possible that men had brought the volcanic glass all the way from Yellowstone? It was. One of the trails they followed to the quarry at Obsidian Cliff was worn so deep into the earth that it could still be seen in historic times.

Few present-day archeologists have doubted that Indians carried on trade and traveled great distances for things they wanted. Nevertheless, James B. Griffin of the University of Michigan decided to test various obsidian samples by a process called neutron activation. Working with members of the university's chemistry department, he has proved that Obsidian Cliff and two less well-known places in Yellowstone are indeed the sources of obsidian used in many artifacts found at midwestern sites.

WYOMING STATE MUSEUM

State Office Bldg., 23rd and Central avenues, Cheyenne. Open free, 9 a.m. to 5 p.m., Monday through Saturday, noon to 5 p.m., Sunday, summer; 9 a.m. to 5 p.m., Monday through Friday, noon to 5 p.m., Sunday, winter.

This museum, which is in the process of renovation, displays random local finds and also has exhibits which deal with the nature of the science of archeology, both prehistoric and historic. New exhibits will be devoted to prehistoric chronology from Paleo times to the arrival of Europeans. These additions to the displays will be made from materials recovered during scientifically conducted excavations.

Tree-Ring Dating

Trees grow by adding layers of wood outside the layers that are already there. Some trees add a layer each year, and in years that are wet during the growing season, the layers are thick. In dry years they are thin. Over areas where weather conditions are uniform, all trees that are weather-sensitive in this way tend to have the same pattern of thick and thin rings. By matching the ring pattern in a living tree with the ring pattern in a tree that was felled some time ago, it is often possible to tell the exact year in which the dead tree was cut.

Working backward from living trees, scientists have found a pattern of tree-ring growth in much of the Southwest that prevailed for more than 2,000 years. They have made a master chart showing patterns of clusters of thick rings and thin rings. These patterns are called signatures, and each tree-ring signature differs from every other just as each handwritten signature differs from every other. By comparing the pattern of growth rings in a tree with the master chart it is possible to determine the exact years during which the tree was alive. In this way you can find out the exact year when the tree died or was cut down.

If the tree was used as a beam in a room, you can be sure it was not used before it was cut down. You have the beginning of a date for the room. If you find other beams in the same room all with the same date, you can be fairly sure when the roof was put on the building. If you find charcoal in the fireplace of the building that gives the same date as the roof beams, you can be reasonably sure that the building was finished and used in about the year given by the tree rings in the beams. This also means that you have some idea about the date of artifacts found in the room. The entire contents of the room were not likely to have been placed there before the room was built.

Tree ring dating is also called dendrochronology.

Stratigraphy

When people live in the same place a long time, the rubbish they throw away piles up. The oldest garbage is at the bottom of the pile. The newest at the top.

When people change their fashions, or adopt new foods, or take up the use of new implements, there is a change in what they throw away.

Layers may form in a trash pile, easily distinguished from each other by the differences in objects they contain. Layers may form, too, when dust or silt covers a trash heap and clearly separates old trash that lies below the dust or silt from newer trash above it.

When layers form for any reason, they are called strata. Those deposits in which there are strata are said to be stratified, and the study of strata is called stratigraphy. With the help of stratigraphy, archeologists can often tell a great deal about the sequence of events in prehistory.

THE SOUTHEAST

 At the end of the Ice Age Indians wandered eastward as well as westward from the Plains, following the trails of big game. By 8000 B.C. (possibly earlier) these Paleo hunters had appeared east of the Mississippi River and south of the Ohio. Perhaps they crossed the great water barriers on the ice in winter or perhaps they had watercraft made of logs or of skins stretched around a framework of branches. No one knows how they reached the Southeast, but there is evidence that early Americans were not limited to land in their travels. Paleo-Indian artifacts 7,000 years old have been found on islands in the Caribbean Sea, obviously left there by people who had watercraft, although no vestiges of their boats or rafts have been found.

Paleo-Indian Period

No glaciers ever reached into the Southeast, but there was heavy rainfall which nourished a dense forest cover. In the shady woods mastodons could find enough to eat, for they were browsers living on twigs and leaves. In open, unshaded areas there was grass for mammoths. Both animals must have been game for Paleo-Indians in the Southeast. Although unmistakable proof of this has not yet been found, collectors have picked up innumerable projectile points of the kind that the Big-Game Hunters alone used. Indeed, the concentration of fluted points of the Clovis type is greater at certain places in the Southeast than it is anywhere in the Southwest.

Archaic Period

After the big game disappeared, descendants of Paleo-Indians gradually had to make adjustments to a changing climate and to many new environments. At first hunters of the next —the Archaic—stage faced their changing world with no better equipment than that of their ancestors. In time, however, they elaborated new tools and new ways of getting nourishment in a land no longer rich in the huge animals that had brought such great rewards for a single kill. Sometime between 6000 B.C. and 4000 B.C. knowledge became widespread that mollusks could be harvested. People who camped often or long on the same site near rivers began to eat freshwater clams and mussels, and here the change in climate played a special role. Rainfall was decreasing. As a result, rivers dwindled and grew

The debris in Russell Cave, Alabama, contained so many nutshells that archeologists think the cave was not a year-round shelter but was visited mainly in fall when nuts would be ripe.

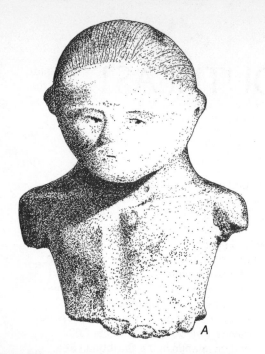

A

B

A. Prehistoric people in the Macon, Georgia, area modeled this head as part of a pottery vessel. Original in the museum, Ocmulgee National Monument, Macon. B. This ceremonial earthlodge at Ocmulgee National Monument has been reconstructed over the original clay floor. National Park Service photo. C. Interior view of the earthlodge at the Ocmulgee National Monument. The raised platform, shaped like an eagle or a buzzard, has three places where dignitaries sat during ceremonies or councils. The floor is of a special type of clay. National Park Service photo.

C

sluggish, and in the shallow, slow-moving waters shellfish were easy to gather. Since it took a great many mollusks to feed a family, the piles of discarded shells grew higher and higher as long as the weather remained warm and dry. But when rainfall increased again, streams grew deeper and their currents sped up. It was more difficult now to pick shellfish off the bottom. People turned to other food sources, and the inland shell mounds ceased to grow.

Along the coasts of the Atlantic Ocean and the Gulf of Mexico the harvest of saltwater mollusks continued uninterrupted. There the shell mounds kept increasing in size right into historic times. Their extent in some places is monumental. Even though centuries of habitation contributed to their growth, it is hard to believe that so many oysters and clams could have been consumed.

This is not to say that all Archaic people concentrated on shellfish. They didn't. Many were meat-eaters, hunters of deer and smaller game, who supplemented their diet with nuts, roots, and seeds. They, too, left debris where they camped, and many a hummock in a modern farmer's field has turned out to be a mound of Archaic garbage partially converted into soil.

The Eastern Archaic hunters differed from Paleo-Indians in their social relationships. Big-Game Hunters probably worked together in groups as they pursued large animals. But men who lived in wooded areas found it more efficient to search as individuals for their smaller quarry. For them hunting was a solitary, not a collective, enterprise. So, too, was a good deal of the foraging that went on. Large-scale cooperation was not required for harvesting nuts, seeds, and roots. Moreover, these were usually not abundant enough to support a large band that remained long in one place.

An exception was the shellfish eaters. During at least part of each year, they could live in larger groups than had ever been possible in the past. But at certain seasons many of them seem to have dispersed as they turned away from mollusks and sought other foods.

Life changed in many ways in the Archaic Period. There was a general, very intensive search for new things to eat. At the same time there was an increase in the number and variety of implements used to gather and process the new foods. For example, Archaic people harvested hard-shelled seeds, for which they needed crushing tools. To make nutcrackers they first pecked several small depressions in a stone. Nuts fixed in these depressions could then be easily cracked by a blow from a hammerstone. Grinding stones and mortars and pestles came into use for pulverizing small seeds. In pots carved from steatite (soapstone) tough seeds could be cooked to a soft mush.

Still further specialization marked the end of this stage. The old simple and rather fluid ways of the hunter began to disappear. Instead of depending entirely on what grew naturally, men created a new source of food by planting gardens. Larger groups could now live together, for part of the year at least, in semi-permanent villages. In some places women began to make a crude sort of pottery from clay that was mixed with grass or moss and then baked in a fire. (This was called fiber-tempered pottery.)

With the arrival of squash, beans, and corn from Mexico there was a large jump in available calories. Population increased. So did the activities and responsibilities that men invented for themselves. As settled communities developed, some individuals could now spend a good deal of time in pursuits other than food-getting, and many of the activities they chose centered around burials and burial ceremonies.

At the same time women had more leisure for making pottery in better and more beautiful forms than before. Good pottery vessels, in turn, increased the available food by providing better means of storing it. They also made cooking easier and so brought a more varied diet. The quality of life changed.

Woodland Period

With the appearance of pottery and of true agriculture, not just gardening, there began what is known as the Woodland Stage. Within this widespread general cultural pattern, some interesting developments came to many parts of the Southeast. One was the custom of building earthen mounds over the bodies, the bones, or the remains from cremations of the dead.

At first, during Early Woodland times, burial mounds in the Southeast were small and conical in shape. They were heaped up by the thousand, often a little way outside villages, wherever people dwelt along rivers, large streams, or the ridges of hills. As time passed, mound construction grew more complex. First a low platform was built, in preparation for a mass funeral. After bodies were placed on it, they were covered with earth. Later burials might be made in the mound and more layers added, until the structure rose as much as 20 feet.

The burial-mound idea seems to have spread to the Southeast from Illinois and Ohio, where it had already become very important in the lives of people who followed a lifeway called Hopewellian. For mortuary offerings, which they placed in graves, these people required a great deal of material obtainable only in distant places—shells from the seacoast, for example. Perhaps the Hopewellians made long journeys for the shells, or they may have got them by trade. In either event, information about their religious customs traveled along the routes that led to the source of the shells. And where the burial-mound cult spread, so, too, did its trappings—elaborate ornaments, tobacco pipes, tools and weapons of polished stone, ornaments of mica, and specially made mortuary vessels.

The intense activity of burial-mound rituals finally began to wear out in one place, then in another. But as this stage was ending another had already begun.

The Mississippian Period

Religious and ceremonial practices in much of the Southeast now centered around a new kind of mound. Probably inspired by ideas from Mexico, people constructed large, flat-topped, earthen pyramids which served as platforms for temples—buildings with thatched roofs on which effigies of birds were sometimes perched. Since the temple-mound idea took form and then spread out vigorously from places along the Mississippi

B

A

C

River, the cultural developments that went with it have been called Mississippian.

Men who followed the Mississippian lifeway became expert farmers and organizers. Population grew tremendously around ceremonial centers, and huge pyramids were built by people who moved vast quantities of earth in baskets. Sometimes 20 or more large mounds marked a great ceremonial site. Arts and crafts flourished as the Mississippian cultures reached a climax.

In some areas temple-mound building became associated with a complex of human activities called the Southern Cult. This final development in ceremonial and religious practices was quite possibly stimulated by the arrival of new notions from Mexico. It has also been called the Southern Death Cult or the Buzzard Cult, and with good reason. Those who practiced it were preoccupied with death.

A great proliferation of grave goods accompanied the spread of the cult, and many of the new artifacts were both elaborate and most skillfully made. Native copper was hammered into ornate headdresses, plaques, ear spools, and celts (a kind of axe). Craftsmen engraved

intricate symbolic designs on shell, which was imported from the Gulf Coast. Sculptors shaped stone into excellent likenesses of people and animals. They also carved and polished stone axes complete with stone handles. Such monolithic axes were useless for real work but obviously important for some ceremonial purpose. Symbols abounded—among them skulls, bones, an eye in the palm of a hand. An eye that wept appeared everywhere in engravings and on pottery. So, too, did spiders and warriors with wings. Workers in flint created graceful fantasies in this intractable material—ceremonial knives adorned with crescents and curlicues.

Human sacrifice was illustrated in various ways on artifacts, and it obviously was practiced in this death-centered culture. Pottery appeared in a great variety of nonutilitarian forms made only for burial with the dead. Exuberant life was expressed in many ways—all celebrating the negation of life. The Death Cult seemed to be imaginative about preparing for its own death, and die it did.

With a dramatic suddenness that still baffles investigators, the building of earthen pyramids ceased, and the lifeway

D

F

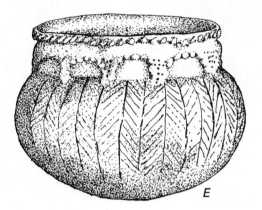

E

A. Diorama of an Indian ceremony at Ocmulgee National Monument. National Park Service photo by Jack E. Boucher. B. Indians who followed the Mississippian lifeway pecked these designs on a rock in Alabama. Frank Jones and Spencer Waters photo; courtesy Campbell Grant. C. This pottery bottle is from Moundsville State Monument, Alabama. Original in the Museum of the American Indian. D. Mound building took many forms in the Southeast. Rock Eagle Effigy Mound near Eatonton, Georgia, can be seen in its entirety from the top of a tower which has been built for the convenience of visitors. The effigy is made up of thousands of white quartz rocks. E. Another type of pottery made by Mississippian people. Original in the University of Mississippi Museum. F. These figurines, each two feet high and carved from marble, were found at Etowah Mounds Archeological Area, Cartersville, Georgia, and are on display there. They may be portraits of the man and woman with whom they were buried.

associated with them vanished. Various theories have been put forward to explain what happened. Perhaps some great prehistoric epidemic sapped the vitality of the people. (This disease theory still lacks supporting evidence.) Perhaps the shock of the European invasion spread panic and sealed the fate of the culture which was already in decline. Certainly the presence of Spanish troops under De Soto was disastrous to large numbers of Indian people in the Southeast. When De Soto arrived in 1539, some mound-building was still going on, but little if any was done after his men withdrew at the end of their vain search for loot—a search which led them from Florida to Georgia, then all the way west into Arkansas. Not only did the Europeans disrupt Indian life by killing and enslaving great numbers of people, they were also an enormous drain on food resources. Wherever the Spanish army went, the Indian economy had to provide food for 700 soldiers, for a large number of slaves, for 200 horses, and for hogs that ate corn and multiplied much faster than the Spanish butchered them.

The invaders also brought with them

diseases to which the Indians had not developed any immunity, and as a result the population suddenly began to dwindle. If there was still vitality in the customs and beliefs that encouraged men to build temple mounds and to pursue the ecstasies of the Death Cult, that vitality was now gone.

Historic Indian tribes lived on in the vicinity of the mounds, which soon became as ancient and mysterious to them as to the Europeans who were overwhelming the land. It is these huge earthen structures that make up most of the archeological sites now open to the public in the Southeast.

Some of the historic Indian tribes in the Southeast were surely descendants of the people who once engaged in the prodigious labor of piling up mounds. However, proof is usually lacking that a particular tribe is related to the builders of mounds near which it lived. On the other hand, scientific excavation has been able to disprove one myth: There was no mysterious vanished race of Mound Builders. These cultures developed out of earlier Indian cultures in eastern North America and also in Mexico.

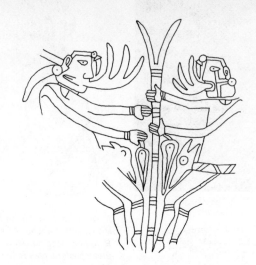

One element of the busk ceremony is shown in this design, which was engraved on a conch shell. It was found at Spiro Mound, Oklahoma. Original in the Museum of the American Indian in New York City.

Busk

For many eastern Indians in historic times the most important ceremony of the year was the summer corn festival. Among the Creeks, who may be directly descended from one group of temple mound builders, the ceremony was called the "pushkita." English-speaking people shortened this word to "busk."

Apparently some of the ideas for the busk came from Mexico where temple mounds originated. The ceremony, a kind of New Year celebration, took place when corn first ripened. People put out all fires and engaged in various rites which were supposed to purify. They drank the Black Drink, took ceremonial baths, then, as a sign that they had rid themselves of evil, they started new fires. Boys who had reached puberty took new names during the busk and were henceforth regarded as men. The ceremonies lasted for eight days and ended with dancing.

Model Archeology Program

Anyone who wants to watch a dig—or to do volunteer work in one—may be able to do so in Arkansas.

Arkansas has what is perhaps the best archeology program in any state or province north of Mexico. The Arkansas Archeological Survey employs a staff of full-time archeologists, with one of them attached to each state-supported college and university. This network is salvaging a great deal of valuable information that would otherwise be lost as grading machines turn scores of thousands of acres of land into absolutely level fields. Any farmer or amateur archeologist who finds material that may be of scientific interest can phone the nearest college, and an expert will normally be out to investigate within two hours. In addition, of course, the Archeological Survey team gathers information from places where roads are being made or foundations dug or artifacts discovered by amateurs.

If a dig is visitable, Dr. Charles R. McGimsey III, Director of the Arkansas Archeological Survey, at the University of Arkansas Museum, Fayetteville, can send you to it. Or call the office of the Archeological Survey in any of the other state institutions of higher learning for the necessary information.

Alabama

ALABAMA DEPARTMENT OF ARCHIVES AND HISTORY

624 Washington St., Montgomery. Open free, 8 a.m. to 4:30 p.m., Monday through Friday; 8 a.m. to 11:30 a.m., 12:30 p.m. to 4:30 p.m., Saturday, Sunday, and state holidays. Closed Jan. 1, Dec. 25.

In the State of Alabama Department of Archives and History are random local archeological finds, reflecting the culture of one or another of the tribes in the Creek Indian Confederacy. Displays are not primarily interpretive, and are exhibited with Choctaw, Chickasaw, and Seminole ethnological materials.

Special Interest. Some artifacts on exhibit were collected by a man who accompanied John James Audubon on a trip through the West.

ALABAMA MUSEUM OF NATURAL HISTORY

University of Alabama campus, Tuscaloosa. Open free, 8 a.m. to 5 p.m., daily, when the university is in session; closed Dec. 25.

Displayed here are artifacts from the important Moundville Site, which was excavated by the University of Alabama. The museum also contains materials from other sites that the university excavated and from many other areas throughout the Americas. There is particular emphasis on interpreting the archeology of Alabama.

Special Interest. Using prehistoric artifacts from the museum, Mr. David de Jarnette, Curator of Anthropology, has arranged a traveling exhibit which traces Indian life in Alabama from Paleo times, before 8000 B.C., through all the major cultural developments, including the historic period. Information about the schedule of this exhibit may be obtained from the museum.

BIRMINGHAM MUSEUM OF ART

2000 Eighth Ave. N., Birmingham. Open free, 10 a.m. to 5 p.m., Monday through Saturday; 5 p.m. to 9 p.m., Thursday; 2 p.m. to 6 p.m., Sunday. Closed Dec 25.

On exhibit here is material which illuminates the lifeway of people who lived, as did the inhabitants of Moundville, between A.D. 1200 and A.D. 1500.

MONTGOMERY MUSEUM OF FINE ARTS

440 S. McDonough St., Montgomery. Open free, 10 a.m. to 5 p.m., Tuesday through Saturday; 2:30 p.m. to 5 p.m., Sunday; closed Jan. 1, July 4, Labor Day, Thanksgiving, Dec. 25, and the last two weeks in Aug.

Exhibits emphasizing Alabama archeology are arranged in chronological order, beginning with the Archaic Period. In addition there are two restored burials—one with a dog, another illustrating how an archeologist excavates a skeleton and the grave goods associated with it. A display of stone tools shows how they were made, and an exhibit of pottery tells how to identify important types. Several exhibits show materials recovered from specific local sites and make clear what was recovered from each of the excavations involved.

MOUND STATE MONUMENT

National Historic Landmark.
From Tuscaloosa drive 17 miles south on Alabama 69 to the monument at Moundville. Open 9 a.m. to 5 p.m., daily, all year; closed Dec. 25. Admission: adults, $1; children, 50¢. Camping allowed, but no prepared areas.

This combination archeological site and museum is a division of the University of Alabama Museums. The museum building is constructed over two actual excavations. Artifacts from these and other digs in the area illustrate the cultural traits and physical characteristics of the prehistoric people who lived here. On top of the principal mound in the monument is a restoration of a temple which includes a life-sized exhibit of a ceremony of the kind that once went on there.

The Story. Between the years A.D. 1200 and A.D. 1400 a large settlement prospered in peace at this site. People in the village were, by present-day, non-Indian standards, good-looking, muscular, and of medium height. Though naturally handsome they often followed a custom which they thought improved their appearance: they altered the shapes of babies' heads by strapping them to wooden cradleboards. The soft baby bones were readily and permanently flattened.

Men and women wore clothing made of woven fabrics and cured animal skins. For warmth in cold weather they had robes made of feathers. They adorned themselves with delicate shell necklaces and pendants, copper bracelets and armbands, and ear decorations called earplugs. Hairdos received a good deal of attention, and women used long bone hairpins.

The houses in this community consisted of frames made of logs over which there was a covering of reeds and canes woven into mats and then plastered with mixed clay and sand.

Food was plentiful. Men hunted in the nearby forest and fished in Black Warrior River, on the banks of which their village stood. They shaped barbless fishhooks of bone, wove fishnets, and made traps, snares, bows, and arrows. Corn, beans, and pumpkins grew readily in soil that was exceedingly fertile. To harvest their various crops they made tools much like those used by Indians elsewhere in eastern America. They also had woodworking tools and grinding implements for making cornmeal. Eating utensils were cut from shell.

Women apparently had time and energy for making pots that were often very lovely. Everyone seems to have had the time necessary for ceremonies and rituals and for the labor of building the 40 mounds on which they placed temples and other important structures. Although they did not build burial mounds, these people were followers of the Southern Cult and devoted a great deal of effort to mortuary customs. As in many other Indian societies, precious belongings were buried with the dead. These grave goods give us much of our information about the lifeway of the people who made and used them.

In the preserved burials that can be seen at the monument, many of the articles appear with skeletons, exactly as archeologists encountered them. Other examples of grave goods are on display in the museum. Still other artifacts recovered at Moundville are on exhibit in the Alabama Museum of Natural History in Tuscaloosa, and some can be seen in the Museum of the American Indian in New York.

A

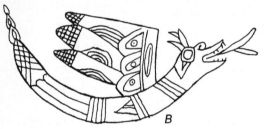

B

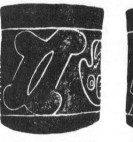 

D

E

A. This diorama in the museum at Mound State Monument shows how archeologists think the village may have looked 500 years ago. The structure on top of the mound at right was a religious and political center of the community. University of Alabama, Museum of Natural History photo.   B. The winged serpent appears in a variety of forms in many prehistoric Indian cultures. A follower of the Mississippian lifeway made this design. After Clarence B. Moore. C. A Park Ranger at Russell Cave National Monument, Alabama, indicates the layers of debris accumulated in more than 8,000 years of human occupation of the cave. National Park Service photo.   D. This black pottery vessel from Mound State Monument has incised designs, shown here in white to make them more visible. E. Three random designs used on pottery made by Mississippian Indians. Pots are on display in the museum at Moundsville State Monument.

C

RUSSELL CAVE NATIONAL MONUMENT

From Bridgeport, drive west on US 72, then north on County Road 91 to Mt. Carmel, then turn right onto County Road 75 which leads to the monument entrance. Total distance from Bridgeport about 8 miles. Open free, 8 a.m. to 6 p.m., May 30 through Labor Day; 8 a.m. to 5 p.m., daily, rest of year. Camping.

A record of about 8,500 years of human life is preserved in this monument. In Russell Cave itself an exhibit shows how archeologists did the excavation there. The museum beside the cave houses other exhibits.

The Story. Long ago hunters found that the gaping hole now called Russell Cave provided shelter, and they camped on its rock-strewn floor. Bits of charcoal, dated by the carbon-14 method, show that men, women, and children warmed themselves at fires here sometime between 8,460 and 8,960 years ago. Usually their visits were in fall and winter, when quantities of nuts could be harvested in the neighboring forest. Hunting at that time of year was good, too, and fish and shellfish were easy to harvest in the nearby Tennessee River.

Year after year families kept visiting the cave, cooking over fires, dropping trash, losing tools. After a while the floor on which they camped was so littered that tidying-up seemed necessary. Loads of dirt were brought in to cover the debris, and the cave floor rose high above its original level.

At last, about 500 B.C., the lifeway of the cave's visitors changed a great deal. They began to make pottery, and many sherds littered the floor. The bow and arrow was now the favorite weapon instead of the spear and spearthrower, which had been used until then. Tools became more varied as people learned to garden as well as hunt.

Farming increased in importance, and beginning about A.D. 1000, people stopped at Russell Cave less and less often. This was a time when many communities in the Southeast were building temple mounds. Some evidence of the temple-mound lifeway was left in the cave, but not a great deal. The final occupants, Cherokee Indians, took shelter there, even in historic times.

During all these centuries of occupation, debris piled up on the floor until it reached a depth of 14 feet. In 1953 four members of the Tennessee Archaeological Society began to dig into the litter. A little excavating was enough to tell them that the job was too big for such a small crew and too important to be left undone. The amateurs called in the Smithsonian Institution, which, together with the National Geographic Society, excavated the cave and by so doing added greatly to our knowledge of the early inhabitants of the Southeast. In all of North America no excavation before this had provided such a detailed record of human life over such a long period. No excavation in the Southeast had provided an earlier date. After the dig was completed, the cave became a national monument.

Arkansas

ARKANSAS STATE UNIVERSITY MUSEUM

On the campus, Jonesboro. Open free, 9 a.m. to noon, 1 p.m. to 5 p.m., Monday through Friday; 1 p.m. to 5 p.m., Sunday; closed Jan. 1, Easter, July 4, Labor Day, Thanksgiving, Dec. 25.

The archeological exhibits in this general museum serve as an excellent introduction to prehistory in northeastern Arkansas, from the Paleo through the Archaic, Woodland, and Mississippian mound-building stages. Maps indicate the various culture areas and tell which artifacts are related to which time period.

A large display is devoted to the Ballard Site, an early temple mound dating from A.D. 700 to 800. A cutaway in this display shows various strata, the artifacts associated with each one, and tools used by archeologists in excavating a burial and grave goods. Another exhibit explains the five steps in making temple-mound pottery. (A note on the pottery used for cooking offers an explanation of the corrugations on the outside of these vessels: The rough surface kept the pot from slipping out of a woman's hands when it was slick with grease.)

CADDO BURIAL MOUNDS

On Arkansas 27, just west of Murphreesboro, turn north, following directional signs. Total distance 1½ miles. Open 9 a.m. to 7 p.m. daily. Camping nearby.

This privately owned and operated archeological site is the only one in Arkansas that is open to the public. Excavation, which continues, is not under the supervision of the Arkansas Archeological Survey.

A number of mounds associated with the important Caddoan people have been partially dug. Some have been covered by buildings that preserve burials as they were found by excavators. Artifacts, including ornaments, pipes, and effigy pots, can be seen in the museum and souvenir shop.

To the consternation of many archeologists, this enterprise encourages vandalism by advertising that it has a surface hunting area where visitors may look for artifacts and may keep what they find.

HAMPSON MUSEUM

From West Memphis drive 34 miles north on Interstate 55, then 7 miles east on local road to Wilson, and follow directional sign to museum. Open free, 10 a.m. to noon, 1 p.m. to 5 p.m., Tuesday through Saturday; 1 p.m. to 5 p.m., Sunday.

Material from Nodena Mound, which has been declared a National Historic Landmark, is on display here in the Henry Clay Hampson II Memorial Museum of Archaeology. The museum, 7 miles from the mound, is owned by the state of Arkansas and operated by Frances Hampson, widow of Dr. J. K. Hampson who excavated the material.

Dr. Hampson began collecting Indian artifacts when he was nine years old, and he continued in this avocation for 70 years. His greatest activity centered at Nodena Mound, a site that covers more than two acres on the Hampson family plantation. In the course of his excavation here Dr. Hampson uncovered 813 burials. Because he was a physician he was particularly interested in what the study of bones could tell him about prehistoric people in the vicinity. He found, for one thing, that they seem to have been peaceful. In all the burials he uncovered, he found only two evidences of death by violence, and these can now be seen in the museum. One is a bone dagger thrust through the breast bone of a victim; the other, a projectile point buried in a skull.

A. An effigy vessel in the shape of a frog, found in a burial mound in Arkansas. Original in the Museum of the American Indian. B. This unusual-shaped water jar was found in Arkansas. Original in the Museum of the American Indian. C. The winged serpent design was engraved on a counch shell found at Spiro Mound. Original in the University of Arkansas museum, Fayetteville, Arkansas. D. The Arkansas Archeological Survey invites visitors to watch and help archeologists as they work. Here an experienced amateur uses a brush and fine-pointed tool to expose a prehistoric skeleton—a task that requires patience and skill. Arkansas Archeological Survey photo.

D

Other exhibits show various evidences of disease in the bones of prehistoric people. Five percent of all the skulls Dr. Hampson found had been artificially flattened, at the back or at the back and on the forehead as well, by the binding of the head to boards when an infant was very young.

Numerous pots, including many effigy jars, are on display, along with other artifacts that represent the Mississippian lifeway at Nodena Mound and elsewhere.

HENDERSON STATE COLLEGE MUSEUM

On the campus, Arkadelphia. Open free, 2 p.m. to 5 p.m., Monday and Thursday; closed national holidays.

This museum has on display about 100 good examples of Caddoan pottery and an exhibit of Caddoan stone, bone, and shell tools and ornaments.

The Caddoan archeological area is named after the Indians of historic times who spoke a Caddoan language and who apparently were descendants of prehistoric groups in Texas, Arkansas, and Oklahoma. Some archeologists believe that prehistoric Caddoan pottery shows a strong influence from Mexico. The people who made it also built ceremonial mounds that resembled the ceremonial pyramids of Mexico.

This combination of pottery and pyramids, along with ceremonial masks representing a long-nosed god sacred to Mexican traders, leads to some interesting questions: Did Mexican ideas come with traders across Texas and Arkansas? Did the Caddoans absorb these ideas, develop them, then pass them along throughout the Southeast? Were Caddoans the originators of ceremonial mound-building and of the religious movement known as the Southern Cult? Some specialists think so.

HOT SPRINGS NATIONAL PARK MUSEUM

In the Visitor Center, Central and Reserve avenues, Hot Springs National Park. Open free, 8 a.m. to 5 p.m., daily; closed Dec. 25.

In the Visitor Center a few Caddoan artifacts are on display, together with explanations of the prehistoric use by man of the water from the hot springs. Drawings show how Indians made stone implements from a very hard stone called novaculite.

MUSEUM OF SCIENCE AND NATURAL HISTORY

MacArthur Park, 500 E. 9th St., Little Rock. Open free, 10 a.m. to 5 p.m., Tuesday through Saturday; 2 p.m. to 5 p.m., Sunday.

One hall in this museum is devoted to material found in prehistoric mounds in Arkansas.

UNIVERSITY OF ARKANSAS MUSEUM

University Hall, University of Arkansas, Fayetteville. Open free 9 a.m. to 5 p.m., Monday through Saturday; 1 p.m. to 5 p.m., Sunday; closed Dec. 25.

Unusual material in this museum comes from what are called bluff shelters in the Arkansas Ozark Mountains. These shelters are areas at the bases of overhanging rock ledges under bluffs or cliffs. Many are quite dry—completely protected from rain and snow—and for that reason they attracted prehistoric people. The absence of moisture also meant that baskets, sandals, clothing, garbage—any organic material left there—did not decay. Things which ordinarily would have been lost to the archeologist have survived, and they tell a story of the life of nonfarming people who inhabited the shelters from about 8000 B.C. to about 1000 B.C.

Ozark Bluff hunters used spears and darts tipped with large stone points. Women gathered nuts and wild plants, made excellent baskets and mats, and wove blankets of feather and hemp. Some of their textiles, cordage, and baskets are on display in the museum. Several exhibits show burials. Unfortunately the Ozark Bluff people did not bury grave goods with the dead. A blanket, a mat, and a basketry pillow are about the only offerings found in the graves, and so less is known about this culture than about some others. Perhaps a little more could have been found out if collectors had not looted the shelters before archeologists got there.

Several displays in the museum contain material from the famous Spiro Mound Site in Oklahoma, which yielded much fascinating material even after vandals had carted off quantities of beautiful things. Among the Spiro artifacts here are small masks carved from wood and overlaid with copper, a piece of cloth woven from a combination of bison and rabbit hair thread, shell ornaments, and beads of many kinds.

One exhibit shows how Indian women made pottery. Others contain artifacts representative of the Eskimo, of Southwestern peoples, and of several different late prehistoric cultures in Louisiana and Arkansas, including Mississippian and Caddoan.

The state headquarters of the Arkansas Archeological Survey is at this museum.

Florida

CRYSTAL RIVER HISTORIC MEMORIAL

From the town of Crystal River drive northwest a short distance on US 19 to directional sign, then turn west on a paved road which leads directly to the museum. Open 8 a.m. to 5 p.m., daily. Admission: 25¢; children under 12, free.

In addition to housing interpretive exhibits and artifacts excavated in the vicinity, the museum in this Florida state park offers a view through its windows of three different types of mound—refuse mounds, burial mounds, and a temple mound. Trails lead from the museum to the various mounds.

The Story. Beginning about 2,100 years ago, Indians developed a settlement here on the bank of the Crystal River. In time this became a very important ceremonial center, and activities continued here for about 1,600 years.

In the course of excavations, which began in 1903, more than 450 burials have been found. Some of the grave goods have proved that there was trade between Crystal River Indians and Indians who lived in distant places—as far north as Ohio. Two stone slabs may indicate that these people were also affected by ideas from Mexico. Carvings on one of the slabs resemble those on stones called steles, which were erected in ancient Mexico to commemorate special events.

FLORIDA STATE MUSEUM

Seagle Building, University of Florida campus, Gainesville. Open free, 9:30 a.m. to 5 p.m., Monday through Saturday; 1 p.m. to 5 p.m., Sunday and holidays. Closed Dec. 25.

Included in this general museum are exhibits of Florida archeology.

HISTORICAL MUSEUM OF SOUTHERN FLORIDA AND THE CARIBBEAN

2010 N. Bayshore Dr., Miami. Open free, noon to 4 p.m., Tuesday through Saturday; 1 p.m. to 5 p.m., Sunday; closed national holidays.

Random local finds and materials professionally excavated throw light on the lifeways of the Calusa and Tequesta Indians from about 600 B.C. to the historic period. The Calusas lived on the west coast of Florida, south of Tampa Bay; the Tequestas on the east coast from the upper Florida keys to what is now Martin County. The exhibits show how people adjusted to an environment that lacked metal and hard stone by substituting seashells and wood for materials that would have been used in other areas.

MADIRA BICKEL MOUND HISTORIC MEMORIAL

From Bradenton drive 6 miles north on US 41 to Rubonia, then turn west and follow state park directional signs to the mound site, which is on Terra Ceia Island. Open free. 8 a.m. to 5 p.m., daily, all year. Camping nearby.

Some Indians apparently occupied this site, which is near present-day St. Petersburg, from about A.D. 1 to about 1600. The earliest inhabitants lived as shellfish harvesters. Abundant food from the sea nourished them, and they left only a few tools behind in their piles of discarded shells. Slowly their lifeway changed, and they began to adopt customs that made existence a good deal more complicated. Like many others in the Southeast, they became greatly occupied with burying the dead.

After about A.D. 700 their rituals and their pottery closely resembled those of the Weeden Island people, who also lived close to St. Petersburg. Sometimes single bodies of the dead were placed within low mounds of sand. Often the bones from a number of skeletons would be bundled together for burial in a mound. Artifacts associated with these burials included specially made pottery, polished stone celts, shell beads, and shell cups. Pottery of the Weeden Island type is unusually attractive, and it was found here in abundance.

Sometime after A.D. 1400 this area came under the influence of dynamic new ideas associated with the building of temple mounds. The people became much more proficient farmers, adopted a new style of pottery making, and spent a great deal of time and energy heaping up an earthen pyramid on which they placed a ceremonial structure. At the time the Spaniards first visited Florida, temple-mound builders still lived here, and some historians believe the site was the village called Ocita, where De Soto first camped in 1539.

SAFETY HARBOR SITE

In Philippe Park, 1 mile northeast of Safety Harbor on County Road 30. Open free, 7 a.m. to dark, daily.

Here on a point of land which extends into Tampa Bay, Timucua Indians built a temple mound in late prehistoric times. The mound, which is 150 feet in diameter and 25 feet high, is protected by the Pinellas County Park Department.

Part of the area has been excavated and a large amount of material recovered. Some of it is on display in the County Courthouse in Clearwater.

ST. PETERSBURG HISTORICAL SOCIETY

335 Second Ave., N.E., St. Petersburg. Open 11 a.m. to 5 p.m., Monday through Saturday; 2 p.m. to 5 p.m., Sunday; closed Dec. 25. Admission: adults, 50¢; children, 15¢.

Included in this historical museum are some prehistoric skulls, artifacts, and potsherds, collected in Pinellas County. Some materials reflect the important Weeden Island and Safety Harbor cultures, which developed nearby. Most are from the early 1500s.

SOUTH FLORIDA MUSEUM AND PLANETARIUM

201 Tenth St. W., Bradenton. Open 9 a.m. to 5 p.m., Monday through Friday; 1 p.m. to 5 p.m., Saturday and Sunday. Admission: adults, $1; students, 50¢; combination tickets, adults, $1.50; children, 75¢.

Prehistoric artifacts are on display here, together with information about the different types of mounds built in Florida before the arrival of Europeans. Dioramas give an artist's interpretation of a Calusa village scene and of a wedding among the Timucua people in Florida in prehistoric times.

TEMPLE MOUND MUSEUM AND PARK

National Historic Landmark.
At intersection of US 98 and US 85, in Fort Walton Beach. Open 11 a.m. to 4 p.m., Monday through Saturday; 1 p.m. to 4 p.m., Sunday, Memorial Day to Labor Day; 11 a.m. to 4 p.m., Saturday; 3 p.m. to 5 p.m., Sunday, winter. Admission: 25¢; children 4th grade and under, free.

This museum, which is operated by the city of Fort Walton Beach, introduces the visitor to 10,000 years of Indian life on the Gulf Coast. Beginning with artifacts from Paleo-Indian times, the exhibits carry prehistory forward chronologically to historic time. Of particular interest are the Weeden Island culture ceramic artifacts. There is also a large exhibit of Fort Walton pottery.

The mound on top of which a temple once stood has been restored. Archeologists have estimated that Indians constructed the mound by moving 500,000 basketloads of earth.

TURTLE MOUND HISTORIC MEMORIAL

From New Smyrna Beach drive 9 miles south on Florida A1A. Open free, 8 a.m. to 5 p.m., daily, all year.

A very large mound grew up here as Indians harvested oysters and discarded the shells over a period of several thousand years.

The site is largely unexcavated, and doubtless contains much material that can throw light on prehistoric Florida. It would now be lost to science had it not been for a campaign by local citizens when an attempt was made to quarry its shells for road construction. Their efforts brought state protection to the site, but other mounds have disappeared as road builders hauled their contents away.

Special Feature. Yaupon plants, which belong to the holly family, now grow on Turtle Mound. It was from the leaves of this plant, or its close rela-

A. People who lived on Weeden Island, Florida, about 1,000 years ago, modeled this clay bottle in the shape of a dove. Original in the Museum of the American Indian. B. This clay vessel was created in the form of a kneeling figure. Original in the Museum of the American Indian. C. Turtle Mound, south of New Smyrna Beach, Florida, grew to its present height of 50 feet as prehistoric Indians of the area harvested oysters and discarded the shells. Several years ago it was threatened with destruction, but a campaign on the part of local citizens led to state protection of the site. Turtle Mound Historic Site photo.

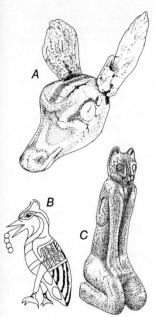

Florida Key Dwellers

Visitors to the keys and glades of southern Florida in the late 19th century were often amazed at the vast deposits of shells which had been left there by prehistoric people. In some places these refuse heaps had been turned into built-up living and ceremonial areas. On one key, for example, men had constructed a monumental sea wall more than ten feet high, mostly of conch shells. It was "as level and broad on top as a turnpike," said the archeologist Frank Cushing who explored it. Beyond the wall were terraces, with a graded way leading to five large mounds and an especially big pyramidal mound which probably supported a temple.

Cushing speculated that at first men built up the keys with shells, then extended the sea walls to make enclosures that served as fish traps into which they paddled their canoes, driving the fish ahead of them. As mud and debris accumulated in canals between shell heaps, they dug it out and formed little garden patches. They also built platforms for dwellings and cisterns to catch rain for drinking water. As time passed the settlements grew more and more elaborate, and so did the lives of the people who occupied them. At Key Marco, where Cushing did a famous job of excavating, he uncovered a wealth of beautiful and fascinating material. Much of it looked as if it had just been finished. Even perishable things such as cordage, mats, and objects made of wood had been preserved in the salty bogs. The woodcarvers of the keys were great artists. Although no one knows for sure, they probably used the sharpened edges of shells and shark teeth as knives.

Some of the spectacular finds at Key Marco can be seen in the Museum of Natural History of the Smithsonian Institution; the University Museum, University of Pennsylvania; and the Museum of the American Indian, New York.

A. The Key Marco artist who carved this deer's head made the ears movable. Original in the University Museum, Philadelphia. B. A woodpecker painted on wood, from Key Marco. After Cushing. C. This pantherlike figure was carved by a Key dweller. D. A humorous shell painting from Key Marco. Original in the University Museum, Philadelphia.

Focus, Phase, Aspect

Archeologists almost never know what a prehistoric tribe called itself or what other prehistoric people called it. But when similar materials appear in several places, all near each other and all left at about the same time, there is reason to suspect that these materials once belonged to members of the same tribe. However, there is always a chance that different tribes that lived close together at the same time may have left identical objects. So archeologists avoid jumping to conclusions that may be wrong. They talk about "focus" instead of "tribe."

Some archeologists use the word "phase" instead of focus. To others "focus" may mean something quite different. What it does mean is not always clear, but don't worry. Archeologists are trying to get words they can all agree on.

The word "aspect" also turns up in museum labels and in books about archeology. The simplest way to understand "aspect" is to think of a group of related small tribes ("foci" or "phases")—in other words a large tribe.

tive the cassina holly, that Indians in the Southeast made the Black Drink which played an important part in certain ceremonies. First the leaves were parched, then steeped in a large jar of water. The result was a liquid containing a great deal of caffein.

Before performing certain ceremonies, Indians drank some of this Black Drink from conch shell cups. Somtimes other herbs were added to make it an emetic. The vomiting it induced was supposed to have a purifying effect. Without the emetic herbs, people often used the Black Drink just as we use coffee or tea today.

Georgia

ALBANY AREA JUNIOR MUSEUM, INC.

516 Flint Ave., Albany. Open free, 10 a.m. to noon; 2 p.m. to 5 p.m., Monday through Friday; closed Jan. 1, July 4, all of August, early Dec., Dec. 25.

This museum, in which ethnographic exhibits emphasize Creek and Cherokee material, also displays artifacts of Paleo, Archaic, Woodland, and Mississippian cultures.

COLUMBUS MUSEUM OF ARTS AND CRAFTS

1251 Wynnton Rd., Columbus. Open free, 10 a.m. to 5 p.m., Tuesday through Saturday; 3 p.m. to 6 p.m., Sunday; closed July 4, Labor Day, Dec. 25, Jan. 1, and last two weeks in August.

Here are displays of artifacts from Paleo through Mississippian cultures. Dioramas show how a site is excavated and how Archaic and Mississippian people lived.

Special Feature. The museum is excavating and restoring a large temple mound and ceremonial center, 7 miles south of Lumpkin, Georgia, that can be visited free, by appointment.

ETOWAH MOUNDS ARCHEOLOGICAL AREA
(ET-oh-wah)

National Historic Landmark
From US 41 at Cartersville, drive 1 mile west on Georgia 61 Spur, then continue 2 miles following directional signs to museum and headquarters. Open 9 a.m. to 5:30 p.m., May through Oct.; 9 a.m. to 5 p.m., Nov. through April. Closed Thanksgiving, Dec. 25. Admission: adults, 50¢; children under 16, 10¢. Camping nearby.

The museum at this site gives an excellent general view of prehistoric life in the area beginning about 5000 B.C., and at the same time it provides real insight into what archeologists do as they search for information about the past. Of special interest is the period beginning about A.D. 1350, when Etowah was occupied by people who built temple mounds and practiced the rituals of the Southern Cult.

During excavation archeologists were astonished at the richness of the grave goods they found buried in tombs, particularly those discovered at the foot of the mound. Exhibits in the museum show something of the society that produced this wealth and the gorgeous costumes of priests who carried out the rituals. Some of the symbolic meaning of the priests' attire is explained.

Two unusual human figures, a man and a woman, carved from Georgia marble were particularly interesting finds. These two-foot-high figures were discovered in a burial and are believed to be actual portraits of the people with whom they were buried.

Ornaments and ceremonial objects were often made of materials from distant places, and one exhibit traces the amazing extent of trade—obsidian and grizzly bear teeth from the Rocky Mountains, for example, and marine products from Florida.

Besides the burial rituals, other religious practices appear in fascinating detail, with explanations of ceremonial paraphernalia, including beautifully worked axes, the chunkey game, and objects used for magic.

Separated from the main museum is a building which protects a cemetery area. The skeletons here have been left exactly as they were found.

A superb view of the entire area rewards the visitor who makes the steep climb to the top of the largest mound in the Etowah complex.

KOLOMOKI MOUNDS STATE PARK
(koh-loh-MOH-kee)

National Historic Landmark
From Blakely drive 2 miles north on US 27, then follow directional signs 4 miles to the Visitor-Center Museum and mounds. Open 10 a.m. to 6 p.m., Tuesday through Sunday; closed national holidays. Admission: 25¢. Park and mounds open free, 7 a.m. to 10 p.m. Camping, Mar. 15 to Nov. 1.

This site includes the largest mound group in the Gulf Coast area and is also noteworthy because of the very careful detective work done by the archeologists who have excavated and interpreted it.

The Story. Hunters probably camped here several thousand years ago beside an artesian spring near Little Kolomoki Creek, but the earliest visitors left only the scantiest of traces. Then a succession of peoples visited the area, at least briefly, during a period of several thousand years. By about A.D. 700 a small village had been established, and women were making pottery that resembled the kind made at Weeden Island, farther south. From then on the population grew, and a distinct Kolomoki lifeway developed.

The daily existence of the ordinary people must have differed greatly from that of the leaders. Commoners did the work of farming, doubtless following patterns of behavior that were widespread throughout the Southeast. The leaders, on the other hand, probably did no farm work. Rather they acted as executives who directed public projects and supervised and organized ceremonies and rituals in the temple on top of the platform mound or in the plaza at the foot of the mound.

One of the complex operations connected with ritual activity was the manufacture of grave goods. First the raw material had to be obtained—shell from the Gulf of Mexico, copper, galena, and mica from much more distant places. These materials were transformed by craftsmen into ornaments and other artifacts buried with the bodies of important people.

All of this activity was coordinated by members of the ruling group. They supervised at least a thousand men, women, and children who must have been involved in the final construction of the pyramid. At that time the work force dug, carried, and dumped the heavy clay necessary to create a cap six feet thick covering the top of the pyramid, which measured 325 feet by 200 feet at its base.

An almost equally large crew of workers had to be directed when it came time to raise a mound for the burial of an important personage at Kolomoki. For such a burial laborers first dug a large pit about seven feet deep. Then the cremated bones were laid in the bottom, together with ornaments, beads, and precious possessions. Next, large rocks were brought in (one measured 6×3×2 feet) to fill the hole about halfway. When this had been covered with a large, rounded heap of clay and more stones, graves at the side were made for wives and other members of the household who were sacrificed. Quantities of specially made mortuary pottery accompanied these burials. Continuous processions of workers added layers of earth and clay, some of which they had to bring from a spot half a mile away in the side of a steep bluff.

The finished burial mounds were as much as 50 feet in diameter and from 6 to 20 feet high. To complete the mortuary ceremonies more men were sacrificed. Why do archeologists think there were sacrifices? Excavation shows that numerous heads with no bodies attached had been buried in the mounds. Many of the heads bore decorations in just the positions they would have had if held there by skin and hair. Where copper ornaments were present, there were even bits of skin and hair left on the bone as a result of the preservative action of the copper. In other words, recently severed heads had been buried, not fleshless skulls. A likely explanation was that the heads were cut off in the course of human sacrifice.

The Museum. To show how archeologists work and what they find, one of the burial mounds, with skeletons and grave goods in place, has been roofed over and made part of the museum. Exhibits here and elsewhere in the building illustrate many aspects of Kolomoki life—hunting, cooking, fishing, planting, house building, pottery making, working with copper, and making decorations of shell. Dioramas and paintings show construction of mounds, and there are fine displays of pottery, especially the kind used only as mortuary ware. Exhibits also give an idea of life in several earlier periods, when people with quite different cultural patterns lived here.

OCMULGEE NATIONAL MONUMENT
(ohk-MULL-ghee)

At the southeast edge of Macon on US 80. Open 9 a.m. to 5 p.m., Wednesday through Sunday; closed Dec. 25. Admission: adults, 50¢; children under 16, free if accompanied by an adult. Camping nearby.

Ocmulgee was the first large site in the Southeast to be scientifically investigated. Temple mounds, a reconstructed ceremonial building, and exhibits in the museum at the Visitor Center recreate the whole history of Indian life in central Georgia.

The Story. The first people to enter Georgia seem to have arrived about 8000 B.C. They were Paleo-Indians, hunters of mammoths and other Ice-Age game. A very small wandering population remained in the area for about 3,000 years. Some who camped near Ocmulgee left behind a projectile point, many scrapers, and a few other tools.

When the big game disappeared, hunters turned to new ways of getting food. In some parts of the Southeast they discovered they could lead an easier life by harvesting freshwater clams and

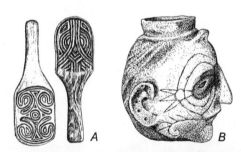

A. Women who once lived at Swift Creek, Georgia, used implements like these to press designs into their pottery while the clay was still moist. Archeologists reconstructed these stamps, now on display in Ocmulgee National Monument. B. A pottery vessel, modeled in the shape of a head, was incised before firing. Original in the museum, Ocmulgee National Monument. C. Present-day visitors at Etowah Mounds Archeological Area in Georgia can climb steps on the same ramp used by prehistoric Indians when they went to the building which stood on the flat top of the large mound, center right in this aerial photograph. Georgia Historical Commission photo.

C

Axe, Adze, and Celt

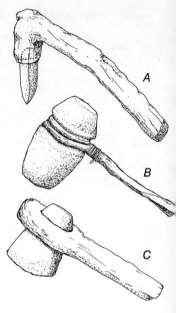

Prehistoric Indians cut and shaped wood with all three of these tools, which they fashioned from stone. Each was attached to a handle in its own special way. The axe was shaped by chipping, or by chipping and grinding and polishing. It was sometimes sharpened on one end, sometimes on both ends, and it had a groove which made it easier to attach a handle. (This is called hafting.) The groove might go all the way around the axe or only partway.

A celt was usually polished, had no groove, and was hafted as the illustration shows.

Although neither an axe nor a celt looks very efficient to anyone who is used to steel tools, both work surprisingly well. Archeologists who have tried stone axes found they could chop down a six-inch tree in less than 20 minutes.

The cutting edge of an axe or a celt is parallel to the handle; the cutting edge of an adze is at right angles to its handle. An adze is not designed for chopping down trees, but it is effective, for example, in hollowing out logs to make dugout canoes.

A. An adze. B. A grooved axe. C. An un-grooved axe, or celt. After Linda Murphy in Indians of Arkansas *by* Charles R. McGimsey III.

The Dog and the Prehistoric Indian

Some archeologists think that about 8,500 years ago men and arctic wolves discovered benefits in living close to each other. The wolves got refuse to eat; men had scavenging done for them. From this partnership a breed of dogs developed and spread throughout Europe and America.

No one knows exactly when dogs first appeared in North America, but they were here by 2000 B.C., perhaps earlier.

Dogs may have helped hunters pursue game. No one is sure about this, but there is no doubt that dogs were companions for adults and playmates for children. Before they were ever used in hunting (if they were so used), dogs had an important place in the religious ceremonies of some tribes. They were occasionally sacrificed in somewhat the same way that animals were sacrificed in biblical times. Sometimes dogs were buried with special honors. Sometimes they were eaten ceremonially—or simply as food. In some areas, particularly in the Southwest and on the Northwest Coast, Indians raised special long-haired dogs. They used the hair in weaving blankets and belts.

Dogs were known throughout much of America, especially where men were hunters. In some farming areas archeologists have found no dog skeletons at all. Wherever they existed dogs were the most important domesticated animal, often the only domesticated animal. In the Plains area they carried loads on special pole frames called travois (truh-VOY).

One curious fact: In many places the very earliest dogs were very small. Later, dogs in the warmer parts of the continent were small, but farther north they were large, and the largest of all lived farthest north.

Pottery in the form of a dog made by an artist of the Mississippian culture in Tennessee. Original in the Peabody Museum, Harvard University.

mussels. However, those who camped at Ocmulgee did not become shellfish eaters. The equipment they left behind shows that they continued hunting, although their food now came from the smaller animals. When game was scarce in one place the hunters moved on to another, following a route that brought them back repeatedly to their old campsite at Ocmulgee.

Not long after 1000 B.C. a whole new way of life began in this part of Georgia. Men had learned to grow food in gardens. They cultivated pumpkins, beans, and sunflowers, and this food supply made it possible to live in villages. Settlement allowed women to adopt an invention that had been in use much earlier in other parts of the Southeast—crude pottery. These Early Farmers, as they are called in the Ocmulgee Museum (or Swift Creek people, as they are also called), gradually expanded their gardens, and now they had more free time. Arts and crafts developed. Their pottery improved.

About A.D. 900 some aggressive people (called by the museum Master Farmers and also referred to as Macon Plateau people) invaded the area. Just where they came from no one knows for sure, possibly from the Mississippi Valley near the mouth of the Missouri River, possibly from Tennessee. Whatever their origin, they drove out the earlier inhabitants and began intensive and very successful corn farming.

The newcomers also brought along elaborate political and religious customs and the habit of building very large ceremonial lodges entirely covered with earth. Here at Ocmulgee one of these earthlodges, constructed rather like a huge Eskimo igloo, has been restored. The roof is new, but it was possible to keep the original floor intact. This was made of a special clay called kaolin, which packs down very hard when walked on—or danced on—as this floor no doubt was.

Meticulous work in excavating the earthlodge revealed that it was used for about 30 years and then burned—perhaps accidentally, but more probably as part of a ritual or as a safety measure. The earthen roof was heavy and often damp, and the supporting beams must have rotted quickly. Fortunately for archeologists, the burned wood collapsed and preserved the circular floor with its molded seats for 47 people around the edge. At one end is a platform in the shape of an eagle, designed in a way that was popular all over the Southeast in late prehistoric times. Apparently important men sat on the platform, where there are seats for three.

The lodge was a place for religious ceremonies and civic gatherings, particularly those held in winter. Because of its thousand-year-old floor, it has been called the oldest public building site in the United States.

Across an open space opposite the earthlodge stands a large flat-topped mound nearly 50 feet tall. Like many other great mounds in the Southeast, this one served as the foundation for a temple. The original temple stood on a low platform. After a time this building was burned, perhaps when a leader died, and the site was entirely covered with earth which served as the foundation for a new temple. This pattern of destruction and rebuilding went on, again and again, as long as the village was occupied by the Master Farmers.

Over a period of 200 years other smaller mounds supported additional temples, and at one end of the village is a mound which apparently served as a cemetery. All of this building took a vast amount of time. More work, too, went into digging moats or ditches, which may have served for protection. Warfare certainly occupied these

people, perhaps because the descendants of the earlier inhabitants were trying to return. What happened in the end at Ocmulgee is something of a mystery. For some unexplained reason everyone left, and the site was never occupied again except for one brief period much later.

Possibly descendants of the Early Farmers mingled with the Master Farmers and settled nearby. Certainly people who shared traits with both the Early Farmers and the Master Farmers developed what is known as the Lamar lifeway and built mounds nearby. Some of their descendants became Creek Indians of historic times.

The Museum. All of this story—and much more—is told in the museum. Models and dioramas illuminate various aspects of the lives of those who inhabited the area for 10,000 years. Exhibits display many artifacts, including a large collection of pipes. Apparently the Ocmulgeeans were heavy smokers and did not limit themselves to the ceremonial use of tobacco, as many Indians did.

Among the special exhibits of pottery of many kinds is one showing how women at Ocmulgee made and decorated their vessels. Visitors who are familiar with pottery making in other parts of the country will find interesting differences here.

The Name. Ocmulgee comes from a Creek Indian word that means "Bubbling Spring," because there is a never-failing spring near the site. After the Creeks were forced to leave the Southeast in the 1800s, they made new homes for themselves in Oklahoma, where they called one of their towns Okmulgee—the old name, spelled differently.

ROCK EAGLE EFFIGY MOUND

From Eatonton drive 6 miles north on US 441 to directional marker. Open free, at all times. Camping nearby.

Prehistoric Indians carried great numbers of white quartz rocks a considerable distance to use in building this effigy. It is in the shape of a huge bird which is called an eagle by some archeologists, a buzzard by others. The wings stretch out across a flat hilltop for 120 feet, tip to tip, and the depth of the original rockpile is thought to have been about eight feet. At the foot of the bird a modern tower has been constructed so that visitors can see the whole of it, looking down from above. Another bird effigy of this sort is in the vicinity, but it cannot be visited by the public.

TRACK ROCK ARCHAEOLOGICAL AREA, CHATTAHOOCHEE NATIONAL FOREST

From Blairsville drive 3 miles south on US 19, then east 5 miles on Forest Service Road 95 to marker. Open free, at all times. Camping nearby.

Here in a 52-acre area are preserved petroglyphs —rock carvings—of ancient Indian origin; they resemble animal and bird tracks, crosses, circles, and human footprints.

Louisiana

LOUISIANA STATE EXHIBIT MUSEUM

3015 Greenwood Rd., Shreveport. Open free, 9 a.m. to 5 p.m., Monday through Saturday; 1 p.m. to 5 p.m., Sunday; closed Jan. 1, Dec. 25.

Displays of Paleo-Indian and other projectile points can be seen in the Capitol Historical Gallery of this museum, which is operated by the Louisiana Department of Agriculture and Immigration. Exhibits from mounds, including the Gahagan Mound in Red River Parish, show examples of ornaments, pottery, and other artifacts.

Special Feature. A large diorama, built under the guidance of an archeologist, shows the Poverty Point Site in northern Louisiana when it was a flourishing village. Until the site, which is a National Historic Landmark, is prepared for the public, this exhibit is probably the best introduction to one of the most intriguing of prehistoric settlements.

Although no one can be sure exactly what the Poverty Point dwellings looked like, those in the diorama show the probable shape of huts thatched with grass, palmetto leaves, or bark. The appearance of the women is based on figurines made of baked clay found at the site. (No male figures seem to have been made.) The women wore short, belted skirts in summer and probably heavier deerskin clothing in cold weather. One of the figurines shows a woman carrying a baby on a cradleboard.

The bow and arrow were not known at Poverty Point. Like other Archaic people, the men used spears, darts, and spear throwers. Hunters may also have captured large birds with bolas. These were weights, either oval or pear-shaped, tied at the ends of strings in groups of three or more. The hunter whirled the weighted strings around and released them at just the right moment to make them wrap themselves around the birds.

The special heavy stone used for the bola weights had to be imported from northern Arkansas or southern Missouri, some distance away. Other material that Poverty Point people wanted came from even more remote places. They got flint from Ohio, slate from the vicinity of Lake Michigan, and copper from Lake Superior. Soapstone for making pots may have come by dugout canoe or raft as much as two or three thousand miles from a quarry in the Appalachian Mountains.

At the Poverty Point Site itself, a local road cuts through six long, low hummocks of earth. A little farther along it crosses another six. These ridges, and a mound nearby, went almost unnoticed until 1953 when an alert archeologist examined an aerial photograph of the spot taken by Army mapmakers. The photograph revealed that the ridges had been laid out in a very definite geometric pattern. They were a series of man-made terraces built in the form of six concentric octagons. The whole configuration measured more than half a mile across, and its very size concealed its real nature.

Archeological work at the site soon told an amazing story. Apparently several thousand people at a time lived in this settlement for more than a thousand years beginning perhaps about 1500 B.C., and the construction they did was remarkable.

To form the terraces, on which they placed their dwellings, people carried earth and heaped it to a height of 6 feet or more. Each terrace was about 80 feet wide at the base, and there were six of them, one inside the other. The total linear measurement of these concentric ridges added up to more than 11 miles.

On the west side of the village these same people built a flat-topped ceremonial mound, 700 feet by 800 feet at the base and 70 feet high. About a mile away they put up another large mound, also used for ceremonies. Still others which were smaller and cone-shaped, covered places where the dead were cremated. Archeologists have esti-

mated that workers transported 20 million basketloads of earth, 50 pounds at a time.

The soil close to the Mississippi River had almost no stone—a fact which led to a curious invention called the Poverty Point object. Each of these objects was molded from a small handful of clay, then baked as hard as rock. Some were roughly spherical. Others were carefully made in other geometric shapes. When hot, the baked clay balls were used in the way stones were used elsewhere: They were dropped into a vessel containing stew or mush to make it boil. Lacking pottery vessels, women cooked in watertight baskets or carved stone bowls.

There is also evidence that cooking was done in another way. First the women dug a pit in the ground. Next they fashioned some of the balls from clay, laid them in the pit, and built a fire over them. Presently they raked out the coals and the hard-baked balls, lined the hot pit with grass, laid food on the grass, covered it with the heated balls and left it to cook, clam-bake style. Whichever way the objects were used, women made, according to estimates, 24,000,000 of them during the period the village was occupied.

Another unusual trait of Poverty Point people was their use of very small, sharp stone tools called microflints.

Recent researches indicate that the Poverty Point culture received much stimulation from Mexico and was ancestral to the Adena and Hopewell cultures which followed later in areas to the north. No direct evidence of agriculture has been found at Poverty Point, but its inhabitants no doubt raised crops. They lived on fertile land and had many customs characteristic of farmers elsewhere. For example, they made female figurines, probably thinking thus to encourage fertility. They had grinding implements as did people who raised corn in Mexico. The very fact that they built geometric mounds suggests agriculture. Their mounds were so constructed that the equinox could be recognized when the sun rose directly in line with certain features of the earthworks. Such information about the seasons was always of importance to farmers.

MARKSVILLE PREHISTORIC INDIAN PARK STATE MONUMENT

National Historic Landmark
From Marksville drive 1 mile east on Louisiana 1 to park entrance. Open 10 a.m. to 4 p.m., Monday through Saturday; 10 a.m. to 6 p.m., Sunday. Admission: adults, 50¢; children under 12, free.

Prehistoric earthen walls enclose a 40-acre tract in which there are a number of burial and temple mounds and a museum.

The Story. As early as 1500 B.C. people seem to have used this site, which was then close to the Mississippi River. Eventually the river shifted course, and its banks are now 30 miles away. Today Old River Lake is all that remains of the ancient channel. About 400 B.C. a permanent village began to grow here along the riverbank, and in unbroken sequence, until about the time Europeans arrived, the Marksville people increased their food supply and the range and variety of their implements, art forms, and religious customs.

Quite early an ambitious earthen barricade was placed around the village, apparently for defensive purposes. Within this protected area three types of mound were built at different times over a period of two millenia. Some mounds are refuse heaps or middens, some conical burial mounds, some temple mounds. One, no longer in its original shape, was a conical mound atop a truncated pyramid.

Archeologists have found this site of great interest, and excavation, which is not yet complete, was done by the Philadelphia Academy of Natural Sciences, the Smithsonian Institution, and Louisiana State University in cooperation with the Works Progress Administration.

Exhibits installed under the supervision of Dr. James A. Ford, of the American Museum of Natural History, display material recovered in the course of the excavations and illustrate the many changes in the lives of those who lived here for such a long time.

During the period of occupation when people were building burial mounds, they were greatly influenced by the Hopewell culture, which centered far to the north. A special variant of this culture has been called Marksville, after this site where it was first identified.

Aerial photographs in the museum show the large number of mounds in and near the monument and the relation of these mounds to the former bed of the Mississippi River.

Mississippi

BYNUM MOUNDS

From Tupelo drive 34 miles southwest on Natchez (NATCH-ez) Trace Parkway to directional marker. Open free, during daylight hours. Camping nearby.

Here is a group of burial mounds, two of which can easily be seen from a hard-surfaced path. An interpretive panel gives information about the far-flung trading activities of the Indians who once lived at the site.

The Story. About A.D. 700, people who followed the Middle Woodland way of life settled here and built circular houses thatched with grass. They hunted, fished, and gathered wild fruits and nuts, and they may also have maintained small gardens. After a time they adopted the custom, popular elsewhere at this period, of building earthen mounds over the remains of the dead. Altogether six of these burial mounds were constructed in the neighborhood of their village.

Gradually life became richer and more complex for the Bynum people. They obtained materials for weapons, ornaments, and tools by trading with other Indians who lived in distant places. Flint came from Ohio; marine shells, from the Gulf Coast; greenstone for their grooved and polished axes, from Alabama. Like the people at Emerald Mound, which is also on the Natchez Trace Parkway, they imported copper from Lake Superior. Why and exactly when they abandoned this site no one yet knows.

EMERALD MOUND

From Natchez drive 12 miles northeast on the Natchez Trace Parkway. Open free, during daylight hours, daily, all year.

Emerald Mound is the third largest temple mound in the United States. Its base measures 730 × 435 feet and covers nearly eight acres. Only Monks Mound, in Cahokia Mounds State Park in Illinois, and Poverty Point Mound, in Louisiana, are larger. Two interpretive panels at the site tell how Indians constructed this immense earthwork.

The Story. People who followed the Mississippian

lifeway began to build Emerald Mound about A.D. 1300, and they continued to live here until about A.D. 1600. After finishing the huge flat-topped platform, they went on to add at one end of it a second mound, itself as large as many of those in the Southeast, which rest directly on the ground. On the principal mound there may once have been many ceremonial structures, and on top of the second one there was certainly a temple.

The whole Emerald Mound complex served as a ceremonial center for farmers who lived nearby in thatch-covered houses, which had walls plastered with clay. These people made fine pottery and were skilled at fabricating a variety of tools and ornaments. As did the earlier farmers at Bynum Mounds, they obtained some of their materials from the Gulf Coast, and their copper came from far away to the north near Lake Superior. What happened to them in the end is something of a mystery, but Emerald Mound, like many others, was still in use when De Soto's marauding expedition passed through the Southeast in A.D. 1540–1541. Many other mounds, including the important Anna Mound group, dot this vicinity, but since none of them have been prepared for the public they cannot be visited.

NATCHEZ TRACE VISITOR CENTER

On the Natchez Trace Parkway, 3 miles north of the Tupelo entrance (from US 78). Open free, 8 a.m. to 5 p.m., daily, all year.

On display here are some of the artifacts and other objects found in the excavation of prehistoric Indian mounds and villages along the Natchez Trace Parkway. A free film program introduces both the prehistory and the history of the Trace. A library contains all the research reports on the excavations along the parkway.

The parkway itself follows old Indian trails. It also passes two groups of prehistoric mounds which have been prepared for visitation. When completed, the parkway will run for about 450 miles between Nashville, Tenn., and Natchez, Miss. As this book goes to press, 312 miles of roadway have been finished. For up-to-date information about the progress of road construction and about any new sites that may have been prepared for the public, write to Natchez Trace Parkway, RR 5, NT-143, Tupelo, Miss. 38801. The completer portions of the parkway are open free, at all times.

OWL CREEK INDIAN MOUNDS, TOMBIGBEE NATIONAL FOREST

From Houston on Mississippi 8 drive 10 miles north on Mississippi 15 to Old Houlka, then east on Forest Service Rd. 903 for 4½ miles to the parking area near the mounds. Open free, at all times. Camping at Davis Lake, 1½ miles from the mounds.

Here, near the place where De Soto made his winter camp, are two reconstructed ceremonial mounds. These, together with three other mounds, once surrounded a village plaza. An interpretive sign at the largest mound describes how the area appeared in prehistoric times. The site is one of an increasing number of archeological areas which the U.S. Forest Service has prepared for visitors.

STATE HISTORICAL MUSEUM

Capitol and N. State streets, Jackson. Open free, 9:30 a.m. to 4:30 p.m., Tuesday through Saturday;

1 p.m. to 5 p.m., Sunday, May through Oct.; 9:30 a.m. to 4:30 p.m., Tuesday through Saturday; 12:30 p.m. to 4:30 p.m., Sunday, Nov. through April; closed Jan. 1, July 4, Labor Day, Thanksgiving, Dec. 25.

Within the room devoted to Mississippi Indians are random archeological finds from various parts of the state. There are also exhibits that show a burial mound, Mississippi pottery and how it was made, and the excavation of a prehistoric site.

UNIVERSITY OF MISSISSIPPI ANTHROPOLOGICAL MUSEUM

Education Building, West University Ave., University. Open free, 1:30 p.m. to 4:30 p.m., Monday through Friday, Sept. through May; at other times by appointment; closed on university holidays.

Exhibits here include both random local finds and materials recovered in Mississippi by scientific excavation. There are some artifacts representing each of the cultural periods from Paleo-Indian to the present, with a particular concentration of Mississippian material. Displays are arranged to show how one cultural form succeeded another. One collection includes a large number of pots of the type called Walls. A diorama shows an Indian village and the daily life connected with it.

Special Feature. One exhibit depicts prehistoric women using Poverty Point objects in cooking.

North Carolina

CATAWBA COLLEGE MUSEUM

At the north edge of Salisbury on US 601 on the East Campus of Catawba College. Open free (except for rare special exhibitions), 2 p.m. to 6 p.m. most Saturdays and Sundays. For information about weekday schedules inquire by mail.

Archeological exhibits in this museum emphasize the South Atlantic area and include paintings, with almost life-size figures of Stone Age people, including Paleo-Indians.
Visitors who have special interests are given guided tours that include the Research Laboratory of Archaeology.

CHARLOTTE NATURE MUSEUM, INC.

1658 Sterling Rd., Charlotte. Open free, 9 a.m. to 5 p.m., Monday through Saturday; 2 p.m. to 5 p.m., Sunday; closed Jan. 1, July 4, Labor Day, Thanksgiving, Dec. 25.

Exhibits of projectile points and tools collected in the Carolina Piedmont area are representative of the major culture periods from Paleo-Indian to historic times. There are also artifacts of the Basketmaker people of the Southwest and projectile points from Pennsylvania and Virginia.

Special Feature. This was one of the first museums in the Southeast to offer special programs and workshops for children.

GREENSBORO HISTORICAL MUSEUM

130 Summit Ave., Greensboro. Open free, 10 a.m. to 5 p.m., Tuesday through Saturday; 2 p.m. to 5 p.m., Sunday; closed Jan. 1, Easter, Thanksgiving, Dec. 25.

Exhibits of artifacts collected in the Piedmont area represent 16 culture groups from Paleo-Indian times to about A.D. 1700.

MORROW MOUNTAIN STATE PARK NATURAL HISTORY MUSEUM

From Albemarle on US 52 to junction with North Carolina 740, follow directional signs to park entrance. Open free, 10 a.m. to 6 p.m., June through Aug.; 9 a.m. to 5 p.m., Saturday and Sunday, Labor Day through May.

In this small natural history museum an archeological display contains artifacts from each of the local cultures, along with explanations of their use.

OCONALUFTEE INDIAN VILLAGE

From Cherokee north on US 441, turn at directional sign and drive one-half mile to village entrance. Open 9 a.m. to 5:30 p.m., mid-May through Labor Day. Admission: adults, $2; children 6 to 13, 50¢. Camping nearby.

Although this reconstructed Cherokee village shows Indian life after the beginning of the historic period, there is a spot within the village where prehistoric hunters camped. On the height above the ceremonial plaza excavators found evidence that men had used the site frequently beginning about 5,000 years ago.

SCHIELE MUSEUM OF NATURAL HISTORY

1300 Kendrick Dr., Gastonia. Open free, 9 a.m. to 5:30 p.m., Tuesday through Sunday.

Materials from various sites in North Carolina illustrate Paleo-Indian, Archaic, Early and Late Woodland cultures. Exhibits show how artifacts were made and used; a diorama pictures the domestic activities of a Cherokee family about A.D. 1450.

TOWN CREEK INDIAN MOUND STATE HISTORIC SITE

National Historic Landmark
From Mount Gilead drive east on North Carolina 73, then north on State Rd. 1160 toward North Carolina 731 to directional sign; total distance, about 5½ miles from Mount Gilead. Open free, 9 a.m. to 5 p.m., Monday through Saturday; 1:30 p.m. to 5 p.m., Sunday and holidays; closed Dec. 25. Guided tours on weekdays by reservation. Camping nearby.

The Story. Early in the 16th century a group of energetic, aggressive people entered this area, driving out the earlier inhabitants. These newcomers, like the invaders who took over Ocmulgee in Georgia, had been influenced by the Mississippian culture. They were farmers who had extraordinary ability to make the land productive. They also had some very distinctive customs. Along with their practical skill they brought a whole constellation of religious ideas, building habits, ceremonial practices, and even a game called chunkey.
On a high bluff, near the place where a stream now called Town Creek joins the Little River, the newcomers made a clearing and surrounded it with a high palisade of logs interwoven with cane. Two openings in the palisade served as entrances,

but there was also a third, half underground, along the bluff. Inside the palisade they leveled off a plaza and around it, as time passed, they built ceremonial structures. The main one was a mound, constructed in one layer after another, starting with a low platform on which a religious building or temple stood. Later the mound was enlarged and made higher, as a base for another temple. A second mound across the plaza served as the base for a smaller temple, and at the center of the plaza stood a group of ceremonial buildings arranged in a square.

The newcomers occupied their village at Town Creek for only about 100 years. During that time they seem to have been at war often with their neighbors. But whether they gave up in defeat or left for some other reason no one knows. After their departure in the early 17th century, bands of people who had very different customs moved in. They spoke a language related to the language of the Sioux Indians of the West, and they were living there when Europeans first came.

The Museum. In the Visitor Center are displays of artifacts discovered during excavation of the site. Archeologists have investigated the entire area and have reconstructed the settlement as they think it must have looked 300 years ago. A palisade surrounds the ceremonial plaza, and on top of the great mound stands a reproduction of the ancient temple. A ceremonial ball field, similar to the one which was probably used by the inhabitants, has been reconstructed. Atop the goalpost, which has been placed in the hole where the original one stood, is an animal skull, just as in ancient times.

UNIVERSITY OF NORTH CAROLINA, RESEARCH LABORATORIES OF ANTHROPOLOGY

Person Hall, on the campus, Chapel Hill. Open free, 8:30 a.m. to 4:30 p.m., Monday through Friday; 8:30 a.m. to 12:30 p.m., Saturday.

Displays here include bones, pottery, and artifacts found in North Carolina.

Oklahoma See page 92.

South Carolina

NATURE MUSEUM OF YORK COUNTY

Mount Hill Rd., Rock Hill. Open free, 10 a.m. to 5 p.m., Tuesday through Saturday; 2 p.m. to 5 p.m., Sunday.

In addition to exhibits which reflect the life of various tribes in the historic period, there are exhibits here which touch on the life of Indians in Paleo, Archaic, and Woodland periods.

SEWEE MOUND ARCHAEOLOGICAL AREA, FRANCIS MARION NATIONAL FOREST

From Charleston drive 21 miles north on US 17, then turn right and drive southeast 4 miles on South Carolina 432. Open free, at all times. Camping.

The U.S. Forest Service has opened this well-

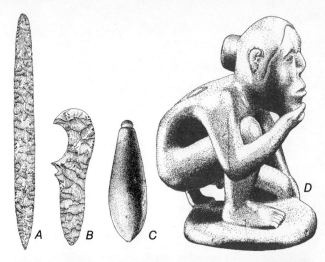

A. and B. Delicately flaked flint artifacts, apparently for ceremonial purposes, were found in Tennessee. Originals in the McClung Museum, Knoxville. C. Small objects of this sort are often called plummets. They may have been used as sinkers on fishlines or fishnets. D. A tobacco pipe, carved in stone, from about A.D. 1600. Found in a mound at Shiloh National Military Park. E. At Town Creek Indian Mound is a reconstructed palisade surrounding a temple that looks the same as it did 400 years ago. North Carolina Dept. of Agriculture photo. F. A restored painting in the temple, also restored, at Town Creek Indian Mound. North Carolina Dept. of Agriculture photo.

preserved shell mound to the public. Visitors are reminded that the Antiquities Act provides severe penalties for collecting any artifacts from the area.

Tennessee

CHILDREN'S MUSEUM

Second Ave. and Lindsley, Nashville. Open free, 10 a.m. to 5 p.m., Tuesday through Saturday; 2 p.m. to 5 p.m., Sunday. Closed Jan. 1, Dec. 25.

In this general museum is an exhibit devoted to early mound builders. Also on display are about 100 projectile points arranged according to culture. The points, which were collected in Tennessee, Alabama, Georgia, and Mississippi, begin with Paleo-Indian, include Archaic, and continue through Late Woodland times.

CHUCALISSA INDIAN TOWN AND MUSEUM
(CHOO-kah-LEE-sah)

From US 61 at the southern edge of Memphis, drive 4½ miles west on Mitchell Rd. and follow directional signs to museum entrance. Open 9 a.m. to 5 p.m., Tuesday through Saturday; 1 p.m. to 5 p.m., Sunday. Admission to the museum is free, but there is a charge for the town: adults, 25¢; children 6-12, 10¢; under 6, free. Camping at T. O. Fuller State Park, which adjoins the site.

The Story. People settled here about A.D. 900 and occupied the site continuously for more than 700 years. Their village developed in two parts—one for ordinary folk, the other for religious and political leaders. The houses of the leaders bordered a large plaza in front of a huge, circular ceremonial building and were made of poles or posts, finished outside with mud-and-straw plaster, and roofed with overlapping bundles of long, heavy grass. The ceremonial building, often called a temple, was constructed in the same way, but was very much larger.

At first the temple stood on a low platform made of earth. As years went by, one temple after another was purposely burned, perhaps when a leader died, and the whole platform was then covered with a mantle of new earth. Each mantle added height and breadth to the foundation for the next temple that was built, until at last a sizable mound dominated the village.

The women of Chucalissa cooked and wove baskets, mats, and textiles. They also made quantities of pottery, some of it very lovely, some very plain, for use as kitchenware.

The men did some hunting, made tools of bone and stone and wood, and cared for crops in their fields. Like other people who built temple mounds at this time, they must have been expert farmers. They may even have raised a variety of corn that was unusually productive. At any rate, they had adequate food to support a community of about a thousand common people, as well as a large number of religious and political leaders who spent much time and energy on ceremonies.

Probably a fire was kept burning in the temple day and night, and men in relays had to tend it carefully. For rituals and festivals crowds gathered in the plaza and shared in such events as the Busk or ripe corn ceremony.

For some reason not known, these people left their homes and temples before the arrival of the

first French explorers in 1673, and so we cannot be certain which modern Indians are their descendants. One possibility is the Tunica tribe. Today Choctaw Indians act as guides and conduct tours around the site which may have been the home of their ancestors.

The Name. "Chucalissa" is a word from modern Choctaw which means "house abandoned."

The Museum. A large part of the Chucalissa site has been made into an outdoor museum. Ten of the prehistoric houses have been reconstructed. So that visitors may see what archeologists have uncovered, 40 burials have been left in place at one side of the plaza, roofed over for protection.

An indoor museum displays material recovered from the site and also from other sites in the Southeast. Some of the most informative exhibits to be found anywhere show the "how's" of archeology: how a scientist-sculptor can reconstruct the face of a prehistoric man after examining a skull carefully; how potsherds tell a story of the people who made the pots; how cane was split and woven into baskets; how blowguns were made. In one room of the museum visitors may hear a lecture, illustrated with slides, about the archeology of the site and the life of its former inhabitants.

Special Feature. The site is being continuously excavated by Memphis State University, and during the summer months visitors may see archeologists and students at work. The first excavation here began with the support of the Tennesse Division of State Parks and with the help of prisoners from the Penal Farm. The scientist in charge of the project wrote: "Undoubtedly it was, for many, the most creative work they had ever undertaken, and they dug carefully, painstakingly, taking enormous and justifiable pride in their digs. . . . One particular prisoner—Driver by name—found the archeologist's conventional tools totally unacceptable and so devised and made his own, instruments which now form the backbone of our tool kit!"

LOOKOUT MOUNTAIN MUSEUM

From Chattanooga drive south on Tennessee 58 to the top of Lookout Mountain, then follow directional signs to Point Park. The museum is opposite the park entrance. Open 8 a.m. to sundown, daily, all year, closed Dec. 25. Admission: adults, 25¢; children 6 to 16, 10¢; children under 6, free.

Some archeological materials in this museum are Paleo-Indian from the LeCroy Site near Chattanooga. Most of the other prehistoric materials also come from the Chattanooga area. They include Archaic and Mississippian artifacts collected over a period of 50 years by an amateur archeologist, J. P. Brown. One diorama shows how Indians shaped stone artifacts by flaking, pressure, grinding, and drilling. Another, with life-sized models, shows an Archaic family engaged in various domestic activities.

McCLUNG MUSEUM

On campus, University of Tennessee, 1327 Circle Park Dr., Knoxville. Open free, 9 a.m. to 5 p.m., Monday through Friday; 9 a.m. to noon, Saturday; 2 p.m. to 5 p.m., Sunday, during the academic year.

Materials in the Frank H. McClung Museum, gathered by careful scientific excavation, throw light on Archaic, Woodland, and Mississippian cultures in the Southeast. Exhibits show how artifacts were made and used and how they related to their environments at different times. Many important finds came to the museum at the time when the Tennessee Valley Authority was building flood-control dams. In a crash program of salvage archeology, thousands of relief workers dug at many sites in the river basins, saving what could be excavated before the water rose.

Special Feature. The museum houses the collections of Thomas M. N. Lewis and Madeline Kneberg Lewis, archeologists who contributed greatly to knowledge of Southeastern cultures. Their work at the famous Eva Site in Benton County disclosed a long period of development of lifeways in that part of Tennessee, beginning about 5200 B.C. Some of the Eva people who settled along riverbanks harvested tremendous quantities of clams and mussels, and their heaps of discarded shells offered a convenient place for burials. In some of those which the Lewises excavated were found an amazing number of skeletons of adults who lived to be 60 or 70 years old. (Usually prehistoric people died at a much earlier age.)

At Hiwassee Island, where the Lewises also worked, no burials at all were found. With no grave goods to study the archeologists could discover little about the appearance or dress of the people who lived there for 4,000 years, but their household debris does tell a good deal about their daily life.

OLD STONE FORT STATE PARK

Just west of the city limits of Manchester, on US 41. Open free, during daylight hours.

The Story. On a high bluff that rises where the Little Duck River flows into the Duck River, early pioneers found sections of a wall that had obviously been built by man. Legends grew up about the site. Some said it was built by Vikings to protect themselves from Indians. Others said it was constructed by a Welshman named Madoc who they believed discovered America about A.D. 1170.

In 1966 archeologists from the University of Tennessee settled the question. They excavated the site, which includes more than 2,000 feet of wall on just one of its sides, and found that the wall had been built over a long period of time, beginning about A.D. 1 and ending sometimes before A.D. 400. The people who did all this vast labor were Indians, not Vikings or Welshmen, and they seem to have been influenced by the Hopewell lifeway centered in the Ohio River valley.

Apparently the builders of the Old Stone Fort did not live at the site, but archeologists have not discovered exactly what they did there. Although it could have served for defense, it also resembled Hopewell ceremonial sites. But what kind of ceremony took place inside the walls? Only further excavation can provide an answer.

SHILOH MOUNDS,
SHILOH NATIONAL MILITARY PARK (SHY-low)

From Savannah drive 4 miles west on US 64, then 6 miles south on Tennessee 22. Open free, 8 a.m. to 6 p.m. daily in summer; 8 a.m. to 5 p.m. daily in winter; closed Dec. 25.

At the Visitor Center are displayed materials recovered from excavations of a cluster of mounds which lie about three-quarters of a mile away. One fine effigy pipe in the exhibit was excavated in 1899, but most of the digging was done in 1934 by Works Progress Administration labor under the direction of Dr. Frank H. H. Roberts of the Smithsonian Institution.

In all, there are more than 30 mounds in the Shiloh group. Six large ones have flat tops, and temples once stood on them. The seventh large mound, in the shape of an oval dome, was used for burial of the dead. Many smaller mounds were dwelling sites.

The Story. The people who began to live here (perhaps 600 to 800 years ago) followed cultural patterns resembling those of many other mound-building Indians in the Southeast. They constructed platforms for temples, then periodically burned the buildings and added a new layer to the whole outside of the mound. They buried important leaders in graves stocked with pottery, ornaments, and ceremonial objects. Like the inhabitants of Etowah in Georgia they seem to have held great feasts in the plaza around the mounds, and afterward they threw the refuse into deep pits. As a result of studying the remains of the feasts archeologists know that these people must have been corn farmers, that they also fished, gathered clams, and hunted for wild game.

The dwellings near the large mounds were made of upright posts, with saplings and split cane woven in between. This lattice work was then daubed over with clay. For roofs, the builders made a close wickerwork of canes and branches which they covered with leaves and grass, and then over this they plastered clay.

People here, as at many other Southeastern towns, played a game called chunkey, using a discoidal (wheel-shaped) stone. According to Europeans who witnessed the game in historic times, contestants holding greased spears gathered at one end of a long, flat field. A signal was given, and a man rolled the chunkey stone down the field. A moment later the players hurled their spears, each one hoping to estimate the distance the stone would roll before it stopped. The winner —the man who landed his spear closest to the spot where the stone came to a halt—then collected the bets he had made with the other contestants. A number of chunkey stones turned up in the excavations at Shiloh, as did evidence of another gambling game played with marked counters which resembled dice.

By the time Europeans arrived in Tennessee the inhabitants of this site had left. Investigators have not yet been able to say for sure which of the historic Indian tribes may have been descendants of the builders of Shiloh Mounds.

The Name. After driving the Indians from Tennessee, white men settled in the neighborhood of this group of ancient mounds and built Shiloh Church, named for the biblical Shiloh which, perhaps coincidentally, was the site of a temple on a mountain. In 1862, a bloody Civil War battle was fought here at Shiloh, and to commemorate it the site was made a National Military Park. Visitors to the park can get a glimpse of history and of prehistory as well.

TRAVELLERS' REST HISTORIC HOUSE

From Nashville drive 6 miles south on Farrell Parkway to marker. Open, 8:30 a.m. to 5 p.m., Monday through Saturday; 1 p.m. to 5 p.m., Sunday. Admission: adults, $1; children, 25¢.

In the Indian museum, which is part of Travellers' Rest, is a display devoted to the culture of people who built temple mounds from about A.D. 1200 to A.D. 1600. In addition to artifacts which throw light on the Mississippian culture, a large mural shows an artist's interpretation of village life in the vicinity of Nashville in prehistoric times.

NORTH CENTRAL

 A young newspaperman named Ephraim George Squier moved from Connecticut to the small Ohio town of Chillicothe in 1845 and began to edit the newspaper there. Near his new home he saw a number of large earthen mounds— man-made, he was told—and he immediately grew curious about them. A physician, Dr. E. H. Davis, also of Chillicothe, shared Squier's interest.

Working as a team, these two amateurs started to investigate. Inside the mounds they discovered human bones and artifacts. Surveys in Ohio and other states revealed more and more sites where vast quantities of earth had been piled up by human hands. Before long Squier and Davis had dug into more than 200 of the mounds, and these were only a sampling of what existed in the Midwest.

Obviously a sizeable and well-organized population had carried out these tremendous projects. Innumerable craftsmen must have been engaged in making the grave goods lavished on burials. Why did an apparent obsession with funeral ceremonies move these people? And what mysterious fate overtook them in th end? Neither white settlers nor the Indians they encountered in the area had any clues to offer.

Squier and Davis needed financial help for their investigations, and they got it from the young American Ethnological Society. Within a year Squier had a report ready. Soon it had expanded into a big book, and in 1848 the newly established Smithsonian Institution brought it out under the title *Ancient Monuments of the Mississippi Valley.*

The Squier and Davis report was the Smithsonian's first publication. It also marked the beginning of widespread interest in the earthworks which were a very prominent feature in America's 19th-century landscape. The two men visited, dug into, and surveyed mound after mound in the central part of the United States. Then Squier drafted beautiful maps of the sites and wrote careful descriptions. In addition, a good many theories came from his facile pen, and here he shared the views of those who were at that time busy driving the original Americans off the land. Indians, in Squier's opinion, were such inferior creatures that they could never have built the great earthen structures in the Mississippi and Ohio valleys. Nor could they have made the sculptured pipes, the pottery, and the handsome ornaments he and Davis were finding in ancient graves. Another people—a separate race of Mound Builders— must have been the creators of such works.

Prehistoric houses and a stockade area are reconstructed at Aztalan State Park. Ancient residents at Aztalan followed the Mississippian lifeway.

More than a hundred years later archeologists were still plagued with the myth of the Mound Builders which Squier and Davis and the Smithsonian Institution had done much to circulate. So persistent was the notion of a mysterious extinct race that Robert Silverberg has found ample material for tracing its history in a fascinating book, *The Mound Builders of Ancient America.*

The fact, of course, is that Indians were quite capable of the esthetic and social achievements which Squier and Davis and a host of other investigators observed. It was also true that by the 19th century all mound building had ceased. The art forms associated with mounds were no longer remembered in central United States, and Indians knew as little as white men about what had happened to earlier dwellers on the land.

Interpretation of the Mounds

There are still a great many unanswered questions. Archeologists do not all agree in their interpretations of material which continuing excavation turns up. However, what has so far emerged as a result of recent scientific study is roughly this:

Toward the end of the Archaic Period, about 3,000 years ago, groups of people in parts of northeastern and north central United States seem to have developed special burial practices. They covered the dead with mounds of earth. Other customs later came to be linked with mound burial. People began to place offerings in graves—such things as food and weapons and ornaments. Ceremonial activities were added to the making and burying of grave goods. Fire took on importance in these rituals. Bodies were sometimes cremated, and mortuary offerings were broken and burned. In many places bodies were first exposed until the flesh had decayed or had been removed by scavengers. Then the bones were covered with a kind of paint made from the mineral known as red ocher, which is an oxide of iron. Sometimes red ocher powder was sprinkled in quantity over both the remains and the grave goods.

No one knows why this mineral was considered important for burials. One suggestion is that red blood is associated with life, and therefore blood-colored ocher in a burial may have been a wordless way of trying to summon continued life for the person who was being buried.

The Red Ocher people in Illinois made pottery which they often placed in their small, low, burial mounds, along with projectile points and beads of copper and shell. Pottery, of course, is hard to transport. Those who make it do not usually travel much. This means that Red Ocher people must have been able to get all the food they needed within a small area. They were good hunters and skilled in the use of every kind of wild food. Eventually some of their descendants, whose lifeway is known as the Morton culture, learned to grow food in gardens, and by 500 B.C. full-scale farming was being done in much of the central Illinois valley. Throughout all this time the cult of the dead persisted. Bigger mounds were built. Grave goods became more elaborate.

Meanwhile, in the Ohio Valley to the east, groups of hunters had been developing lifeways that were similar to those in Illinois. They started with simple graves in small mounds. Later they placed the dead in log tombs over which they heaped earth. On top of the first burial they added others, gradually building up a high structure shaped like a cone. Groups of these conical mounds covered whole mortuary areas near villages. Here, too, ceremonies and the creation of grave goods—including pottery—occupied large numbers of people and led to the distinctive culture now called Adena.

The Woodland Lifeway

Adena people began to make pottery about 1000 B.C., as did many other groups in the eastern two-thirds of North America. For archeologists, pottery marks the beginning of a new period. Some call it Woodland; some call it Ceramic. All agree that it is distinguished also by the development of agriculture. Woodland is perhaps an unfortunate term for a lifeway that extended from the eastern forest lands onto the treeless plains, but since the name appears in most books and museums, it is hard to avoid.

After the Adena had established themselves in Ohio, another lifeway called Hopewell appeared. Hopewell was named for a farmer, M. C. Hopewell, on whose land near Chillicothe archeologists excavated one of the richest of all burial mounds. Hopewell grave goods were beautiful, lavish, and sophisticated. Experts have found them baffling as well. At first all the evidence indicated that this new culture had developed from the simpler Adena culture in the Ohio Valley. This proved not to be so. On further study, Hopewell traits in Ohio seemed to spring from nowhere. Suddenly, about 100 B.C., large Hopewell burial mounds were being constructed in groups and surrounded by earthen walls built in the form of immense circles, octagons, and squares. For a long time this culture co-existed with Adena. Activity around mounds went on for six or seven hundred years, and then the Hopewell way of life vanished, leaving no trace except the great structures that were soon covered with forest or sod.

With no evidence that Hopewell began in Ohio, the question arose: Where did the Hopewell phenomenon originate? Some archeologists came to the conclusion that it began with people who moved into Illinois from somewhere around Lake Ontario. After establishing themselves, they spread outward with great vigor to Ohio and other areas as well. Another theory was that it developed on the spot among people who had been living in Illinois for a long time and who got new vigor from new food resources, perhaps a very productive variety of corn. Still other archeologists now think that its origins lay in the Poverty Point culture which centered in the lower Mississippi Valley.

As Hopewell farms along the various rivers prospered, men had more and more time in which to make and accumulate goods. They also had time and energy to use in expanding their ceremonies for the dead and in building huge earthworks connected with the ceremonies.

Much of Hopewell material wealth went into the burial mounds. Funerary offerings included daggers and knives chipped from huge pieces of obsidian, tobacco pipes carved from stone in the shapes of animals and birds, sheets of mica precisely cut in the outlines of birds or serpents or human hands, possibly for use as stencils. In one burial alone archeologists found 48,000 fresh-water pearls.

A great deal of the raw material for grave goods came from distant places. Mica and quartz crystal were brought from the Appalachian Mountains. The obsidian had to be transported all the way from the Southwest or from the Yellowstone area in Wyoming. Silver for beads came from Ontario, copper for beads and other ornaments from around Lake Superior. Florida provided shells and the teeth of shark and alligator, while sources closer to home furnished bear teeth for necklaces, feathers for gorgeous feather-cloth robes, pearls by the hundreds of thousands. And all this was then buried under earth and stone laboriously heaped up in layer after layer to form large mounds.

Ceremonies and Trade

As burial practices became more complex, so did community life. Groups were now divided into social classes, and the funerals of those who belonged to the highest class were held with enormous pomp and grandeur. At the same time Hopewell ceremonialism stimulated a very intricate economy. Men engaged in trade over a wide area. A relentless search for raw material had to go on because the need could never be satisfied, as a steady stream of manufactured objects disappeared underground.

With trade the dynamic Hopewellian lifeway traveled outward. Their ceremonial ideas eventually dominated people from Weeden Island in Florida all the way to the Canadian border, and from Kansas City to New York State. Wherever the Hopewell influence went, the local people seem to have kept their own basic patterns of existence while they adopted— or perhaps submitted to—the new religious practices. (Some archeologists compare Hopewell influence to that of the Muslims in Africa and the Middle East. Hopewell, they believe, was a cult rather than a culture.) In the Ohio Valley Hopewell and Adena existed side by side and probably borrowed notions from each

A. Serpent Mound in Ohio. It is nearly one-quarter of a mile long, 20 feet wide, and 4 to 5 feet high. The date it was built is not known. Ohio Historical Society photo. B. A Hopewell man wearing copper earspools, necklace of copper and pearls, and headdress of deer antlers. The reconstructed figurine is in the Field Museum of Natural History, Chicago.

other, although their relationship may not always have been completely friendly. In the end large numbers of Adena seem to have given in to pressure of some sort. Groups of them migrated southward into Kentucky; others went eastward all the way to Chesapeake Bay.

For more than 700 years Hopewellians in the huge Midwest area lived intricate lives that centered around death. Then for reasons no one yet understands, their influence declined and finally disappeared, not only in Ohio but also in all their religious centers. What could have happened?

One suggestion is that a slight change of climate may have brought a long period of crop failure. Without a stable food base people could no longer afford the luxuries the cult demanded. And so the cult died, although its practitioners lived on.

Another suggestion related to supposed climate change is that crop failure brought about greatly increased competition for food. This meant raids or warfare. There is evidence of burning and massacre and the building of defenses at several Hopewell centers. But warfare could have had another disruptive effect on the cult. Raids and fighting could have stopped the trading for raw materials that were essential to the manufacture of elaborate grave goods. Without these necessary exotic materials the religion itself ground to a halt.

Or it may be simply that everyone got tired of the whole business. Perhaps a kind of disillusionment set in: Why squander life to celebrate death? Men may well have found unendurable the contradiction between creating wealth and destroying it for the glory in death of priests or chiefs who probably weren't very lovable taskmasters when they were alive. Whatever the reason, by A.D. 750 the Hopewell influence had ended almost everywhere.

The period from about A.D. 600 to 800 in Illinois has been called a kind of "Dark Age." People apparently built no mounds, wore no rich ceremonial dress, made no elegant grave goods. Villages housed only small groups, and men who had once been skilled farmers raised only small field crops to supplement their hunting. In other words, they lived much as their ancestors had done 2,000 years before.

The Mississippian Culture

Then change began again along the Mississippi River near the mouth of the Missouri, in the area where several important age-old travel routes came together. This was also a region where the soil was particularly good for growing corn. Here, about A.D. 800, a new way of life appeared. Before long there was new mound building. Separate social classes developed once more, along with intense ceremonialism, including once again an emphasis on death. However, the new religiosity had many very distinct features. Rituals were aimed at insuring the productivity of crops. The new flat-topped pyramidal mounds served chiefly as platforms for religious structures, although priests or leaders were sometimes buried in them. The prosperity of communities often led to a wealth of beautiful artifacts, but they were not all intended primarily to be grave goods.

The origin of this lifeway, which archeologists call Mississippian, has not been established to everyone's satisfaction. It seems to have been based in part at least on ideas that came from Mexico, possibly in association with a kind of corn farming that was enormously productive. At any rate, Mississippian habits of farming, of temple-mound building, of pottery making, and of religious ritual spread widely throughout much of the Mississippi drainage system and spilled over into other areas of the Southeast as well.

Between A.D. 1200 and 1500 these people flourished. Then their society, like that of the Hopewell, began to decline. Although temple mounds in some places were still built and used in historic times, by the late 17th century all the great centers were abandoned, and Mississippian ceremonialism had withered and died.

In the 19th century all these giant earthworks—and the spectacular quantities of loot that came from them—were bound to intrigue both professional and amateur investigators. They also attracted mound-miners who were animated by the spirit of free enterprise. These men dug up objects not for what they could learn by studying them but for what they could earn by selling them. There was a market for archeological goodies, and much that scientists would like to have in museums has now disappeared. The amazing thing is that unrifled burials do still exist, and very often professional people are called in to excavate them.

Mound builders, however, were not the only prehistoric inhabitants of the North Central area. Near the town of Modoc in southern Illinois, for example, ancient hunters 10,000 years ago discovered a shelter under overhanging rock in the bluffs along the Mississippi River. Off and on, until about 3000 B.C., families slept, ate, and made tools and weapons in this dry, protected spot. Later, small bands of hunters used it in spring and fall. All of them left the trash of daily living, and by the time archeologists discovered the Modoc shelter, 27 feet of refuse had piled up on the floor.

South of Modoc, along the Ohio River, hunters now known as Baumer people settled in semipermanent villages about 3,000 years ago. Men continued to search for game, but they came home to solid dwellings made of upright logs where women and children lived the year round. This kind of existence was possible because the Baumer people and some of their neighbors had learned to store large supplies of acorns and hickory nuts in pits underground. In winter when the earth was frozen, empty pits were sometimes used as graves.

Farther up the Ohio, particularly in Kentucky, groups of people lived mainly by harvesting freshwater shellfish. As the piles of discarded shells grew higher, they camped on top of the heaps. Very few of these shell mounds can now be seen, but many have been studied by scientists. One, called Indian Knoll, on the Green River in Kentucky, is so well known that it has been declared a National Historic Landmark. About 3000 B.C., its occupants buried their dead under the shells as a matter of convenience. Eight hundred graves have been found there, although the mound was primarily a habitation site, not a cemetery.

Everywhere, as men exploited their environment, they sought not only new foods but also new materials for tools and weapons. Near the Great Lakes, about 3000 B.C., they found one material little known elsewhere—deposits of pure copper that could be mined with stone tools. By a process of heating and hammering the metal, they fashioned it into knives, projectile points, drills, and adzes. Later they used it—and traded it to others for use—in beads and ornaments and ceremonial objects.

Visitable copper mines, flint quarries, burial mounds, ceremonial centers—all offer glimpses of the larger aspects of prehistoric life in the great North Central area. The many excellent museums give smaller, intimate insights into ways of living very different from our own. Together these macro- and micro-remnants of the past are enough for a picture to take form, and we can begin to see men, no matter how alien their customs, as part of nature, always adjusting and experimenting, always in motion.

Illinois

BURPEE NATURAL HISTORY MUSEUM

Rockford Park District Building, 813 N. Main St., Rockford. Open free, 1 p.m. to 5 p.m., Tuesday through Saturday; 2 p.m. to 5 p.m., Sunday; closed major holidays.

Random finds, identified by county of origin, are on display together with some Woodland materials—largely Middle Woodland—from limited excavations.

CAHOKIA MOUNDS STATE PARK
(kah-HO-kee-uh)

National Historic Landmark
From St. Louis, Mo., drive 4 miles east on US (business) 40 to 7850 Collinsville Rd., which is between East St. Louis and Collinsville. The museum is open free, 8 a.m. to 6 p.m., daily; the park closes at 10 p.m. Camping.

This easily visitable park, which covers 589 acres, is one of the most important sites in the United States. It includes the largest mound in the country—a man-made pyramid of earth more than 100 feet high—and a number of smaller mounds. At one time the population here was more dense than at any other place in America north of the Valley of Mexico, reflecting a wealth and vigor that made Cahokia a center from which its culture, known as Mississippian, spread over a vast area.

The Story. About A.D. 800 Late Woodland people planted corn in a very fertile area called the American Bottoms, which lies along the east side of the Mississippi River opposite St. Louis. Apparently these people had acquired a variety of corn that was extraordinarily productive. They increased their yields further by using an efficient type of flint hoe to kill weeds that competed with corn plants for sunlight and nourishment.

Raw material for the hoes came from the area near the present town of Mill Creek, in southern Illinois. There, in a deposit of soft clay, men discovered flint nodules which were somewhat flat. This shape easily lent itself to the making of large oval hoe blades which could be attached to wooden handles. To get at the nodules, they dug shafts, some almost 30 feet deep, often with side corridors at the bottom.

With good tools to use and good seed to plant, farmers produced large crops on the fertile land near Cahokia. There was enough corn to feed a great many families. As the population grew, more and more complexities marked the ways in which people related to each other and to their environment. At first, dwellings dotted the landscape in small, haphazard clusters. Then groups of habitations became recognizable villages in which certain important structures were used for community, civic, and religious affairs. To emphasize their importance, village leaders had these public buildings placed on earthen platforms which elevated them above the flat landscape—an idea that probably came from Mexico. Large open plazas in front of the buildings gave them further distinction.

From this busy and growing settlement it was possible for traders to take long canoe trips on the Mississippi and its tributaries—the Missouri, Ohio, Illinois, Tennessee, and Arkansas rivers. Raw materials reached Cahokia from the Gulf of Mexico, the Appalachian Mountains, the Great Lakes, and the Rockies. With trade came an exchange of ideas. Cahokians exported art forms, even attitudes toward life, along the routes they used, and they in turn received stimulation from many places, some very distant.

As time passed, the number of mounds increased until there were about 120 within an area of 3,700 acres. Possibly the region around them became overpopulated. For that reason or some other, groups of Cahokians began to move away. In the new communities they set up, they continued to follow the Mississippian style of life.

Some of these colonies were established in regions where people were still living in Late Woodland ways. One such place was Aztalan in Wisconsin. Another colony seems to have grown up about A.D. 1200 on the Ohio River, near the place where Brookport, Ill., is presently located. Here a major temple mound community developed and apparently served as a trading station on the river. This community, known as the Kincaid Site, is now a National Historic Landmark, but it is *not* open to the public. It in turn seems to have had an important influence on other communities, including Angel Mounds, in Indiana, which is visitable.

Cahokia itself continued to prosper until about 1550, when sudden disaster seems to have ended its existence. Enemies apparently attacked the city and burned it. Who the enemies were is uncertain, and the fate of the survivors is not known. Possibly the Illiniwek Indians of historic times were descendants of the Cahokians. Certainly those who succeeded the Cahokians lived much simpler lives than did their ancestors. The first Europeans to enter the area saw no signs of the high culture that once made Cahokia the center of stimulation in much of eastern North America.

Nineteenth-century settlers found good farmland in the American Bottoms, and they leveled some of the mounds with their plows. For a while Trappist monks planted fields on top of the huge main temple mound, now called Monks Mound. At one time there was danger that it might be torn apart to make fill for a railroad bed. Highway builders and industrial developers destroyed many of the other earthworks. Those which remain are now protected by the State Park.

For years both amateur and professional archeologists worked at the site, and since 1960 intensive scientific work has been going on there. Very likely digging will continue in the summer months. Interested visitors might do well to ask the ranger at the park if it is possible to watch.

Excavation so far has established a good deal about daily life at Cahokia. Its first settlers lived in houses built partially underground. Perhaps the frequent floods in this lowland area convinced people that pithouses were not practical. At any rate, they began to build houses with floors at ground level. For walls they set posts upright in the earth and wove branches in between, basket-fashion. Over this they spread a layer of mud plaster. Then to protect the mud from rain, they added an outer covering of mats. Roofs were thatched with dried grass and supported by a large center post.

This kind of dwelling didn't last long. The roof caught fire easily, and the whole building might burn. When that happened a new home was put up on the same site. Houses were built, over and over again, one above another, for hundreds of years, leaving a series of hints about existence in the one settlement north of Mexico that might be called a city.

Other hints need further study. For example, there seems to be evidence that Cahokians sought good crops by conducting ceremonies that included sacrifice of the most valuable of all things

The Meaning of a Mound

What does a mound show about the people who built it?

A mound has a definite shape. It is planned. It is not spontaneous or haphazard. This means that there was a social mechanism for planning and for getting plans carried out.

A mound means division of labor. There were planners or leaders involved in its construction, and there were those who carried out the plans—who were led. In other words, there were social classes, at least in rudimentary form. There were rulers and ruled.

Rulers had to have time in which to do their ruling. They had to be able to eat without spending all of their days obtaining food. This meant either that leaders were very successful part-time food getters or they were fed out of the stores grown or collected by others. Moreover the food supply had to be large enough to sustain the common people while they expended an immense amount of energy in piling up huge quantities of earth.

Mounds also meant that their builders had religious beliefs. They had adopted or invented ways to feel comfortable amid the baffling complexities of life and the painfully recurrent fact of death. To judge from what we know has happened among similar groups of people who have been directly observed, the leisure-time activities of some members of the mound-builder community must have gone into developing reassuring myths and shamanistic procedures. As time went by, these may have led to ceremonies and rituals supervised by full-time specialists whom we would call priests.

The religious beliefs which mound builders held provided motivation for the great trouble they took in burying their dead, often amid riches and almost always under great heaps of earth. By such activity people must have sought either to influence events in some magic way or to do something that seemed to fit the living satisfactorily into the immutable flow of events.

Mound builders also had thoughts for the welfare of loved ones—or feared ones—who had died. They were solicitous for the continuing comfort of those whom they regarded as in some way important. In imagination they created circumstances that lay ahead for those who had ceased to live in the flesh, and then they laid palpable conveniences—garments, meals, weapons, implements, amulets—close to the bodies or bones of the deceased. Here were real objects that could be taken as testimony to the reality of some kind of ongoing existence.

Mounds tell us all this about people who lived within nature and at the same time erected a world outside it—a world of the supernatural. Mounds say that their builders elaborated life in ways that were different from those worked out by earlier people. The simplicity of the shape of the mound belies the intricacy of the society that produced it.

A

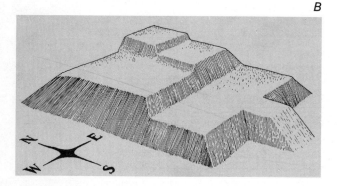

B

—human life. This practice was known in Mexico where maize agriculture originated. However, the full extent and meaning of human sacrifice in the Mississippian culture is not yet understood.

Possibly associated with agriculture was another discovery reported in 1964 by Warren L. Wittry of the Cranbrook Institute of Science. Four very large circles, once defined by upright posts, turned up in the course of excavation. To create one of these perfect geometrical forms, the builders apparently drove a peg into the ground, attached one end of a rope to it, then holding the free end of the rope taut, walked in a circle to outline the circumference. One of the circles was 410 feet across. If a Cahokian had stood by a post that was set near its center, then sighted the sun behind one of the posts on the circumference, he could have worked out a sort of calendar that would have indicated the day on which corn planting was best done.

The Name. When French explorers entered Illinois in 1673 they met several Algonquian-speaking tribes which had formed a confederacy. These Indians called themselves the Illini (ILL-in-ee) or Illiniwek. One tribe, known as the Cahokia, lived in the American Bottoms near the mounds—which by association became known as the Cahokia Mounds.

Archeologists aren't sure, but some of them think that the ancestors of the Cahokia Indians of 1673 may indeed have been the builders of the mounds that bear their name.

The Museum. A small museum in the park gives some introduction to the site and to prehistoric Indian life.

CHICAGO NATURAL HISTORY MUSEUM

See Field Museum of Natural History, page 133.

DICKSON MOUNDS MUSEUM OF THE ILLINOIS INDIAN

From Lewistown drive 3 miles east on US 24, then 2 miles south on Illinois 78 to directional sign. Or from US 136 just west of Havana drive 5 miles north on Illinois 78 to directional sign. Open free, 8:30 a.m. to 5 p.m., daily; closed Jan. 1, Easter, Thanksgiving, Dec. 25. Camping nearby.

A new building, designed to suggest the shape of a prehistoric mound, houses the museum and encloses the burial mound which has made this place famous. Inside the building it is possible to see 234 burials exactly as they were found by archeologists.

Not far from the museum is the Eveland prehistoric village which can also be visited. In a new building there, a color-slide show with a taped commentary gives a good deal of information about the history of the whole site. The Dickson Mounds Museum is a branch of the Illinois State Museum.

The Story. About 15,000 years ago the front edge of the last major Ice Age glacier reached into the northern part of Fulton County in Illinois. On the tundra, which stretched southward from the ice, herds of grass-eating animals grazed, and small bands of Paleo-Indians hunted them. When the ice began to melt and move northward, a forest of fir, spruce, and pine grew up where the tundra had been. Now mastodons, elk, and deer browsed on shrubbery and the lower branches of the trees, and men hunted the browsers.

About 7,000 years ago Archaic hunters and gatherers managed existence here, living on

A. Figurines like this one, which was found at Knight Mounds in Illinois, have provided archeologists with information about the appearance of Indians who followed the Hopewell lifeway. After a reproduction in the Field Museum of Natural History, Chicago. B. Monks Mound at Cahokia, Illinois, was approximately this shape in its final stage. It was almost as big as the largest pyramid in Egypt. The mound is named for the Trappist monks who once used its top surface for planting crops. After Knoblock. C. Red Paint people of the Archaic Period hunted moose using spears and spear throwers (atlatls). This diorama is in the Field Museum of Natural History, Chicago. Field Museum of Natural History photo.

C

smaller game, nuts, seeds, and shellfish. Some of these Archaic people left evidence of their camp-sites along the Illinois River, near what is now Dickson Mounds Museum.

By 1000 B.C. their successors were following a new pattern of life which archeologists call Wood-land. They made pottery, using designs that were a little different from Woodland designs elsewhere. They cultivated plants and paid a good deal of attention to the burial of their dead. One such group lived for a while in a village within the mu-seum grounds. Their particular variety of Early Woodland culture has been called Black Sand because some of their burials were found on a sandy black layer of earth.

Between 200 B.C. and A.D. 400, people here followed a new pattern—the Middle Woodland. They buried their dead in a large mound, and around it they built a pentagonal earthen enclosure or wall 800 feet across. Like others before them, they left tools and weapons and other evidence of their daily lives.

Between A.D. 850 and A.D. 950 Late Woodland people occupied a village around which they built a palisade. Apparently life was not peaceful for them. Perhaps men who were spreading out from Cahokia threatened this group, just as they threatened other Woodland people at Aztalan in Wisconsin.

About A.D. 900 Cahokians, or people like them who followed the Mississippian lifeway, moved in and settled here, merging to some extent with the resident Woodland population. At this point a memorable development began. The Mississippians started a cemetery in the form of a crescent-shaped mound which kept growing as burials were added to it. Because of the peculiar chemical composi-tion of the wind-blown soil used to cover these burials, large numbers of skeletons were beauti-fully preserved. More than a thousand have been found.

Farmland was good in this neighborhood. There was also an ample supply of waterfowl and mus-sels and forest mammals. People lived in relative prosperity until about A.D. 1300, when something up-set their relationship to the world around them. Pos-sibly a slight change in climate made farming more difficult. Possibly poor conservation practices, such as the custom of setting fire to forests in order to get farmland, reduced productivity near Dickson Mounds. Perhaps some disease swept through the community and reduced the population and the vitality of the survivors. Whatever the reason, ac-tivity at Dickson Mounds ended. Occasional bands of hunters were the only inhabitants until Euro-peans arrived.

The Name. In 1833 the Dickson family settled on land around the burial mound. In 1927 Dr. Don F. Dickson, a physician, began scientific investigation of the human bones that he found on the place. What started out as medical curiosity about pos-sible evidence of disease in prehistoric skeletons ended in archeological curiosity about all aspects of life here. Dr. Dickson did a great deal of exca-vating and did it so well that he attracted the in-terest and admiration of professional archeologists. When it came time to choose an official name for the museum at the site, it was easily agreed that the Dickson name should be used.

The form of the name is plural, although only one mound is covered by the museum. Another was once visible about a mile away, and this may be why people got into the habit, which has stuck, of referring to Dickson Mounds—with an *s.*

Special Interest. Dickson Mounds has proved to be a rich source of information. There is appar-ently so much more that can be learned here by scientist and layman alike that the Illinois State Museum, with funds provided by the Illinois Gen-eral Assembly, has established research facilities at the site. Work continues at Dickson Mounds and elsewhere in the vicinity. There are known to be 1,000 mounds and village sites in Fulton County alone.

FIELD MUSEUM OF NATURAL HISTORY

Roosevelt Rd. and Lake Shore Dr., Chicago. Open 9 a.m. to 4 p.m., Monday through Thursday, Nov., Dec., Jan., Feb.; 9 a.m. to 5 p.m., Monday through Thursday, March, April, Sept., Oct.; 9 a.m. to 6 p.m., Monday through Thursday, May, June, July, Aug.; 9 a.m. to 9 p.m., Friday, all year; 9 a.m. to 5 p.m., Saturday and Sunday, all year. Admission: adults, $1; children 6 to 17, 35¢; under 6, free. Maximum family rate: $2.50.

Exhibits and dioramas in several halls of this great museum throw light on the prehistory of Indians north of Mexico. Taken all together they tell a gen-eral story of man on this continent before the arrival of Europeans, with particular emphasis on people who inhabited the North Central region. One display deals with prehistoric man in the Chi-cago area. Another presents animals which were hunted by early man. Still others show the lives of various tribes on the High Plains, in the Great Basin and California, in the Southwest, and along the Northwest coast to the Arctic.

In addition, the exhibits on ancient people in Mexico and Central America and on stone-age man in the Old World contain material which relates to prehistory in North America.

The museum's large library may be used by anyone seriously interested in archeology. Its read-ing room is open Monday through Friday.

Special Interest. Anyone who comes here after visiting sites open to visitors in other parts of the country will find certain things which could not be seen at the sites themselves. For example, the museum has in its collection material from the original Hopewell Site, and its Hopewell exhibit gives a good idea of how these people built their burial mounds, how they dressed, and what their ornaments were like.

ILLINOIS STATE MUSEUM

Spring and Edwards streets, Springfield. Open free, 8:30 a.m. to 5 p.m., Monday through Saturday; 2 p.m. to 5 p.m., Sunday; closed Jan. 1, Easter, Thanksgiving, Dec. 25.

Archeological exhibits in this general museum cover the whole range from Paleo-Indian times to the his-toric period. A series of dioramas shows the major steps in man's cultural development.

Archeologists connected with the museum have excavated many important sites in Illinois and else-where, and some of the material they have found is included in exhibits. Of special importance is their work at the Modoc Rock Shelter, where they helped to uncover one of the longest records of human existence in North America.

Modoc Rock Shelter was formed when the Mississippi River, carrying great torrents of water from the melting ice of Pleistocene glaciers, ate into the base of a high sandstone bluff on the Illinois side, south of St. Louis. When the water went down, it left a protected area 25 feet deep and about 300 feet long. Ten thousand years ago

Archaic hunters and gatherers began to live under this overhang, which is named for the nearby village of Modoc.

For 5,000 years the shelter served groups of people, at first as a permanent base, later as a seasonal campsite. Then for some reason it was not used for a while, until Woodland Indians began to stop there on occasion and to leave broken pottery and other signs of their visits.

Sheltered from the rain, layer on layer of man's history piled up to a depth of 27 feet. Archeologists now read the story with special attention because it reveals that Archaic Indians in the East followed the same general pattern of existence as that of Archaic people in the West. Clear evidence of this had not appeared before the Modoc Rock Shelter was excavated.

Here also was evidence of steadily changing adjustments to an environment that remained essentially unchanged. The people who lived on the bank of the great waterway could pick up ideas from travelers. Theirs was a relatively rich world, and they learned how to get the most out of it. For example, about 5,000 years ago they used rough chipped stone axes to chop down saplings for the frames of the shelters they built even in their sheltered dwelling place. Then they improved the axes and made them more efficient. To reduce the friction of stone against wood, they began to grind and polish the axe to make it smooth. In time they polished other stone artifacts as well.

Modoc Rock Shelter is not open to the public. Nor are other sites such as the Knight burial mounds in Calhoun County along the Mississippi, where archeologists discovered Hopewell figurines. Reconstructions of these famous figurines can be seen in the museum, along with Hopewell artifacts from other sites.

The Illinois State Museum also directs a new museum at Dickson Mounds near Lewistown, Ill. The facility will feature a series of new exhibits on the development of Indian culture, especially as related to Illinois.

Special Feature. The Illinois State Museum operates a Museumobile—a traveling museum on wheels—designed to enrich young people's knowledge of their state, including its prehistory.

LAKEVIEW CENTER FOR THE ARTS AND SCIENCES

1125 Lake Ave., Peoria. Open 9 a.m. to 5 p.m., Tuesday through Saturday; 1 p.m. to 6 p.m., Sunday; 7 p.m. to 9 p.m., Wednesday; closed Jan. 1, Thanksgiving, Dec. 25. Admission free, Tuesday through Friday; adults, 50¢, Saturday and Sunday.

In the gallery of this institution there is a section devoted to Illinois archeology. Exhibits change from time to time.

MADISON COUNTY HISTORICAL MUSEUM

715 N. Main St., Edwardsville. Open free, 9 a.m. to 5 p.m., Wednesday and Friday; 1 p.m. to 5 p.m., Saturday; 2 p.m. to 5 p.m., Sunday; closed national and local holidays.

Nearly 3,000 artifacts in the Indian collection of this museum are grouped by types—axes together, bannerstones together, and so on. Although some of the material seems to be at least 4,000 years old, no attempt is made to arrange it chronologically or by cultures. A number of artifacts are from Cahokia Mounds. In addition to Illinois material, mostly from Madison County, there are some artifacts from the prehistoric Southwest.

MISSISSIPPI PALISADES STATE PARK

From Savanna drive 2 miles north on Illinois 84 to directional sign on the right. Open free, all year. Roads may be closed during periods of freezing and thawing. Camping.

Within the park are old Indian trails and numerous mounds in which archeologists have done little excavating.

PERE MARQUETTE STATE PARK (PEER mar-KET)

From Alton drive 19 miles northwest via Great River Rd. to Grafton, then 5 miles west on Illinois 100 to the park entrance. Open free, all year except when roads are closed during freezing and thawing. Camping.

Beginning around A.D. 1, Indians left evidence of their presence at 18 different sites in this park, which is named for the 17th-century French explorer, Father Jacques Marquette. A folder issued by the Illinois Department of Conservation summarizing the history of Indian occupation of the area is available at park headquarters.

When Marquette traveled the Illinois and Mississippi rivers, two distinct mound-builder cultures had developed, flourished, and died along their banks. A group known as the Jersey Bluff people once made their homes in the rocky palisades near the park, and they may have been the forerunners of the great mound builders at Cahokia a little way to the south. In adjacent Calhoun County a much earlier people who followed the Hopewell lifeway buried their dead in less prominent earthworks. But the gifts they put into the graves were spectacular. At one of the sites—the Knight mound, which is not visitable—they buried small baked-clay figurines. These portrait statues were purposely broken at the time of burial, but they have been reconstructed and are one of the chief sources of information about Hopewell appearance and dress. Replicas of the Knight figurines can be seen in the Illinois State Museum.

SOUTHERN ILLINOIS UNIVERSITY MUSEUM

Altgeld Hall, on the campus, Carbondale. Open free, 8 a.m. to 5 p.m., Monday through Saturday; 1 p.m .to 5 p.m., Sunday; closed national holidays.

This museum has extensive archeological collections from the Midwest.

STARVED ROCK STATE PARK

From Ottawa drive 6 miles west on Illinois 71 to the east entrance of the park. Or from La Salle drive 6 miles east on Illinois 71, then three-quarters of a mile north on Illinois 178 to west entrance. Open free, all year. Camping.

In this beautiful place on the bank of the Illinois River are old Indian trails through the woods, shelter caves and open sites where prehistoric people camped, and the remains of several burial mounds.

The Story. When the first wandering hunters entered Illinois, perhaps 10,000 years ago, a band of them discovered Starved Rock and camped there. The Rock is a section of the Illinois River bluff which rises 125 feet straight up from the water. It can be approached only from one side, and so its flat circular top made it an ideal lookout spot.

During the Archaic Period, people sometimes camped on the Rock. At other times men probably camped below, brought chunks of stone to the top

Illinois Archeological Survey photo.

Portrait of a Leader

In 1952 archeologists digging at a site on the Illinois River uncovered the skeleton of an Indian who had been buried there at some time between A.D. 900 and A.D. 1200. With only his bones and a few artifacts to study, the scientists have put together an amazingly complete picture of the man.

Evidence that he was a leader is in the articles placed beside him in the grave: two necklaces with a total of 468 beads, each laboriously shaped of shell brought from the Gulf of Mexico; bracelets and anklets of shell beads; four projectile points; a stone for use in grinding red pigment; a pottery jar. Other objects are the sort of thing that might be given to someone who held office—a large stone ceremonial blade, a piece of galena ore imported from the north, a tobacco pipe, an animal rib that had been carved for some purpose, and a long rod made of horn. Negative evidence that the man was important lay in the other burials nearby. They contained much less wealth in the form of grave goods.

After examining the skull, Bartlett Frost of the Detroit Historical Museum modeled the bust shown here, basing his work on information that physical anthropologists have put together. Size of facial muscles, for example, is indicated by bony structure where the muscles are attached. Skin thickness and nose shape are determined by other measurements. The result is this portrait of an Indian leader in Illinois a thousand years ago.

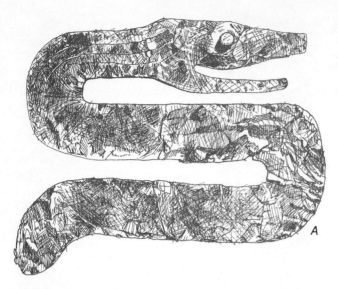

of the bluff, and sat about making projectile points and tools. The remains of their workshops have turned up in archeological excavations. One such group also left behind a copper spearpoint, one of the earliest known. Others, over a period of two or three thousand years, lost or discarded their hammerstones, scrapers, drills, and grinding tools around their campsites on the Rock.

Later, when people began to follow the Woodland way of life, women cooked here and threw away their broken pots. On the flatlands near by, the dead were buried in mounds. Still later, other groups visited the Rock, at least occasionally, up until historic times.

The Name. According to legend, the Illini Indians who lived along the river were attacked by Ottawa and Potawatomi warriors. The Illini fled to the top of the Rock, which they were able to defend until their food gave out. In the end many died of hunger. Hence the name Starved Rock.

UNIVERSITY OF ILLINOIS
MUSEUM OF NATURAL HISTORY

Natural History Building, on the campus, Urbana. Open free, 8 a.m. to 5 p.m., Monday through Saturday; closed national holidays.

In the museum's Hall of the Past several cases display material related to the life of prehistoric Indians in Illinois, beginning with Paleo times about 8000 B.C. There are exhibits of the tools, clothing, hunting gear, and homes of Archaic people, of Woodland people from 2500 B.C. to A.D. 1300, and of the Mississippian culture from A.D. 900 to A.D. 1500. Special displays identify various types of pottery and stone artifacts and tell how certain artifacts were made.

A portion of the hall is devoted to prehistoric man in the Southwest.

Indiana

ANGEL MOUNDS STATE MEMORIAL

National Historic Landmark
From downtown Evansville drive 7 miles east on Indiana 662 to a point 2½ miles west of Newburgh, then south three-quarters of a mile on Fuqua Rd. to Pollack Ave., then east about one-half mile to site entrance. Open free, 8 a.m. to 5 p.m., Thursday through Saturday, all year. Camping nearby.

People who followed the lifeway which archeologists call Mississippian lived here on the bank of the Ohio River from about A.D. 1400 to A.D. 1600. Like others in their day, they were farmers, traders, and builders of temple mounds. What makes this site unusual and important is its fate in modern times. It lies in a spot that industry has not invaded. It escaped extreme depredation by relic hunters. And for 20 years it was turned over, with adequate financing, to archeologist Glenn A. Black to excavate. Foot by foot he studied the village, which probably marks the most northeasterly extension of the Mississippian culture.

Black dug into the mounds. He stripped away soil from the living areas, and unearthed more than 2½ million pieces of material. Still there is much to be discovered, and scientists will continue to work at the site for some time to come. Meanwhile a good deal can be told about the life that went on there.

A. An ornament in the shape of a snake, cut from a sheet of mica. The original, found at Turner Mound, Ohio, is now in the Peabody Museum, Harvard University. B. These rounded heaps of earth are part of nine mounds built by Indians nearly 2,000 years ago in an area used for ceremonies and funeral rites. The site is now part of Mounds State Park, Indiana. Indiana Natural Resources photo.

The people who built the mounds were emigrants, probably from Illinois. They may not have been entirely welcome, for they chose to build in a spot that was easy to defend. In front of their village an island in the river shielded them from approach across open water. A stream, now dry, protected the site from the rear. For extra safety the settlers surrounded the village with a palisade. This wall, about a mile in length, was made of stout posts placed upright in the ground. Branches were woven between the posts and then plastered over with mud. At intervals in the palisade were bastions, or lookout towers

In times of peace the river channel between shore and the island offered an easy place to fish. The surrounding land, which lay above the water level of most spring floods, was good for farming. In the woods not far away men found game.

Inside the palisade these hard-working people built 11 mounds, the largest with three distinct terraces. A religious structure may have stood on the lowest terrace. Possibly the house of the principal chief occupied the terrace above that. Higher still, on the northeast corner, was a conical mound. Perhaps the chief made ceremonial use of this prominence, the top of which was 44 feet above the surrounding land. Some experts think he may have mounted it daily to greet the rising sun.

A second large mound is believed to be the location of the main religious structure in the town. Between this temple mound and the chief's mound was the town square, where important ceremonies took place. On ordinary days people gambled in the square and young men played games. Members of the upper class probably lived close to the square; common people, farther away.

The town as a whole seems to have served as the religious center for an area that extended outward for 50 or 60 miles. What happened to it in the end is not known. Like other Mississippian settlements it was deserted when Europeans reached the Ohio Valley.

The Museum. A small museum at the site contains models of the mounds and the other features of the town. Representative artifacts are on display, and some exhibits show how the artifacts, which are common in southern Indiana, changed with the passage of time. A new, enlarged building is being constructed here. Other material from the site may be seen by appointment at the museum of the Indiana Historical Society.

The Name. Angel was the family name of people who once owned the mounds. Now the state of Indiana owns the site, and students in archeology at Indiana University dig here.

CHILDREN'S MUSEUM OF INDIANAPOLIS

3010 N. Meridian St., Indianapolis. Open free, 9 a.m. to 5 p.m., Tuesday through Saturday; 9 a.m. to 9 p.m., Friday; 2 p.m. to 5 p.m., Sunday; closed Friday nights and Sundays, June, July, Aug., and national holidays.

Indian artifacts, both prehistoric and historic, are displayed in this museum. Exhibits and dioramas have been designed to show grade-school children how tools, weapons, and utensils were made and how they were related to the everyday life of the people who used them.

INDIANA HISTORICAL SOCIETY

140 N. Senate Ave., Indianapolis. Open free, by appointment.

Here may be seen some of the materials recovered from Angel Mounds.

INDIANA STATE MUSEUM

202 N. Alabama St., Indianapolis. Open free, 9 a.m. to 5 p.m., Tuesday through Saturday; closed Jan. 1, Dec. 25.

This museum contains a display of prehistoric polished stone artifacts from Indiana. The staff is in the process of adding exhibits devoted to various prehistoric cultures and the changes in them as illustrated by the changing use of materials.

INDIANA UNIVERSITY MUSEUM

Student Building, on the campus, Bloomington. Open free, 8 a.m. to noon, 1 p.m. to 4:30 p.m., Monday through Saturday; 1 p.m. to 4:30 p.m., Sunday; closed holidays.

In this general science museum are archeological materials, fully explained, which have been recovered from scientific excavations in various parts of the New World, including areas north of Mexico.

MIAMI COUNTY HISTORICAL MUSEUM

Court House (4th Floor), Peru. Open free, 9 a.m. to noon, Monday through Saturday; closed holidays.

Prehistoric materials on display here include some artifacts from each of these cultures: Paleo-Indian, Adena, Hopewell, Mississippian, and Fort Ancient.

MOUNDS STATE PARK

From Anderson drive 4 miles east on Indiana 232. Open at all times. Admission: $1.25 per car, June through Aug., and on weekends April, May, Sept., Oct. Camping.

Nine well-preserved mounds can be visited here. Five of them are circular, two fiddle-shaped, one rectangular, and one resembles a figure eight.

The largest, the Great Mound, seems to have served at first as the site of an important man's burial. After a tomb of logs was built over his body, the structure was burned and covered with earth before the fire had gone out. Later the earthen mound was enlarged and surrounded by a kind of fence. Its summit became a crematory for people whose remains were then buried in other mounds.

Artifacts found at the site include sheets of mica, a tobacco pipe, and some rather unusual ornaments which seem to have been attached to clothing rather than worn around the neck. These and the burials indicate that the people who conducted their ceremonies here probably followed the Hopewell lifeway.

PUTERBAUGH MUSEUM

11 N. Huntington St., Peru. Open free, 1 p.m. to 5 p.m., daily except Wednesday and Sunday; closed holidays.

Artifacts on display represent the Paleo-Indian, Woodland, and Mississippian cultures.

WYANDOTTE CAVE

From Evansville drive 80 miles east on US 460 to Wyandotte, then follow directional signs. Or from

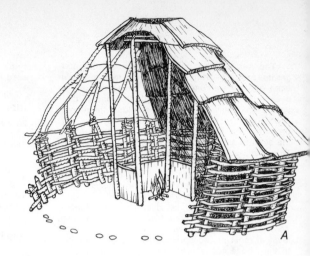

Adena

One of the 19th-century governors of Ohio lived near Chillicothe on a large estate, which he called Adena. Like other property nearby, his grounds had been occupied in prehistoric times by people who built large cone-shaped earthen mounds in which they buried their dead. But unlike most mounds, the one at Adena remained more or less undisturbed until 1901, when an archeologist was allowed to excavate it. The material he uncovered seemed to be the work of a people with very definite and identifiable traits.

When artifacts and burials from other mounds were compared to those at Adena, a general pattern emerged. People with similar traits had lived in prehistoric times throughout much of Ohio, eastern Indiana, northern Kentucky, western Pennsylvania, and parts of West Virginia.

Much of Adena life centered around rituals in honor of the dead. Few people ever had more ways of handling burials. Sometimes they placed an individual in a bark-lined pit on the floor of a house which was then covered with a mound of earth. They cremated other bodies, then buried the remains. Sometimes part of a body was cremated and part buried. Often bodies were left to decay, perhaps lying on raised platforms, and then the cleaned bones were buried. Ritual bowls were made from some skulls, and bone from the skullcap might be shaped and engraved to make gorgets.

Toward the end of their long history, the Adena seem to have paid honor mainly to a few important people who were buried in stout log tombs surrounded by their possessions. These grave goods included copper bracelets and rings, beads of shell and copper, tobacco pipes, ornaments of mica, polished stone, and other materials.

Archeologists have found the skeletons in log tombs especially interesting. Many were tall—men and women both over six feet. Almost all the skulls were flattened at the back, as a result of binding to a cradleboard in infancy. Some also had a groove at the sides which seems to indicate further binding to give the skull a rounded shape.

Tobacco played a part in ceremonies, and the Adena made innumerable pipes, some of clay and some of stone. Often a man's pipe was buried with him, but occasionally archeologists have found large numbers of them associated with a single burial, perhaps because the dead man was a pipe-maker.

In some of their ceremonies, possibly designed to bring good hunting, men wore headdresses imitating deer antlers and masks imitating wolf or puma heads. The jaws of bears and other animals were also carefully cut and ground to make ornaments or charms of some sort.

The original Adena mound cannot be visited, but the house on the estate for which it was named is open to the public.

A. Archeologists believe that one type of Adena house looked like this. Often mud plaster was added to the walls. No original dwelling now exists, but some were destroyed by fire which baked the mud and preserved the imprint of posts and interwoven branches. After Webb. B. This stone pipe is from the original Adena Mound in Ohio. Ohio Historical Society photo.

B

New Albany drive 27 miles west on US 460 to directional sign. Open 8 a.m. to 5 p.m., daily, all year. Admission: varies, depending on length of tour taken. Camping.

Although people usually visit this privately owned cave to see the cave itself, it is of archeological interest on more than one count. Apparently two different groups of people came here at two different times to do two different types of mining. One group hammered out and carried away large quantities of a soft mineral called calcite. What they used it for is not known, possibly because calcite turns to dust under certain conditions. The other group dug out nodules of flint embedded in the walls in a different section of the cave. The flint was, of course, raw material for projectile points, scrapers, and other tools.

At still another place, in the dried mud on the floor of a corridor that had long been blocked off by a calcite formation, Indian moccasin footprints were found, going farther into the cave but not returning. One possible explanation is that the footprints led to a cave exit which was later closed by a rockfall.

Iowa

DAVENPORT PUBLIC MUSEUM

1717 W. 12th St., Davenport. Open 9 a.m. to 5 p.m., Monday through Saturday; 2 p.m. to 5 p.m., Sunday. Admission: adults, 35¢; children, 10¢.

Examples of Mississippian pottery of several kinds from Tennessee and Arkansas are on display here. Also there are exhibits of random local archeological finds.

EFFIGY MOUNDS NATIONAL MONUMENT

From Marquette drive 3 miles north on Iowa 76 to monument entrance. Open free, 8 a.m. to 5 p.m., winter; 8 a.m. to 7 p.m., June through Labor Day; closed Dec. 25. Camping nearby.

Here on high land, which was bypassed instead of being scoured down by glaciers of the Ice Age, Indians built nearly 200 mounds during a period of at least 1,500 years. Some of these mounds are likenesses—effigies—of birds or bears. Others are cone-shaped and were built by people whose customs differed from those of the effigy mound builders. It is possible to see a good sample of both types by walking along a trail that starts at the monument's Visitor Center.

The Story. Twelve thousand years ago in Iowa, Paleo-Indians hunted mammoths and giant bison which grazed on prairie grasses. But changes in climate brought changes in vegetation, and forest slowly covered much of the land along the banks of the Yellow River where it flows into the Mississippi. The big game of earlier times disappeared and people turned to hunting smaller animals.

The earliest tools that have been discovered near Effigy Mounds are woodworking implements—axes, adzes, gouges. Obviously the people who made this kind of tool lived in wooded country. Other evidence shows that they hunted forest mammals, fished, and gathered freshwater mussels. Plants, too, made up part of their diet—wild rice, nuts, fruits, berries. They sewed clothing and wove baskets, using awls that were made of bone or copper.

Their medicine men conducted ceremonies aimed at curing illness and warding off bad luck, but if they had any special burial customs few signs of them have survived.

Their successors, however, began to take a deep interest in death ceremonials. By 2,000 years ago they were following the pattern of many other groups of the North Central area. First they allowed the flesh of their dead to disintegrate. Then they gathered up the bones in bundles, which they buried along with spear points and large stone knifelike artifacts. Often they covered the bones with red ocher.

Later, knowledge of how to make pottery came into this area, and over the years potters improved their techniques and changed the styles of the vessels they made. Gradually people adopted other new customs and accepted new beliefs. Between 100 B.C. and A.D. 600 they participated in the Hopewell Cult.

Hopewell ideas about death and burial included the belief that a wealth of beautiful objects should be placed in graves. To get the material for their grave goods, Hopewellians in Iowa, like those in other places, engaged in trade. Mica for their decorations came from the distant Appalachian Mountains. They used obsidian from Yellowstone Park, conch shells from the Gulf of Mexico, and copper from the Great Lakes area. As in other Hopewellian settlements, mounds were built over the dead. Three such burial mounds can be seen near the Visitor Center in the monument.

A new fashion in mound building began here about A.D. 500, while the Hopewell Cult was still active. The new style dictated that burial mounds should be in the form of effigies—huge earthen likenesses of birds or bears. Twenty-seven such effigy mounds are in the monument.

The Effigy Mound people apparently lived in ways that resembled those of the Hopewellians, but they differed in some ways too, and not only in the kind of mound they built. They did not bury grave goods with their dead. They put copper to practical use in tools instead of merely shaping it into decorations.

By A.D. 1400, Indians who lived here were following the Oneota lifeway. Now they spent more time farming than earlier people had, and they lived in larger communities. Apparently, among the descendants of the Oneota were the Iowa Indians whom Europeans later encountered in the region and from whom the state of Iowa gets its name.

The Museum. Exhibits in the Visitor Center throw light on the prehistory of the monument area, and an audiovisual presentation interprets the archeological findings. Two paintings show what people may have looked like, what they wore, and how they built mounds.

FISH FARM MOUNDS

From New Albin drive 3 miles south on Iowa 26. Open free, 4 a.m. to 10:30 p.m., daily, all year.

At this site which overlooks the Mississippi River are about 30 prehistoric Indian mounds representative of the Woodland culture.

IOWA STATE MUSEUM

E. 12th and Grand Ave., Des Moines. Open free, 8 a.m. to 4 p.m., daily.

Early Woodland, Middle Woodland, and Mississippian artifacts are emphasized in the archeological collections here.

MUSEUM OF HISTORY AND SCIENCE

Park Ave. at South St., Waterloo. Open free, 1 p.m. to 5 p.m., Tuesday through Friday; 10 a.m. to 4 p.m., Saturday; 1 p.m. to 4 p.m., Sunday; closed national holidays.

Four exhibit cases here are devoted to: Early Big-Game Hunters, Bison Hunters, Iowa's First Farmers, and Indians of Ohio.

PIKES PEAK STATE PARK

From McGregor drive 1½ miles south on Iowa 340. Open free, 4 a.m. to 10:30 p.m., daily all year. Camping.

Here, overlooking the Mississippi River, are several mounds, including an impressive effigy mound in the form of a bear.

SIOUX CITY PUBLIC MUSEUM

29th and Jackson streets, Sioux City. Open free, 9 a.m. to noon, 1 p.m. to 5 p.m., Tuesday through Saturday; 2 p.m. to 5 p.m., Sunday.

In addition to ethnological exhibits from the Plains and North Central areas, this museum has some archeological material from northwest Iowa.

STATE UNIVERSITY OF IOWA, MUSEUM OF NATURAL HISTORY

Macbride Hall, on the campus, Iowa City. Open free, 8 a.m. to 4:30 p.m., Monday through Saturday; 1 p.m. to 4:30 p.m., Sunday; closed national holidays.

Of the ten cases in this museum which display archeological material three contain exhibits on cultures north of Mexico. One presents baskets, pottery, and blankets from the Southwest. Another shows clothing, snowshoes, and tools made by Indians of the Far North. The third deals with techniques of pottery decoration. Exhibits in the other cases are changed from time to time.

Kentucky

ADENA PARK

From Lexington drive 8 miles north on US 27, then turn off onto Old Ironworks Rd., and from this turn onto Mount Horeb Pike. The park is on the south side of N. Elkhorn Creek. Open free, by appointment arranged through the Department of Physical Education of the University of Kentucky in Lexington.

In the park is a circular earthwork, of the kind known as a "sacred circle," which surrounds a flat area where a structure once stood. A ditch and an embankment crossed by a causeway form part of the site, which was built and used as a ceremonial center by Adena people. The park is owned by the University of Kentucky.

ANCIENT BURIED CITY

From Cairo, Ill., drive across the Ohio River Bridge, then 7 miles southeast on US 51 to directional sign near Wickliffe. Open 8 a.m. to 6 p.m., daily. Admission: adults, $1.50; children, 75¢.

Here, close to the place where the Ohio River flows into the Mississippi, was once a large community that followed the Mississippian lifeway. Several of the temple mounds and one burial mound built by these people are protected by buildings, in which they may be viewed in a partially excavated state. The site is administered by a commercial enterprise, profits from which go to the Western Baptist Hospital in Paducah, Ky. Excavation, which continues at this site, is not done by professional archeologists, and scientists have been critical of some of the explanations offered to the public by those who interpret the large amount of material that has been recovered and can be seen here.

ASHLAND CENTRAL PARK

Two blocks south of US 60 in Ashland. Open free, 7 a.m. to 10 p.m., daily, all year.

In the playground area in this city park, markers indicate five burial mounds. These are a small fraction of the total number that once existed where the city of Ashland now stands on the bank of the Ohio River. Professional archeologists have not investigated the mounds in Central Park, and it is not known who built them or when.

BEHRINGER MUSEUM OF NATURAL HISTORY

Devou Park, Covington. Open free, 9 a.m. to 5 p.m., Tuesday through Saturday and holidays; 1 p.m. to 5 p.m., Sunday; closed Dec. 1 to April 1.

Included in the archeological displays in this museum is a collection of Adena material.

BLUE LICKS MUSEUM

Blue Licks Battlefield State Park. From Lexington drive 40 miles northeast on US 68 to Blue Licks Spring, then follow directional markers. Open 9 a.m. to 5 p.m., April through Oct. Admission: adults, 50¢; children, 25¢.

Ten thousand years ago a spring of saltwater flowed in the park. Attracted by the salt, mastodons, mammoths, bison, and other animals visited the spring. Big-Game Hunters followed the animals, which sometimes got stuck in the mud and died there.

After the animals of the Ice Age disappeared, hunters continued to camp near the spring from time to time. Finally, about A.D. 1400, people who followed the Fort Ancient lifeway made their homes nearby. Their village, known as the Fox Field Site, has been excavated, and artifacts from it are on exhibit at the museum in the park. Other exhibits contain projectile points used by the early hunters, fishhooks, and stone tools made by later people. Bones of some of the extinct animals are also on display.

Gigantic herds of buffalo in ancient times made a regular path, called a trace, to various salt licks in Kentucky. Near the Falls of the Ohio at Louisville they had a crossing, as did the mammoths and mastodons. Prehistoric peoples also followed trade routes to the crossing. At least one trading expedition may have made its way to the Falls from the neighborhood of Poverty Point far down the Mississippi in Louisiana. Evidence suggesting such a visit was recently discovered—a cache of small baked clay balls of the kind which Poverty Point people used in cooking. Possibly visitors from

Louisiana brought the balls along or they or someone else may have made them on the spot.

On the Indiana side of the river there was once a settlement of shellfish eaters who left piles of discarded mussel shells ten feet deep for almost a mile along the riverbank. Their tools and those of other groups who lived in the area turn up often near the Falls, but no visitable sites remain.

KENTUCKY BUILDING MUSEUM

On the campus, Western Kentucky University, on US 68, Bowling Green. Open free, 9 a.m. to 5 p.m., Monday through Friday; 9 a.m. to 4 p.m., Saturday; 2 p.m. to 4 p.m., Sunday.

In this general museum are displays of prehistoric Indian artifacts representing various cultures in south-central Kentucky.

MAMMOTH CAVE

Mammoth Cave National Park. From Bowling Green drive 22 miles northeast on US 31W to Park City, then north on Kentucky 255 to the park entrance; from here it is 5 miles to park headquarters. From points north and east, take US 31W west to Cave City, then Kentucky 70, 10 miles to park headquarters. Open daily, all year. Admission: Fees for the trips vary, as do hours. Camping.

Indians sometimes camped in the entrance to Mammoth Cave in Archaic times, 3,000 years ago, before they made pottery or did any farming. During one such visit a young girl died. Before moving on, her people buried her in a grass-lined grave at the cave's mouth.

By 400 B.C. men had grown bold enough to enter the dark underground passages. There, on some of the walls, they found curious and beautiful crystals of the mineral gypsum. This soft white substance often appears in shapes that resemble ferns or flowers, and whole corridors are decorated with the ghostly bloom.

Gypsum flowers attracted the Indians, and for some reason they began taking them off the walls. Perhaps they pulverized the mineral and used it as a substitute for salt or as medicine. They may have mixed it into the pigment they used for paint. Possibly they scattered it on their fields after they began to farm nearby. At any rate they ventured farther and farther to get it. Two and a half miles of cave walls show evidence of their mining activity. As tools they used stone hammers and scrapers made of mussel shells. For light they carried torches made from bundles of reeds.

When modern visitors entered, remnants of ancient torches still lay on the cave floor, as did worn-out sandals woven from strips of the inner bark of the pawpaw tree. Here and at nearby Salts Cave, collectors began to find and carry away feather blankets, cloth woven in black and white stripes, dishes made of dried squash rind, string bags, and basket coffins made of cane. Much of this material disappeared into private collections before the caves were put under government protection. Some articles may be seen in the Peabody Museum at Harvard University. A few are on exhibit in the museum at Mammoth Cave Park Headquarters.

In 1935 an explorer came upon the body of an ancient miner who had been killed by a falling rock. Instead of decaying, his flesh had simply dried in the cool, pure cave air. The body has been placed in a sealed glass case which can be seen inside Mammoth Cave.

A

A. Two students in archeology, working at Effigy Mounds National Monument in Iowa, prepare to remove a column of earth intact so that it may be studied in a laboratory. Examining different pollen grains in each layer of the soil discloses what plants grew there at a given time in the past. National Park Service photo.

B. Styles in tobacco pipes varied from one place to another and changed as time went on. This one, in the form of a fish and a bird, was carved by Hopewellian people in Ohio. Original in the Field Museum of Natural History, Chicago.

B

SPEED ART MUSEUM

2035 S. Third St., Louisville. Open free, 10 a.m. to 4 p.m., Tuesday through Saturday; 2 p.m. to 6 p.m., Sunday; closed national holidays.

Prehistoric material on display in the J. B. Speed Art Museum consists mainly of artifacts made by the Adena people in Kentucky and southern Indiana. There is also material of the Paleo-Indian culture.

WESTERN KENTUCKY UNIVERSITY ANTHROPOLOGY MUSEUM

Finley Grise Bldg., on the campus, Bowling Green. Open free, 1 p.m. to 4:30 p.m., Monday through Friday; 8 a.m. to noon Saturday, during the school year; closed during school vacations and after the summer session.

This museum opened in the fall of 1970 with exhibits on the Paleo-Indians and on the Mississippian period in Kentucky, with artifacts from a local site.

Michigan

CRANBROOK INSTITUTE OF SCIENCE

500 Long Pine Rd., Bloomfield Hills. Open 10 a.m. to 5 p.m., Monday through Friday; 1 p.m. to 5 p.m., Saturday, Sunday. Admission: adults, $1.25; children through grade 12, 50¢.

This very active general science museum is interested in archeology and has good exhibits on prehistoric Indian life and culture, including one on Starved Rock (Illinois) stratigraphy and another on the sequence of cultures in Michigan.

FORT MICHILIMACKINAC MUSEUM
(MISH-ill-ee-MACK-in-AW)

National Historic Landmark
On US 75 at the southern end of the Mackinac Bridge, Mackinaw City. Open 8 a.m. to 8 p.m., July, Aug.; 9 a.m. to 5 p.m., May 30 to June 30, Sept. 1 to Oct. 12. Admission: adults, $1; children with parents, free. Administered by the Mackinac Island State Park Commission.

Although the museum here displays Indian material only from the 18th century (Ottawa and Chippewa), visitors can see archeologists at work in the park from June 20 to Aug. 20.

FORT WAYNE MILITARY MUSEUM

6053 W. Jefferson St., Detroit. Open free, 10 a.m. to 6 p.m., Wednesday through Sunday.

On exhibit here is material excavated from a mound on the bank of the Detroit River about 100 yards from the museum.
  Originally a group of mounds, built perhaps 900 years ago, stood on the site. All had been destroyed except this one when the military post was established. Fortunately the commanding officers of the post forbade digging. Then in 1944 the Aboriginal Research Club of Detroit was given permission to excavate.

GRAND RAPIDS PUBLIC MUSEUM

54 Jefferson Ave., Grand Rapids. Open free, 10 a.m. to 5 p.m., Monday through Saturday; 2 p.m. to 5 p.m., Sunday and holidays; closed Dec. 25.

This museum exhibits materials recovered by the Museum of Anthropology of the University of Michigan from Norton Indian Mounds where the Hopewell Cult flourished from about A.D. 1 to A.D. 200. In addition to several hundred artifacts from this site, there are dioramas which show what life may have been like at the mounds nearly 2,000 years ago. There are also exhibits of random local finds.

Special Interest. Every school day in the spring and fall this museum sponsors a bus trip for third-grade school children to Norton Mounds.

ISLE ROYALE NATIONAL PARK

Approaches are only by boat or floatplane from Houghton, Michigan, 73 miles away, or from Grand Portage, Minnesota, 22 miles away. For information on how to reach the park, write to: Superintendent, Isle Royale National Park, Houghton, Michigan 49931. Camping.

Prehistoric copper mines can be seen on Isle Royale, one island in an archipelago in Lake Superior. Beginning perhaps 4,500 years ago, Indians dug pits to expose copper-bearing rock. Then they may have built fires to heat the rock and dashed cold water on it to make it crack into chunks. Finally, using cobbles as hammerstones, they probably broke up the chunks to get at the lumps of pure copper inside.
  Some of the lumps were small. Others were very large. In 1874 one solid mass of copper was found on Isle Royale which weighed 5,720 pounds. On it were clear marks that showed where prehistoric hammerstones had battered off small chunks of the malleable metal. Obviously it had once been even larger than it was when found by white miners. After this immense nugget was exhibited to the public for a while, it was melted down for commercial use.
  There are many of the old mining pits in the park. In or near them has been found evidence that they were worked until historic times. Some of the prehistoric miners may have been ancestors of modern Algonquian and Siouan tribes. There is also evidence of the use of the mines by Iroquois Indians.

KALAMAZOO PUBLIC MUSEUM

315 S. Rose St., Kalamazoo. Open free, 9 a.m. to 6 p.m., Monday through Saturday.

Some archeological material from the Southwest and from the eastern Woodland cultures is included with ethnological exhibits.

MICHIGAN HISTORICAL COMMISSION MUSEUM

505 N. Washington Ave., Lansing. Open free, 9 a.m. to 4:30 p.m., Monday through Friday; noon to 5 p.m., Saturday, Sunday; closed major holidays.

On the first floor in this official, tax-supported museum there are exhibits devoted to the Old Copper culture at sites on the Keweenaw Peninsula and on Isle Royale and to the Hopewell culture in the southern part of the state.

Glacial Kame Culture

When the great ice sheet of the Pleistocene retreated, it left ridges of gravel in many places. Sometimes these ridges are known as glacial kames. *Kame* is a Scottish word for ridge and is pronounced like "came."

Some time after one group of hunting people entered and established themselves in an area which had been glaciated, they began to bury their dead in the gravel ridges. Because they left a distinctive set of grave goods with these burials, archeologists have named them "Glacial Kame" people. Many of their burials have been found in northern parts of Ohio and Indiana, southern parts of Michigan and Ontario, and also in eastern Illinois and southeastern Wisconsin.

As far as is now known, the people who followed the Glacial Kame lifeway lived at some time between 2000 B.C. and 1000 B.C. Their rather elaborate burials included many ornaments but very few tools, a fact which leads some archeologists to think they may have been forerunners of the Adena and Hopewell people who placed great emphasis on funerary practices. It is also possible, though not proved, that the whole later tradition of placing burials in artificial mounds derived from the Glacial Kame practice of using natural mounds.

No Glacial Kame sites have been prepared for the public, but Glacial Kame artifacts can be seen in exhibits in several museums, including the Allen County Museum in Lima, Ohio, and the Ohio Historical Center in Columbus.

Archeology by Satellite

Although the state of Hawaii is excluded from this book because it is not part of the land mass on which Indians lived, archeology on the island state has been linked to the mainland.

Stell Newman, of the University of Hawaii, has experimented with ways of recording archeological data in the field so that it is immediately ready for processing by computer. In 1969 archeologists at a Hawaiian site were in contact by satellite with a computer in Palo Alto, California. They fed in data and promptly received information they needed.

If this amazing technique can be widely applied, archeologists who may be working far from a laboratory or library can get immediate answers to questions that arise in the course of their work, and the answers to these questions may affect the nature of what they do as they dig on in the field. And, of course, this teaming-up of satellite and computer saves labor and time and hastens the day on which new information about the past may be generally available.

A. A pottery head from Seip Mound in Ohio shows how skulls were artificially shaped by binding in infancy. Ohio Historical Society photo.   B. Many Indians liked a certain soft red stone for making the bowls of tobacco pipes. The stone, called catlinite because the artist George Catlin was the first to write about it, occurs in a very large deposit in Pipestone National Monument, Minnesota. This diorama at the monument shows Indians at work quarrying catlinite. National Park Service photo.   C. A Hopewell funeral ceremony is depicted in this diorama in the University of Michigan Exhibits Museum. University of Michigan Museum of Anthropology photo.

MICHIGAN STATE UNIVERSITY MUSEUM

Circle Dr., East Lansing. Open free, 9 a.m. to 5 p.m., Monday through Friday; 1 p.m. to 5 p.m., Saturday, Sunday, holidays; closed Jan. 1, Dec. 25.

Some of the North American prehistoric exhibits in this museum are devoted to Michigan archeology. Others show the culture areas of the continent and techniques used in archeological excavation.

NORTON MOUNDS

National Historic Landmark
From Campau Square in Grand Rapids drive 4 miles south along Grand River on Market St. to the railroad crossing, where Market St. becomes Indian Mound Rd. This is the mound area, and it is undeveloped. Open free, at all times.

Here are 17 mounds, 13 clearly visible, which are all that remain of about 40 once standing in the vicinity. Although the site lies outside Grand Rapids, it is owned by the city. Local citizens are seeking to have the mounds included in a National Monument which would protect and interpret them. Meantime, to avoid littering, the road through the park is closed, and it is necessary to visit the mounds on foot.

The Story. People who practiced the Hopewell Cult moved from the Illinois River valley to this place about 400 B.C. Here as elsewhere they began to pile up earth over the bodies of their dead. Around the mounds they built low earthen enclosures. When a leading member of the community died, lavish funeral ceremonies were held, and gifts were placed in the grave. To get material for their burials, the Hopewell traded with other people in distant places. Copper for beads and tools came from northern Michigan; conch shells for ornaments from the Gulf of Mexico. Decorations and silhouette designs were cut from sheets of mica, which had to be brought from the far-off Appalachian Mountains. Sources close to home provided material for polished stone tools, chipped projectile points, headdresses of deer antlers, and beads of beaver teeth.

For 800 years people continued to build their burial mounds here and at a site, now destroyed, in the center of Grand Rapids. Then for some unknown reason the mound builders stopped.

Archeologists from the University of Michigan have excavated Norton Mounds, and some of the materials they recovered are on exhibit nearby in the Grand Rapids Public Museum. A leaflet about the mounds may be obtained at the museum.

UNIVERSITY QF MICHIGAN EXHIBIT MUSEUM

Washtenaw and N. University avenues, Ann Arbor. Open free, 8 a.m. to 5 p.m., Monday through Saturday; 1:30 p.m. to 5:30 p.m., Sunday; closed national holidays.

In this general natural science museum are exhibits on early Indian sites in Michigan. There are also exhibits of prehistoric Eskimo, Northwest Coast, and Woodland material. Several displays show the manufacture, evolution, and use of Old World tools, some of which were ancestral to prehistoric American tools. Fourteen small dioramas, six of which are devoted to Michigan, show aspects of various Indian cultures before the arrival of Europeans.

The Museum of Anthropology in this same building conducts archeological research. Its collections are for scientific study and are not open to the public.

Minnesota

KATHIO INDIAN MUSEUM

National Historic Landmark
From Minneapolis drive 29 miles northwest on US
52 to Elk River, then 64 miles north on Minnesota
169 to the museum on the west side of Lake Mille
Lacs. Open free, 10 a.m. to 5 p.m., May 16
through Sept. Camping.

In prehistoric times this place was an important
Sioux (Dakota) village, and it remained one until
the 1740s when the Chippewas, who had obtained
guns, drove the still gun-less Sioux westward onto
the plains. The museum, which is operated by the
Minnesota Historical Society, has some prehistoric
material as part of its displays on the history of
the Sioux and Chippewa Indians. A diorama shows
an Indian camp in winter.

Modern Indians in the area still harvest and
preserve wild rice as their ancestors did in prehistoric times, and they offer a demonstration of the
process on several Sundays during the summer at
nearby Mille Lacs Kathio State Park. Also in the
park archeological excavations are conducted from
time to time by the state archeologist and a team of
graduate students from the University of Minnesota.
For dates of the ricing demonstrations and for information about the possibility of observing archeological work in the park, query the Division of Parks
and Recreation, Department of Conservation, St.
Paul, Minn. 55101

MINNESOTA HISTORICAL SOCIETY

690 Cedar St. at Central Ave., St. Paul. Open free,
8:30 a.m. to 5 p.m., Monday through Friday, June to
Oct.; 8:30 a.m. to 5 p.m., Monday through Friday;
10 a.m. to 4 p.m., Saturday; 2 p.m. to 5 p.m., Sunday, Oct. to June; closed national holidays.

Much of the archeological material in this museum
has been recovered from scientifically supervised
excavations. Many prehistoric artifacts are used in
exhibits that tell the story of the Sioux (Dakota)
and the Ojibwa (Chippewa) Indians in the state.
There is also material on mound builders of the
Woodland Period, from about 1000 B.C. A diorama
shows a burial. One exhibit explains how prehistoric tools were made and used.

Special Feature. The skeleton of Minnesota Man
(really a teen-age girl) is on display here.

MINNESOTA MAN SITE

Drive 3 miles north from Pelican Rapids on US 59.
Camping nearby.

Here, where the highway cuts through an embankment, road workers found a skeleton in a bed of
clay that had been laid down during the last part
of the Ice Age. If, as some experts believe, this
skeleton was covered by clay during the Ice Age,
it is very old and very important. Others believe
it was buried in recent times and might be a modern Sioux. All agree that Minnesota Man is a young
female.

Archeologists agree, too, that it is a pity the
excavation of the skeleton was not scientifically
done. It is now difficult to tell with certainty
whether or not the earth above the burial had
been dug or moved. Undisturbed earth would have
given clearer evidence of great age. Moral: When
nonprofessional people make a discovery, they
should call for professional help. If they don't,
what might be an important discovery may end up
only as a puzzle or a hole in the ground.

MOUNDS PARK

Mounds Blvd. and East St., St. Paul. Open free, at
all times.

This park preserves six burial mounds, all that
remain out of 18 or more that once stood in the
area.

PIPESTONE NATIONAL MONUMENT

From Pipestone, at the junction of US 75 and
Minnesota 23, drive about 1 mile north. Open free,
all year. Visitor Center open 8:15 a.m. to 9 p.m.,
summer; 8:15 a.m. to 5 p.m., winter. Camping
nearby.

Among almost all Indians the tobacco pipe had
religious meaning. Very often men smoked it when
an agreement had been made. Thus a pipe was
often a symbol for peace. So important was it in
ceremonial life that Indians traveled great distances to obtain the material they deemed best for
making pipe bowls. Most sought-after was a red-
dish stone that came from a quarry in Minnesota.
The quarry was known apparently over a large
part of the United States and was considered a
sacred spot.

Pipestone is a kind of clay which has been altered by chemical and physical action after having
been laid down under water a very long time ago.
It is soft and easily carved when it first comes
out of a pit, then hardens in contact with air.

Archeologists do not know exactly when Indians began to visit the Pipestone Quarry, but they
feel sure it must have been at least 300 years ago.
There was mining at the site when the first whites
appeared in the area. At that time the Dakota Indians, better known as the Sioux, controlled the
quarry and had a monopoly of the stone, which
they traded to other tribes. After a period when
white men controlled the quarry and sold pipestone to Indians, the site became a national monument. Now only Indians are allowed to dig the
stone, and they do continue to use it.

One of the first whites to see the quarry was
the artist George Catlin, who visited it in 1836.
Catlin made a drawing and a painting which show
the quarry and Indians at work there, no doubt as
they worked in prehistoric times. In his notes, later
expanded into a detailed description, he writes
that behind the quarry rises a natural wall "two
miles in length and thirty feet high, with a beautiful cascade leaping from its top into a basin. On
the prairie, at the base of the wall, the pipeclay is
dug up at two and three feet depth. There are
seen five immense granite bowlders, under which
there are two squaws, according to their tradition,
who eternally dwell there—the guardian spirits of
the place—and must be consulted before the pipestone can be dug up."

Because Catlin did so much to call attention
to the Pipestone Quarry, the stone found there has
been named catlinite.

Beginning at the Visitor Center where there is
a small museum, a circle trail leads to the quarry
pits and other points of interest in the monument.

Missouri

CLAY COUNTY HISTORICAL MUSEUM

West side of the square, Liberty. Open free, 1 p.m. to 5 p.m., Tuesday through Sunday; closed holidays.

In this museum are some materials representative of the Nebo Hill culture which the museum dates at 5000 B.C., also some materials from West Prairie, Mo.

GRAHAM CAVE

National Historic Landmark
Graham Cave State Park. Take the Danville-Montgomery City exit from Interstate 70, then drive 2 miles west on County TT to park entrance. Open free, 8 a.m. to 5 p.m., daily, Memorial Day to Labor Day. Camping.

Graham Cave is a natural rockshelter 20 feet high and 120 feet wide, in which people camped at intervals for 10,000 years. During that time the cave floor was littered with the waste they left, then with chunks of rock that fell from the ceiling, and quantities of fine dust blown in by wind. All this material piled up to a depth of six or seven feet, forming a series of layers in which archeologists could read the story of Missouri's early inhabitants.

Hunters first took shelter here at the end of the Ice Age, when prairie vegetation extended from the present Great Plains to the vicinity of the cave. These hunters had weapons like those used farther west by Paleo-Indians who stalked the big game animals that grazed on prairie grass. Later as forests took the place of grasslands, hunters who followed the Archaic lifeway camped at the cave. Still later people of Woodland culture stopped here from time to time.

One interesting find in the cave is a large flat rock around which smaller rocks are arranged. Quite clearly, ancient campers built fires on the big rock, then sat around it on the small ones, perhaps engaging in some kind of ceremony.

Because the cave contains evidence of human life over such a long span of time and because it lies on the western fringe of the Woodland culture area, this site is of great importance to archeologists.

Special Feature. Excavation continues here, and visitors may watch archeologists at work from June to September.

KANSAS CITY
MUSEUM OF HISTORY AND SCIENCE

3218 Gladstone Blvd., Kansas City. Open 9 a.m. to 5 p.m., Tuesday through Saturday; 2 p.m. to 6 p.m., Sunday; closed Jan. 1, Thanksgiving, Dec. 25. Admission: adults, 50¢; children, 25¢.

Exhibits in one hall in this museum trace the cultural history of man in the general area surrounding Kansas City. One exhibit is devoted to Paleo-Indian hunters who used Clovis points. Another presents the Nebo Hill Complex of northwest Missouri, together with pre-pottery material dated at 5000 B.C. to 1000 B.C. and Early Woodland artifacts from 1000 B.C. to 300 B.C. A life-sized diorama shows what an Osage Indian house was like at the time of the first contact with Europeans. Material found at the Renner Site inside Kansas

A

A. Working from various archeological clues, an artist painted this version of an Oneota harvest ceremony for the Field Museum of Natural History, Chicago. Field Museum of Natural History photo.

B. Graham Cave in Missouri was created by an overhanging rock. The cave is 120 feet wide and 20 feet high. It attracted hunters from the time of the Ice Age on, and for more than 10,000 years debris and remains of human life accumulated there. Graham Cave State Park photo.

B

City is also on display. The people who lived at this site from about A.D. 1 to A.D. 500 were followers of the Hopewell Cult. They were surrounded by other Woodland people whose lifeway was quite different. The site is on private land and cannot be visited, but a burial was removed from it and is exhibited in the museum just as it was when archeologists encountered it.

LYMAN ARCHAEOLOGICAL RESEARCH CENTER AND HAMILTON FIELD SCHOOL (Utz Site)

National Historic Landmark
From Marshall drive 8 miles north on Missouri 41 to junction with Missouri 122, then 4 miles west to Van Meter State Park. The center is on the northeast edge of the park. Open free, 8 a.m. to 5 p.m., Tuesday through Sunday, June 1 to Sept. 1; at other times by appointment, except in Dec., Jan., Feb. The address of the director is Route 2, Miami, Mo. 65344. Camping in Van Meter State Park.

This archeological center and school is located on the site of a large prehistoric Indian village known as the Utz Site. Scientific excavation goes on here every year from June 15 to Aug. 1. Visitors are invited to watch the work as it proceeds, and tours are conducted by professionally trained guides. The project is a joint endeavor of the University of Missouri and the Missouri State Park Board.
   Materials from the dig are displayed in the archeological museum nearby. They include artifacts representing these cultures: Archaic, Hopewell, Woodland, and Oneota.
   The Oneota culture appears more clearly here at the Utz Site than anywhere else in Missouri. Apparently it resulted in late prehistoric times from a shift to the Northwest of traits which had earlier been widespread in the Southeast. At its greatest extent the Oneota way of life existed as far west as Kansas City, and as far north as central Wisconsin.
   One artifact found in Oneota villages shows the kind of mixed elements out of which the culture was formed: Oneota people obtained catlinite, a stone used in making pipes, from Minnesota, far to the north. On this soft stone they engraved the forked-eye symbol which was popular throughout much of the Southeast.
   There seems to be agreement among experts that the Missouri tribe of Indians was directly descended from people who followed the Oneota lifeway. And the chief settlement of the Missouri tribe, at the time of first contact with Europeans, was here at this site.

MISSOURI HISTORICAL SOCIETY

Lindell at De Balivere, St. Louis. Open free, 9 a.m. to 5 p.m. daily; closed Jan. 1, July 4, Thanksgiving, Dec. 25.

Artifacts on display here come primarily from digs in Missouri or the middle Mississippi Valley. Paleo, Archaic, Woodland, and Mississippian periods are represented.

MISSOURI STATE MUSEUM

State Capitol Bldg., Jefferson City. Open free, 8 a.m. to 5 p.m., daily; closed Jan. 1, Dec. 25.

Using dioramas, this museum presents an Indian paint mine, pottery making, and Archaic Indian life. A reconstructed burial comes from a Missouri site now flooded by a reservoir. Several exhibits show how baskets and other artifacts were made.

MUSEUM OF SCIENCE AND NATURAL HISTORY

Clayton and Big Bend roads, St. Louis. Open 9 a.m. to 5 p.m., Tuesday through Saturday; 1 p.m. to 5 p.m., Sunday; closed national holidays. Admission: adults, 50¢; children, 25¢; children accompanied by an adult, free; Tuesdays free.

Many midwestern cultures are represented in this museum, which displays prehistoric material dating from 8000 B.C. to A.D. 1500. The greatest concentration of artifacts is Mississippian, and the areas best represented are Missouri and Illinois. There is some material from the Southwest. Much of what is exhibited comes from private collections made by amateurs; however, some artifacts and a complete burial are from scientific digs conducted during the Depression with labor provided by workers from the Works Progress Administration.

ST. JOSEPH MUSEUM

Eleventh and Charles streets, St. Joseph. Open free, 9 a.m. to 5 p.m., Monday through Saturday; 2 p.m. to 5 p.m., Sunday, May through mid-Sept.; 1 p.m. to 5 p.m., Tuesday through Saturday; 2 p.m. to 5 p.m., Sunday, mid-Sept. through April.

The American Indian collections in this museum are national in scope and include some archeological material. They touch on a wide variety of cultures and present some material from all time periods.

SCHOOL OF THE OZARKS, RALPH FOSTER MUSEUM

From Springfield drive 40 miles south on US 65. The school is 3 miles south of Branson at Point Lookout. Open free, 8 a.m. to 5 p.m., Monday through Saturday; 1 p.m. to 5 p.m., Sunday.

This museum has on display 625 pieces of pottery from the Mississippian culture. There are also exhibits of artifacts made by Ozark Bluff Dwellers and materials from other later cultures.

TOWOSAHGY STATE PARK (toe-wah-SOG-ee)

From East Prairie drive 6 miles east on Missouri 80, then 2 miles south on County Rd. AA, then 3 miles south on County Rd. FF; turn east and go 1 mile on gravel road, then south 1 mile on gravel. Open free, 8 a.m. to 5 p.m., Tuesday through Sunday, Memorial Day to Labor Day. Camping.

About A.D. 900 people who followed the Mississippian lifeway were living in a 30-acre village at this place. They built mounds around a large central plaza, and on one at least they placed a structure which was probably a temple. A moat surrounds the village, possibly for protection. It may, however, be only a by-product of mound-building—the borrow pit from which earth was dug for the mounds. The women of the village farmed nearby and made pottery in fashions that were popular in other villages on the Mississippi River. (The river no longer flows in the course it followed a thousand years ago. Its channel is now several miles away.)
   In 1967 scientific excavation of the site began, and much investigation remains to be done. The Missouri State Park Board has announced plans for a museum and other facilities in the park. Visitors who are interested mainly in watching excavation in progress might do well to inquire ahead of time about the actual stage of the work.

UNIVERSITY OF MISSOURI MUSEUM OF ANTHROPOLOGY

100 Swallow Hall, on the campus, Columbia. Open free, 9 a.m. to 5 p.m., Monday through Friday; tours by appointment for groups during the week, weekends, or evenings.

This museum gives special attention to Indian cultures of Missouri and the Midwest. Its archeological exhibits include artifacts from Paleo-Indian times to A.D. 1800. There is a special wealth of material in the Mississippian period (A.D. 1100 to 1500). Dioramas show a Paleo-Indian hunt, a Woodland mound, and a Mississippian mound. There is also a full-sized reconstruction of a Mississippian house of about A.D. 1200.

UTZ SITE

See *Lyman Archaeological Research Center, page 147.*

WASHINGTON STATE PARK MUSEUM

From DeSoto drive 1 mile west on County Rd. H, then 10 miles south on Missouri 21. Open free, 8 a.m. to 5 p.m., Tuesday through Sunday, Memorial Day to Labor Day. Camping.

In this park are petroglyphs (rock carvings) and a museum which includes archeological exhibits. A folder available at the park gives directions to the petroglyph sites.

At Site 1 several hundred symbols were carved in the rock, presumably between A.D. 1000 and A.D. 1600. The designs include birds, arrows, squares, ovals, circles, footprints, claws, and human figures. The birds may represent the eagle, buzzard, or hawk, which were important in many Indian cultures over a wide area. Speech scrolls issue from the mouths of several human figures and one bird. Like the balloons in modern day comic strips, they seem to indicate that talking is going on.

Site 2 has symbols that were connected with the Southern Cult—maces, bi-lobed arrows, crosses.

Some archeologists believe ancient trails crossed in this area and that people came together here for special rites or ceremonies. Possibly the symbols were associated with such ceremonies. Or they may have been devices to help men memorize certain songs or rituals.

Ohio

ALLEN COUNTY MUSEUM

620 W. Market St., Lima. Open free, 1:30 p.m. to 5 p.m., Tuesday through Sunday; closed national holidays.

A feature of this museum is a diorama showing how Glacial Kame people buried the dead, together with material from a Glacial Kame grave found near Lima. Other displays contain materials from these cultures: Paleo-Indian, Archaic, Adena, Hopewell, Cole Creek, Fort Ancient, and Erie.

CAMPBELL MOUND

On McKinley Ave., one-half mile south of Trabue Rd., Columbus. Open free, at all times.

This example of an Adena mound is administered by the Ohio Historical Society.

CINCINNATI MUSEUM OF NATURAL HISTORY

1720 Gilbert Ave., Cincinnati. Open 9 a.m. to 4:30 p.m., Tuesday through Saturday; 1 p.m. to 5 p.m., Sunday; closed national holidays. Admission: adults, 25¢; children under 12, 10¢.

Most of the archeological materials on display here have been collected by the museum's own field workers in the Ohio Valley. The Adena, Hopewell, and Fort Ancient cultures are represented. Leaflets describing the lifeways of these people are available. Some material from the Southwest and the Northwest Coast is also on exhibit.

Special Feature. The museum building stands not far from the site of an ancient Adena burial mound. In the mound was discovered a small, carefully-shaped piece of stone on which a design had been engraved. This tablet, one of 12 found in various mounds, is now in the museum.

Some Adena tablets appear to have been coated with a red pigment. This may indicate that they were used as stamps to print red-colored designs on clothing or on the bodies either of the dead or of those taking part in funeral ceremonies. Some connection with burial practices seems likely because Adena people sprinkled red ocher over the remains of the dead and even over the grave goods placed in tombs.

Careful study of the designs on tablets indicates that many if not all of them represent birds of prey, such as the vulture, duck hawk, and carrion crow. On some tablets the figures are quite realistic. On others, such as the Cincinnati tablet, the design seems to contain very stylized elements of wings, beaks, and eyes. Flesh-eating birds seem to have been important in all the burial mound cults, possibly because they acted as scavengers and helped to clean the bones of bodies which were exposed and allowed to decompose before burial or cremation.

CLEVELAND MUSEUM OF ART

11150 E. Blvd. at University Circle, Cleveland. Open free, 10 a.m. to 6 p.m., Tuesday through Friday; 9 a.m. to 5 p.m., Saturday; 10 a.m. to 10 p.m., Wednesday; 1 p.m. to 6 p.m., Sunday and Memorial Day; closed July 4, Thanksgiving, Dec. 25.

A number of prehistoric objects are displayed in this museum because of their artistic interest. These include Mimbres and other Southwestern pottery, bannerstones, birdstones, and pipes from Ohio.

DAYTON ART INSTITUTE

405 W. Riverview Ave., Dayton. Open free, 12:30 p.m. to 5 p.m., Tuesday through Friday; 9 a.m. to 5 p.m., Saturday; 1 p.m. to 6 p.m., Sunday; 7:30 p.m. to 10 p.m., Tuesday evenings in winter; closed national holidays.

A number of prehistoric objects are displayed in the museum because of their esthetic interest. Some of these are from the Northwest Coast. There are baskets from the Southwest, and a few artifacts which were recovered from Midwestern mounds.

DAYTON MUSEUM OF NATURAL HISTORY

2629 Ridge Ave., Dayton. Open free, 9 a.m. to 6 p.m., Monday, Wednesday, Thursday, Saturday; 9 a.m. to 9 p.m., Tuesday, Friday; closed national holidays. Open 2 p.m. to 6 p.m., Sunday. Admission: adults, 50¢; children, 25¢.

Exhibits include Ohio material from Paleo times through Early Woodland, Adena, Hopewell, and late prehistoric periods.

Special Feature. As part of an educational program for children and young people, the museum conducts archeological excavations in which students participate.

FIRELANDS MUSEUM

4 Case Ave. (at the rear of the Public Library), Norwalk. Open noon to 6 p.m., May, June, Sept., Oct.; 9 a.m. to 6 p.m., daily except Sunday morning, July and Aug.; Saturday and Sunday afternoon, April and Nov.; by appointment Dec. to March. Admission: adults, 50¢; children under 12, free.

One room here includes archeological materials from the Archaic, Early Woodland, and Hopewell cultures.

FLINT RIDGE MEMORIAL

From Brownsville drive 2 miles north on County 668. Open 9 a.m. to 5 p.m., Tuesday through Sunday. Admission: adults, 50¢; children, 15¢.

In hilly country between Newark and Zanesville, Indians once mined the fine translucent, varicolored flint that covered an area of five square miles in deposits from one to ten feet thick. To break off chunks of the flint, men first drove wooden or bone wedges into natural cracks in the rock, using hammerstones, some of which weighed as much as 25 pounds. Then with smaller hammerstones they shaped what are called blades or blanks, each one about a foot long. This work was done at the quarry, and some of the blanks were further chipped to make finished artifacts on the spot. Men carried other blanks back to their villages where they did the painstaking work of chipping them into projectile points or knives or drills or scrapers.

Miners also shaped flint into blocks called cores, which were sometimes carried for considerable distances. When a man wanted a new knife, he struck a flake off one of these cores and had a cutting tool almost as sharp as a steel blade.

In prehistoric times the flint from this huge quarry was so prized that it was traded over great distances—as far east as the Atlantic Coast, as far west as the present site of Kansas City, and as far south as Louisiana.

At some of the Indian workshops on Flint Ridge the heaps of discarded chips were very large—so large that modern engineers who were building the National Road through the area made use of the wastage in the road's construction.

The Museum. At the quarry the Ohio Historical Society maintains a museum which tells the geological story of the formation of the flint and the archeological story of the use that men made of it over a very long period of time. Exhibits show how flint was mined and then made into artifacts.

FORT ANCIENT STATE MEMORIAL

National Historic Landmark
From Lebanon drive 7 miles southeast on Ohio 350. The earthworks are open during daylight hours, daily; the museum is open 9:30 a.m. to 5 p.m., Tuesday through Sunday. Admission: adults,

A

A. A model in the museum at Fort Hill State Memorial in Ohio shows what a building in a large Hopewell ceremonial area once looked like. Ohio Historical Society photo. B. Two stages in mound building. First, Indians cremated and buried a body within a sacred enclosure. Then they heaped up basketloads of earth over the burial, forming a mound. The lower drawing shows how funerary offerings were placed on the altars, right front and upper right. Part of an exhibit in the Field Museum of Natural History, Chicago. Field Museum of Natural History photo.

B

MOUND OF EARTH BUILT OVER SACRED ENCLOSURE

25¢; children, 10¢. Administered by the Ohio Historical Society. Camping nearby.

The Story. Here a bluff rises 275 feet above the Little Miami River. On this natural eminence two different Indian peoples lived at two different times.

The first settlers arrived about 300 B.C. From that time until about A.D. 600 they followed the Hopewell way of life. All around the top of the bluff they built a wall of limestone slabs and earth that varies in height from 4 to 23 feet. Apparently the wall served a defensive purpose, but it was also designed to have some significance in relation to social and religious activities. The Hopewell people here, as elsewhere, enclosed the areas where they performed rituals and conducted elaborate funeral ceremonies.

The area within the wall has three distinct subdivisions now called the North Fort, the Middle Fort, and the South Fort. Also within the wall are ditches, areas paved with stone, and the burial mounds.

The Hopewell people raised corn, were skilled artisans, and traded throughout a very wide area. The grizzly bear teeth they used in ornaments came from the Rocky Mountains; they got shark teeth from the Atlantic Coast, shells from the Gulf of Mexico, copper from the Lake Superior region. But here, as elsewhere in the Ohio Valley, they came to some sudden and unknown end.

After the Hopewell settlement was abandoned, apparently no one lived on the hilltop for a long time. Then about A.D. 1000 a group of Indians who followed what is called the Fort Ancient lifeway settled on part of the site—the South Fort. They also built homes in the valley below the bluff. These Fort Ancient people introduced the bow and arrow to the vicinity. They grew corn as had the earlier people, and they hunted and fished and made a variety of artifacts, but none of them were so skillfully fashioned as the earlier Hopewell tools and ornaments.

About A.D. 1600 Fort Ancient people left the site, for what reason no one knows. It was uninhabited when the first Europeans entered the area.

The Museum. Here are exhibits which give a good deal of information about the two distinct cultures connected with the site. Another display deals with the chronology of this area over a 10,000-year span of time.

FORT HILL STATE MEMORIAL

From Hillsboro drive 16 miles southeast on Ohio 124, then 2 miles north on Ohio 41. Or from Chillicothe drive 20 miles southwest on US 50, to Bainbridge, then 12 miles south on Ohio 41. Open 9:30 a.m. to 5:30 p.m., Tuesday through Sunday. Admission to museum: adults, 50¢; children alone, 15¢; children with adult, free; organized children's groups, free; adult groups can arrange special rates with the Ohio Historical Society which administers the site. Camping nearby.

At a date not yet known, Fort Hill became an important Hopewell ceremonial center for burial of the dead. Around the flat top of the hill, which stands out from the surrounding land, people built a wall of earth and rock. At its base the wall is about 40 feet thick, and in places it is 15 feet high. Earthworks of this kind were common at Hopewell sites. Many of them seem to have had only ritual use, but here the embankment may have served also for defense.

On the flat land below the hill two structures were built. One was circular, possibly used as

temporary housing for visitors who came for ceremonies. No other such circular building is known in Ohio. The second was exceedingly large—120 feet long and 80 feet wide. At other Hopewell sites this kind of structure was often simply an enclosure inside which the dead were prepared for burial.

The Museum. Archeological exhibits here illuminate the Hopewell lifeway. Models show the site and its structures as they may have looked when it was occupied. One display includes material on older cultures in Ohio.

INSCRIPTION ROCK AND GLACIAL GROOVES

Kelleys Island, in Lake Erie, north of Sandusky. Open free, at all times. Administered by the Ohio Historical Society. Camping nearby.

Inscription Rock is a large boulder on which prehistoric people carved symbols and figures of animals, birds, and men. No one knows exactly what the inscriptions mean or who made them, but they probably date from A.D. 1000 to A.D. 1650. There is an interpretive sign at the site.

LEO PETROGLYPH

From Jackson on US 35 drive 5 miles north on Ohio 93 to Coalton, then northwest on Ohio 337 to Leo. The site is on an unpaved road northwest of Leo. Open free, during daylight hours, all year. Administered by the Ohio Historical Society.

This site is similar to Inscription Rock. Here prehistoric Indians carved symbols and figures on a stone slab, but their date and meaning are not known.

LICKING COUNTY
HISTORICAL SOCIETY MUSEUM

Sixth and Church streets, Newark. Open 1 p.m. to 4 p.m., Monday, Wednesday, Friday, Saturday, Sunday. Admission: adults, 50¢; Historical Society members and children, free.

This museum near the Newark Earthworks has both Hopewell and Adena artifacts, including ornaments of copper, mica, and pearls. Paintings show an artist's conception of life in Ohio during eight different prehistoric culture periods.

MIAMI COUNTY ARCHAEOLOGICAL MUSEUM

From Pleasant Hill drive one mile west on Louver Rd. to directional sign just west of the Stillwater River bridge. Open free, 2 p.m. to 4 p.m., the last Sunday of the month, May to Oct.; at other times by appointment.

Some of the materials on display here are random local finds from each of five prehistoric Indian cultures of the area beginning with Paleo-Indian and ending with Fort Ancient. One exhibit shows how real artifacts can be distinguished from fakes. Another shows a Fort Ancient burial, excavated by the local archeological society.

MIAMISBURG MOUND STATE MEMORIAL

One mile southeast of Miamisburg on Ohio 725. Open free, during daylight hours, all year. Administered by the Ohio Historical Society. Camping nearby.

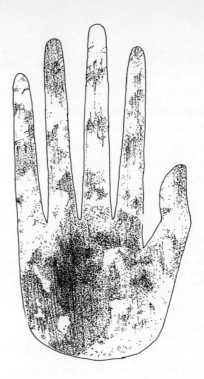

This mica grave offering, in the form of a hand, was made by the Hopewell Indians of Ohio. Original in the Field Museum of Natural History, Chicago.

How's That, Again?

Museums receive communications of many kinds. Here are excerpts from letters about Indians which children have written to the Southwest Museum in Los Angeles:

California Indians ground acorns with a mortal and pistol.

Tepees were used instead of houses because the Indians did not have furniture.

Indians made spoons of the horns of buffalo to eat the rest of him with.

Indians grew feathers for ceremonial use only.

The poor Indians did not know they were savages until missionaries were sent to them.

God likes Indians better than White People for he did not make them work.

Indians were prohibitionists until White settlers made them stop.

So they could get groceries the Indians sold buffalo pills. These they made from the hides.

Indians did not put pockets in their clothes because there was nothing to carry in them.

Indians never told time for there wasn't anything to be late to.

The Indians are now suffering from a depression of buffaloes and war-paths.

Indians had no civilization until Columbus was introduced.

Seems like I could never be an Indian for none of them are Jewish.

I read a book that said an Indian girl loved her sweetheart silently. That don't seem natural.

Indians never fell out of bed because they had none.

Hopi Indians live on high mesas where it is their custom to be born and die.

In another part of the country a teacher reported that a child said this on a test paper: "Compared to the Painted Desert, people have lived in Arizona for only a drop in the bucket."

This cone-shaped Adena mound, 68 feet high, is the largest of its kind in Ohio. There is an interpretive sign at the site.

MOUND BUILDERS STATE MEMORIAL

See Newark Earthworks, this page.

MOUND CITY GROUP NATIONAL MONUMENT

From Chillicothe (chil-ee-KOTH-ee) drive 3 miles north on Ohio 104. Open free, at all times. The Visitor Center is open free, 8 a.m. to 5 p.m., daily; closed Dec. 25. Camping.

The Story. By about 300 B.C. some Indians here in the Scioto River Valley had begun to follow the Hopewell way of life. They paid great attention to personal decoration and became very skillful at fashioning beautiful ornaments. They also devoted themselves to performing elaborate ceremonials for the dead. Many burials were accompanied by pottery, carvings, jewelry, and other objects made by sophisticated craftsmen. The Mound City Site was a major burial ground and was connected with Hopeton Earthworks, a ceremonial center which lies across the river. (Hopeton is on private property and is not open to the public.)

Although the first excavation of the Mound City Group began in 1846, there is no Ohio Hopewell site in a better state of preservation than this one. Because it had been so little disturbed, archeologists from the Ohio State Museum undertook an excavation program there in 1963. Materials recovered from these recent digs are on view in the Ohio Historical Center. The artifacts recovered in 1846 cannot be seen in the United States. They are in the British Museum in London.

The Museum. In the Visitor Center are exhibits designed to help visitors understand the site and the life of the Hopewell people who once lived here. Some material from the site may also be seen at the Ross County Historical Society Museum in nearby Chillicothe.

Special Feature. On a self-guided tour, visitors may see within a square earthen enclosure 24 mounds, of which 11 are interpreted. One contained a grave in which the cremated remains of four bodies were placed on sheets of mica. A second mound is the site of a crematory where the dead were prepared for burial. In another, excavators found many beautifully carved tobacco pipes. Replicas of some of these are on display in the Visitor Center. In one called Death Mask Mound, early excavators found pieces of a human skull. Later, archeologist Raymond Baby put the bits together and discovered they formed a mask which may have been worn at burial ceremonies by a shaman or medicine man. Offerings to the dead varied from one burial and from one mound to another. Beautiful pottery accompanied one. With another were fragments of tusks of a mammoth or mastodon that had died thousands of years before the time of the Hopewell people.

MUSEUM OF HEALTH AND NATURAL HISTORY

Toledo Zoological Park, 2700 Broadway, Toledo. Open 10 a.m. to 5 p.m., winter; 10 a.m. to 6 p.m., summer. Admission: adults, 75¢; children 2 to 11, 25¢.

Materials here include many random finds in the Toledo area representing Archaic, Hopewell, and prehistoric Potawatomi, Algonquian, and Iroquoian cultures. Dioramas show prehistoric Wyandot and Algonquian village life on the banks of the Maumee River.

NATURAL SCIENCE MUSEUM

10600 E. Blvd., Cleveland. Open 10 a.m. to 5 p.m., Monday through Saturday; 1 p.m. to 5:30 p.m., Sunday; closed national holidays. Admission: adults, 50¢; children over 6, 25¢; Tuesdays free.

On display here are materials on prehistoric peoples in Ohio and other North American areas. Dioramas show reconstructions of ancient life. Some exhibits of current field work change from time to time.

NEWARK EARTHWORKS

Newark Earthworks is the collective name for three separate sections of a huge prehistoric site on which the modern city of Newark has been built. The three areas are now preserved as public parks. Their names, with road directions, are given below. All are open free, 8 a.m. to 9 p.m., daily.

An amazing group of people settled near Newark about 1,800 years ago. They followed the Hopewell lifeway, but apparently with more than usual energy and a taste for grandiose public works. Like other Hopewellians, they buried their dead under mounds of earth in special ceremonial areas. Here they conducted death rituals inside tremendous enclosures made by heaping up earth into walls or embankments 8 to 14 feet high. One of the enclosures was a square, another an octagon, several were circular. All were linked together by long corridors between high parallel earthen walls. A separate corridor extended from the site to the bank of the Licking River in an almost straight avenue, two and a half miles long.

A few important individuals seem to have lived at the religious center itself. Possibly they were leaders of the groups that regarded the area as a focal point in their elaborate ceremonial life. The dwellings of ordinary people were built in outlying areas.

Like Hopewell people in other places, those at Newark were superb craftsmen. They made personal ornaments of many kinds—earrings, combs, necklaces, headdresses. They were skilled weavers, using thread they made from various plant fibers including the bark of certain trees. Many if not most of the splendid things they created were made only to be buried with the dead.

When an important personage died, he was dressed in rich clothing and covered with decorations. He might then be placed in a tomb. More likely he was cremated. At first small mounds of earth were heaped over the remains of the dead. Later, much more earth was added to cover a group of the small heaps, creating one sizeable mound.

Archeologists believe that the ceremonies which required such great expenditure of effort and great destruction of wealth were reserved for members of an upper class. Funerals for common people were certainly more simple.

Much of the original complex of structures at Newark has been destroyed by the expansion of the city. The three portions that survive are administered by the Ohio Historical Society. They are:

Mound Builders State Memorial

Enter from the junction of S. 21st St. and Cooper.

This is the area known as the Great Circle Earthworks. The circular embankment encloses ceremonial grounds 1,200 feet in diameter covering about 26 acres. Within the enclosure is a mound built in the shape of an eagle—Eagle Effigy Mound. High earthen walls once lined a corridor that led from the Great Circle to a smaller enclosure now called Wright Earthworks.

Wright Earthworks

From West Main St. drive south on S. Williams St., then east on Waldo to park entrance.

Only part of the original square enclosure survives here. Before modern settlement began, it was possible to see that the square was linked by corridors to another area of unknown shape and by a very long passageway to still another built in the shape of an octagon.

Octagon Mound State Memorial

From Church St. drive south on 30th St. to Parkview, then west to park entrance.

Here an eight-sided enclosure of 50 acres adjoins another which is circular in form and covers about 20 acres. Several small mounds stand inside the octagon. This well-preserved area is now the municipal golf course.

OHIO HISTORICAL CENTER
(Formerly the Ohio State Museum)

Interstate 71 and 17th Ave., Columbus. Open free, 9 a.m. to 5 p.m., Monday, Tuesday, Thursday, Friday, and Saturday; 9 a.m. to 9 p.m., Wednesday; 1 p.m. to 5 p.m., Sunday and holidays.

This new building opened in August, 1970. Displays of prehistoric material are arranged in mall areas, and there is a unique pit system which permits visitors to examine objects without the intrusion of glass separations.

Excellent exhibits relate to these cultures: Paleo-Indian, Archaic, Glacial Kame, Adena, Hopewell, Cole, Fort Ancient, and Erie. Materials from many important sites are on display, including finds from new excavation which the museum has been conducting in the Mound City Group.

Anyone who has visited Ohio sites and is eager to know more about them will find the dioramas of special interest. Some of them interpret prehistoric life at Fort Ancient, Seip Mound, Hopewell Mound Group, Harness Mound. Others show an Adena house, a rockshelter, a Fort Ancient grave, a cremation basin, an infant burial. Many cases, each with a distinct theme, introduce the visitor to important archeological ideas and to a great variety of archeological materials.

SEIP MOUND (sipe)

From Bainbridge drive 3 miles east on US 50. Open free, 8 a.m. to 6 p.m., daily, all year. Administered by the Ohio Historical Society.

This burial site is part of a group of Hopewell mounds that was once very extensive. Several are still visible, the largest an oval 150 feet wide, 250 feet long, and 32 feet high. An earthwork in the form of a circle 2,000 feet in diameter surrounds the mound. In addition there is a smaller earthen circle and a partly preserved earthen square.

From the Seip mounds came much of the early information about the Hopewell lifeway. One grave yielded a great collection of ornaments made of mica, copper, and silver and so many thousands of pearls that it was called "the great pearl burial."

There is a small museum at the site. Material from the mounds can also be seen in the Ohio Historical Center in Columbus.

SERPENT MOUND STATE MEMORIAL

From Peebles drive northeast about 7 miles to Locust Grove then drive 5 miles northwest on Ohio 73. The mound is open during daylight hours daily, all year. The museum is open 9:30 a.m. to 5 p.m., Tuesday through Sunday. Admission: Adults, 50¢; children, 15¢.

At this place long ago (the exact date is not known), Indians used small stones and lumps of clay to trace on the ground an outline of a huge snake. Then they covered these markers with great quantities of yellow clay which they dug up nearby. The result was a modeled form which resembled a writhing snake with open mouth apparently about to swallow an egg.

Many Indian groups attached great significance to snakes. Many built snake effigies, but none is larger than this one. It is nearly one-quarter of a mile long, 20 feet wide, and 4 or 5 feet high. The people who labored to pile up so much earth did not leave in the mound itself any clues to their identity or to the time when they did their work. However, archeologists think it is likely that whoever shaped the serpent also built the burial mound found nearby, and that mound did offer clues.

Among the things in the grave were some leaf-shaped projectile points, some points that had stems, chunks of sandstone in which there were deep grooves, bone tubes and awls, and a pigment called red ocher. All these were objects that usually turned up in the graves of Adena people, who are known to have lived in this part of Ohio from about 1000 B.C. to A.D. 400. The evidence uncovered so far does not prove that people who built the burial mound also constructed Serpent Mound, but archeologists believe they did.

The Museum. Exhibits include an interpretation of the site, models of the steps taken in reconstruction of the effigy and nearby burial mound, some Adena artifacts and their use, and chronology. A diorama shows a conical burial mound with an Adena grave to which another burial was later added by Fort Ancient people.

Special Interest. The preservation of Serpent Mound was one of the first American archeological conservation projects. When white men first learned about the mound, it lay in the midst of a forest and seemed to be in no danger. Then, just before the Civil War, a tornado mowed down the big trees along its whole length. Farmers completed the job and began to cultivate the area. Some years later F. W. Putnam, an archeologist from Harvard University, visited the mound and then went home to talk about the need for protecting it. As he tells it, "Several of Boston's noble and earnest women issued a private circular." They soon collected enough money to buy the mound which was given in trust to the Peabody Museum at Harvard. Later the museum turned it over to the Ohio Historical Society, which now administers it.

STORY MOUND

Delano Ave., one block south of Allen Ave., Chillicothe. Open free, at all times. Administered by the Ohio Historical Society.

Here, easily visible from the street, is an Adena burial mound. In size and shape it is similar to the original Adena mound, which has been destroyed by excavation.

TARLTON CROSS MOUND

From Circleville drive southeast on Ohio 56 to junction with Ohio 159. Go north on Ohio 159 to Tarlton. Drive north on Ohio 159 one mile. Open free, during daylight hours, daily. Administered by the Ohio Historical Society.

This effigy mound, in the shape of a Greek cross, measures 90 feet in width and 3 feet in height. Although it has never been excavated, archeologists believe it was built by Hopewell people. Nearby are four small conical mounds.

WARREN COUNTY HISTORICAL SOCIETY

Harmon Hall, South Broadway, Lebanon. Open free, 9 a.m. to 4 p.m., Tuesday through Sunday; closed Dec. 25.

The cultures represented in the exhibits of prehistoric material in this museum are Hopewell and Fort Ancient.

WESTERN RESERVE HISTORICAL SOCIETY

10825 East Blvd., Cleveland. Open free, 10 a.m. to 5 p.m., Tuesday through Friday.

A feature of this historical museum is an introduction to American Indian cultures which has been arranged for children. It includes eight small dioramas presenting scenes of Indian life from a wide variety of geographic areas. In addition there is special emphasis on Indian life in northern Ohio, both at the time of contact with Europeans and earlier.

WRIGHT EARTHWORKS

See page 153.

WYANDOT COUNTY HISTORICAL SOCIETY

130 S. Seventh St., Upper Sandusky. Open free, 10 a.m. to noon, 1 p.m. to 5 p.m., Tuesday through Saturday; 1 p.m. to 5 p.m., Sunday.

Here are random local archeological finds including some material from mounds and a Glacial Kame skeleton.

West Virginia

CEMETERY MOUND

City Cemetery, Romney.

Here in the municipal cemetery is a prehistoric Indian mound.

GRAVE CREEK MOUND STATE PARK
(Also known as Mammoth Mound)

Tomlinson and Tenth streets, Moundsville. Open free, 11 a.m. to 6 p.m., April through Dec. Admission to museum: adults, 30¢; children with an adult, free. Camping nearby.

Grave Creek Mound is the largest of all those known to have been built by Adena people. When first measured in 1838, it stood 69 feet high and had a flat top 60 feet in diameter. Around its summit ran a low wall or parapet. A circular ditch surrounded the base.

The mound is not as high as it was once, because of extensive pot-hunting and clumsy excavation. This great man-made pile of earth intrigued the first white men who saw it, and they soon began digging to find out what secrets it held. They carved out pits, drove tunnels into the center, and kept few records or none at all. Much of what they found in their excavations has disappeared.

Among the many missing objects is a tablet which was supposed to have been found there. On it appeared strange signs that were widely believed to be letters in some undeciphered language. This "writing" served well to attract tourists to the site when it was being commercially exploited, but scholars never found that the tablet served the interests of science. They politely or impolitely called it a fake.

According to Don W. Dragoo, an authority on Adena culture, the mound was probably begun in late Archaic times. In several distinct stages, people made additions which they used as burial places for hundreds of years.

Grave Creek Mound, also known as Mammoth Mound, was one of 47 which stood on the present site of the city of Moundsville. Most of these ancient earthworks have been destroyed by modern industrial construction. But enough remains to show that the area was a population center of importance to those who followed the Adena lifeway.

Because Grave Creek Mound has been greatly disturbed, archeologists' understanding of it had to come from a study of a similar mound built in the same period in the same area. Such was Cresap Mound, 6½ miles away. Although it is not open to the public, anyone who is interested can read about Cresap in a detailed report made by Don W. Dragoo, who excavated the site. Material found there can be seen in the Carnegie Museum in Pittsburgh.

The Museum. Beside the Grave Creek Mound is a museum which includes information about the archeology and history of this site. It also offers an exhibit on nearby Cresap Mound.

A model of an Adena house accompanies a display showing Adena burial practices. In addition there are exhibits on other nearby Adena mounds: Natrium, Half Moon, Beech Bottom. A group of exhibits throws light on Indian artifacts and how they were made and used.

MUSEUM, DEPARTMENT OF ARCHIVES AND HISTORY

Room E-400, State Capitol, Charleston. Open free, 9 a.m. to 5 p.m., Monday through Saturday and holidays; 1 p.m. to 5 p.m., Sunday; closed Dec. 25.

Some West Virginia prehistoric artifacts are displayed here.

UNIVERSITY OF WEST VIRGINIA, ARCHEOLOGY MUSEUM

Mineral Industries Bldg., Willey St., on the downtown campus, Morgantown. Open free, 8:30 a.m. to 5 p.m., Monday through Saturday when the university is in session; closed national holidays.

In this excellent small museum one exhibit answers the question, "What is archeology?" Another makes clear how archeologists can get information about diseases in prehistory by studying the bones they excavate. A whole burial is arranged at tabletop height so that it can be easily viewed. A separate exhibit is devoted to each of the following cultures or subjects: Paleo-Indian, Archaic, Ohio Adena, Early Woodland, Middle Woodland, trade routes. Paintings show reconstructions of villages. For the late prehistoric period there are exhibits on the Fort Ancient and the Monongahela cultures.

One display is devoted to the St. Albans Archaic Site, one of the most important in North America. The strata at this site are among the deepest anywhere in the United States—43 feet below the original surface of the soil. There is a carbon-14 date of 7900 B.C. for material in a stratum 23 feet below the original surface, which in itself makes the site very early. But core drillings show human occupation 19 feet farther down. This lowest level, not yet dated, has not been excavated, largely because of great problems with water seeping into the dig from the Kanawha River which flows close by. If it ever becomes possible to complete work at the site, some very interesting information and very early dates may be obtained.

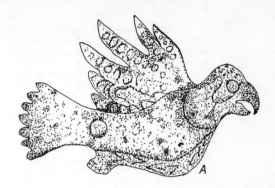

A. The bird of prey often appeared as an element in mound builders' designs. This ornament was cut from a sheet of hammered copper. Original in Ohio Historical Center. B. The bird motif, sometimes very stylized, was also carved by Adena mound builders on small pieces of stone. These engraved Adena tablets, found in burials, were probably used somehow in funeral ceremonies. After Webb and Baby. C. This imaginary creature carved in stone came from Turner Mounds, Madisonville, Ohio. Original in the Peabody Museum, Harvard University.

Wisconsin

AZTALAN STATE PARK (AZ-ta-lan)

National Historic Landmark.
From Lake Mills drive 3 miles east on County Trunk B to the center of Aztalan, then south to park entrance. Open free, 4 a.m. to 11 p.m., daily, all year.

This is one of the most important sites in Wisconsin. Seven hundred years ago a busy town stood here, completely protected by a palisade built of upright poles 12 to 19 feet high, placed close together. Branches were woven between the poles then the entire structure was covered with a thick plaster of clay. Watchtowers built at frequent intervals reinforced this stockade which surrounded not only the dwellings but also fields and ceremonial mounds and burial areas as well.

Portions of the stockade have now been restored, as have two large pyramidal mounds. One of these rises in a series of terraces, the other in an unbroken slope. Ten conical mounds also remain, although 74 once stood in a double line within the palisade.

An exhibit case in the park interprets Aztalan culture for summer visitors but is removed in winter. There is no official museum. However, random local finds of material from the Aztalan area are exhibited in the Lake Mills-Aztalan Historical Museum adjoining the park. A famous burial called the "Princess," which was found close to the museum building, is now on display in the Milwaukee Public Museum.

The Story. Sometime after A.D. 1100 a group of people, probably from Cahokia in Illinois, started out in search of a new home. Possibly they had been under pressure from newcomers. (Archeologists have evidence that outsiders did invade Cahokia at about this time.) Possibly the emigrants left because there was too large a population at Cahokia to be supported by the surrounding farmlands, rich though they were. Or perhaps some kind of feud had developed in the community.

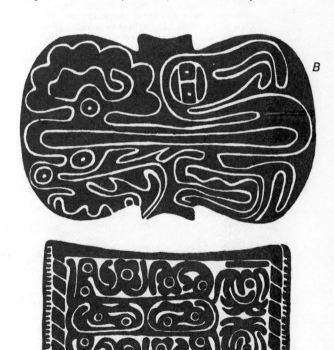

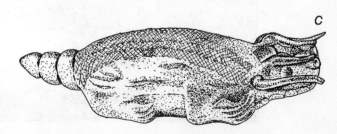

Nobody is sure why some people moved away, but move they did—up the Mississippi River, then up the Rock River and finally up a tributary of the Rock, the Crawfish River. Finally, on the banks of the Crawfish, the wanderers found a site to their liking. It offered good farmland, good fishing, and good hunting in the nearby woods. All around, however, were Indians who followed the Woodland lifeway, which was very different from the Mississippian.

The Woodland people were less advanced than the newcomers. Their arts were less developed. Their ceremonial life was much more simple. The two groups did not get along. This explains the strong outer palisades and watchtowers and the additional inner palisades that divided up the settlement into smaller areas that were easy to defend.

For nearly 200 years the Mississippian farmers, who with their families never numbered more than 500, managed to live on, surrounded by a hostile community. They kept to their own ways and continued to conduct their own kind of ceremony, including one which may have been religious in nature but was certainly not reassuring to their neighbors. The Mississippians practiced cannibalism, and since the victims in cannibalistic rites were very likely captured Woodland Indians, the latter may have had good reason for taking a dim view of the alien culture in their midst. In the end they seem to have destroyed it completely. The entire town of Aztalan, including the log palisades, was burned to the ground, and no one knows what became of those who once lived there.

The Name. In the early part of the 19th century readers of books and magazines in the United States were excited by reports of mysterious pyramids supposedly built by the ancient Aztecs of Mexico. Two men in Wisconsin had these stories in mind when they discovered the flat-topped pyramidal mounds on the banks of the Crawfish. With very little trouble the two enthusiastic pioneers developed the theory that their site was the original homeland of the Aztecs, and they called the place Aztalan.

There was, indeed, a connection between Aztalan and the Indians in Mexico, but it worked the other way around. There is little doubt that the idea of building pyramids as bases for temples and of using certain artistic motifs spread from Mexico northward. Possibly the notion that ceremonial cannibalism was pleasing to the gods had also come from Mexico to settlements on the Mississippi River and its tributaries. The influence was all from south to north.

Special Feature. You may wonder how archeologists can be sure that the log palisade around Aztalan was 12 to 19 feet high and plastered over with clay. After all, the wood should have decayed in 600 years, and clay would long ago have been washed away by rain.

The fact is that the fire which burned Aztalan was so intense that it baked the clay brick-hard. Chunks of this "Aztalan brick" still show the marks of the wooden posts, and when pieced together, they tell exactly how high the palisade was.

BELOIT COLLEGE, LOGAN MUSEUM OF ANTHROPOLOGY

South end of Beloit campus, Beloit. Open free, 9 a.m. to noon, 1 p.m. to 4 p.m., Monday through Friday; 9 a.m. to noon, Saturday; 1:30 p.m. to 4:30 p.m., Sunday; closed school vacation periods.

Along with extensive archeological displays of materials from many parts of the world, this museum has these Wisconsin exhibits: Paleo-Indian, Effigy Mound culture, Archaic Period, Middle Woodland Period, Middle Mississippian, Oneota cul-

ture. Dioramas of archeological subjects include one showing an effigy mound on the Beloit campus. On the second floor of the museum are Southwestern archeological exhibits. Among these is a full scale Hopi house.

COPPER CULTURE STATE PARK

National Historic Landmark.
From junction of US 41 and Wisconsin 22 in Oconto, drive two-tenths mile west on Wisconsin 22 (Main Street), then follow directional signs. Open free, daily, all year. Camping nearby.

This small park contains the site of an important archeological discovery. It was undeveloped as this book went to press, but construction is scheduled.

The Story. For a great many years Midwestern farmers found strange green objects in their fields when they plowed. Nobody was sure what these objects were. Then in 1945 the Mississippi River washed away part of its bank near Potosi, Wis., and exposed what is called the Osceola Site. Excavation revealed chipped stone tools and human burials. With them were some objects which proved to be copper tools turned green by corrosion.

A few years later a boy at Oconto found some bones in a gravel pit. His first thought was that he had stumbled upon evidence of a murder, and he reported his discovery to the sheriff. It was an archeologist, however, who solved the mystery. The bones belonged to an Indian who had been buried for a very long time. In the same gravel pit were other burials, many of them, and made in three different ways. Some of the bodies had been cremated. Some had been buried only after the flesh was removed from the bones. About half had been buried while the flesh was still intact. This was all interesting, but most exciting to ar-

cheologists was the discovery of copper tools with many of the burials.

Archeologists now began to talk about an Old Copper culture, because the tools were much more ancient than others made of copper by such people as the Hopewell. Carbon-14 dates show that the Old Copper people lived perhaps 5,000 years ago.

This date suggested that Indians in Wisconsin were using metal almost as early as any people in the Old World, but the Indians never learned to smelt it. Nor did they harden it by adding another metal to form an alloy. Perhaps the softness of copper led men to abandon it in favor of stone. Perhaps a hostile group got control of the mines and kept the Old Copper people away from their source of supply until they forgot about the metal. For whatever reason, Indians in Wisconsin had stopped making much use of copper long before the arrival of Europeans in the area.

DEVILS LAKE STATE PARK

From Baraboo drive 3 miles south on Wisconsin 123 to park entrance. Open 4 a.m. to 11 p.m., daily, all year. Admission: $1 per car. The Nature Center is open free, 1 p.m. to 5 p.m., Monday through Saturday, summer. Camping.

A. Working with information supplied by archeologists, an artist painted this view of Aztalan as it may have looked during the period from A.D. 1100 to A.D. 1300. Milwaukee Public Museum photo. B. Reconstructed exterior (left) and cutaway (right) of a house at Aztalan. After R. R. Burke. C. At some time in the distant past this deer head was incised in stone at a rockshelter near Disco, Wisconsin. Photo by Warren Wittry, courtesy Campbell Grant.

A

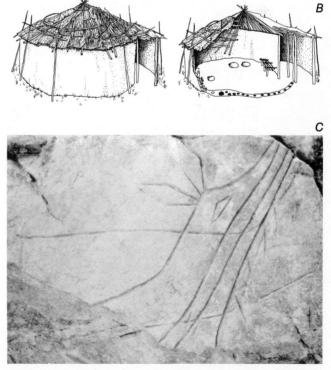

B

C

A diorama in the Milwaukee Public Museum designed to explain mound building in the Wisconsin area. In the foreground the mound is shown in cross section, with a view of a skeleton, grave goods, and a crematory area. Milwaukee Public Museum photo.

Effigy mounds in the park are indicated by explanatory signs. One in the shape of a bear and another which resembles a lynx are at the north end of the lake. A bird-shaped mound is at the south end.

In the Visitor Center a diorama shows Indians building the bear effigy mound.

DURST ROCKSHELTER

From Sauk City on US 12, drive west on County Trunk O, then north on County Trunk C to Leland, then one-half mile north on County Trunk PF to local road leading to the site. Open free, at all times. Camping nearby.

This rockshelter was occupied from Archaic through Late Woodland times.

GULLICKSON'S GLEN

From Black River Falls drive 2 miles south on Wisconsin 54, then west about 7 miles on C Road. At Disco Store turn south and drive about 1 mile to parking lot at the site.

Here in a narrow gorge on high sandstone cliffs a large collection of petroglyphs is preserved in a county park. Among the figures are recognizable bison, elk, cranes, a wild turkey, a human figure with bow and arrow, an eagle dancer, and a thunderbird. Excavation at the site produced numerous artifacts from the late-prehistoric Oneota culture. These included quartzite tools that may have been used in carving the rock. Materials from the dig are in the possession of the Wisconsin Historical Society at Madison.

HIGH CLIFF STATE PARK

From Menasha (men-ASH-a) drive about 10 miles east on Wisconsin 114 to park entrance; or from Stockbridge drive north on Wisconsin 55 to park entrance. Open 4 a.m. to 11 p.m., daily, all year. Admission: $1 per car. Camping.

On top of the bluff in the park, 200 feet above Lake Winnebago, prehistoric people built 13 effigy mounds. Some are in the shape of lizards; others represent birds. All are about two feet high, but they vary in length from 25 feet to 285 feet.

HOARD HISTORICAL MUSEUM

407 Merchants Ave., Fort Atkinson. Open free, 9 a.m. to 5 p.m., Wednesday, Saturday; closed national holidays.

About 10,000 artifacts found in Jefferson County represent the Old Copper, Woodland, and Mississippian cultures.

LAKE MILLS—AZTALAN
HISTORICAL SOCIETY MUSEUM

From Lake Mills drive 3 miles east on County Trunk B to junction with Aztalan Mound Rd. Open 9 a.m. to 5 p.m., daily, May 1 to Oct. 1. Admission: adults, 25¢; children 8-12, 10¢; children under 8, free.

Random local finds of Mississippian and Woodland material are in this small historical museum, which adjoins Aztalan State Park. Some of the "brick" from the burned walls of the Aztalan palisade is on exhibit.

LIZARD MOUND STATE PARK

From West Bend drive 4 miles northeast on Wisconsin 144, then 1 mile east on County Trunk A to directional marker. Open free, 4 a.m. to 11 p.m., all year except when snows are heavy.

In this park there are 31 good examples of effigy mounds, three to four feet high, which represent birds, panthers, and lizards. A number are geometrical—either linear or conical in form. When archeologists finished excavating the site they left one burial in place as a permanent outdoor exhibit protected by glass.

About 5,000 effigy mounds have been found in southern Wisconsin—approximately 98% of all that are known in North America. Some of them are so large that it was presumably from the vantage point of treetops that their builders were able to view them as a whole—if view they did. In any event, they seemed to have had clear patterns in mind as they worked.

The creators of effigy mounds usually buried the dead in them, but often they did not leave offerings in the graves. As a result, archeologists know less about the Effigy Mound people than they do about people who left abundant gifts with burials. One important question is when the building of effigy mounds began. At least one specialist believes that the custom may have started a very long while ago, perhaps in Archaic times, and that it continued almost up to historic times.

Generally speaking, the people who built effigy mounds were part of the widespread Woodland culture. They had pottery, engaged in hunting and fishing, and also did some farming. In winter and in summer they scattered and lived in small bands. At planting time in the spring, and again at harvest time in the fall, the bands seem to have come together, forming temporary communities. At such times there was a good deal of manpower and womanpower available—enough to do the considerable work involved in building mounds.

No one knows for sure why effigy mounds take the shapes they do. Perhaps they represented creatures sacred to the person buried in them. The burials, incidentally, were often made at spots in the effigies which were possibly considered vital to the creatures whose shapes had been modeled in earth. Skeletons have been found where wings or legs joined effigy bodies, or in the areas of the head, heart, or groin.

MAN MOUND

From Baraboo drive east on Eighth Ave. (Wisconsin 33), then north on County Trunk T to the first intersection, then east to the mound. Open free, at all times. Camping nearby.

This large effigy mound in a county park is unusual because it resembles a human figure. Most other effigy mounds are likenesses of birds, serpents, or four-legged mammals.

MENASHA MOUNDS

Smith Park, Menasha. Open free, at all times.

In municipally owned Smith Park are three effigy mounds said to resemble panthers. The largest is 180 feet long. A marker in the park indicates that they were built about A.D. 900.

MENDOTA STATE HOSPITAL MOUND

On the grounds of Mendota State Hospital, Madison. Open free, at all times.

Here, on the hospital grounds, is a 6-foot high effigy mound in the form of a bird which has a wingspread of 624 feet.

MILWAUKEE PUBLIC MUSEUM

800 West Wells St., Milwaukee. Open free, 9 a.m. to 5 p.m., daily, June 16 to Aug. 25; noon to 8 p.m., Monday; 9 a.m. to 5 p.m., Tuesday through Sunday, Aug. 26 to June 15.

With a multi-media approach to dramatizing prehistoric life, this museum uses film strips, motion pictures, talks and music on sound tape, dioramas, and extensive life-sized models, along with artifact displays. Even the floor in part of the Indian area is textured to give visitors the illusion of walking on the adobe soil of the Southwest. The cafeteria is a fascinating exhibit area decorated with Indian themes.

One hall is devoted to Wisconsin archeology with exhibits showing the sequence of cultures in the state. Specimens on display come from scientific excavations, and they include some unusual material found at Wisconsin sites.

Dioramas interpret the Effigy Mound builders, copper mining on Isle Royale in Michigan, life at Mesa Verde, Colo., wild rice threshing among the Menominee Indians of Wisconsin, and village life among the Kwakiutls of the Northwest Coast. Outside the museum is a highly colored Haida totem pole from British Columbia. A special hall shows in capsule form, with a series of exhibits, how culture makes man unique among animals.

MUSCODA MOUNDS (MUSS-koh-dah)

From Muscoda drive one mile west on Wisconsin 60 across the Wisconsin River to directional sign. Open free, at all times. Camping nearby.

This group of effigy mounds, on private land, has not been developed but is open to the public. The mounds can be seen from an unsurfaced road which passes them.

NELSON DEWEY STATE PARK

From Cassville, drive 2 miles northwest on County Trunk VV to the park. Open 4 a.m. to 11 p.m., daily, all year. Admission: $1 per car. Camping.

In this park overlooking the Mississippi River are a number of prehistoric effigy mounds.

NEVILLE PUBLIC MUSEUM

129 S. Jefferson St., Green Bay. Open free, 9 a.m. to 5 p.m., Monday through Saturday; 2 p.m. to 5 p.m., Sunday; closed major holidays.

In this general museum is an important display of artifacts from the Old Copper culture. There are also materials from another Archaic culture, the Red Ocher. The North Bay culture of the Middle Woodland Period is represented by material from the Mero Site, and there is Oneota material also.

OCONTO COUNTY
HISTORICAL SOCIETY MUSEUM (oh-KAHN-toh)

917 Park Ave., Oconto. Open 9 a.m. to 5 p.m., June to Sept. 15. Admission: adults, 75¢; children, 25¢.

In this museum are examples of Old Copper culture material found at the Oconto Site on the western edge of the town. This site is now part of Copper Culture State Park.

OSHKOSH PUBLIC MUSEUM

1331 Algoma Blvd., Oshkosh. Open free, 9 a.m. to

At Aztalan in Wisconsin, which was inhabited for about 200 years, archeologists have found very few burials. One that they did uncover revealed the skeleton of a teen-age girl. She is called the Princess—not for any scientific reason but because she was buried with a wealth of 2,000 shell beads wrapped in four strands around her body. Careful examination revealed that the "princess" suffered from a deformed spinal column. She is now on display in the Milwaukee Public Museum. The museum also has on exhibit a great deal of material found at various Wisconsin sites, and one of its halls is entirely devoted to Wisconsin archeology, with exhibits showing the sequence of cultures in the state. Milwaukee Public Museum photo.

noon; 1:30 p.m. to 5 p.m., Monday through Saturday; 1 p.m. to 5 p.m., Sunday.

Various members of the staff of this museum have gathered material from several excavations in the area. This material, plus some collected by early Wisconsin archeologists and supplemented by random local finds, illustrates cultures from Paleo-Indian times through Archaic, Woodland, and Mississippian up to the present.

PANTHER INTAGLIO

From Fort Atkinson drive west on Wisconsin 106 to the site. Open free, at all times. Camping nearby.

Here is what may be the only example of a large effigy dug into the earth instead of raised above it. The intaglio effect is created by a depression about a foot deep. No burials have been found at the site. In the vicinity are effigies of the usual kind modeled in the form of a mound.

PERROT STATE PARK (pair-OH)

From Trempealeau drive 2 miles north on Wisconsin 93 to park entrance. Open 4 a.m. to 11 p.m., daily, all year. Admission: $1 per car. Camping.

In this park are a few conical mounds.

RAHR CIVIC CENTER AND PUBLIC MUSEUM

610 N. Eighth St., Manitowac (MAN-i-to-WAHK). Open free, 9 a.m. to noon; 1 p.m. to 5 p.m., Monday through Friday; 2 p.m. to 5 p.m., Sunday; closed national holidays, Jan. 1, Easter, Dec. 25.

In the prehistory room of this museum are exhibits based to some extent on random local finds of materials from the Old Copper, Hopewell, Middle and Upper Mississippian cultures. Dioramas show Old Copper and Aztalan life.

Special Interest. At Two Creeks, near Manitowac, a forest grew during a warm period between the last two temporary advances of the last Pleistocene glacier. The final advance covered the trees with rock and clay. This buried forest is of great interest to geologists and archeologists because wood from it has been radiocarbon dated. The trees were living 11,500 years ago. This Two Creeks date establishes the time *after* which the last glacial advance took place. Thus it helps to date events in the lives of Paleo-Indians who once lived in the area but who did not move in until the glacier had moved out.

SHEBOYGAN COUNTY MUSEUM (she-BOY-gun)

3110 Erie Ave., Sheboygan. Open 10 a.m. to 5 p.m., Tuesday through Saturday; 1 p.m. to 5 p.m., Sunday, April 1 to Sept. 30. Admission: adults, 25¢; children, 10¢.

In this museum are random local finds from Old Copper, Hopewellian, and Upper Mississippian cultures.

SHEBOYGAN MOUND PARK

From Sheboygan drive south on US Business 141, then east on County Trunk EE, then south on S. 12th St. to Riverdale Country Club. Here turn east on Panther Ave., then south on S. Ninth St. to the park entrance. Open free, at all times. Camping nearby.

In this city park are 33 effigy mounds, called the Kletzien Group. Some resemble deer and panthers. Others are conical and linear in shape. As with many effigy mound burials elsewhere, there were very few artifacts found in the graves here. Therefore, little is known about the people who built these earthen structures. From Carbon-14 dates obtained at other sites, it is supposed that the Sheboygan Mounds were built between A.D. 500 and A.D. 1000.

STATE HISTORICAL SOCIETY OF WISCONSIN

816 State St., Madison. Open free, 8 a.m. to 10 p.m., Monday through Friday; 8 a.m. to 5 p.m., Saturday; closed Sundays, national holidays.

This museum displays a large collection of surface finds of Old Copper artifacts. In addition it has materials from sites that have been excavated by the museum staff. The exhibits represent all periods in Wisconsin prehistory, and separate displays show how pottery, stone, and copper artifacts were made.

Dioramas show the excavation of a rockshelter, prehistoric economic activities in each season, and the life cycle of an Indian man.

UNIVERSITY OF WISCONSIN ARBORETUM

On the shore of Lake Winagra. Madison. Open free, at all times.

There are three groups of mounds in the University Arboretum, all of which can be visited. No effort has been made to interpret them.

UNIVERSITY OF WISCONSIN CAMPUS

Madison. Open free, at all times.

At four places on the campus there are prehistoric mounds, several of them near the Elm Drive dormitories. One is on Observatory Hill, two groups on Picnic Point, and one group near Eagle Heights, the student housing units. Some, but not all, are marked by plaques.

WISCONSIN STATE UNIVERSITY MUSEUM OF ANTHROPOLOGY

Clow Science Bldg., Room 241, on the campus, Oshkosh. Open free, 8 a.m. to 4 p.m., Monday through Friday during regular semesters.

On display in this museum are a burial of a Wisconsin Indian woman who died about AD 1200, several prehistoric Wisconsin skulls, a dugout canoe, and numerous local artifacts of copper, stone, bone, and pottery.

Special Feature. A number of the artifacts exhibited are from a collection made by Angus Lookaround, an Indian.

WYALUSING STATE PARK (WYE-uh-LOOSE-ing)

From Prairie du Chien (duh-SHEEN) drive 6 miles southeast on US 18, then 5 miles west on County Trunk C, then three-quarters of a mile to County Trunk X, then to junction with State Park Road which leads to park entrance. Open 4 a.m. to 11 p.m., daily, April 1 to Oct. 31. Admission: $1 per car. Camping.

Sentinel Ridge, a high divide in the park, was used by prehistoric people as a burial spot. Here they built mounds over the bodies of the dead. One large group known as "a procession of mounds" stretches out in a line along the ridge and can be reached by auto and an easy trail from the parking lot.

NORTHEAST

After the last Ice Age glacier disappeared, one feature was common to all of northeastern North America from Labrador south to Virginia. The area was forested. Everyone who lived in the region during the next 10,000 years had to adjust in one way or another to that fact. As a result, there were similarities in the prehistoric cultures of the Northeast, but there were also marked differences in lifeways. These arose in part from necessarily different responses to climate and food resources. They also arose from the influences of diverse cultures in neighboring areas.

Men arrived in the northern part of the Northeast even before trees began to grow on land recently laid bare by retreating ice. The first to come were Paleo hunters who sometimes tracked their quarry very close indeed to the edge of the ice. For example, the Debert (deh-BURT) site in Nova Scotia yielded evidence that men camped there 11,000 years ago when snowfields were just five miles away, and it was only 65 miles to the ice itself. Even in such a chilly world tundra vegetation fed herds of grazing animals which in turn provided food for men.

Other groups of Paleo-Indians stayed behind in the region farther south. After the glaciers contracted, this area was the first to be covered by trees which eventually spread northward into Canada. What we know about these Big-Game Hunters in the Northeast comes from a small number of sites including the Williamson Site in Virginia, the Shoop Site in Pennsylvania, Bull Brook and Wapanucket No. 8 in Massachusetts, and Reagen in Vermont. None of the sites is prepared for the public, but artifacts from some of them can be seen in major northeastern museums.

Archaic Period

As they did elsewhere, Paleo-Indians in all of the Northeast slowly developed new lifeways in the forest environment, and during the next period, known as the Archaic, they learned to exploit new resources. Along some rivers and seashores they harvested quantities of mollusks, and the shells they discarded piled up in heaps. Many of these heaps, all the way from Virginia to the Maritime Provinces of Canada, have now disappeared because sea level has risen in relation to the land, but where they survived archeologists have studied them—along the banks of the Hudson River, for example, and on Cape Cod and the coast of Maine.

These refuse pits at the Cole Gravel Pit Site in New York were used during the Archaic Period. Several hundred pits were found, some with burials.

At one place, unfortunately not open to the public, the shell middens tell a story of considerable social change. At Ellsworth Falls, Maine, excavation has revealed four distinct stages of social development. In the oldest, known as the Kelley Phase and dated before 3000 B.C., men made heavy, chipped tools. The implements they used for scraping hides or wood were large and crude. Their hammerstones were essentially large pebbles or cobbles. Flakes struck from the cobbles seem to have served as knives.

By about 2000 B.C. a much more elaborate tool kit had developed at this site. Men had adzes and gouges—woodworking tools useful in making dugout canoes, among other things. Six hundred years later they had refined their tools still further: They used plummets possibly as weights on fishing nets or possibly as bolas. They made weights to improve the balance and efficiency of their atlatls, and in time they began to use pottery. Finally men at Ellsworth Falls began to hunt with smaller projectile points. This suggests that they had bows and arrows. They may even have done some gardening. They had entered what is called the Woodland cultural period.

Fish Trapping

In broad outline this one site tells what happened in varying ways at varying times all over the Northeast. Where Boston now stands, Archaic people who depended on the sea for food made an elaborate adjustment to their environment and reached a high level of social organization earlier than did those at Ellsworth Falls. At Boston—and elsewhere—they trapped fish in devices called weirs. These were arrangements of various kinds built so that fish could more easily swim into them than out of them.

The Boston Site, known as the Boylston Street Fish Weir, is now covered by the New England Mutual Life Insurance Company building. When construction workers were digging the foundation for this building they encountered evidence of earlier construction. Archeologists studied the site, dug further, and found that 65,000 wooden stakes had been driven into clay, above which shallow tidal

waters once rose and fell. Between the upright stakes branches had been woven basket-fashion, permitting water to pass through but creating an obstacle for fish. Later 12 feet of silt had been deposited above the tops of the stakes. This meant that the water had risen in relation to the land. Then, as Boston expanded in historic times, landfill had been dumped on top of the silt, driving the water away from the area.

Estimates by geologists and dates obtained by the radiocarbon method place the time of construction of the Boylston Street Fish Weir between 4000 B.C. and 2000 B.C. The Archaic people who used the trap had obviously achieved a rather highly organized society; otherwise they could not have built and maintained such a large and complicated device for obtaining food.

Snowshoes

A quite different invention—snowshoes —helped those who lived inland to get food in the dead of winter. Some experts think snowshoes may have come into the Northeast from northern Eurasia. Others believe they may have been an independent invention made by northeastern Indians during early Archaic times. Whichever it was, hunters could now walk and even run on top of soft snow. They could actually travel faster than the game they hunted.

At the time when people were harvesting fish in Boston and mollusks at Ellsworth Falls, other groups had begun to develop a lifeway known as Laurentian in northern New York, Ontario, Quebec, and parts of New England and Pennsylvania. Men hunted with broad, heavy projectile points, and they supplemented their meat diet with fish, nuts, berries, and seeds. At many Laurentian campsites evidence points to short stays by small groups. Here and there, however, where they found an abundance of fish or waterfowl or acorns, several groups gathered in large settlements for part of the year.

In central New York and northern Pennsylvania a quite distinct lifeway known as the Lamoka developed in a few places, paralleling in time and in some of

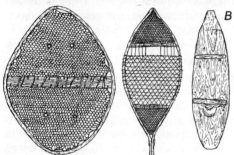

A. Fish traps of several kinds were used in rivers and estuaries along the Atlantic Coast. This one, built by Indians in Virginia, was sketched by Hariot, one of the first French artists to visit America. Fishermen drove stakes into the river bottom and then wove branches between the stakes, basket-fashion, allowing the water to pass through but creating an obstacle for the fish. After Hariot. B. Various types of snowshoes: a bearpaw snowshoe, used by Naskapi Indians, with four eyelets through which lashings were placed to hold it firmly on the foot (left); a woven snowshoe made by Onondaga Indians (center); and a wooden snowshoe from Manitoba (right). After Birket-Smith, Turner, Beauchamp.

its traits the Laurentian culture. Lamoka people were hunters and fishermen. At one time or another they consumed more than 30 different kinds of animal and left the bones in trash heaps. They were also great eaters of acorns and other nuts and seeds, which they parched and ground into meal. Some of their grinding stones were very large, and they seem to have pounded some of their food with big stone pestles, using hollow stumps for mortars.

Toward the end of the Archaic Period, about 1000 B.C., hunters in some areas began to travel more and more in canoes. In Pennsylvania, New York, and New Jersey, for example, they tended to camp along riverbanks and to make short expeditions into the forests for food.

At about this same time women acquired a new kind of cooking vessel. For centuries in the past they had been preparing stews and soups in watertight kettles of skin or wood or bark, into which they dropped hot stones to make the liquid boil. Now they began to use large, heavy vessels carved from a soft stone

called steatite or soapstone. The old-fashioned method of stone boiling continued, but it was easier to do in the large steatite pots which also held heat much better than vessels of wood or skin. Canoes made it possible to take the heavy vessels along when it was necessary to move camp. If a pot broke, it was cut up to make beads, gorgets, ladles, and spoons.

Woodland Period

This time of change, called by some archeologists the Transitional Period, merged into another period known as the Woodland. If any one thing sets off the Early Woodland lifeway it is the acquisition of pottery. Vessels of baked clay replaced the cumbersome steatite pots, and since they could be set directly over the fire they gave new freedom to the women who made and used them.

Another new concern of Early Woodland women was gardening. Just how or when they came by the idea is not known, but between about 1000 B.C. and 500 B.C.

they were caring for little patches of sunflowers, Jerusalem artichoke, and several other plants which we customarily think of as weeds.

With a more stable food supply came further changes in life. People could settle down on small farms, although men made constant trips into the forests for game. Before long the farming areas increased. Trees were cleared along stream banks to make larger fields, and corn and beans began to take the place of older food plants. During these Middle Woodland times, which lasted from about 500 B.C. to about A.D. 700, agriculture became important from Virginia as far north as the St. Lawrence River. Abbott Farm in New Jersey, which archeologists have been studying for a hundred years, was inhabited during this time. In New York, Ontario, and New England the lifeway known as Point Peninsula began to develop from a purely hunting culture into one that accepted the idea of farming.

Development of Villages

From now on, with a few exceptions, lifeways all over the Northeast developed slowly but steadily in much the same directions. Villages, some of them quite large, took the place of single farms. Many of these settlements were fortified by log stockades. Corn and beans became more and more important in man's diet. In western Pennsylvania one Late Woodland culture is known as the Monongahela. In New York and around the lower Great Lakes the Owasco culture evolved from earlier lifeways.

It was from the Owasco that the prehistoric Iroquois developed. By the time Europeans came to New York and the St. Lawrence River area, some of their great towns had a thousand inhabitants, with fields covering several hundred acres of cleared and cultivated ground.

From Paleo times until the day when Europeans arrived on the Atlantic coast, the numbers of northeastern Indians increased a great deal. This does not seem to have been the result of large migration from other areas. Rather it was a steady growth of resident populations as they improved their methods of obtaining food.

Although people did not move into the Northeast, ideas and customs and inventions did. From the south in Early Woodland times knowledge of pottery-making entered Virginia and moved up the coast. Possibly the pottery idea also entered the northern part of the region from some place far to the west in Canada. Corn and beans—and some of the notions and social behavior connected with agriculture —came ultimately from Mexico. Cultures, such as the Adena, which were stimulated by agriculture in the Ohio Valley affected people in part of the Northeast. There were also minor influences from the Hopewell Cult of Ohio. The custom of burying the dead in mounds appeared in a number of places. Virginia was one. There in a burial mound Thomas Jefferson conducted the first scientific excavation in the United States.

Possibly there were influences in pottery styles or implement design that came somehow from northwestern or northeastern Eurasia. Immigration did take place at more than one time across the Bering Strait, and immigrants who followed that route certainly brought their cultures with them. It is not so easy to see how ideas could have crossed westward from northern Europe, but the use of small craft for island-hopping has been suggested as a possibility. Also scholars have suggested that people may have crossed the water barrier in the north when it was covered with ice floes, following the edge of the ice and subsisting, as Eskimos did, on the sea mammals and fish available there.

The Northeast never attained the population density of the Mississippi Valley. Nor did arts and crafts and social organization reach such levels of development as in the major centers of Indian life. But much more happened in 12,000 years in the Northeast than one would guess from the number of visitable archeological sites. These are few indeed, and an important reason is that a humid climate and generally acid soil in the region have conspired to destroy most organic matter left by prehistoric peoples.

But even though site areas are minimal, some of the best museums in America are in the Northeast. They serve as excellent introductions to the area and to Indian life elsewhere as well.

Birdstones, Boatstones, Bannerstones

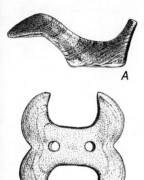

A

B

A. Birdstones have been found throughout the North Central area, and their exact use and function are still disputed. This birdstone may have been used as a weight on an atlatl. Original in the Milwaukee Public Museum. B. The bannerstone, also, is an artifact that has thus far defied exact identification. This one was cut from slate and finely polished. It is of the type called "winged"; others were shaped like butterflies. Original in the Museum of the American Indian, New York.

In 1840 some theological students from Connecticut found in an Indian burial a highly polished stone that somewhat resembled a bird. In 1848 Squier and Davis included illustrations of similar stones in their *Ancient Monuments of the Mississippi Valley.* From that time on farmers and others began to collect these strange objects. Birdstones turned up all over Ohio and Indiana and in western New York, western Pennsylvania, eastern Illinois, southeastern Wisconsin, southern Michigan and lower Canada.

The carefully shaped images sometimes resembled creatures other than birds. Some looked a little like boats. (These were called boatstones.) Others, less representational in form, got the name bannerstone possibly because they were thought to resemble the small banners that in some societies were attached to ceremonial staffs. The kind of stone used in these objects was very often attractive. Banded slate was a favorite material. So was porphyry which had a mottled, varicolored appearance. The range of shades in these artifacts was wide and so was the range of shapes.

But what was their origin, their use, their meaning? The answers to these questions were as numerous as the facts about them were scarce. They were called handles for knives, emblems of maternity designed to be worn in women's hair, stone bayonets, totemic emblems, cornhuskers, necklace ornaments, fetishes, decorations for the tops of staffs used by medicine men. One man argued that the birdstones were somehow connected with the widespread thunderbird myth.

Arthur Parker, an archeologist and himself an Indian, speculated that at least one type of bannerstone was attached to the shaft of a spear. Its purpose was to give the spear weight and also to keep it on course, as feathers keep an arrow. Parker experimented with this arrangement and discovered that the spear went much straighter, faster, and about 25 percent farther than an unweighted shaft.

Another theory is that a good many birdstones/bannerstones were used as weights on atlatls (and not on spears themselves) to give added momentum for launching the weapon. Some evidence does suggest that some bannerstones were so used. It also seems possible that some birdstones had no such mechanical value but were for magical or ceremonial purposes.

Archeologist Thorne Deuel believes that bannerstones developed from atlatl weights but were either decorations or ceremonial objects carried by men to show they were good hunters. Later, he thinks, they evolved still further into flat forms that had bannerstone outlines but were worn as gorgets.

The practice of making birdstones seems to have begun in the Late Archaic Period when people were still using spears, and it continued up until Late Woodland times. However, not much more about these often very lovely objects is known. One thing is certain however: Many forgers have gone into the business of making birdstones and have found it very profitable.

Caveat emptor!

Connecticut

BRUCE MUSEUM

Bruce Park, Greenwich. Open free, 10 a.m. to 5 p.m., Monday through Friday; 2 p.m. to 5 p.m., Sunday; closed Saturday and most legal holidays.

Dioramas in this museum show how Woodland Indians made canoes and built bark huts. In addition to random collections from local rockshelters and middens, there are materials from the vicinity of Rolla, Mo., and Hohokam materials from Arizona.

CHILDREN'S MUSEUM OF HARTFORD

950 Trout Brook Dr., West Hartford. Open free, 9 a.m. to 5 p.m., Monday through Saturday; 1 p.m. to 5 p.m., Sunday and holidays; closed July 4, Labor Day weekend, weekends July, Aug., Thanksgiving, Dec. 25.

General material interprets the life of North American Indians in all areas. One exhibit explains an archeological dig and shows the use of artifacts and their relationship to the seasonal activities of the Indians of Connecticut.

CONNECTICUT STATE LIBRARY MUSEUM

231 Capitol Ave., Hartford. Open free, 8:30 a.m. to 5 p.m., Monday through Friday; 9 a.m. to 1 p.m., Saturday; closed Sunday, holidays.

A new addition containing archeological materials is now open.

A diorama in the Museum of Natural History of the Smithsonian Institution shows a prehistoric Indian settlement in what is now Washington, D. C. The museum has many dioramas and displays on the major prehistoric cultures of the United States. Smithsonian Institution photo.

GUNN MEMORIAL LIBRARY MUSEUM

Washington Green, Washington. Open free, 2 p.m. to 5 p.m., Tuesday, Thursday, Saturday, and by appointment.

In addition to a collection given by Oglalla Sioux Indians, the museum exhibits Connecticut material covering all periods from 4000 B.C. to A.D. 1500. Displays include artifacts from an excavation conducted by a local amateur archeology group.

MATTATUCK MUSEUM OF THE MATTATUCK HISTORICAL SOCIETY

119 West Main St., Waterbury. Open free, noon to 5 p.m., Tuesday through Saturday; 2 p.m. to 5 p.m., Sunday; closed all holidays.

Eight cases contain displays of Indian artifacts, mostly from the Northeast.

NEW BRITAIN CHILDREN'S MUSEUM

Hawley Memorial Library Bldg., 28 High St., New Britain. Open free, 9 a.m. to 5 p.m., Monday through Saturday; 1 p.m. to 5 p.m., Sunday, winter; closed Saturday, Sunday, summer.

This small but active museum has changing exhibits which include dioramas and prehistoric Indian material.

Special Interest. The museum prepares display kits on prehistoric Indian life which schools, churches, or other institutions may borrow for educational use. The staff conducts a training program for teen-agers in museum work and encourages those interested in archeology.

PEABODY MUSEUM OF NATURAL HISTORY, YALE UNIVERSITY

170 Whitney Ave., New Haven. Open 9 a.m. to 5 p.m., Monday through Saturday; 1 p.m. to 5 p.m.,

Sunday; closed, Jan. 1, July 4, Thanksgiving, Dec. 25. Admission: Monday, Wednesday, Friday, free; other days, adults, 25¢; children, 10¢.

Money contributed by George Peabody in the 19th century financed this museum, which bears his name. It houses an extensive archeological collection from which are taken the materials for exhibits both permanent and changing.

A number of displays illuminate prehistoric Indian life in Connecticut, with artifacts, photographs, and drawings of a rockshelter, a soapstone quarry, a shell heap, a burial, and a village site. Other exhibits explain the process of making bone needles, wampum, clay pottery, soapstone vessels, chipped stone tools. Of particular interest is the display of snowshoe making, together with types of snowshoes which were apparently invented in Europe and Asia as well as in North America.

Some material on exhibit comes from important sites that are not open to the public. There are artifacts from Deer Island, Me.; from Florida shell mounds; and from a Mississippian site in Perry County, Mo.

Special Interest. The museum has a division which lends material to schools for study and which offers special programs for school children.

STAMFORD MUSEUM AND NATURE CENTER

High Ridge at Scofieldtown Rd., Stamford. Open free, 9 a.m. to 5 p.m., Monday through Saturday; 2 p.m. to 6 p.m., Sunday and holidays; closed, Jan. 1, Thanksgiving, Dec. 25. Parking fee: 75¢, in-state cars; $1.50, out-of-state.

Several Indian rooms here contain displays of prehistoric artifacts, including local finds. One exhibit demonstrates how stone was chipped to make tools and weapons. Dioramas showing typical village scenes depict the lives of Woodland people in the Northeast and Southeast, mound builders, and Indians of the Plains, Southwest, California, and Northwest.

Delaware

DELAWARE STATE MUSEUM

316 S. Governors Ave., Dover. Open free, 11 a.m. to 5 p.m., Tuesday through Saturday; 2 p.m. to 5 p.m., Sunday.

This museum has a display of prehistoric weapons, implements, and pottery made by Delaware Indians. One exhibit shows a cache of stone blades; another an Indian burial.

HAGLEY MUSEUM

Barley Mill Rd., Greenville, Wilmington. Open free, 9:30 a.m. to 4:30 p.m., Tuesday through Saturday; 1 p.m. to 5 p.m., Sunday.

Although primarily historic in emphasis, this museum has some prehistoric material dating back as far as the Archaic Period. A diorama shows an Indian habitation in a rockshelter.

IRON HILL MUSEUM

From Newark drive south on Delaware 896, past the intersection with Interstate 95, then west on the Old Baltimore Pike. The museum is between Cooch's Bridge, Del., and Elkton, Md. Open free, 7 p.m. to 9 p.m., Tuesday and Thursday; 1 p.m. to 5 p.m., Saturday and Sunday.

In 1964 an all-Negro school ceased to operate in this building and a group of volunteers from the Archaeological Society of Delaware and the Delaware Mineralological Society turned it into a museum. Since then exhibits designed primarily for school children have been developed, showing the lives of Woodland Indians of the vicinity. One exhibit centers around the Harlan Mill Steatite Quarry where prehistoric Indians obtained soapstone from which they made vessels for cooking. A general exhibit traces the history of Indians from Paleo times to the historic period. Indian foods are displayed, and there are dioramas on Delaware (Lenni Lenape) village life and trapping methods.

ISLAND FIELD SITE

From the north, proceed to Dover on US 13, then drive 12 miles south on US 113 to the Murderkill River; cross the river on the Frederica bypass, then take the first road to the left and follow signs to the site. From the south, drive 2 miles north on US 113 from Milford, turn right on the South Bowers-Thompsonville Rd., and follow signs to the site. Open free, 12:30 p.m. to 4:30 p.m., Wednesday through Sunday, June, July, Aug.; 12:30 p.m. to 4:30 p.m., Saturday, Sunday, April, May, Sept., Oct.

At this site, which has been occupied by various groups for 3,000 years or more, it is possible to see how archeologists have made a series of discoveries.

First to be excavated were ancient storage pits and trash dumps where people left artifacts among discarded mollusk shells. During a later dig, rains exposed what turned out to be a large cemetery. Excavation revealed burials made in a number of different ways. Some graves contained skeletons of bodies buried in the flesh. In others were bones that had been bundled together after the flesh was removed. Still others contained the remains of cremations. In several a number of individuals had been buried together.

With many of the burials were grave offerings, including bone awls and needles, harpoons made of deer antler, pipes carved from stone, and a variety of tools, weapons, and ornaments.

The cemetery was apparently used between A.D. 700 and A.D. 1000 by people who followed the Woodland lifeway. They were prosperous farmers, hunters, and fishermen, and their grave offerings show that they did widespread trading. Some of their ideas and practices may also have been influenced by trade. Like people in the Ohio Valley and elsewhere in the Midwest, they seem to have valued mica and shark teeth, conch shell, and bits of crystal.

Near the cemetery there was a village at a later time, approximately A.D. 1200, about which information is still being gathered.

Material from this important site is on exhibit at the Zwaanendael Museum.

Special Feature. Archeologists are often working at the site during summer months, and visitors are welcome to watch. Guided tours may be arranged during most of the year by writing in advance to Educational Coordinator, Delaware Archaeological Board, R.D. No. 2, Box 166A, Dover, Del. 19901.

ZWAANENDAEL MUSEUM (ZWAN-en-dale)

Savannah Rd. and Kings Hwy., Lewes. Open free, 10 a.m. to 5 p.m., Tuesday through Saturday; 12:30 p.m. to 5 p.m., Sunday.

This museum contains a representative display of artifacts from the important Island Field Site. Also on exhibit are artifacts from the Townsend Site, which dates from A.D. 1550 to 1600.

District of Columbia

MUSEUM OF NATURAL HISTORY, UNITED STATES NATIONAL MUSEUM, SMITHSONIAN INSTITUTION

Constitution Ave. at Tenth St., N.W., on the Mall. Open free, 9 a.m. to 4:30 p.m., daily, Sept. through March; 9 a.m. to 10 p.m., daily, April through Aug.; closed Dec. 25.

In the archeology halls in this great museum, materials are displayed by geographic areas and generally by the main cultural periods within these areas, except for the Paleo-Indian culture, which has a separate exhibit of its own and is not represented in the exhibits for each geographical area.

Special exhibits give detailed information about the physical characteristics and origins of the American Indian, explaining blood groups and such traits as tooth shape and facial characteristics.

An exhibit shows how rapidly the Indians increased in number once they had entered America, but also how sparse the Indian population was compared to the total population today. (North of Mexico in 1492 there were probably no more than a million people.)

A large map divides the country into areas according to the predominant food available in each in prehistoric times: sea mammal area, caribou area, salmon area, wild seed area, and others.

One exhibit is devoted to ceremonial shell art of the Southeast, with numerous examples and labels explaining the relationship of this art form to similar work done in copper, stone, and pottery. Exhibits also make clear how shells were used in the Black Drink Ceremony.

Southeast sculpture appears in a separate exhibit and woodcarving in another. Life-sized figures in a number of exhibits show Indians engaged in typical occupations in different areas.

Dioramas and displays introduce visitors to copper mining, to Old Copper, Adena, Hopewell, and Fort Ancient cultures, and to Great Plains village life.

This vast museum can serve as an excellent introduction to many of the most important aspects of prehistoric life all over America, as well as to the lifeway of people who inhabited the area around Washington, D.C., 500 years ago.

NATIONAL GEOGRAPHIC SOCIETY

17th and M St., N.W. Open free, 9 a.m. to 6 p.m., Monday through Friday; 9 a.m. to 5 p.m., Saturday and holidays; noon to 5 p.m., Sunday.

Included in exhibits of material gathered in world-wide exploration is a life-sized model of an Anasazi kiva showing various activities conducted by men and older boys in the underground ceremonial chamber. From time to time there are special exhibits in Explorers' Hall. These may include archeology north of Mexico.

Maine

ABBE MUSEUM

Acadia National Park. From Bar Harbor drive south on Maine 3 to Sieur de Monts Spring. Open free, 9 a.m. to 5 p.m., daily, Memorial Day to Labor Day. Camping in Acadia National Park.

The Robert Abbe Museum of Stone Age Antiquities contains materials from Woodland sites, both coastal and interior. One diorama shows summer activity in prehistoric times; another shows a scene of coastal activity.

ANCIENT PEMAQUID RESTORATION
(pem-ah-QUID)

Round Pond. Open 9 a.m. to 5 p.m., daily, June 15 through Labor Day. Admission: adults, 50¢; children, 25¢. Camping nearby.

The Wawenocks, a subtribe of the Abnakis, once lived at this site and left refuse heaped up in a midden. A few artifacts recovered from the midden are on display in the museum which is devoted primarily to the English occupation of the area in the early 17th century.

AROOSTOOK HISTORICAL AND ART MUSEUM OF HOULTON

109 Main St., Houlton. Open free, 1 p.m. to 5 p.m., Tuesday and Saturday; closed holidays.

Stone tools on exhibit here were made by people of the Red Paint culture.

BANGOR HISTORICAL SOCIETY

159 Union St., Bangor. Open free, 2 p.m. to 4 p.m., Monday through Saturday; closed national holidays.

Exhibits include prehistoric artifacts from a professional excavation in the Penobscot River drainage.

DAMARISCOTTA RIVER SHELL MOUNDS
(or Oyster Shell Banks) (dam-uh-riss-COTT-uh)

From Damariscotta drive 1.2 miles east on US Business 1. Open free, at all times.

Mounds, which consist mostly of oyster shells, were left here by people of the Red Paint culture. The mounds can be seen from across the Damariscotta River. An interpretive sign tells about the prehistoric occupation. Artifacts from the site are in the Peabody Museum, Harvard University.

WILSON MUSEUM

Perkins St., Castine (kas-TEEN). Open free, 2 p.m. to 5 p.m., Tuesday through Sunday, May 27 to Sept. 15.

Exhibits of prehistoric artifacts represent some of the major Indian cultures in North America. They include material from the Northeast, from Ohio mounds, Southwestern pueblos, the Great Plains, and Eskimo areas in Canada.

Special Feature. One display of material found in a Red Paint grave contains fire lighters. These were pieces of iron pyrite which were struck with flint to make sparks.

Maryland

MARYLAND ACADEMY OF SCIENCES

7 W. Mulberry St., Baltimore. Open free, 9 a.m. to 4:30 p.m., Monday through Friday.

The present exhibits contain only a small part of the archeological collection belonging to the Maryland Academy of Sciences. However, in January, 1973, the museum will move to a new building at Key Highway and Light St. There it will be open 9 a.m. to 4:30 p.m., Monday through Saturday. There will be a small admission fee, except on Saturday when admission will be free. At the new location large displays will be devoted to the archeology of eastern United States with special emphasis on Maryland and surrounding states.

MUSEUM OF NATURAL HISTORY

Maryland House, Druid Hill Park, Baltimore. Open free, 10 a.m. to 4 p.m., Monday through Saturday; 1 p.m. to 5 p.m., Sunday; closed Monday, Nov. 1 through April.

This museum has one room devoted to Indian materials, primarily from the Maryland area. Many prehistoric artifacts are included in the exhibits.

PISCATAWAY PARK (pis-CAT-ah-way)

From Alexandria, Va., drive east on Interstate 495 to Exit 37, then 12 miles south on Maryland 210 to park entrance. Open free, 7:30 a.m. to dark, daily.

About 5,000 years ago hunters camped here on the bank of the Potomac River. Later people buried their dead in a cemetery not far from what is now the site of old Fort Washington. Still later, when George Washington built his home at Mount Vernon just across the river, there were Indians living in the park area, and they continued to do so until almost 1800. Although archeologists have done excavation here, there is no special site prepared for view.

Massachusetts

BRONSON MUSEUM

8. N. Main Street Building, Attleboro. Open free, 9:30 a.m. to 4:30 p.m., Monday, Tuesday, Thursday; other days by appointment.

This unusual museum is operated by the Massachusetts Archaeological Society, and a great deal of its material comes from sites which the society has excavated. For comparative purposes some displays contain artifacts from areas outside New England, but the main concentration is on pre-

historic man in Massachusetts from Paleo times through the Woodland Period. A large diorama shows a village as it may have looked about 2300 B.C. at Assowampsett Lake, where the society has been excavating for 19 years.

Other dioramas show a quarry where men dug steatite (soapstone) from which they made large cooking vessels; a Woodland burial; and a Titicut Site village scene, and a scene based on information gained by the society in excavating a site in Massachusetts known as Wapanucket #6. Exhibits include a number of restored soapstone bowls found with cremations, tools and weapons which are explained, and a group of implements for which hafting has been reconstructed.

Special Interest. The Massachusetts Archaeological Society offers lectures at the museum from time to time and sponsors conducted group visits.

CAPE COD NATIONAL SEASHORE

Follow US 6 on Cape Cod to Eastham, where the Salt Pond Visitor Center is located. Visitor Center

Detail from a diorama in the Hagley Museum in Wilmington, Delaware, that shows Indian life in a rockshelter. The woman is making corn meal by breaking up kernels of corn in a hollow tree stump. Hagley Museum photo.

open free, 8 a.m. to 8 p.m., daily, summer; 9 a.m. to 4:45 p.m., Wednesday through Sunday, winter.

The Indians first encountered by the Pilgrims were Wampanoags. These people may have lived on Cape Cod for 3,000 years or more before a boatload of the *Mayflower's* passengers disembarked and helped themselves to corn which the Indians had stored underground in a large basket. The Wampanoags were hunters and fishermen as well as farmers. Their arrowheads, fishline sinkers, and other implements are still to be found at sites on Cape Cod even after more than 300 years of European occupation. A collection of their artifacts is on exhibit in the museum at the Visitor Center and more will be added as archeologists excavate sites owned by the National Park Service. A large display in the museum shows how some of the implements were used.

From the Visitor Center it is a short drive to Indian Rock at Skiff Hill. The rock, a 20-ton glacial granite boulder, has deep grooves where Indians sharpened bone harpoon heads, fishhooks, and stone axes. Originally the giant whetstone stood a hundred feet down the hill at the edge of Nauset Marsh. It was moved when it seemed in danger of being lost in the swamp. Indian Rock is only one of several such sharpening stones in the neighborhood.

Along the beaches of the National Seashore there are several heaps of discarded shells where prehistoric people camped and ate seafood. These have not been excavated. Visitors are earnestly requested not to disturb them.

CHILDREN'S MUSEUM

60 Burroughs and Jamaicaway, Boston. Open, 1 p.m. to 5 p.m., Monday through Friday, during the

In the Children's Museum in Boston young people can learn how Indians made materials they used in their daily lives. Here a boy scrapes a skin that has been hung on a frame made of tree branches. Photo by Julie Snow.

school year; 1 p.m. to 5 p.m., Saturday, Sunday, and on Boston public school vacation days, winter; 10 a.m. to 5 p.m., daily, summer; closed Sept. Admission: adults, $1.25; children, 75¢.

This museum has exhibits representing ten major culture areas north of Mexico. Some prehistoric materials are included in the displays. A full-sized reconstruction shows an Algonquian wigwam from southern New England as it may have been just before the arrival of Europeans.

CHILDREN'S MUSEUM, INC.

Russells Mills Rd., Dartmouth. Open free, 11 a.m. to 4 p.m., Tuesday through Friday; 2 p.m. to 4 p.m., Saturday and Sunday; closed Easter, July 4, Thanksgiving, and from late December to early February.

In addition to historic Indian materials from the Plains and the Southwest, this museum has a few prehistoric Wampanoag Indian artifacts from the immediate vicinity.

COHASSET HISTORICAL SOCIETY, MARITIME MUSEUM

Elm St., Cohasset. Open, 1:30 p.m. to 4:30 p.m., Tuesday, Wednesday, Thursday, from the last week in June through the first week in September. Admission: adults, 50¢, children, 25¢.

This museum devoted to local history includes a case of Indian artifacts found in the area. These are primarily Algonquian and seem to date from about A.D. 1500 to 1700.

DIGHTON ROCK STATE PARK (DIE-ton)

Go north from Fall River on Massachusetts 24, take Main St. Exit at Assonet and follow directional signs to park. Open free, daily during daylight hours. Camping nearby.

In the Taunton River at this spot stands a rock on which Indians carved petroglyphs at some unknown time in the past. These markings were known in the 17th century and prompted Cotton Mather to speculate about their origin.

Non-Indian inscriptions have also been chipped in the rock. According to the book *Dighton Rock* by E. B. Delabarre of Brown University, one of these inscriptions indicates that a Portuguese explorer, Miguel Cortereal, visited the spot in A.D. 1511. Not all scholars agree with Dr. Delabarre's interpretation.

The best time to examine the rock is at extreme low tide.

Special Interest. At one time certain markings on the rock were supposed to have been made by Vikings. This prompted the 19th-century violinist Ole Bull to buy it for the Royal Society of Copenhagen. When scholars disproved the idea of Norse origin, the society gave the rock to the Old Colony Historical Society of Taunton, which then presented it to the Commonwealth of Massachusetts.

FRUITLANDS MUSEUM

Prospect Hill Rd., Harvard. Open, 1 p.m. to 5 p.m., Tuesday through Sunday, May 30 to Sept. 30, and Monday when it is a holiday. Admission: adults, 50¢, children, 25¢.

Some miscellaneous prehistoric materials in this museum are supplemented by a diorama showing

Indian life in the Nashua Valley which was prepared by S. J. Guernsey, a well-known archeologist. Another diorama showing the Sun Dance of the Sioux is in preparation.

HOLYOKE MUSEUM

238 Cabot St., Holyoke. Open free, 1 p.m. to 5 p.m., Monday through Saturday; 2 p.m. to 5 p.m., Sunday; closed national holidays and July.

The Museum of Fine Arts in the Victorian Mansion has archeological exhibits which contain Indian artifacts used in ceremonies, in agriculture, and in hunting, and there is a display that shows how men chipped flint to make weapons and tools.

PEABODY MUSEUM, SALEM

161 Essex St., Salem. Open free, 9 a.m. to 5 p.m., Monday through Saturday; 2 p.m. to 5 p.m., Sunday and holidays, March 1 to Nov. 1; 9 a.m. to 4 p.m., Monday through Saturday; 2 p.m. to 4 p.m., Sunday and holidays, Nov. 1 to March 1; closed Jan. 1, Thanksgiving, Dec. 25.

Exhibits of American Indian material here are ethnological rather than archeological, although some of the artifacts shown are similar to those used in prehistoric times. In one small display of prehistoric Japanese ceramics is an example of Jomon pottery, a type which has recently caused certain archeologists to ask: "Did the inspiration for the first American Indian pottery come from Japan?" The question was raised by the discovery on the coast of Ecuador of Jomon-type potsherds which have been dated at 2500 B.C., earlier than any other ceramics in South or North America. It is possible, some students say, for ocean currents to have helped a vessel to make a voyage across the Pacific from Japan to South America.

The museum has in storage considerable archeological material from Essex County, Mass., and from Red Paint sites in Maine. This may be used by students but is not on exhibit for the general public.

The Name. Originally the museum, known as East India Marine Hall, was the meeting place for a society of sailing ship captains who gathered "curiosities" from all over the world. In 1867 it was renamed for George Peabody, a New England philanthropist who endowed it as well as two other museums which bear his name—one at Harvard and one at Yale.

PEABODY MUSEUM OF ARCHAEOLOGY AND ETHNOLOGY, HARVARD UNIVERSITY

11 Divinity St., Cambridge. Open free, 9 a.m. to 4:30 p.m., Monday through Saturday; 1 p.m. to 4:30 p.m., Sunday. Closed holidays.

This very important museum exhibits archeological materials from all over the world. Three large rooms are devoted to areas north of Mexico.

For those who have not yet visited archeological sites in various parts of the country, the displays offer a good idea of what to look for when examining an excavation. In addition to a wealth of artifacts, there are models of Southwestern pueblos, the great Serpent Mound in Ohio, the ancient cliff dwelling at Betatakin in Arizona, and Montezuma Well. Displays of material from important sites open to the public include Moundville in Alabama, Casa Grande and Tonto National Monument in Arizona, and Alkali Ridge in Utah.

For those who are already familiar with visitable places, the displays are rewarding because they include much material from sites that are not open to the public. Some of the more important of these are: Marsh Pass (Arizona), Stallings Island (Georgia), Weeden Island (Florida), Poverty Point (Louisiana), Dick Creek, Cumberland, and Obion (Tennessee), Marietta Mound (Ohio), and a Red Paint site (Maine).

Some exhibits contain especially interesting items from nonvisitable sites. For example, a rare fragment of lace comes from Ceremonial Cave in the Hueco Mountains in Texas. Four figurines from the Turner Mound in Ohio helped archeologists to understand what the Hopewell people looked like.

Since the displays present an unusual number of artifacts, they are of special interest to those who read more than they travel. Materials in the wide-ranging exhibits represent a variety of cultures including: Old Copper, Hohokam, Owasco, Mimbres, Fremont, Mississippian, Santa Rosa, Swift Creek, Nodena, Caddoan, Point Peninsula, Adena. Various periods are represented for each of the major areas on the continent.

PHILLIPS ACADEMY, ROBERT S. PEABODY FOUNDATION FOR ARCHAEOLOGY

Main St., Andover. Open free, 9 a.m. to 4:30 p.m., Monday through Friday; 9 a.m. to 11:45 a.m., Saturday; 2 p.m. to 5 p.m., Sunday; closed July 4, Labor Day, Thanksgiving, Dec. 25.

Materials drawn from the extensive collections of the museum are arranged in displays that illustrate the daily lives of people of various cultures, the techniques of archeologists who dig up and study prehistoric man, and the theories that finally emerge.

Exhibits from sites which cannot be visited include the Boylston Street Fish Weir in Boston, Ellsworth Falls in Maine, the Bull Brook Site in Massachusetts which yielded much important information about Paleo people in New England, Labrador Eskimo sites, and the Debert Site in Nova Scotia.

Material on the Boreal Archaic people shows how they differed from southern Archaic people because of their heavy reliance on hunting and fishing rather than on plant foods, while at the same time they used many of the same tools.

Exhibits showing cultural influences in New England indicate the spread of burial cult ideas from the Adena in Ohio, of copper artifacts from the Great Lakes, and of agriculture from areas to the south.

A diorama of Pecos Pueblo is based on information gathered during excavations conducted by the museum. Among other major sites in other areas represented are Etowah, Moundville, and Serpent Mound.

PLIMOTH PLANTATION, INC.

Warren Ave., Plymouth. Open, 9 a.m. to 5 p.m., daily, April 15 through Nov. 30; 9 a.m. to 6 p.m., late spring and early fall; 9 a.m. to 7 p.m., summer. Admission: adults, $1.25; children, 50¢; under 5, free.

In addition to extensive reconstruction of the village of Plymouth as it was in the early 17th century, there is an outdoor exhibit which contains a one-family summer house of the kind made by Wampanoag Indians just prior to the arrival of Europeans. The house is located in the middle of the family's cornfield. Planted with the corn are squash, beans, gourds, sunflowers, pumpkins, and tobacco. A drying rack shows how fish were dried in the sun. Additions have been planned for this warm-weather seasonal exhibit.

New Brunswick

NEW BRUNSWICK MUSEUM

277 Douglas Ave., St. John. Open, 10 a.m. to 9 p.m., Monday through Saturday; 2 p.m. to 9 p.m., Sunday, June 15 to Sept. 15; 2 p.m. to 5 p.m., daily, Sept. 16 to June 14. Admission: adults, 25¢; children, 10¢.

Exhibits in this museum are changed frequently, but there are always some archeological materials on display. Of particular interest are the artifacts from shell heap sites along the Bay of Fundy. For study purposes the museum has an extensive collection of pre-Algonquian artifacts from the New Brunswick area.

Newfoundland

L'ANSE AUX MEADOWS (LANSS oh meadows)

At the terminus of Newfoundland 81 on the northern tip of the Great Northern Peninsula. Open free, 9 a.m. to 9 p.m., summer.

Here, protected by seven big, barnlike structures, is a site where Vikings established a settlement in North America nearly 1,000 years ago. The discovery was made in the early 1960s when Helge Ingstad and his wife followed clues they picked up from old Norse sagas and from local fishermen. As a result of their detective work, they found and excavated a Norse house foundation 55 feet wide and 70 feet long. In the center was a typical Norse hearth, lined with slate. Nearby stood the remains of a smithy.

Apparently at least one woman had lived here and had lost a spindle whorl which turned up in the excavation. This implement, used in making yarn, meant that the site was no temporary camp established by sailors. It was a permanent settlement.

After much speculation and many fruitless searches by many scholars, proof had at last been found that Norsemen landed on and lived in America. So important is the site that the Canadian government has announced plans to establish it as a National Historic Park.

NEWFOUNDLAND MUSEUM

Duckworth St., St. John's. Open free, 10 a.m. to 12:30 p.m., 2:30 p.m. to 5 p.m., Monday through Saturday; 2:30 p.m. to 5 p.m., Sunday.

Collections of artifacts made by the Beothuck (bee-AWTH-uk) Indians, whose last survivor died in 1829, are being augmented by archeological materials which this museum is excavating in cooperation with the National Museum of Canada. Also on exhibit are Nascapi Indian artifacts from Labrador.

The Beothuck Indians spoke a distinct language, unrelated to any other in the area. They hunted caribou by building a fence or barrier of fallen trees that extended along the Exploits River for 40 miles. In spring and fall the hunters waited at gaps which had been purposely created in this fence for the migrating caribou herds to pass through. As the animals crowded into the narrow openings, hunters found it easy to kill as many as they wanted. The meat was smoked and cached for use later.

PORT AU CHOIX CEMETERY (PORT oh shwah)

In Port au Choix on Newfoundland 73, on the west coast of the Great Northern Peninsula. Open free, 9 a.m. to 9 p.m., summer; at other seasons on request.

Here at the site of a large prehistoric Indian burial ground, the Provincial Government has erected what it calls an appreciation center in which are exhibits interpreting the culture of the people who once lived—and died—here.

Somewhat as did the Red Paint people who lived farther south in New England, these Archaic hunters and fishermen deposited a pigment called red ocher in graves. They also left gifts for the dead. Their choice of gifts, however, was sometimes unusual. Instead of placing a woman's tools with her body, supposedly for use in an afterlife, and a man's tools with his body, they frequently did just the opposite. They put men's axes and hunting charms and amulets in women's graves. And some needles for sewing were recovered from men's graves. Some of the burials of children were accompanied by lavish gifts of all kinds. Apparently an article's supposed usefulness in afterlife was not the only criterion for grave goods. These people also gave things they treasured when they buried those they loved.

Among the artifacts recovered at the site were beautifully carved stone effigies of whales, small images of birds, and other hunting charms; a wealth of harpoons, points, and daggers made from bone and ivory; and animal teeth, especially beaver incisors, which seem to have been made into woodworking tools.

To judge from the type of material found in the graves, these people may have lived inland in the winter, existing mainly on caribou meat. In summer they lived here on the coast where they fished and caught marine mammals. The fact that they were able to venture out to sea in boats of some sort is obvious, for Newfoundland is an island, and at its nearest point the mainland is ten miles away.

Apparently use of the cemetery went on for about a thousand years. A radiocarbon date places the oldest burial at between 2450 B.C. and 2130 B.C. A radiocarbon date of between 1500 B.C. and 1060 B.C. has been obtained for the most recent burial.

The culture of these seacoast dwellers resembled that of other Archaic people, and they may have come originally from the Great Lakes region. However, they also had distinctive traits of their own. For that reason some archeologists are inclined to put them in a special category called Maritime Archaic.

Many of the Maritime Archaic artifacts resembled those of Eskimos who lived in the area at a later time. However, there is no evidence that Eskimos borrowed these implements from their predecessors. Apparently the two peoples, living in the same environment, developed the same kinds of tool for dealing with it.

New Hampshire

DARTMOUTH COLLEGE MUSEUM

East Wheelock St., Hanover. Open free, 9 a.m. to 5 p.m., Monday through Saturday; 2 p.m. to 5 p.m., Sunday, when college is in session; 9 a.m. to 5 p.m., Monday through Friday, summer vacation; closed national holidays.

In addition to several permanent displays of material from important archeological sites in Central and South America, this general museum has an exhibit of Southwestern pottery from the period A.D. 800 to 900. An exhibit on archeological method shows a typical sequence of cultures in the New England area.

LIBBY MUSEUM

From Wolfeboro drive 4 miles north on New Hampshire 109. Open free, 10 a.m. to 5 p.m., Tuesday through Sunday, July, Aug., July 4, and Labor Day.

In addition to local Indian artifacts, this museum has a map of Indian trails and campsites in the area.

MANCHESTER HISTORIC ASSOCIATION

129 Amherst St., Manchester. Open free, 9 a.m. to 4 p.m., Tuesday through Friday; 10 a.m. to 4 p.m., Saturday; closed national holidays.

In addition to random local finds, this museum displays materials from one careful dig near the Amoskeag Falls at Manchester. The falls apparently provided a good fishing spot and attracted prehistoric Indians from as far away as Maine and New York. Visits to the region obviously began a very long time ago, for a Clovis point was found in the excavation at the falls. Projectile points of this type found elsewhere were associated with hunters of big game which has long been extinct. Later materials which resembled artifacts made by the Iroquois were also recovered at the site.

WOODMAN INSTITUTE

182-192 Central Ave., Dover. Open free, 2 p.m. to 5 p.m., Tuesday through Sunday; closed Jan. 1, Thanksgiving, Dec. 25.

Artifacts of the Red Paint people of Maine and other prehistoric New England materials are on display here in the Annie E. Woodman Institute.

New Jersey

CUMBERLAND COUNTY HISTORICAL SOCIETY

Main St., Greenwich. Open, 2 p.m. to 5 p.m., Wednesday, Saturday, Sunday, April to Oct. Admission: adults, 25¢; students 12-18, 10¢; children, free.

Exhibits here contain random local finds of Lenni Lenape material from the period before 1685.

MORRIS MUSEUM OF ARTS AND SCIENCES

Normandy Heights and Columbia roads, Morristown. Open free, 10 a.m. to 5 p.m., Monday through Saturday, Sept. through June; 2 p.m. to 5 p.m., Sunday; 10 a.m. to 4 p.m., Tuesday through Saturday, July and Aug.; closed major holidays.

This museum has on exhibit stone artifacts of the Woodland Period in New Jersey, with pictures and explanations of their use. A diorama shows a Lenni Lenape village.

Special Interest. The museum sponsors a high school age archeological club which is excavating an Archaic village in the Great Swamp. A changing exhibit of materials recovered from this dig is maintained in the museum.

NEWARK MUSEUM

49 Washington St., Newark. Open free, noon to 5 p.m., Monday through Saturday; 2 p.m. to 6 p.m., Sunday and holidays; closed Thanksgiving, July 4, Dec. 25.

On exhibit are artifacts from a wide range of culture areas and time periods. A model shows life in a prehistoric Hackensack village.

NEW JERSEY STATE MUSEUM

West State St., Trenton. Open free, 9 a.m. to 5 p.m., Monday through Saturday; 2 p.m. to 5 p.m., Sunday and holidays; closed Jan. 1, Dec. 25.

In this general museum is an Indian Room devoted to New Jersey Indians, which focuses attention on the prehistoric Lenni Lenape and on the methods used to learn about them. One exhibit traces archeological work—from locating a site, through excavating it, to laboratory study of materials recovered from it. Another exhibit shows a child burial from Tocks Island in the Delaware River and explains with photographs how burials are uncovered and removed.

Several exhibits deal with specific aspects of Indian life. One concentrates on the cooking of fish, corn, and clams. Another shows how pottery was made, and a separate case presents distinctive examples of local pottery types, including a very large vessel used for underground storage. Still another display makes clear how Indians transformed a water-worn cobble into an axe by pecking away at it with another stone until a cutting edge was formed at one end and a groove around the other. This groove helped to keep bindings in place when a handle was attached.

Displays show typical artifacts recovered from the Pahaquarra, Rosenkrans Ferry, and other sites. A cache of 126 almost identical argillite blades is displayed much as it looked when it was found on the famous Abbott Farm Site at the edge of Trenton. In this cache was a 14-inch-long copper rod, with an eye in one end, the use of which is unknown. Also shown is a dugout canoe which had been preserved in mud in the southern part of the state. Separate displays concentrate on artifacts from the Early Woodland Period which began in New Jersey about 1000 B.C.; the Middle Woodland, which began about 500 B.C.; and the Late Woodland, which began about A.D. 500 and lasted up to A.D. 1625.

Small models show a thatched dwelling and a village with a ceremony going on in the Big House. A map makes clear where trails crossed the state linking settlements to each other and to sources of raw material. Life-size models depict a family group in a rockshelter.

PRINCETON UNIVERSITY
MUSEUM OF NATURAL HISTORY

Guyot Hall, on the campus, Princeton. Open free, 9 a.m. to 4:30 p.m., Monday through Saturday; 2 p.m. to 4 p.m., Sunday.

On exhibit here is a special display of Cody Complex material from Wyoming, 8,000 years old. Some prehistoric materials from the Northwest Coast and from sites in New Jersey are also displayed.

SETON HALL UNIVERSITY MUSEUM

In the library on the campus, South Orange. Open free, 8 a.m. to 10 p.m., Monday through Saturday; 1 p.m. to 5 p.m., Sunday, during the academic year.

From time to time this museum changes its exhibit of prehistoric New Jersey artifacts. Some of the material displayed is likely to be from digs conducted by the museum on the Delaware River. On permanent display are the only two petroglyphs that have been found in New Jersey.

SPACE FARMS
ZOOLOGICAL PARK AND MUSEUM

Midway between Sussex and Branchville on County 519. Open free, 9 a.m. to dark, daily, May 1 to Oct. 30.

The museum includes materials collected by the owner, Ralph Space, during 60 years of amateur archeological activity along the Delaware and Neversink Rivers in New Jersey and New York, in Wythe and Smythe counties in southwest Virginia, and in Tennessee.

SUSSEX COUNTY HISTORICAL SOCIETY

Hill Memorial Building, 82 Main St., Newton. Open free, 9 a.m. to 4 p.m., Monday through Friday.

This museum displays surface finds, made in the Wallkill Valley, of material from the Archaic through the Woodland periods. There is a life-sized model of Indians inhabiting a rockshelter. Another display shows a Woodland burial.

THUNDERBIRD MUSEUM

Mt. Laurel Road, east of Moorestown. Open 1 p.m. to 4 p.m., Saturday and Sunday; at other times by appointment. Admission: adults, $1; children 5 to 14, 75¢.

A wide variety of prehistoric artifacts from New Jersey and also from other areas is on display in this privately owned museum.

WATSON HOUSE (Abbott Farm Site)

151 Westcott St., Trenton. Open free, by appointment. Write, or phone (609) 888-2062.

This house, which was built in 1708, now serves as a headquarters and museum for the Daughters of the American Revolution. Its grounds overlap an extensive archeological area known as the Abbott Farm Site. Prehistoric artifacts on display in the museum were recovered in 1966 by the Unami Chapter of the Archeological Society of New Jersey from the area immediately surrounding the house.

Excavation at the site has gone on at intervals

for the last 100 years and has attracted wide attention. Much of the early material recovered is in the Peabody Museum at Harvard. A small amount of material found later can be seen in the New Jersey State Museum, Trenton.

In 1872 a physician, Dr. Charles Conrad Abbott, owner of a farm which included part of the site, published a book, *The Stone Age in New Jersey*, about the artifacts he was finding in the area. Thereafter he gave up the practice of medicine and devoted the rest of his life to archeology. Dr. Abbott put forth several different theories to explain the material, some of which seemed spectacularly old. More recent researches have not supported his ideas.

In 1936, with funds provided by the Works Progress Administration, Dr. Dorothy Cross began extensive excavation of the site which extends for 3½ miles along a bluff above the Delaware River. She recovered materials which showed that somewhere between 8000 B.C. and 3000 B.C. Indians walked along the bluff and dropped projectile points in one small area. At about A.D. 100, Woodland people carved steatite (soapstone) bowls at the site and adorned themselves with steatite beads and gorgets and pendants. Somewhat later the knowledge of clay pottery making came to them from other Indians who lived to the south. Soon after A.D. 350, they began to garden. Their pottery became more varied in form and style.

Although they were far from the centers of the most active Indian life in the Ohio and Mississippi valleys, the people at Abbott Farm were not entirely isolated. They traveled and traded, and travelers came to them. One visitor from central New York State brought with him a variety of personal belongings which showed he was a man of importance. While he was there, he died and was buried with his exotic finery.

Material recovered from Abbott burials and large photographs showing how burials are excavated are on display at the New Jersey State Museum in Trenton.

New York

AMERICAN MUSEUM OF NATURAL HISTORY

Central Park West at 79th St., New York. Open free, 10 a.m. to 5 p.m., Monday through Saturday; 1 p.m. to 5 p.m., Sunday and holidays.

In its exhibits of Indian and Eskimo life, this great museum integrates material obtained from excavations of prehistoric sites with more recent material. The Eskimo Hall contains artifacts from the Ipiutak Site in Alaska together with casts of Denbigh flint material.

A Hall of Eastern Woodland Indians has a display on Paleo-Indians and Archaic people which includes several varieties of early projectile points, including Clovis, Cumberland, Meserve, and Dalton.

The burial mound cult display contains Hopewellian copper artifacts, sculpture, ornaments, pottery, and a model of a Hopewell burial mound.

The Temple Mound exhibit shows pottery, engraved shells, sculpture, and other items from southeastern United States.

In the Hall of the Great Plains Indians another Paleo-Indian display includes a replica of the famous projectile point found at Folsom, N. Mex., shown in position among bones of an extinct type of bison.

BEAR MOUNTAIN TRAILSIDE HISTORICAL MUSEUM

In Bear Mountain State Park, 45 miles north of New York City. The museum entrance is just off US 202 near Bear Mountain Bridge tollhouse. Daily bus service and boat service from New York City in summer. Open free, 9 a.m. to 5 p.m., daily.

Indian artifacts, mainly from Orange, Rockland, and Ulster counties, are used in exhibits that show prehistoric shelter, food, weapons, and art in New York State. The Paleo, Archaic, and Woodland periods, from about 7000 B.C. to the 17th century, are represented.

BROOKLYN CHILDREN'S MUSEUM

1530 Bedford Ave., Brooklyn. Open free, 10 a.m. to 10 p.m., Tuesday through Friday; 10 a.m. to 5 p.m., Saturday; 1 p.m. to 5 p.m., Sunday; closed Monday, Sept. 1 to May 31; 10 a.m. to 8 p.m., Monday through Friday; 10 a.m. to 5 p.m., Saturday; closed Sunday, June 1 to Aug. 31.

In this children's science museum, displays change frequently and there are many "see-and-touch" programs. Materials exhibited include prehistoric artifacts of the Eastern Woodland culture area.

A

Special Interest. Serious students of any age can apply to the curator for an appointment to view collections that are not on exhibit.

BROOKLYN MUSEUM

188 Eastern Pkwy., Brooklyn. Open, 10 a.m. to 5 p.m., Monday through Saturday; 1 p.m. to 5 p.m., Sunday, holidays; closed Dec. 25.

In this large general museum are several exhibits of North American archeological materials, including Southwestern Basketmaker artifacts, and a diorama showing a pueblo.

BUFFALO MUSEUM OF SCIENCE

Humboldt Park, Buffalo. Open free, 10 a.m. to 5 p.m., Monday through Saturday; 5 p.m. to 10 p.m., Wednesday; 1:30 to 5:30 p.m., Sunday and holidays. Children under 18 must be accompanied by an adult.

In this museum there is special emphasis on the Iroquois Indians, including their prehistory. One exhibit shows the cultural sequences of all five Iroquois tribes. Paintings by a Seneca Indian artist depict Iroquois legends. Four dioramas show pre-contact Iroquois life. There are also exhibits which include prehistoric life in California, the Northwest Coast, and Southwestern areas.

CASTILE HISTORICAL HOUSE (kass-TILE)

17 E. Park Rd., Castile. Open free, 2 p.m. to 5 p.m., Tuesday through Sunday; other times by appointment.

Although most of the material in this museum is from the historic period, some of it throws light on Seneca Indian prehistory. Three miles away in Letchworth State Park is a Seneca council house dating from the time of the American Revolution.

A. In Samuel de Champlain's Voyages *is this drawing of an Indian village; it may be the same prehistoric village which once stood at Nichols Pond, New York. Smithsonian Inst. National Anthropological Archives. B. Owasco Indian village at Auburn, New York. New York State Dept. of Commerce photo by Sid Lane.*

B

CAYUGA MUSEUM OF HISTORY AND ART
(kah-YOO-gah)

203 Genesee St., Auburn. Open free, 1 p.m. to 5 p.m., Tuesday through Friday; 9 a.m. to noon, 1 p.m. to 5 p.m., Saturday; 2 p.m. to 5 p.m., Sunday; closed holidays.

Some materials from the Owasco culture (A.D. 1000 to 1300) and the later Iroquoian culture are displayed here.

CHAUTAUQUA COUNTY HISTORICAL SOCIETY
(shuh-TAW-quah)

Main and Portage streets, Westfield. Open 10 a.m. to noon, 1 p.m. to 4 p.m., Tuesday through Saturday, May through Oct.; 2 p.m. to 5 p.m., Sunday, July, Aug.; closed national holidays. Admission: adults, 50¢; children, 10¢.

Displays of prehistoric and historic Algonquian and Iroquoian material include restored Iroquoian pottery.

CHEMUNG COUNTY HISTORICAL SOCIETY, INC.
(shuh-MUNG)

Historical Center, 304 William St., Elmira. Open free, 1 p.m. to 4:30 p.m., Tuesday, Wednesday, Friday; 2 p.m. to 5 p.m., Sunday; closed national holidays.

Of special interest here are materials from the Lamoka Lake Site which was occupied about 5,000 years ago. Other displays contain artifacts of the Algonquian and Seneca Indians who lived in the Chemung and Susquehanna river valleys at a much later period. There are also Paleo-Indian materials from Nebraska, Colorado, and Washington State, artifacts from the important quarry at Flint Ridge, Ohio, and miscellaneous material from many other areas. A special exhibit displays artifacts of the Mimbres culture in southwestern New Mexico.
    Exhibits explain how the artifacts were made and used and how they related to the environment in which the users lived.

COOPERSTOWN INDIAN MUSEUM

1 Pioneer St., Cooperstown. Open, 1 p.m. to 5 p.m., daily, May through Oct. 15; 10 a.m. to 8 p.m., daily, July, Aug. Admission: adults, 50¢; children, 10¢.

Indian artifacts from the New York State area are arranged in cultural sequence. Exhibits of historic Iroquois material together with displays of Plains Indian material are designed to show visitors the difference between Indian life in New York and the life of Indians on the Great Plains.
    Archeological materials here come mostly from an area within 30 miles of Cooperstown and represent cultures from the Paleo-Indian Period of about 8000 B.C. through the Late Woodland Period in the 17th century. Dioramas show a typical Iroquois village, how a dugout canoe was made, a flint quarry, how baskets and pottery were made, a bear hunt, and how hides were tanned.

DURHAM CENTER MUSEUM, INC.

From Exit 21 at Catskill on the New York Thruway, drive 20 miles north on New York 145. Open free, 9 a.m. to 5 p.m., Saturday, Sunday, May 30 to Labor Day; by appointment at other times.

Displays contain random finds, largely from Greene and Schoharie counties. Materials represent the Lamoka and later cultures.

FORT STANWIX MUSEUM

117 E. Dominick St., Rome. Open free, 9 a.m. to 4 p.m., Tuesday through Friday; 1 p.m. to 4 p.m., Saturday, Sunday; closed national holidays.

With paintings, dioramas, and displays of random local finds of artifacts, this museum sketches the life of prehistoric Indians in the area from Paleo times, about 7,000 years ago, to the Iroquois occupation of the historic period.

Special Interest. The museum, operated by the Rome Historical Society, is built on the site of a pre-Revolutionary British fort. The area was important because it was what the Indians called the "Great Carry"—the route over which they portaged their canoes between two water routes, one going south and east, the other northwest.

FORT WILLIAM HENRY
RESTORATION AND MUSEUM

Canada St., Lake George. Open, 9 a.m. to 6 p.m., daily, May through Oct.; 9 a.m. to 10 p.m., daily, July, Aug. Museum admission: adults, $1.25; children, 35¢; family, $3.00; Iroquois village admission: adults, 35¢; family, $1.00.

Included with historic exhibits are displays of archeological material relating to the aboriginal occupation of northern New York and the Lake George-Lake Champlain area in particular. A diorama shows how small animals were caught in a dead fall trap.
    The Indian village surrounded by a wooden stockade is a reconstruction of an 18th-century Iroquois settlement which closely resembled villages of late prehistoric times.

HARTWICK COLLEGE, YAGER MUSEUM

Library-Museum Building, on the campus, Oneonta. Open free, 10 a.m. to 3 p.m., Monday through Friday; 10 a.m. to noon, Saturday; 2 p.m. to 4 p.m., Sunday.

In addition to exhibits of materials from Central and South America, this museum has on permanent display prehistoric materials from the Upper Susquehanna Valley, representing the Archaic Period, the Early Woodland, and the Late Woodland. Some materials from the Upper Susquehanna River drainage not yet on display may be seen by appointment.

HOWE PUBLIC LIBRARY

155 N. Main St., Wellsville. Open free, 10 a.m. to 9 p.m., Monday, Tuesday, Thursday, Friday; 10 a.m. to 6 p.m., Saturday, winter; 10 a.m. to 9 p.m., Monday through Friday, summer; closed national holidays.

A feature of the David A. Howe Public Library is a small display of identified local artifacts from the Paleo Period to the historic Iroquois.

MUSEUM OF THE AMERICAN INDIAN,
HEYE FOUNDATION

Broadway at W. 155th St., New York. Open free, 1 p.m. to 5 p.m., Tuesday through Sunday; closed in Aug. and on national holidays.

Animals for Food

As they explored their different environments on this continent, Indians seem to have tried just about every likely source of nourishment. The food resources in a desert area were of course quite different from those near a large river in the Southeast. Plains dwellers had foods quite unlike those available to inhabitants of the Northwest Coast.

Archeologists study all the animal bones they find in an excavation in an effort to discover the diet of the people who lived there, and also to find out about prehistoric ecology.

Here is a list of animal remains found at one site in Massachusetts which was inhabited between A.D. 900 and A.D. 1500: beaver, dog, red fox, grey fox, black bear, mink, harbor seal, white-tailed deer, red-throated loon, great blue heron, mallard, black duck, red-tailed hawk, bald eagle, great auk, snapping turtle, Plymouth turtle, roughtail sting ray, Atlantic sturgeon, black sea bass, sculpin, sea robin, scup, wolffish, bay scallop, blue mussel, quahog, surf clam, long clam, lobed moon shell, moon shell, boat shell, thick-lipped drill, conch, channeled conch.

Albany to Buffalo

The Mohawk Trail, another name for US 90 and New York 5, provides an easy, gently graded route from Albany to Buffalo. As the name implies, it follows a prehistoric Indian trail which once linked the villages of all the tribes belonging to what white men called the Iroquois Confederacy.

Many other modern travel routes in the United States follow old Indian trails. A usual sequence was this: First, animals made paths to and from watering places or feeding grounds or salt licks. Indian hunters followed the animals, widening the trails, some of which later proved useful as means of communications between Indian settlements. Pioneers of European origin then used the Indian paths—on foot at first, later on horseback. Next wagons went along the same trails. Still later, when railroads were built, civil engineers often found that the best routes had been followed by the drivers of the horse-drawn wagons. Finally, when automobile roads were needed, highways often took the same easy grades that the Indians discovered long ago.

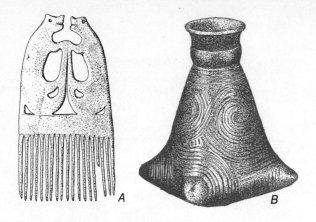

A. An ancestor of the Iroquois Indians carved this ornamental comb from bone. Original in the Museum of the American Indian, New York. B. The Museum of the American Indian has this water jar from Louisiana in its collection. The prehistoric potter incised the intricate design on the moist clay before firing the vessel. C. Iroquois Indians carved masks such as this in living basswood trees then removed them and used them as part of curing ceremonies. Original in the Rochester Museum and Science Center.

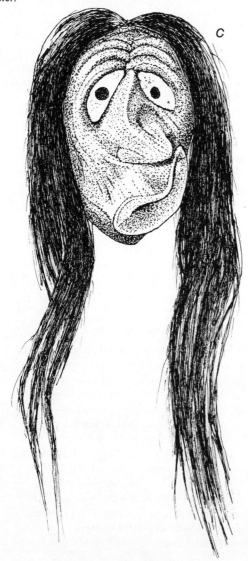

This museum, devoted exclusively to the American Indian, is probably the largest and most complete of its kind in the United States and Canada.

Many of the ethnologic exhibits throw light on prehistoric cultures. The extensive archeological displays contain materials from several sites which cannot be visited—for example, Spiro Mound in Oklahoma—various sites on the Northwest Coast, and Mimbres sites in the Southwest. Many artifacts have been chosen for their superior artistic quality. Two exhibits are of special interest—one on North American calendrical devices, another on wampum, its uses and manufacture in both prehistoric and historic times.

On the third floor are archeological materials from south of the United States whence came many influences that affected North American cultures. In addition to its illuminating displays, the museum has in storage more than 3½ million items which are available to scholars for study.

NASSAU COUNTY HISTORICAL MUSEUM

Nassau County Park, Salisbury, East Meadow. Open 10 a.m. to 6 p.m., daily, summer; 9 a.m. to 5 p.m., daily, winter. Free to residents of Nassau County and their guests.

Included in this historical museum are displays which explain the daily life of the prehistoric Indians in the area.

NEW YORK STATE
MUSEUM AND SCIENCE SERVICE

31 Washington Ave., Albany. Open free, 9 a.m. to 4:30 p.m., daily; closed Jan. 1, Thanksgiving, Dec. 25.

Although this general museum has and sometimes exhibits archeological material from all over the United States, its primary Indian displays concentrate on material from New York State, from the Paleo-Indian Period to the present. Six life-size dioramas show aspects of the daily life and ceremonial activity of the Iroquois.

Special Feature. A full-size replica of an Iroquois bark house in the museum is open to groups of school children by appointment.

NIAGARA COUNTY HISTORICAL CENTER

Pioneer Building, 215 Niagara St., Lockport. Open free, 10 a.m. to 5 p.m., Tuesday through Friday; 1 p.m. to 5 p.m., Saturday, Sunday; closed holidays.

Artifacts from local prehistoric Indian sites are on exhibit here, together with a diorama showing an Iroquois Indian village.

NICHOLS POND

From Morrisville on US 20 drive north on county road toward Canastota to directional sign, then west to the Champlain-Oneida Battleground and Nichols Pond. Open free, at all times, weather permitting. Camping.

An Oneida or Mohawk Indian village stood at this place in late prehistoric times, and there is some reason to think that it was attacked by the French explorer Samuel de Champlain in A.D. 1615. Champlain was accompanied by about 500 Huron and Algonquian Indians from Canada, in addition to a dozen men of his own, who were armed with arquebuses. Since the village seemed very well protected by a high palisade, Champlain tried a special strategem. He ordered a tower built close to the palisade. Standing on the tower, his gunners could fire down into the village. More than this was needed, however, to overcome the inhabitants. They withstood the siege, and the French adventurer was forced to return to Canada. The illustration of the palisaded village which appears in Champlain's *Voyages* is probably a fairly accurate picture of the village which once stood here and which dates from prehistoric times.

OLD FORT JOHNSON

From Amsterdam drive 2 miles west on New York 5. Open 1 p.m. to 5 p.m., daily, May to Nov.; 10 a.m. to 5 p.m., Tuesday through Saturday; 1 p.m. to 5 p.m., Sunday, Monday, July and Aug. Admission: adults, 50¢; children under 12 accompanied by an adult, free.

In this colonial mansion, operated by the Montgomery County Historical Society, is an exhibit on Indians of the Mohawk Valley. Many of the artifacts displayed were collected in the vicinity. Others are on loan from the New York State Museum, which also gave help in preparing the exhibit. A museum booklet interpreting the material provides a brief survey of prehistory in New York State from Paleo times to the historic period.

ONTARIO COUNTY HISTORICAL SOCIETY

55 N. Main St., Canandaigua (can-an-DAY-gwah). Open free, 1 p.m. to 5 p.m., Tuesday through Saturday.

Many artifacts from the site of a Seneca village that existed in and before 1687 are on display here, together with random local finds of two different types of projectile point.

OSSINING HISTORICAL SOCIETY MUSEUM

83 Croton Ave., Ossining. Open free, 2 p.m. to 4 p.m., Monday, Sept. through June, and by appointment.

This museum has locally collected artifacts, some of which have been dated at 3900 B.C., and some of which were made in contact times by the Sint Sinck tribe of the Wappinger Confederacy.

OWASCO INDIAN VILLAGE (oh-WAHS-ko)

Emerson Park, near the foot of Owasco Lake, 2 miles south of Auburn. Open, 9 a.m. to 5 p.m., daily, summer; at other times by appointment. Admission: adults, 50¢; children, 25¢.

Owasco Indian Village is a reconstruction of an Owasco village as it was about A.D. 1050. The Owasco culture is believed to be ancestral to the culture of the Iroquois Indians who lived in this area in early historic times.

Inside the stockade are two reconstructed longhouses. One has been left unfinished so that visitors may see how it was built and how it was used as a living area by many families at the same time. There is also a medicine man's hut in the village and a garden area. Displays show how pottery developed and how hunting and other crafts were practiced. One exhibit shows how the prehistoric Indians played lacrosse and what equipment they used.

OYSTERPONDS HISTORICAL SOCIETY, INC.

Village Lane, Orient, L.I. Open 2 p.m. to 5 p.m., Tuesday, Thursday, Saturday, Sunday, holidays. Admission: adults (nonmember), 50¢; children, 10¢.

Local Indian artifacts on display here include a Clovis point, stone pots and tools dated at about 4000 B.C. and some material dating from 1000 B.C. to A.D. 1600.

POWELL HOUSE

434 Park Ave., Huntington, L.I. Office open, 9 a.m. to 5 p.m., Tuesday through Friday; tours arranged by appointment. Admission: adults, 25¢; children, 10¢. Fee may change for special activities.

On exhibit here are materials recovered from excavations in the vicinity. The museum, which stands at the intersection of old Indian trails, is operated by the Huntington Historical Society.

ROBERSON CENTER
FOR THE ARTS AND SCIENCES

30 Front St., Binghamton. Open free, 10 a.m. to 5 p.m., Monday through Friday; noon to 5 p.m., Saturday, Sunday.

Archeological materials of local origin are arranged according to culture periods—Paleo, Archaic, Laurentian, and Transitional. There are also Woodland materials (Point Peninsula) and Late Woodland (Clempson Island, Carpenter Brook, Owasco, and Castle Creek).

A diorama shows life in an Owasco village about A.D. 1300. Another shows how a longhouse was constructed.

ROCHESTER MUSEUM AND SCIENCE CENTER

657 East Ave., Rochester. Open free, 9 a.m. to 5 p.m., Monday through Saturday; 2 p.m. to 5 p.m., Sunday; closed national holidays and Sunday, June through Aug.

Numerous displays cover all New York State Indian cultures from the Archaic to the historic period, including Adena, Hopewell, Point Peninsula, Owasco, and prehistoric Iroquois.

Exhibits are arranged to show how man fitted into his environment and how his tools are clues to the way he managed life. Of particular interest are cases which show the sequence of New York projectile points, how wampum was made, radiocarbon dating of sites, and evidence of illness in prehistoric times. One entire alcove is devoted to the life of hunters during the Archaic, before the use of the bow and arrow. Other exhibits are devoted to the Arctic, Northwest Coast, Southwest, Plains, and Southeastern culture areas.

In addition to prehistoric material, many exhibits show Indian life at the time of first contact with Europeans and later.

Dioramas show the construction of a prehistoric Iroquois longhouse, the life-size interior of a prehistoric longhouse, a Haida Indian village, the Zuni pueblo, how an archeological site is excavated, and burials.

Special Interest. This museum achieved national prominence under the directorship of Arthur C. Parker, a Seneca Indian.

SIX NATIONS INDIAN MUSEUM

Off New York 3, 1 mile east of Onchiota. Open 9

a.m. to 8 p.m., daily. Admission: adults, 75¢; children, 35¢.

This museum, dedicated to preserving all aspects of Iroquois culture, has exhibits of prehistoric Iroquois pottery and other artifacts, as well as some pre-Iroquois material, largely from the St. Lawrence River Valley and the Lake Champlain regions. Displays show how various articles were made and used. A diorama is devoted to the carving of a false face mask from a living tree.

Special Feature. This museum will supply on request a catalog of a series of educational pamphlets and charts which it publishes on Iroquois history and culture. One of these publications, entitled *Six Nations Indian Monuments,* is a kind of guidebook to sites which are important in Iroquois history and legend. It covers parts of New York State, Pennsylvania, Ohio, and Canada.

SUFFOLK MUSEUM

Christian Ave., Stony Brook, L.I. Open 10 a.m. to 5 p.m., daily. Admission: adults, 75¢; children, 50¢.

A life-size diorama is the center of various exhibits which show Long Island Indian life at the time Europeans arrived. Artifacts on display were excavated in the area. These include Archaic material from the Stony Brook Site which has been radiocarbon dated at about 3,000 years ago, and Woodland material tentatively dated at A.D. 1550-1660.

TIOGA COUNTY HISTORICAL SOCIETY MUSEUM
(tie-OH-gah)

110-112 Front St., Owego. Open free, 10 a.m. to noon, 1:30 p.m. to 4:30 p.m., Tuesday through Friday; 7 p.m. to 9 p.m., Wednesday.

Artifacts collected in the immediate area represent cultures from about 2500 B.C. to historic times. A special display is devoted to the Engelbert Site, which is about ten miles from Owego. In this display are materials representing Lamoka, Late Owasco, prehistoric Iroquois, and Susquehannock cultures.

YATES COUNTY
GENEALOGICAL AND HISTORICAL SOCIETY

200 Main St., Penn Yan. Open free, 2 p.m. to 4 p.m., Tuesday and Thursday, summer; 2 p.m. to 4 p.m. last Saturday of the month.

Locally collected material on display here includes both Algonquian and Seneca material found at one site.

Nova Scotia

CITADEL HILL BRANCH, NOVA SCOTIA MUSEUM

Citadel Hill National Historic Park, Halifax. Open free, 1 p.m. to 5 p.m., Monday through Saturday; noon to 5 p.m., Sunday, Sept. through May; 9 a.m. to 9 p.m., daily, June through Aug.

In addition to ethnological materials, this museum exhibits some Nova Scotia archeological items. One diorama shows an Indian camp at the time of contact with Europeans. Another shows, a mid-17th-century burial.

NOVA SCOTIA MUSEUM

1747 Summer St., Halifax. Open free, 9 a.m. to 5 p.m., Monday through Friday.

In this new location, a section of the main exhibit area is devoted to the prehistory of Nova Scotia from Paleo-Indian through the Archaic and Ceramic or Woodland stages.

Ontario

ALGONQUIN PROVINCIAL PARK MUSEUM

Algonquin Provincial Park, Whitney. Open, 10 a.m. to 6 p.m., daily, June 15-30; 10 a.m. to 8 p.m., July through Labor Day; 10 a.m. to 8 p.m., Saturday, Sunday, May 15 to June 15. Admission to the park, 50¢; the museum is free.

This museum exhibits materials recovered from campsites on Grand Lake and Lake Traverse, some of which date from 2500 B.C., some of which are later.

ASSIGNACK HISTORICAL SOCIETY
(ass-SIG-in-ack)

Nelson and Queen streets, Manitowaning (MAN-it-toh-WAH-ning). Open, 10 a.m. to 5 p.m., daily, June 1 to Sept. 6. Admission: 50¢.

Here may be seen artifacts from the nearby Sheguiandah Site on loan from the Royal Ontario Museum.

BRANT MUSEUM

1240 North Shore Blvd., Burlington. Open free, 10 a.m. to 5 p.m., daily, June 1 to Sept. 30; Sunday afternoons, Oct. to June.

One gallery in the Joseph Brant Museum is devoted to prehistoric Indian culture. All artifacts on display are of local origin, some from the Paleo Period and some from the Old Copper culture. A diorama shows how Indians made a dugout canoe using fire and stone tools. Another shows methods used in hunting big game.

BRUCE COUNTY MUSEUM

Southampton. Open, 2 p.m. to 5 p.m., daily, May, June, Sept.; 2 p.m. to 9 p.m., daily, July, Aug. Admission: adults, 25¢; school children, 10¢; preschool children, free.

Artifacts on display here come from the Laurentian, Early Woodland, Point Peninsula, and early Iroquoian cultures.

CHATHAM-KENT MUSEUM

59 William St., North, Chatham. Open free, 2 p.m. to 5 p.m., Tuesday, Thursday, Saturday; 2 p.m. to 5 p.m., first and third Sundays.

The main concern in this museum is with local history, but there are archeological exhibits which include the skeleton of a middle-aged Glacial Kame woman of about 1500 B.C.; a display of identified artifacts; a display that shows how prehistoric tools were made and used; a display on the evolution of pottery from 1000 B.C. to about

A.D. 1500. A special exhibit shows the stratigraphy of a prehistoric village site near Clearville, Kent County, Ontario.

HURONIA MUSEUM

Little Lake Park, at King St. entrance, Midland. Open 9 a.m. to 5 p.m., Monday through Saturday; 1 p.m. to 5 p.m., Sunday, May 16 to Oct. 12. Admission: adults, 50¢; students, 25¢; children, 10¢.

Displayed here are random finds of local prehistoric material. Near the museum a Huron Indian village has been reconstructed.

LENNOX AND ADDINGTON HISTORICAL SOCIETY

County Memorial Bldg., 41 Dundas West, Napanee. Open free, 2 p.m. to 5 p.m., May 24 through Sept. 30; noon to 3 p.m., Wednesday; 2 p.m. to 5 p.m., Saturday, Oct. through May 23; closed Jan. 1, Thanksgiving, Dec. 25.

On display here are a limited number of artifacts from Laurentian, Point Peninsula, late prehistoric Huron, Mississaugas, and Oneida cultures.

LITTLE CURRENT-HOWLAND CENTENNIAL MUSEUM

See Shequiandah Site, page 184.

McMASTER UNIVERSITY MUSEUM

Department of Anthropology, on the campus, Hamilton. Open free, during classroom hours.

Display cases contain archeological material from the Southwest, from western Canada, and from Ontario. These will be housed later in a museum-laboratory now under construction.

MUSEUM OF INDIAN ARCHAEOLOGY AND PIONEER LIFE

University of Western Ontario, London. Open free, 9 a.m. to 5 p.m., Monday through Friday.

Here are exhibits illustrative of the archeology of the surrounding area.

NATIONAL MUSEUM OF MAN

Metcalf and McLeod streets, Ottawa. Following alterations, this museum will be open, at hours to be announced, in January 1972.

In this museum are several galleries which contain interpretations of the prehistoric as well as the more recent life of Canada's aboriginal peoples. In the Eskimo gallery exhibits show how Eskimos who lived in a harsh environment made use of whatever was available to them. They built igloos of snow. Using driftwood and sealskins they made boats, one type called the kayak for hunting, another type called the umiak for carrying freight. From seal and caribou they obtained clothing, meat, and fuel. A diorama in this gallery shows an Eskimo dwelling of 500 years ago and modern archeologists excavating that dwelling.

Beautiful art created by Coastal Indians of northwestern North America fills another gallery and indicates the kind of work these Indians did before contact with Europeans as well as more recently.

Exhibits in the Plains Indian gallery illustrate the many uses people made of the buffalo in pre-

A

B

A. Designs scratched on slate by prehistoric Indians near Lake Kedgemakooge in Nova Scotia. Photo by Arthur Kelsall, courtesy of Campbell Grant. B. A knife (top) and projectile point (bottom) of copper, typical artifacts of the Old Copper culture. Note sockets for hafting. C. A diorama of an Iroquois village of longhouses surrounded by a palisade, from the National Museum of Canada in Ottawa. National Museum of Canada photo. D. In 1934 the Seine River band of Ojibwa Indians in Ontario were still building longhouses much like those used in prehistoric times. Here the pole framework of a ceremonial longhouse has been completed. National Museum of Canada photo.

C

D

historic times, and also show the changes in their lives after they obtained horses.

Exhibits in the Iroquois gallery suggest the remarkable political life of these Indians who lived in palisaded villages and ruled over a very large territory. Displays show how the Iroquois obtained much of their food by farming. Special exhibits are devoted to artifacts of the Ontario Iroquois. There is also a display of prehistoric materials from the village of Hochelaga which was on the site of Montreal.

Dioramas show the corn harvest in a Huron village in 1615, the False Face curing ceremony, a later prehistoric Huron village of 11 very large houses, the interior of a longhouse, Indians in the eastern part of subarctic Canada hunting caribou, and artifacts made and used by the Ojibwa and Cree Indians in the eastern subarctic between A.D. 900 and 1750.

PERTH MUSEUM
(The Archibald M. Campbell Memorial Museum)

5 Gore St. East, Perth. Open, 10 a.m. to noon, 1 p.m. to 5 p.m., Monday through Saturday; 2 p.m. to 5 p.m., Sunday, about May 24 to Nov. 1; 10 a.m. to noon, 1 p.m. to 5 p.m., Saturday; 2 p.m. to 5 p.m., Sunday, Nov. 1 to May 24. Admission: adults, 50¢; children, 25¢.

In addition to random local finds this museum houses some archeological material from the southwestern part of the United States.

ROYAL ONTARIO MUSEUM

100 Queen's Park, Toronto. Open, 10 a.m. to 5 p.m., Monday through Saturday; 1 p.m. to 5 p.m., Sunday; closed Dec. 25. Admission: adults, 25¢; children, free.

Rich ethnological resources in this museum throw light on prehistory, and space is also allotted for unusual displays of material from archeological excavations. Some of these reflect current work being done in Ontario.

Dioramas, life size, are devoted to a Mohawk family and their house, prehistoric cliff dwellers in the Southwest, a Hopi snake dance, Plains Indians, Hupas of California, and Haidas on the Northwest Coast.

One case is devoted to materials from the very interesting Sheguiandah Site.

Many paintings by Paul Kane show Canadian Indians as they appeared when first seen by Europeans.

SERPENT MOUND

From Peterboro drive southeast to the north shore of Rice Lake. Open free, at all times.

Here about 80 feet above the lake is a mound which depicts a snake. It is 189 feet in length, averages 5 feet in height, and 24 feet in width. Near the head is an oval mound which contained four burials.

Serpent Mound seems not to be the work of Effigy Mound people who were active in Wisconsin. It is instead a rare example of a mound built by people who followed a lifeway called Point Peninsula. A cremation in the mound has a radiocarbon date of A.D. 130.

SHEGUIANDAH SITE (SHEG-wee-AN-duh)

From Sudbury drive 41 miles west on Trans-Canada 17, then 43 miles south on Provincial Road 68 through Little Current to the Little Current-Howland Centennial Museum at the edge of the town of Sheguiandah. The museum is open free, noon to 5 p.m., May, June; 10 a.m. to 9 p.m., July, Aug.; noon to 5 p.m., Sept.

At this site, near the museum, an excavation conducted for several years has produced considerable controversy in archeological circles. Dr. Thomas E. Lee, who was in charge of the dig, reported that he had found crude choppers and scrapers made of quartzite *underneath* several levels of deposits in which there were signs of human occupation. These crude tools had been tumbled about and mixed in what appeared to be glacial till—that is, an aggregation of clay, sand, and rock deposited by a glacier. It looked to Dr. Lee—and to some eminent geologists—as if the front edge of a glacier had pushed a very ancient campsite for a short distance, thus disturbing the artifacts which had been left there. If this is what happened, the men who made these quartzite tools lived in Canada *before* the last great glacial advance.

The archeologists who believed that Dr. Lee had found very old artifacts estimated their age at 30,000 years, at the very least. According to some responsible estimates, they were much older than that. Not all archeologists, however, agreed that the Sheguiandah materials were of such antiquity.

One thing is certain. If Dr. Lee's discovery proves to be what he and others think it is, he has shown that man was on this continent much earlier than has generally been believed. And if this is so, some of the basic theories about Early Man will have to be revised.

The Museum. Some of the artifacts recovered from the Sheguiandah Site are on exhibit here, together with photographs of the dig. Visitors are urged to phone or write ahead to the curator, Mrs. Fred Stevens, who will arrange for a guide to the site, which is protected by the provincial government. The guides are high school boys and girls, some of them Ojibwa and Ottawa Indians who live in the nearby Sheguiandah Reserve. Mrs. Stevens is an Ojibwa.

SIMCOE COUNTY MUSEUM AND ARCHIVES
(SIM-coe)

From Barrie drive 4 miles north on Ontario 27 to West Hwy. 26, then one-half mile west to museum, adjacent to Springwater Park. Open, 1 p.m. to 5 p.m., Tuesday through Sunday, April, May, Sept., Oct., Nov., Dec.; 9 a.m. to 5 p.m., Monday through Saturday; 1 p.m. to 9 p.m., Sunday, June; 9 a.m. to 9 p.m., Monday through Saturday, 1 p.m. to 9 p.m., Sunday, July, Aug.; 10 a.m. to noon, 1 p.m. to 5 p.m., Saturday; 1 p.m. to 5 p.m., Sunday, Jan. through March. Admission: adults, 35¢; children, free.

Materials from a number of systematically excavated sites may be seen here. The cultures represented are: Laurentian, Middleport, Lalonde, and Huron. The earliest materials have been dated at sometime between 3000 and 2000 B.C. An electrified map shows the location of the sites and clearly indicates what culture and period are represented at each site.

THUNDER BAY HISTORICAL SOCIETY

216 S. Brodie St., Thunder Bay. Open free, 2 p.m. to 5 p.m., Monday, Friday; 7 p.m. to 9 p.m., Tuesday, Sept. 1 to July 1; 2 p.m. to 5 p.m., Monday through Friday, July 1 to Sept. 1; closed holidays.

Artifacts of the Paleo and the Copper culture periods found at the Cummins Site in the vicinity are displayed here. Also on exhibit are Woodland materials from the Black Duck culture and trade goods, both prehistoric and historic.

UNITED COUNTIES MUSEUM

731 Second St. W., Cornwall. Open, 10 a.m. to noon, 1 p.m. to 5 p.m., Monday through Saturday; 2 p.m. to 5 p.m., Sunday, May 24 through Sept.

On display here are some Point Peninsula artifacts.

WOODWINDS HISTORICAL MUSEUM

From Gravenhurst, drive north on Ontario 69. The museum is on the shore of Lake Muskoka at Barlochan, 2½ miles off Highway 69. Open, 1 p.m. to 8 p.m., daily, July, Aug.; 1 p.m. to 8 p.m., weekends, May 15 to July and Sept. to Oct. 15; and by appointment. Admission: adults, 35¢; children, 25¢.

Exhibited here are random local finds of hunting implements. The vicinity of the museum was apparently a summer hunting area, but not a place where permanent habitations were built.

Pennsylvania

CARNEGIE MUSEUM

4400 Forbes Ave., Pittsburgh. Open free, 10 a.m. to 5 p.m., Monday through Saturday; 2 p.m. to 5 p.m., Sunday; 5 p.m. to 9 p.m., Tuesday; closed national holidays.

In the main archeological exhibit of this important museum a series of cases contain artifacts from, and explanations of, each major culture period in the Upper Ohio Valley from Paleo-Indian through Archaic, Early Woodland, Middle Woodland, and late prehistoric to historic. A typical site for each period is represented with artifacts, text, and illustrations. There is also general information about each period.

Special exhibits depict certain phases of New World archeology, such as Adena. In this connection the materials from Cresap Mound in West Virginia are on display. Also there is full treatment of the late prehistoric Monongahela culture. Special exhibits on various aspects of Eastern archeology change every few months.

FORT LIGONIER MEMORIAL FOUNDATION, INC.
(lig-oh-NEER)

At intersection of US 30 and Pennsylvania 711 in Ligonier. Open, 9 a.m. to dusk, daily; closed Jan. 1, Thanksgiving, Dec. 25. Admission: adults, $1; children under 18, 35¢; special rates for groups.

In this reconstruction of a fort of the period of the French and Indian War, one building contains exhibits of prehistoric materials from 30 sites in the area. These materials cover all major local cultures and periods from Paleo through Late Woodland.

FRANKLIN AND MARSHALL COLLEGE

See North Museum, this page.

INDIAN STEPS MUSEUM

(East of York) From Airville, where Pennsylvania 74 and Pennsylvania 425 intersect, take a local road east to the museum which is on the west bank of the Susquehanna River. Open free, 10 a.m. to 4 p.m., Tuesday through Saturday; 10 a.m. to 6 p.m., Sunday and holidays, April 1 to Nov. 1.

In seven rooms containing American Indian material are exhibits devoted to the Susquehannock and Cherokee Indians. All periods from Paleo through Late Woodland are represented. Shadow boxes show various aspects of Indian life. One display consists of a burial from the Shenk's Ferry Site. Also on exhibit are plaster casts of petroglyphs which are now submerged under water impounded behind a dam on the Susquehanna River. Before the dam was built it was possible to reach the river's edge by steps which prehistoric people cut in the rock. Hence the name Indian Steps Museum.

Special Interest. This museum was constructed on the site where the Susquehannock tribe, decimated by smallpox, ceased to exist after it lost a battle with the Massowomeke Indians.

MERCER MUSEUM

Pine and Ashland streets, Doylestown. Open, 10 a.m. to 5 p.m., Tuesday through Saturday, March through Dec.; 1 p.m. to 5 p.m., Sunday, April through Oct.; closed all of Jan., Feb., Thanksgiving, Dec. 25. Admission: adults $1; children 50¢.

Here, along with tools and implements which Europeans used in eastern Pennsylvania before the invention of steam power, are tools of the prehistoric Lenni Lenape Indians.

MONROE COUNTY HISTORICAL SOCIETY

Main and Ninth streets, Stroudsburg. Open free, 1 p.m. to 4 p.m., Tuesday.

On exhibit are local finds, mostly of Lenni Lenape origin.

NORTH MUSEUM,
FRANKLIN AND MARSHALL COLLEGE

College and Buchanan avenues, Lancaster. Open free, 9 a.m. to 5 p.m., Wednesday through Saturday; 1:30 p.m. to 5 p.m., Sunday, Sept. through July; 1:30 p.m. to 5 p.m., Saturday, Sunday, Aug.

All periods in the Northeast are represented in archeological exhibits here. Special exhibits are devoted to pottery-making and to the local Shenk's Ferry and Susquehannock cultures. Also there are technical exhibits on Northeastern projectile points and pottery types. A diorama shows a Shenk's Ferry village.

PARKER INDIAN MUSEUM

From Brookville drive 5 miles east on US 322. Open, 9 a.m. to dark, daily; closed Jan., Feb., and Dec. 25.

The E. M. Parker Indian Museum has random local finds, including some Owasco and prehistoric Iroquois material from New York State and a little material from eastern Ohio.

PENNSYLVANIA STATE MUSEUM

See William Penn Memorial Museum, page 186.

A

B

A. This mask, carved of wood, with abalone shell eyes, was worn by a shaman on the Northwest Coast. It is on exhibit at the Walker Museum, Fairlee, Vermont.   B. Eskimos engraved this mask in steatite on Qajartalik Island near Wakeham Bay, Quebec. Bernard Saladin d'Anglure photo, courtesy Campbell Grant. C. At the Micmac Indian Village on Prince Edward Island this prehistoric Indian dwelling has been reconstructed as part of an exhibit. Artifacts found in the area are also on display in a museum there. Micmac Indian Village photo.

C

TIOGA POINT MUSEUM (tie-OH-gah

724 S. Main St., Athens. Open free, 2 p.m. to 5 p.m., Wednesday, Saturday; 7 p.m. to 9 p.m., Monday; group tours by appointment.

The prehistoric Indian collection here consists mainly of random local finds, but there are materials from three systematically excavated sites—Murray Garden, Spanish Hill, and Abbe-Brennan—which provided data about several cultures. One exhibit shows how pottery was made. Another demonstrates the chronologic sequence of different local pottery types.

UNIVERSITY MUSEUM, UNIVERSITY OF PENNSYLVANIA

Spruce and 33rd streets, Philadelphia. Open free, 10 a.m. to 5 p.m., Tuesday through Saturday; 1 p.m. to 5 p.m., Sunday; closed national holidays.

In this museum, which is rich in archeological materials from all over the world, three sections are devoted to Indians north of Mexico. One concentrates on art, one on cultures as the first Europeans found them, and the third is devoted to prehistory. Displays of artifacts, with explanations, trace the history of Indians from their entry into the continent up to the era when Europeans arrived. Paleo materials, excavated by the museum at the Clovis Site, Blackwater Draw, New Mexico, and at the Eden Valley Site in Wyoming, may be seen.

Exhibits give information about six different Archaic cultures. Woodland exhibits trace the introduction and development of pottery in the East, together with the development of agriculture. Among especially rare materials shown are wooden artifacts from Key Marco, Florida, which were preserved in mud below sea level. Also on display are organic materials preserved in dry caves in the Southwest. In addition there are Eskimo archeological materials and an excellent Pennsylvania collection.

WILLIAM PENN MEMORIAL MUSEUM
(The Pennsylvania State Museum)

Third and North streets, adjacent to the State Capitol, Harrisburg. Open free, 9:30 a.m. to 5 p.m., Monday through Saturday; 1 p.m. to 5 p.m., Sunday; closed Jan. 1, Dec. 25, and Pennsylvania election days.

The museum is currently developing displays which will cover all major periods in Pennsylvania archeology from Paleo times to the present. Displays will be designed to show various problems which archeologists encounter in excavating a rockshelter and in open sites. A series of dioramas will trace the development of the culture of the Delaware (Lenni Lenape) Indians.

WYOMING HISTORICAL AND GENEALOGICAL SOCIETY

60 South Franklin St., Wilkes Barre. Open free, 10 a.m. to 5 p.m., Tuesday through Saturday.

Archeological exhibits here illuminate the prehistory of the Susquehanna River Valley from the Archaic to the historic period. Included are displays of Owasco and prehistoric Huron material.

Prince Edward Island

MICMAC INDIAN VILLAGE (mick-mack)

Rocky Point, Prince Edward Island. From Charlottetown, drive to Rocky Point on the opposite side of the harbor on Route 19. Open, 9 a.m. to sunset, June 15 to Sept. 15. Admission: adults, 75¢; children 6-12, 25¢; under 6, free.

Here, in an outdoor setting, the proprietors have reconstructed a 16th-century Micmac village. Indoors is a museum with random local finds of prehistoric artifacts.

Quebec

McCORD MUSEUM, McGILL UNIVERSITY

690 Sherbrooke St. West, Montreal. Open, at hours to be announced in 1971.

In the new headquarters of this museum there are to be anthropological exhibits that were formerly in two separate museums. Information about the exhibits will be available from the museum after it opens.

Rhode Island

HAFFENREFFER MUSEUM, BROWN UNIVERSITY

Mount Hope Grant, off Rhode Island 136, Bristol. Open free, 10 a.m. to 4 p.m., Saturday; 1 p.m. to 4 p.m., Sunday, Sept. through May; 1 p.m. to 4 p.m., Tuesday through Sunday, June through Aug.

One of the best places in America to see Arctic archeology is in a modest building on a rambling estate located outside of Bristol, R.I. Here excellent exhibits display the results of Brown University digs in the Far North. Each exhibit is accompanied by a clear explanation. One display deals with beach ridge dating in Alaska at a place where the coast is rising and ocean currents have piled up a series of beaches. The newest beach is closest to the sea. The oldest is farthest away. Because Eskimos are dependent on the sea, they like to live close to it. At this spot they have long built homes near the water. When a new beach formed between them and the shore, they moved to a new house site. The result is a continuous record of life over a long period of time. Archeologists have traced this story by excavating Eskimo remains on beach after beach.

Very tiny blades from the Denbigh culture are on exhibit here, as are harpoon heads, semilunar knives, carved figurines, and other artifacts of later cultures.

Other exhibits are devoted to baskets from California and other parts of the West; Iroquois materials, including masks known as False Faces; and artifacts made by Archaic people. The displays make clear the relationships of these Archaic people to others who entered the area from the West, bringing with them knowledge of farming, copper tools, and smoking tobacco.

In many ways the museum illustrates the varied life patterns of Indians and Eskimos and the manner in which these patterns changed as people kept working out new adjustments to their environments.

Special Feature. One display is devoted to the Red Paint people who lived along the Penobscot River in Maine about 4,000 years ago. They are so called because they used the mineral red ocher in burial ceremonies, sprinkling quantities of it on the dead and over all the gifts they placed in graves. Among the gifts were familiar objects, such as knives, projectile points, and woodworking tools. Less common were net sinkers, polished slate objects that resemble bayonets, implements of flint and iron pyrite for making fire, and mysterious little perfectly rounded pebbles. Since there are no visitable Red Paint sites in the United States, the display here is of special interest. (The Port au Choix Site in Newfoundland was occupied by people who had many of the same cultural patterns.)

RHODE ISLAND HISTORICAL SOCIETY

52 Power St., Providence. Open, 11 a.m. to 4 p.m., Tuesday through Friday; 2 p.m. to 4 p.m., Saturday, Sunday; closed national holidays. Admission: adults, $1; students, 50¢; children, 25¢.

Early Archaic materials are displayed here, together with artifacts of the Late Archaic and Woodland periods. Most of the exhibits are from Rhode Island sites, of which one is the Indian Interment at Arnolda.

ROGER WILLIAMS PARK
MUSEUM AND PLANETARIUM

Roger Williams Park, Providence. Open free, 9 a.m. to 5 p.m., Monday through Saturday; 2 p.m. to 5 p.m., Sunday and holidays, Sept. to June; 9 a.m. to 4 p.m., Monday through Friday, July and Aug.; closed national holidays.

Although most of the material in this museum is postcontact, there are some items and some whole exhibits which throw light on prehistory. One case shows supposed routes by which Indians entered America. Another presents a chronological chart for North American archeology, with appropriate tools and weapons for each period. A third shows the differences in physical appearance among Indians of different regions. There is also an exhibit on the plants domesticated by Indians and a summary of their accomplishments in prehistoric times.

Vermont

DANIELS MUSEUM

From Fair Haven drive 16 miles north on 22A to junction with Vermont 73, then east on Vermont 73, 3.7 miles to the museum. Or from Sudbury on Vermont 30 at junction with Vermont 73, drive west 5.3 miles on Vermont 73. Open, 9 a.m. to 5 p.m., June 1 to Sept. 1; closed, Monday and Friday. Admission: adults, 50¢; children under 8, free.

In addition to random local finds, this museum displays two collections from archeological excavations. There are also some Iroquois and Algonquian artifacts and material from the Red Paint culture.

UNIVERSITY OF VERMONT, ROBERT HULL FLEMING MUSEUM

61 Colchester Ave., Burlington. Open free, 9 a.m. to 4:30 p.m., Monday through Friday; 9 a.m. to 3 p.m., Saturday; 2 p.m. to 5 p.m., Sunday; closed national holidays.

Here may be seen selected random local finds and artifacts from other parts of the Eastern Woodland area, together with prehistoric materials from the Southwest and the Northwest Coast. One diorama shows a Northwest Coast village; another, an Eastern Woodland camp.

VERMONT HISTORICAL SOCIETY

State Administration Building, State St., Montpelier. Open free, 8 a.m. to 4:30 p.m., Monday through Friday, winter; 8 a.m. to 4:30 p.m., daily, summer; closed state and national holidays.

On display are four cases of random local finds which have come from all parts of Vermont. Abnaki and Algonquian materials are best represented, but there are some Iroquois artifacts.

WALKER MUSEUM

From White River Jct. drive 20 miles north on US 5 to the museum in Fairlee. Open, 10 a.m. to 5 p.m., daily, May through Oct. 25. Admission: 50¢.

Included with miscellaneous ethnological material from various parts of the Americas, are some North American prehistoric artifacts.

Virginia

COLONIAL NATIONAL HISTORICAL PARK, JAMESTOWN VISITOR CENTER

From Williamsburg drive 10 miles southwest on the Colonial Pkwy. Or from the south take Virginia 10 and 31 to Scotland, where a ferry crosses the James River to Glasshouse Point near the Jamestown entrance. Open 9 a.m. to 5 p.m., daily, winter; 9 a.m. to 6 p.m., daily, summer; closed, Dec. 25. Admission: adults, 50¢; children, free.

The materials displayed in the Visitor Center consist mainly of 17th-century artifacts of European origin. About 300 Indian artifacts were excavated at Jamestown, and some of these, all Algonquian of the Woodland and historic periods, are on display in one exhibit.

JAMESTOWN FESTIVAL PARK

From Williamsburg drive south 5 miles on Virginia 31 to park entrance. Open, 9 a.m. to 5 p.m., Labor Day through June; 9 a.m. to 5:30 p.m., July to Labor Day. Admission: adults, $1; children 12 to 17, 50¢; 7 to 11, 25¢; under 7, free.

In the New World Pavilion at this park are exhibited 400 prehistoric stone artifacts from Virginia. These date from about 8000 B.C. and represent Early and Late Archaic cultures and Early, Middle, and Late Woodland cultures.

In addition there are dioramas that show Indian tobacco growing at Jamestown and the kind of life that Pocohontas led.

NORFOLK MUSEUM OF ARTS AND SCIENCES

Yarmouth St. and The Hague, Norfolk. Open free, 10 a.m. to 5 p.m., Monday through Saturday; 11 a.m. to 6 p.m., Sunday.

The archeological exhibits in this museum concentrate on Tidewater Virginia and include material from local excavations of Paleo-Indian, Archaic, and Woodland sites. Dioramas show Paleo hunters killing a mastodon trapped in a marsh, Archaic hunters killing a bison on a stream bank, and a scene in a village of the Woodland Period.

PEAKS OF OTTER VISITOR CENTER

At Mile Post 86 on the Blue Ridge Pkwy. Open free, 9 a.m. to 6 p.m., daily, June through Oct.; closed Nov. through May.

In addition to wildlife exhibits, this museum displays materials which archeologists recovered in 1965 from a prehistoric campsite nearby. The site, which was discovered in the course of building a lake, had been occupied by wandering hunters at three different times. The first may have been about 6,500 years ago; the second, about 5,500 years ago, according to a radiocarbon date obtained for charcoal from a firepit. Above this there was a later occupation which has not been exactly dated, although it was in the Archaic Period.

VALENTINE MUSEUM

1015 East Clay St., Richmond. Open, 10 a.m. to 4:45 p.m., Tuesday through Saturday; 2:30 p.m. to 5 p.m., Sunday. Admission: adults, $1; students, 25¢; children under 5 accompanied by an adult, free. Special rates for families and groups.

Archaeological exhibits here emphasize Virginia prehistory and cover the periods from the Paleo to the historic. One display shows the layers of soil and debris revealed by an archeological survey trench. Dioramas portray Indian life of the contact period.

Special Interest. Through its Junior Center the museum has a special program on cultural history for children.

An Invitation To Readers

Do you know about a good prehistoric Indian museum exhibit that is not included in this book? Or an archeological site which is open to the public and adequately protected against vandalism? If you do, please send in full information about it, including if possible the mail address of the curator or superintendent. Write to Franklin Folsom, care of Sylvia McNair, Travel Editor, Rand McNally and Co., Box 7600, Chicago, Ill. 60680.

Such information will be valuable when it comes time to prepare a revised, updated edition of AMERICA'S ANCIENT TREASURES. And everyone who sends in a lead to a museum or site that is added to the next edition will have acknowledgement for the help given.

If you should discover an archeological site, which so far as you know has not been excavated or may not be known to archeologists, LEAVE IT ABSOLUTELY UNDISTURBED, take careful note of its location, and send news of your discovery to the nearest of the addresses given below.

ALABAMA
Department of Anthropology
Box 6136
University of Alabama
University, Alabama 35486

ALASKA
Department of Anthropology
Alaska Methodist University
Anchorage, Alaska 99504

ARIZONA
State Archeologist
Arizona State Museum
University of Arizona
Tucson, Arizona 85721

ARKANSAS
State Archeologist
Arkansas Archeological Survey
University of Arkansas Museum
Fayetteville, Arkansas 72701

CALIFORNIA
State Park Archeologist
Department of Parks and Recreation
P.O. Box 2390
Sacramento, California 95811

COLORADO
Department of Anthropology
University of Colorado
Boulder, Colorado 80302

CONNECTICUT
State Archeologist
Jorgensen Auditorium
University of Connecticut
Storrs, Connecticut 06268

DELAWARE
Delaware Archaeological Board
RD 2, Box 166A
Chestnut Grove Road
Dover, Delaware 19901

FLORIDA
State Archeologist
Bureau of Historic Sites & Properties
Department of State
The Capitol
Tallahassee, Florida 32304

GEORGIA
Department of Sociology & Anthropology
University of Georgia
Atlanta, Georgia 30601

HAWAII
State Archeologist
Department of Land &
Natural Resources
P.O. Box 621
Honolulu, Hawaii 96809

IDAHO
Department of Anthropology
Idaho State University
Pocatello, Idaho 83201

ILLINOIS
Illinois Archaeological Survey
Department of Anthropology
Davenport Hall
University of Illinois
Urbana, Illinois 61801

INDIANA
Department of Anthropology
Rawles Hall 108
Indiana University
Bloomington, Indiana 47401

IOWA
Office of State Archeologist
129 S. Capitol
University of Iowa
Iowa City, Iowa 52240

KANSAS
State Archeologist
Kansas State Historical Society
Topeka, Kansas 66603

KENTUCKY
Kentucky Archeological Survey
Department of Anthropology
University of Kentucky
Lexington, Kentucky 40506

LOUISIANA
Department of
Geography and Anthropology
Louisiana State University
Baton Rouge, Louisiana 70803

MAINE
Department of Anthropology
University of Maine
Orono, Maine 04473

MARYLAND
State Archeologist
Maryland Geological Survey
Latrobe Hall
Johns Hopkins University
Baltimore, Maryland 21218

MASSACHUSETTS
Bronson Museum
8 N. Maine Street
Attleboro, Massachusetts 02708

MICHIGAN
Museum of Anthropology
4011 Museums Building
University of Michigan
Ann Arbor, Michigan 48104

MINNESOTA
State Archeologist
Department of Anthropology
200 Ford Hall
University of Minnesota
Minneapolis, Minnesota 55455

MISSISSIPPI
State Archeologist
Mississippi Archaeological Survey
Department of Archives & History
Jackson, Mississippi 39201

MISSOURI
Director, Archaeological Survey
15 Switzler Hall
University of Missouri
Columbia, Missouri 65201

MONTANA
Montana Statewide Archeological
Survey
Department of Anthropology
University of Montana
Missoula, Montana 59801

NEBRASKA
Nebraska State Historical Society
Lincoln, Nebraska 68501

NEVADA
Nevada Archeological Survey
University of Nevada
Reno, Nevada 89507

NEW HAMPSHIRE
Department of Sociology-Anthropology
Franklin Pierce College
Rindge, New Hampshire 03461

NEW JERSEY
Bureau of Research-Archeology
New Jersey State Museum
Trenton, New Jersey 08625

NEW MEXICO
Division of Anthropology
Museum of New Mexico
P.O. Box 2087
Santa Fe, New Mexico 87501

NEW YORK
State Archeologist
Social Science 369
New York State Museum
Albany, New York 12203

NORTH CAROLINA
State Archeologist
Department of Anthropology
University of North Carolina
Chapel Hill, North Carolina 27514

NORTH DAKOTA
State Historical Society of North Dakota

Liberty Memorial Building
Bismarck, North Dakota 58501

OHIO
Division of Archaeology
The Ohio Historical Center
Columbus, Ohio 43210

OKLAHOMA
State Archaeologist
Oklahoma Archaeological Survey
1335 South Asp
University of Oklahoma
Norman, Oklahoma 73069

OREGON
Museum of Natural History
University of Oregon
Eugene, Oregon 97403

PENNSYLVANIA
State Archeologist
William Penn Memorial Museum
Box 232
Harrisburg, Pennsylvania 17108

RHODE ISLAND
Department of Sociology & Anthropology
Brown University
Providence, Rhode Island 02912

SOUTH CAROLINA
Institute of Archeology & Anthropology
University of South Carolina
Columbia, South Carolina 29208

SOUTH DAKOTA
W.H. Over-Dakota Museum
University of South Dakota
Vermillion, South Dakota 57069

TENNESSEE
The McClung Museum
University of Tennessee
Knoxville, Tennessee 37916

TEXAS
State Archeologist
State Building Commission
P.O. Box 12172
Austin, Texas 78711

UTAH
Statewide Archeological Survey
University of Utah
Salt Lake City, Utah 84112

VERMONT
Department of Sociology & Anthropology
University of Vermont
Burlington, Vermont 05401

VIRGINIA
Archeologist
Virginia State Library
Richmond, Virginia 23219

WASHINGTON
Department of Anthropology
Washington State University
Pullman, Washington 99163

WEST VIRGINIA
Section of Archeology
West Virginia Geological Survey
Box 879
Morgantown, West Virginia 26505

WISCONSIN
State Archeologist
State Historical Society of Wisconsin
Madison, Wisconsin 53706

WYOMING
State Archeologist
Department of Anthropology
University of Wyoming
University Station Box 3431
Laramie, Wyoming 82070

Bibliography

Some of the titles below have been starred because they are popular introductions to archeology as a whole or to some aspect of it. The unstarred titles are more specialized and contain detailed scientific information.

*Akweks, Aren. *Monuments to Six Nation Indians.* Hogansburg, N.Y.: Akwesasne Mohawk Counselor Organization.

Alabama Museum of Natural History. "Mound State Monument, Moundville, Alabama." *Museum Paper,* 1942.

American Antiquity: A periodical, published by the Society for American Archaeology, containing many scientific articles which have been of use to this book.

American Association of Museums and the Smithsonian Institution. *Museums Directory of the United States and Canada,* 1965.

*Bandelier, Adolph F. *The Delight Makers.* New York: Dodd Mead & Co., 1918.

*Belden, L. Burr. "50,000 Years Ago." *Desert Magazine,* December 1968.

*Benedict, Ruth. *Patterns of Culture.* Boston: Houghton Mifflin Co., 1934

Birdsell, Joseph B. "The Problem of the Early Peopling of the Americas as Viewed from Asia." *Papers on the Physical Anthropology of the American Indian.* Viking Fund, Inc., 1951.

*Bordaz, Jacques. "First Tools of Mankind," parts I and II. *Natural History,* January, February 1959.

Borden, C. E. "Fraser River Archaeological Project, Progress Report, April 20, 1961." *Anthropology Papers,* National Museum of Canada, 1961.

*Bray, Robert T. "The Missouri Indian Tribe in Archaeology and History." *Missouri Historical Review,* April 1961.

*Brennan, Louis. *No Stone Unturned.* New York: Random House, Inc., 1959.

Brew, J. O. *The Archaeology of Alkali Ridge, Southeastern Utah.* Peabody Museum Papers, Harvard University, 1946.

Brothwell, Don, and Higgs, Eric, eds. *Science in Archaeology: A Comprehensive Survey of Progress and Research.* New York: Basic Books, Inc., 1963.

Broyles, Bettye J. "The St. Albans Site, Kanawha County, West Virginia." *The West Virginia Archeologist,* Fall 1966.

Bryan, Alan L. "Paleo-American Prehistory." *Occasional Papers.* Idaho State University Museum, 1965.

*Bureau of Indian Affairs. *Indians, Eskimos, and Aleuts of Alaska; Indians of Arizona; Indians of California; Indians of Montana-Wyoming; Indians of New Mexico; Indians of North Carolina; Indians of Oklahoma; Indians of the Central Plains; Indians of the Dakotas; Indians of the Great Lakes Area; Indians of the Gulf Coast States; Indians of the Lower Plateau; Indians of the Northwest.*

Bushnell, Geoffrey, and McBurney, Charles. "New World Origins Seen from the Old World." *Antiquity,* no. 130, 1959.

Butcher, Devereux. *Exploring Our Prehistoric Indian Ruins,* National Parks Association, 1950.

*Chapman, Carl H., and Chapman, Eleanor F. *Indians and Archaeology of Missouri.* University of Missouri Press, 1967.

Chard, Chester S. "New World Origins: A Reappraisal." *Antiquity,* no. 129, 1959.

———. "Routes to Bering Strait." *American Antiquity,* October 1960.

*Childe, V. Gordon. *Piecing Together the Past: The Interpretation of Archaeological Data.* New York: Praeger Publishers, Inc., 1956.

*Clark, Grahame. *Archaeology and Society.* New York: Barnes & Noble, Inc., 1960.

Colton, Harold S. *Black Sand: Prehistory in Northern Arizona.* University of New Mexico Press, 1960.

*———. *Hopi Kachina Dolls.* University of New Mexico Press, 1959.

———. *The Sinagua.* Museum of Northern Arizona, 1946.

Corbett, John M. *Aztec Ruins.* National Park Service Historical Handbook Series, no. 36, 1962.

Cotter, John L. "Archeological Survey of Emerald Mound." *Journal of Mississippi History,* January 1949.

———. "Prehistoric Peoples Along the Natchez Trace." *Journal of Mississippi History,* October 1950.

Cotter, John L., and Corbett, John M. "Archeology of the Bynum Mounds, Mississippi." *Archeological Research Series No. 1,* National Park Service, 1951.

*Cressman, Luther S. *The Sandal and the Cave: The Indians of Oregon.* Portland, Oreg.: Beaver Books, 1962.

Cross, Dorothy. *Archaelogy of New Jersey,* vol. I, 1941; vol. II, 1956. The Archaeological Society of New Jersey and the New Jersey State Museum.

*———. *New Jersey's Indians.* New Jersey State Museum, 1965.

*Daugherty, Richard D. *Early Man in Washington.* Washington State Department of Conservation.

———. "The Intermontane Western Tradition." *American Antiquity,* October, 1962.

Davidson, D. S. "Snowshoes." *Memoirs of the American Philosophical Society.* vol. 6. 1937.

De Borhegyi, Stephan F., and de Borhegyi, Suzanne. *The Rubber Ball Game of Ancient America.* Milwaukee Public Museum, 1963.

DeBusk, Charles R. "Dickson Mounds Prehistory." *The Explorer,* Natural Science Museum, Cleveland, Ohio. Summer 1969.

*Deuel, Thorne. *American Indian Ways of Life.* Illinois State Museum, 1958.

*Dockstader, Frederick J. *Indian Art in America: The Arts and Crafts of the North American Indian.* Greenwich, Conn.: New York Graphic Society Ltd., 1966.

*Douglass, Andrew E. "The Secret of the Southwest Solved by Talkative Tree Rings," *National Geographic Magazine,* December 1929.

*Dragoo, Don W. *Mounds for the Dead.* Annals of the Carnegie Museum, 1963.

Driver, Harold E. *The Americas on the Eve of Discovery.* Englewood Cliffs, N.J.: Prentice-Hall, Inc., 1964.

*———. *Indians of North America.* University of Chicago Press, 1969.

Drucker, Philip. *Indians of the Northwest Coast.* Garden City, N.Y.: Natural History Press, 1955.

*Dutton, Bertha. *Indians of New Mexico.* Museum of New Mexico Press, 1963.

———. *Let's Explore Indian Villages Past and Present.* Museum of New Mexico Press, 1962.

———. *Sun Father's Way.* University of New Mexico Press, 1963.

Eddy, Frank W. *Metates and Manos.* Museum of New Mexico Press, 1964.

Eggan, Fred. *The American Indian.* Chicago: Aldine Publishing Co., 1966.

*Elting, Mary, and Folsom, Michael. *The Mysterious Grain.* New York: M. Evans & Co., Inc., 1967.

*———. *The Secret Story of Pueblo Bonito.* Irvington-on-Hudson: Harvey House, Inc., 1963.

Estrada, Emilio; Meggers, Betty J.; and Evans, Clifford. "Possible Transpacific Contact on the Coast of Ecuador." *Science,* 2 February 1962.

*Euler, Robert C. "The Canyon Dwellers." *The American West,* May 1967.

Fairbanks, Charles H. *Archaeological Excavations in the Funeral Mound, Ocmulgee National Monument.* National Park Service, 1956.

———. "Excavations at the Fort Walton Temple Mound, 1960." *Florida Anthropologist,* December 1965.

*Farb, Peter. *Man's Rise to Civilization as Shown by the Indians of North America, from Primeval Times to the Coming of the Industrial State.* New York: E. P. Dutton & Co., Inc., 1968.

Faulkner, Charles H. *The Old Stone Fort.* University of Tennessee Press, 1968.

Ferdon, Edwin N., Jr. "The Hohokam 'Ball Court,' an Alternate View of its Function." *The Kiva,* October 1967.

Folsom, Franklin. *Exploring American Caves.* New York: Crowell Collier and Macmillan, Inc., 1962.

*———. *Science and the Secret of Man's Past,* Irvington-on-Hudson, N.Y.: Harvey House, Inc., 1966.

Ford, James A., and Webb, Clarence H. *Poverty Point, a Late Archaic Site in Louisiana.* Anthropological Papers, American Museum of Natural History, vol. 46, part I, 1956.

Fowler, Melvin L. *Modoc Rock Shelter: A Summary and Analysis of Four Seasons of Excavations.* Illinois State Museum, Report of Investigations, no. 8, 1959.

*Fundaburk, Emma L., and Foreman, Mary D. *Sun Circles and Human Hands.* Emma L. Fundaburk, Luverne, Ala., 1957.

*Giddings, James Louis. *Ancient Men of the Arctic.* New York: Alfred A. Knopf, Inc., 1967.

*Gladwin, H. S. *A History of the Ancient Southwest.* Freeport, Me.: The Bond Wheelwright Co., 1957.

*Grant, Campbell. *Rock Art of the American Indian.* New York: Thomas Y. Crowell Co., 1967.

———. *Rock Paintings of the Chumash, a Study of a California Indian Culture.* University of California Press, 1965.

Grant, Campbell; Baird, James W.; and Pringle, J. Kenneth. *Rock Drawings of the Coso Range.* Maturango Museum, 1968.

Griffin, James B., ed. *Archaeology of Eastern United States.* University of Chicago Press, 1952.

*Griffin, James B. "Eastern North American Archaeology: A Summary." *Science,* 14 April 1967.

———. *Lake Superior Copper and the Indians.* Anthropological Papers, University of Michigan, 1961.

Grimm, R. E., ed. *Cahokia Brought to Life: An Artifactual Story of America's Great Monument.* Greater St. Louis Archaeological Society, 1950.

*Haury, Emil W. "The Hohokam, First Masters of the American Desert," *National Geographic Magazine,* May 1967.

*———. "The Hohokam, First Masters of the American Desert," *National Geographic Magazine,* May 1967.

———. *The Stratigraphy and Archaeology of Ventana Cave, Arizona.* University of Arizona Press and University of New Mexico Press, 1950.

Haury, Emil W.; Sayles, E. B.; and Wasley, W. W. "The Lehner Mammoth Site, Southeastern Arizona." *American Antiquity,* July 1959.

*Hawkes, Jacquetta, and Woolley, Leonard. *Prehistory and the Beginnings of Civilization,* vol. I, New York: Harper and Row, 1963.

Haynes, C. Vance, Jr. "Fluted Projectile Points: Their Age and Dispersion." *Science,* 25 September 1964.

Heizer, Robert F., ed. *The Archaeologist at Work, a Source Book in Archaeological Method and Interpretation.* New York: Harper and Row, 1959.

———. *A Guide to Archaeological Field Methods.* Palo Alto, Cal.: National Press Books, 1958.

*Heizer, Robert F., and Whipple, M. A. eds. *The California Indians.* University of California Press, 1967.

Hibben, Frank C. "Evidences of Early Occupation in Sandia Cave, New Mexico, and Other Sites in the Sandia-Manzano Region." *Smithsonian Miscellaneous Collections,* vol. 99, no. 23, 1941.

Hodge, Frederick W., ed. *Handbook of American Indians North of Mexico,* 2 vols., reprint. New York: Rowman & Littlefield, Inc., 1968.

*Hole, Frank, and Heizer, Robert F. *An Introduction to Prehistoric Archeology.* New York: Holt, Rinehart, & Winston, Inc., 1965.

*Irwin, Cynthia; Irwin, Henry; and George Agogino. "Wyoming Muck Tells of Battle: Ice Age Man vs. Mammoth." *National Geographic Magazine,* June 1962.

Irwin-Williams, Cynthia. *The Elementary Southwestern Culture: The Configuration of Late Preceramic Development in the Southwestern United States.* Paper presented at 64th annual meeting of American Anthropological Association, 1965.

Jackson, George F. *Wyandotte Cave.* Wynnewood, Pa.: Livingston Publishing Co., 1953.

Jennings, Jesse D. "The Archaeological Survey of the Natchez Trace." *American Antiquity,* April 1944.

———. *Danger Cave.* University of Utah Press and The Society for American Archaeology, 1957.

*———. *Prehistory of North America.* New York: McGraw-Hill Book Co., 1968.

*Jennings, Jesse D., and Norbeck, Edward, eds. *Prehistoric Man in the New World.* University of Chicago Press, 1964.

Johnson, Frederick. "The Excavation of the Fish-weir." *Papers of the Robert S. Peabody Foundation for Archaeology,* 1942.

Johnson, Frederick, ed. "Man in Northeastern North America." *Papers of the Robert S. Peabody Foundation for Archaelogy,* 1946.

*Josephy, Alvin M. *The Indian Heritage of America,* New York: Alfred A. Knopf, Inc., 1968.

Judd, Neil. *The Material Culture of Pueblo Bonito.* Smithsonian Miscellaneous Collections, 1954.

*Kanetzke, Howard W., ed. "Wisconsin Indians." *Badger History,* The State Historical Society of Wisconsin, 1965.

Kelly, A. R., and Larson, Lewis H., Jr. "Explorations at Etowah, Georgia, 1954–1956." Reprinted by the Georgia Historical Commission from *Archaeology,* Spring 1957.

*Kidder, A. V. *An Introduction to the Study of Southwestern Archaeology, with a Preliminary Account of the Excavations at Pecos,* with an introduction on "Southwestern Archaeology Today" by Irving Rouse. Yale University Press, 1962.

Laughlin, William S. "Eskimos and Aleuts: Their Origins and Evolution." *Science,* 8 November 1963.

Leakey, L. S. B.; Simpson, Ruth D.; and Clements, Thomas. "Archaeological Excavations in the Calico Mountains, California: Preliminary Report." *Science,* 31 May 1968.

Lee, Thomas E. "The Antiquity of the Sheguiandah Site." *The Canadian Field-Naturalist,* July-September 1957.

———. "The First Sheguiandah Expedition, Manitoulin Island, Ontario." *American Antiquity,* October 1954.

———. "The Second Sheguiandah Expedition, Manitoulin Island, Ontario." *American Antiquity,* July 1955.

*Lewis, T. M. N., and Kneberg, Madeline. *Tribes That Slumber, Indians of the Tennessee Region.* University of Tennessee Press, 1958.

Lewis, T. M. N., and Lewis, Madeline Kneberg. *Eva, an Archaic Site.* University of Tennessee Press, 1961.

*Lister, Florence C., and Lister, Robert H. *Earl Morris and Southwestern Archaeology.* University of New Mexico Press, 1968.

*Lister, Robert H. "Archeology for Layman and Scientist at Mesa Verde." *Science,* 3 May 1968.

Logan, Wilfred D. *Graham Cave.* Missouri Archaeological Society.

Logan, Wilfred D., and Ingmanson, J. Earl. "Effigy Mounds National Monument." *The Palimpsest.* State Historical Society of Iowa, April 1961.

*McFarland, Elizabeth. *Forever Frontier, The Gila Cliff Dwellings.* University of New Mexico Press, 1967.

*McGregor, J. C. *Southwestern Archaeology.* University of Illinois Press, 1965.

*McKusick, Marshall. *Men of Ancient Iowa.* Iowa State University Press, 1964.

*McNitt, Frank. *Richard Wetherill: Anasazi.* University of New Mexico Press, 1957.

*Martin, Paul S. *Digging into History.* Popular Series in Anthropology, no. 38. Chicago Natural History Museum, 1959.

———. *Lowry Ruin in Southwestern Colorado.* Field Museum of Natural History, Anthropological Series, vol. 23, no. 1. 1936.

*Martin, Paul S.; Quimby, George I.; and Collier, Donald. *Indians Before Columbus: Twenty Thousand Years of North American History Revealed by Archeology.* University of Chicago Press, 1947.

The Masterkey. Many articles in this popular magazine, published by the Southwest Museum in Los Angeles, tell of archeological discoveries.

Midvale, Frank. "Prehistoric Irrigation of the Casa Grande Ruins Area." *The Kiva,* Arizona Archaeological and Historical Society, February 1965.

Miller, Carl. "Life Eight Thousand Years Ago Uncovered in an Alabama Cave." *National Geographic Magazine,* October 1956.

Müller-Beck, Hansjürgen. "Paleohunters in America: Origins and Diffusion." *Science,* 27 May 1966.

Morse, Dan F. "Introducing Northeastern Arkansas Prehistory." *The Arkansas Archeologist,* Spring, Summer, Fall 1969.

*Museum of Anthropology. *Pueblo Pottery, A.D. 400–1967.* University of New Mexico, 1967.

Nash, Charles H., and Gates, Rodney, Jr. "Chucalissa." *Tennessee Historical Quarterly,* June 1962.

*National Park Service. *The National Register of Historic Places 1969.* U.S. Department of the Interior, 1969.

*National Park Service. At each park and monument a descriptive leaflet is available and all these leaflets are also obtainable from the Superintendent of Documents, U.S. Government Printing Office, Washington, D.C., 20402.

Nordquist, Delmar. "Petroglyphs at Roosevelt, Washington." *The Washington Archaeologist,* Spring 1965.

*Norona, Delf. *Moundsville's Mammoth Mound.* West Virginia Archeological Society, August 1957.

Orr, Phil C. "Dwarf Mammoths and Man on Santa Rosa Island." *Anthropological Papers.* University of Utah, 1956.

*Pope, G. D., Jr. *Ocmulgee National Monument, Georgia.* National Park Service, 1956.

*Potter, Martha A. *Ohio's Prehistoric Peoples.* Ohio Historical Society, 1968.

*Prufer, Olaf H. "The Hopewell Cult." *Scientific American,* December 1964.

Quimby, George I. *Indian Life in the Upper Great Lakes, 11,000 B.C. to A.D. 1800.* University of Chicago Press, 1960.

Ritchie, William A. *The Archaeology of Martha's Vineyard: A Framework for the Prehistory of Southern New England.* Garden City, N.Y.: Natural History Press, 1969.

———. *The Archaeology of New York State.* Garden City, N.Y.: Natural History Press, 1965.

Ritzenthaler, Robert E. *Masks of the North American Indians,* Milwaukee Public Museum, 1964.

*———. *Prehistoric Indians of Wisconsin.* Milwaukee Public Museum, 1953.

*———. *Totem Poles.* Milwaukee Public Museum, 1965.

*Robbins, Maurice. *The Amateur Archaeologist's Handbook.* New York: Thomas Y. Crowell Co., 1965.

———. *Wapanucket No. 6, an Archaic Village in Middleboro, Massachusetts.* Massachusetts Archaeological Society, 1959.

*Rogers, Edward S. *Indians of the North Pacific Coast.* Royal Ontario Museum, 1970.

*Ross, Edward Hunter. *Indians of the Passaic Valley.* Newark Museum Association, 1963.

*Rowe, Chandler W. *The Effigy Mound Culture of Wisconsin.* Milwaukee Public Museum, 1956.

*Schroeder, Albert H., and Hastings, Homer F. *Montezuma Castle National Monument.* National Park Service Historical Handbook Series, no. 27, 1961.

*Schultz, Helen A., ed. *The Ancient Aztalan Story.* Lake Mills-Aztalan Historical Society, 1969.

*Schwartz, Douglas W. "Prehistoric Man in Mammoth Cave." *Scientific American,* July 1960.

*———. "Prehistoric Man in the Grand Canyon." *Scientific American,* February 1958.

Sears, William H. *Excavations at Kolomoki, Final Report.* University of Georgia Series in Anthropology, 1956.

*Silverberg, Robert. *Mound Builders of Ancient America: The Archeology of a Myth.* Greenwich, Conn.: New York Graphic Society, Ltd., 1968.

*Smith, Harriet. *Prehistoric People of Illinois.* Field Museum of Natural History, 1963.

South, Stanley. *The Indians of North Carolina.* North Carolina Department of Archives and History.

*Spencer, Robert F., Jennings, Jesse D., et al. *The Native Americans: Prehistory and Ethnology of the North American Indians.* New York: Harper and Row, 1965.

Stalker, Archie MacS. "Geology and Age of the Early Man Site at Taber, Alberta." *American Antiquity,* October 1969.

———. *Quarternary Stratigraphy in Southern Alberta, Report II: Section near Medicine Hat.* Paper 69–76. Geological Survey of Canada, 1969.

Starr, S. F. *The Archeology of Hamilton County, Ohio.* Cincinnati Museum of Natural History, 1960.

The Story of Poverty Point. Louisiana Department of Agriculture and Immigration.

*Suggs, Robert C. *The Archaeology of San Francisco.* New York: Thomas Y. Crowell Co., 1965.

Swanton, John R. *The Indian Tribes of North America.* Bureau of American Ethnology. Bulletin 145, 1952.

Townsend, Earl C., Jr. *Birdstones of the North American Indian.* Privately published, 1959.

*Tuck, James A. "An Archaic Indian Cemetery in Newfoundland." *Scientific American,* June 1970.

*Underhill, Ruth M. *Indians of the Pacific Northwest.* Bureau of Indian Affairs, 1945.

*———. *Red Man's America.* University of Chicago Press, 1953.

*———. *Red Man's Religion.* University of Chicago Press, 1965.

Vivian, Gordon. *Excavations in a Seventeenth Century Jumano Pueblo—Gran Quivira.* National Park Service, 1964.

Wallace, Paul A.W. *Indians in Pennsylvania.* Pennsylvania Historical and Museum Commission, 1961.

Wallace, William J. "Prehistoric Cultural Development in the Southern California Deserts." *American Antiquity,* October 1962.

*Watson, Don. *Cliff Dwellings of the Mesa Verde.* Mesa Verde Museum Association, 1950.

Watson, Patty Jo. "Prehistoric Miners of Salt Flats, Kentucky." *Archaeology,* October 1966.

Webb, Clarence H. "The Extent and Content of Poverty Point Culture." *American Antiquity,* July 1968.

*Wedel, Waldo R. *Prehistoric Man on the Great Plains.* University of Oklahoma Press, 1961.

West, Frederick, ed. "Early Man in the Western American Arctic: A Symposium." *Anthropological Papers,* X, no. 2, University of Alaska Press, 1963.

Wheat, Joe Ben. *Mogollon Culture Prior to A.D. 1000.* Memoirs of the Society for American Archaeology, no. 10, 1955.

*———. "A Paleo-Indian Bison Kill." *Scientific American,* January 1967.

———Prehistoric People of the Northern Southwest. Grand Canyon Natural History Association, 1963.

*Willey, Gordon R. *An Introduction to American Archaeology,* vol. 1. Englewood Cliffs, N.J.: Prentice-Hall, Inc., 1966.

*Wing, Kittridge A. *Bandelier National Monument.* National Park Service, 1955.

*Wissler, Clark. *The American Indian.* New York: The Smith, 1957.

Witthoft, John. *The American Indian as Hunter.* Pennsylvania Historical and Museum Commission, rev. ed. 1967.

———. *Indian Prehistory of Pennsylvania.* Pennsylvania Historical and Museum Commission, 1965.

———. *A Paleo-Indian Site in Eastern Pennsylvania: An Early Hunting Culture.* Proceedings of the American Philosophical Society, no. 4, 1952.

Wormington, H. M. *Ancient Man in North America.* Denver Museum of Natural History, 1957.

*———. *Prehistoric Indians of the Southwest.* Denver Museum of Natural History, 1961.

———. *A Reappraisal of the Fremont Culture.* Denver Museum of Natural History, 1955.

Wormington, H. M., and Forbis, Richard G. *An Introduction to the Archaeology of Alberta, Canada.* Denver Museum of Natural History, 1965.

Wright, Barton, and Roat, Evelyn. *This Is a Hopi Kachina.* Museum of Northern Arizona, 1965.

Index